Spying on Americans

Athan Theoharis

Spying on Americans
Political Surveillance from Hoover to the Huston Plan

TEMPLE UNIVERSITY PRESS
Philadelphia

Library of Congress Cataloging in Publication Data

Theoharis, Athan G
  Spying on Americans.

  Bibliography: p.
  Includes index.
  1. Intelligence service—United States—History.
  2. Internal security—United States—History.
  3. United States. Federal Bureau of Investigation—
  History. 4. Abuse of administrative power—United
  States—History. I. Title.
  JK468.I6T45   327.12′0973   78-12037
  ISBN 0-87722-141-3

Temple University Press, Philadelphia 19122
© 1978 by Temple University. All rights reserved
Published 1978
Printed in the United States of America

To Jeanne, George Thomas, and Elizabeth
for their love and understanding

Contents

Acknowledgments   ix

Preface   xi

Introduction   Presidential Power and Internal Security   3

Chapter One   The Huston Plan   13

Chapter Two   Emergency Detention Programs   40

Chapter Three   Authorizing Political Surveillance   65

Chapter Four   Wiretaps, Mail Openings, and Break-Ins   94

Chapter Five   Political Counterintelligence   133

Chapter Six   Political Uses of Surveillance   156

Chapter Seven   Loyalty and Security Programs   196

Conclusion   The Politics of Intelligence   229

Abbreviations   245

Notes   247

Bibliography   307

Index   317

Acknowledgments

It is impossible to acknowledge by name all the archivists, former students, fellow historians, lawyers, and congressional staff members who assisted in the research and writing of this study. Chapter Two is an expanded version of a paper originally published as "The Truman Administration and the Decline of Civil Liberties: The FBI's Success in Securing Authorization for a Preventive Detention Program," *Journal of American History*, LXIV (March 1978), 1010–1030. Chapter Three is an expanded version of a paper entitled "The FBI's Stretching of Presidential Directives, 1936–1953," *Political Science Quarterly* 91 (Winter 1976–77): 649–672. I would like to thank the editors of these two journals for permission to draw upon these articles. The staffs of the Truman Library, the Eisenhower Library, the Kennedy Library, the Johnson Library, the Milwaukee Public Library, and the Marquette University Library provided invaluable assistance and ensured that I consulted all relevant sources. My colleagues at Marquette and in the history profession provided expert counsel; their penetrating questions compelled me to reassess some of my conclusions. So too did many of my former graduate and undergraduate students. To them I owe a special thanks. I particularly acknowledge the assistance of Kenneth O'Reilly, John Berens, Robert Griffith, Barton Bernstein, Mike Epstein, John Elliff, Mark Gitenstein, Timothy Ingram, Ira Shapiro, Lewis Paper, Alger Hiss, David Kendall, Anthony Marro, Perry Raines, and Carol Schieffer. Financial assistance from the Lyndon Baines Johnson Foundation, Marquette University, and the National Endowment for the Humanities supported my research, while Michael Ames of Temple University Press provided expert editorial assistance. I owe a special debt, however, to my wife Nancy and my three children Jeanne, George Thomas, and Elizabeth. Authors tend to think their contribution to be of world-shattering significance. The contemporary relevance of the subject matter of this study particularly encouraged me to believe this. My family assumed a healthier attitude; not being convinced that my work was all that important, even interesting. They nevertheless humored me; their moral support, moreover, inspired me to contribute in some small way toward the preservation of a democratic and libertarian society.

Athan Theoharis
Milwaukee, Wisconsin
June 14, 1978

Preface

This study will focus exclusively on internal security policy for the years after 1936, and thus principally on the investigative activities and authority of the Federal Bureau of Investigation (FBI). The history of FBI break-ins, wiretapping, politically-motivated investigations, and preventive detention programs will be analyzed in detail. Other federal intelligence agencies—the Central Intelligence Agency (CIA), National Security Agency (NSA), Internal Revenue Service (IRS), and the various military intelligence agencies—will be discussed only when their activities involved domestic surveillance. Because FBI investigations of political activities were only authorized in August 1936 by Franklin Roosevelt's verbal order, this study begins that year rather than with J. Edgar Hoover's appointment as FBI director in 1924. When appointing Hoover in 1924, Attorney General Harlan Fiske Stone had specifically restricted FBI investigations to violations of federal statutes, thereby prohibiting political surveillance.

This study will center on three questions. First, what was the nature of the relationship between the presidency and the intelligence community—and did presidents and attorneys general effectively oversee the internal security bureaucracy? Second, did executive branch officials establish the limits within which internal security bureaucrats operated and ensure compliance either with their orders or the law? Third, what contributed to the expansion of presidential powers as well as to the increased authority and the independent initiatives of the intelligence agencies?

Unfortunately, the first question is least satisfactorily resolved in the ensuing study. This study does document instances both of presidential direction and presidential ignorance. Our knowledge of the scope of activities of the federal intelligence agencies has been only recently acquired. The principal source of that knowledge derives from the declassification of thousands of FBI, CIA, NSA, NSC, and IRS documents during recent congressional investigations. Documents pertaining directly to most presidential policy decisions, however, remain classified. The result is an imperfect record. We know what internal security bureaucrats proposed, and their claimed authority; at present we do not know whether presidents were aware of all these decisions and/or approved them. Nor is the problem simply that of classification restrictions; there are more serious research problems for the historian of federal intelligence policy.

During the years after 1940, federal intelligence agencies devised separate filing systems, the intent of which was to safeguard even "national security" classified documents from public discovery. Documents pertaining to "sensitive," "illegal," or "embarrassing" activities were filed separately from other agency documents, and were not serialized; hence these documents could be (and were to be) destroyed without a retrievable record having ever been created of their existence.[1] Such separate filing and record destruction procedures could serve to preclude not only public but also presidential knowledge of these activities. These procedures accordingly make it impossible for the historian to ascertain definitively the nature of the presidential–internal security bureaucracy relationship.

In addition, the commitment to secrecy of presidents and intelligence officials resulted in a conscious policy *not* to create a complete written record. For example, FBI Director Hoover in a December 29, 1953, memorandum to Attorney General Herbert Brownell cited a National Security Council (NSC) discussion and decision of December 15, 1953, to issue a presidential directive on the FBI's investigative authority. In a May 13, 1954, diary entry, James Hagerty (President Eisenhower's press secretary) also reported a NSC discussion of that day involving a recommendation of Attorney General Brownell and how the president proposed to handle this matter at a forthcoming press conference.[2] The minutes of both these NSC meetings, however, record neither the discussions nor decisions on these matters. The incompleteness of these NSC minutes is crucial, however; increasingly during the Cold War years it was at NSC meetings that important internal and international security policy matters were discussed and where presidential knowledge (and implicit authorization) can clearly be established. In this sense, former NSC staff officials Robert Johnson's, Marion Boggs's, and James Lay's 1975 testimony about how NSC discussions and decisions were recorded is highly important.

During June 18, 1975, testimony before the Senate Select Committee on Intelligence Activities, NSC staff member Robert Johnson claimed that President Eisenhower had ordered the assassination of Congolese leader Patrice Lumumba at an August 18, 1960, NSC meeting. The controversy over whether or not Eisenhower ordered Lumumba's assassination is not germane here; what is, though, are Johnson's, Boggs's, and Lay's accounts of how this particular discussion was recorded. Responsible for writing the memorandum on this August 18, 1960, NSC discussion, Johnson consulted with other senior NSC staff (either Marion Boggs or James Lay) to determine how the president's statement should be handled in the NSC memorandum on the meeting and in the debriefing of the NSC Planning Board. The president's statement was omitted from the debriefing, Johnson testified; "quite likely that it [the President's statement] was handled [in his memorandum on the meeting] through some kind of euphemism or may have been omitted altogether." Not recalling having been consulted by Johnson on this matter, Boggs testified: "I am not saying I was not consulted, I would almost certainly have directed Mr. Johnson to omit the matter from the memorandum of discussion." James Lay also emphasized that had a presidential order to assassinate Lumumba been given, NSC minutes would not record such a decision: "If extremely sensitive matters were discussed at an NSC meeting, it was sometimes the practice that the official NSC minutes would record only the general subject discussed without identifying the specially sensitive subject of the discussion. In highly sensitive cases, no reference to the subject would be made in the NSC minutes."[3]

This commitment to sanitize the record was not atypical, confined only to these three known NSC minutes. The reports of the Senate Select Committee on Intelligence Activities recount numerous other instances either where the recognized "sensitivity" of certain projects resulted in decisions to devise secretive procedures, where intelligence officials were unable to produce documents involving activities or proposals the committee learned about through testimony, where incomplete records were created in part to ensure "plausible deniability" or to confine knowledge to those "who need to know," or wherein contemporary orders were issued to destroy documents pertaining to proposed questionable or abhorrent activities. In a January 14, 1977, report justifying its decision not to prosecute former CIA officials for illegally opening the mail, the Department of Justice emphasized that executive approval of these programs could not be established because, under the practice of "plausible deniability" or "presidential deniability," no "written records [were made] of presidential authorizations of sensitive intelligence-gathering operations. It was thought that the conduct of foreign affairs frequently required the practice of non-recordation of such presidential authorizations." Moreover, when Secretary of Defense Charles Wilson established the so-called Coolidge Committee in 1956 and directed it to review the Defense Department's classification policy, the committee decided not to hold formal hearings. Chairman Coolidge explained this decision: "We had conferences without a stenographer present, to get the opinions of our conferees."[4]

Second, what factors contributed to the internal security agencies' far-reaching abuses of power during the post-1936 years? Were these abuses the direct result of the transformation of the office of the presidency and of the attendant centralization of power in the federal bureaucracy? Had the Cold War fundamentally altered American values and institutions? Why, moreover, had internal security bureaucrats become indifferent to legal and constitutional prohibitions, devising instead procedures to ensure against public knowledge or disclosure of recognizably illegal activities? Did the acceptance of secrecy (whether on "executive privilege" or "national security" grounds) effectively preclude accountability and ensure insubordination?

Third, why did internal security investigations and programs become politicized? Were FBI investigations—whether involving "subversive activities," the so-called COINTELPROs, and the loyalty/security program—and reports to presidents on dissident activities based principally on political criteria? In addition, did the internal security agencies' investigations and reports affect national politics and/or shape public opinion?

I began this study seven years ago intending to survey federal intelligence policy during the Cold War years. Because of stringent classification restrictions, my research was confined principally to the evolution of federal loyalty/security programs and electronic surveillance authority. Aside from the loyalty/security programs, presidential libraries contained virtually no documentation on internal security policy, and our knowledge of electronic surveillance derived from legislative hearings and court cases wherein the government disclosed either that wiretaps or bugs had been used or had been properly authorized.

Appointed a consultant to the Senate Select Committee on Intelligence Activities in July 1975 (the so-called Church Committee) to assist in the investigation of the FBI, I temporarily set aside this research project. Assigned responsibility to research presidential libraries, I learned how limited my knowledge had in fact been about federal surveillance policy and how capricious existing classification restrictions were. For example, one of the areas the committee staff directed me to research involved FBI reports to the White House. Reviewing the very extensive reports from FBI Director Hoover to the Truman White House at the Truman Library during an August 1975 research trip, I requested similar Hoover to the White House reports during my research trip that month to the Eisenhower Library. There were no such reports, I was informed, except for one thin folder of approximately ten classified documents. Returning to the Eisenhower Library in December 1975 (and this time with a security clearance and having authorization to research classified files at the library), I discovered a voluminous correspondence from FBI Director Hoover to the Eisenhower White House, the vast majority of which was political. Because Hoover's reports were forwarded to National Security Council staff members, and not to White House aides as they had been during the Truman years, they were all classified and wholly closed to the academic researcher.

The release of the Select Committee's hearings and reports further convinced me of my earlier limited knowledge; this study's frequent citations from them attest to their importance. Indeed, students of federal intelligence policy should begin their research with these reports and hearings; they provide the necessary background about key policy decisions, make it possible for the researcher to file intelligent Freedom of Information Act (FOIA) and mandatory declassification requests, and outline the areas wherein our knowledge is presently incomplete or deficient. I hope that this study will also stimulate others to initiate the additional research and analysis required to understand this critical period in American history.

Spying on Americans

Introduction
Presidential Power and Internal Security

Until the early 1970s, most Americans—particularly members of Congress, political scientists, historians, and newspaper editorialists—were enamored of the office of the presidency. For them, only presidents could provide the leadership needed to effect national goals, especially in the national security area. Claims to secrecy and unilateral decisions were tolerated, when not encouraged, on the premise that presidents alone possessed the information and the ability to respond quickly to external and internal threats to the national security.

Section 2511 of the Omnibus Crime Control and Safe Streets Act of 1968 (the first legislative authorization ever for electronic surveillance) indirectly confirms a deferential tolerance of claims to expansive presidential powers. This section stipulated:

> Nothing contained in this statute or in section 605 of the Communications Act of 1934 . . . shall limit the constitutional powers of the President to take such measures as he deems necessary to protect the Nation against actual or potential attack or other hostile acts of a foreign power, to obtain foreign intelligence information deemed essential to the security of the United States or to protect national security information against foreign intelligence activities. Nor shall anything in this chapter be deemed to limit the constitutional power of the President to take such action as he deems necessary to protect the United States against the overthrow of the Government by force or by other unlawful means, or against any other clear and present danger to the structure or existence of the Government. The contents of any wire or oral communication intercepted by authority of the President in the exercise of the foregoing powers may be received in evidence . . . only where such interception was reasonable, and shall not be otherwise used or disclosed except as is necessary to implement that power.[1]

The reference to the "constitutional powers of the President" qualifies this section's broad language. Congress had not attempted, however, to confine presidential initiatives or to limit the president's claimed discretionary authority. Presidents had certain "inherent" and expansive powers; it would be unwise to encroach upon them. The Senate Judiciary Committee majority report (of April 28, 1968) further captures this deference, and the underlying "national security" rationale:

3

It is obvious that whatever means are necessary should and must be taken to protect the national security interest. Wiretapping and electronic surveillance are proper means for the acquisition of counter-intelligence against hostile actions of foreign powers. Nothing in the proposed legislation seeks to disturb the power of the President in this area. Limitations that might be deemed proper in the field of domestic affairs become artificial when international relations and internal security are at stake.[2]

Senator Philip Hart pointedly challenged this broad language during floor debate, noting the failure to limit executive authority. By not delineating the basis for a national security exception Congress thereby would permit presidents to authorize electronic surveillance of dissident political activities. Senators John McClellan and Spessard Holland, in response, dismissed Hart's singular fears as unfounded. This language, McClellan observed, had been drafted "by the Administration, the Justice Department"; he "was perfectly willing to recognize the power of the President in this area. If he [the President] felt there was an organization . . . that was plotting to overthrow the government, I would think we would want him to have the right." Holland qualified McClellan's assertion, after Hart queried whether this language granted such powers to the president. Presidential power simply was not restricted, Holland maintained. "There is nothing affirmative in the statement." McClellan concurred with Holland's assessment.[3]

This legislative strategy neither was atypical nor confined to electronic surveillance policy. Since the 1950s liberal and conservative academics had enthusiastically commended the increase in presidential powers, maintaining that dynamic even manipulative executive leadership was needed to effect national goals. Describing his purpose for writing *The American Presidency*, now recognized as the classic study of the institution, the conservative political scientist Clinton Rossiter emphasized his "feeling of veneration, if not exactly reverence, for the authority and dignity of the presidency." Rossiter approvingly quoted Harry Truman's blunt comment to the Jewish War Veterans "I make American foreign policy" and more generally extolled the strong-minded executive who bent Congress and the public to his will and who left as a legacy a strengthened executive office. Similarly, in his thoughtful survey of the U.S. presidency, *1600 Pennsylvania Avenue*, the liberal historian Walter Johnson both praised executive leadership and emphasized the need for a strong, manipulative presidency. These themes were popularized during the 1950s by George Kennan, Walter Lippmann, Thomas Bailey, and Hans Morgenthau. Other scholars have described the president as the "central instrument of democracy," the "national teacher," the American public's "one authentic trumpet," or have lamented either the excessive influence of public opinion in "ruling foreign policy" or the absence of a ruling policy elite. The scholarly former diplomat, George Kennan, has recently echoed this lament. Congress, Kennan argues, is "not constituted for the conduct of foreign policy in the first place"; a system of checks and balances impedes the "promptness and incisiveness . . . necessary to an effective world policy" and undermines the efforts of those "highly competent persons in the Executive branch, who . . . had exclusively the national interest at heart."[4] This deference to the presidency is a recent phenomenon. In the 1930s and 1940s conservative congressmen and commentators sharply assailed Franklin Roosevelt's and Harry Truman's expansion of presidential powers, unilateral decisions, claims to secrecy, and insistence on an unreviewable right to deny "national security" information to congressional committees. President Roosevelt's 1937 proposal to reorganize the executive branch was pointedly denounced as a measure which, if enacted, could result in dictatorship or at least undermine constitutional government. During the late 1940s and early 1950s, conservatives in Congress and in the media attributed the expansion of Soviet power and the origins of the Cold War to Roosevelt's secret, unilateral diplomacy at the Yalta Conference. To prevent the recurrence of this problem they proposed to rein in executive power through proposed congressional resolutions or constitutional amendments. Conservatives also sharply denounced first President Truman's refusal in 1948 and again in 1950 to honor congressional requests for the loyalty reports of specified executive branch employees and then his September 1951 executive order extending classification restrictions to all federal agencies and departments.

Moreover, during congressional consideration of the National Security Act of 1947, conservative Congressman Clarence Brown objected to the failure to prohibit the CIA from conducting domestic surveillance. "I am very much interested in seeing the United States have as fine a foreign military and naval intelligence as they can," Brown warned, "but I am not interested in setting up here in the United States any particular agency under any President and I do not care what his name is, and just allow him to have a Gestapo of his own if he wants to have it. Every now and then you get a man that comes up in power that has an imperialistic idea." To conciliate Brown, the bill was amended to specify that the CIA "shall have no police, subpoena, law-enforcement powers, or internal security functions." Conservatives had even earlier challenged proposals to create a federal intelligence agency. During World War II Senator Robert Taft had warned of the dangers of White House control of intelligence and investigative agencies. On February 9, 1945, moreover, a Walter Trohan byline article titled "New Deal Plans Postwar Super-Spy System: Donovan Proposes Super-Spy System for Post-War New Deal" was carried by the *Chicago Tribune, New York Daily News,* and *Washington Times-Herald.* Based on access to a memorandum proposing the creation of a centralized intelligence agency, Trohan's story characterized the proposed plan as a "Gestapo" which "would supersede all existing Federal police and intelligence units," threaten constitutional liberties, and undermine a government of divided powers.

Although differing over tactics, conservatives (whether politicians, columnists, or intellectuals) shared in common an opposition to executive claims of a right to control the flow of information. Variously, during the 1940s and early 1950s, Richard Nixon, Robert Taft, Joseph McCarthy, Herbert Hoover, Fulton Lewis, Jr., Clarence Manion, William Buckley, Jr., and Felix Morley urged an assertive congressional investigative role, characterized President Truman's refusal to provide requested information to the Congress as an attempted cover-up, and insisted upon full publicity.

Responding to President Truman's September 25, 1951, executive order extending existing classification restrictions to civilian agencies, twenty-five conservative senators pointedly observed: "There is evidence that some persons or groups in authority in our Government are unable to tolerate criticism. This is manifested by the smear tactics and propaganda techniques now being used to silence any critics." They continued: "Uncontrolled public discussion is the American tradition and is the greatest enemy of tyranny. There is evidence that no man can criticize our Government today and escape intemperate reprisals. This is an alarming situation. It cannot be ignored. We, therefore . . . pledge to the American people that we shall fight to guarantee that in the difficult days ahead, no man's voice shall be silenced."[5]

No man's voice was silenced. Rather, those conservatives who had so vociferously denounced Presidents Roosevelt's and Truman's secretive, unilateral conduct of domestic and foreign policy during the 1930s and 1940s became strikingly mute during the 1950s when the conservative Dwight Eisenhower acted in a similar manner. During Eisenhower's presidency the most important foreign policy decisions were increasingly made in secret (without consultation with Congress), the CIA's principal role shifted from intelligence gathering to covert operations (including coups and planned assassinations), and the claim of an unreviewable presidential right to deny any and all information to the Congress was formally asserted. The term "executive privilege" was employed for the first time in 1958 during Eisenhower's tenure: although affirming such a claim during his presidency Truman had then justified it on the basis of separation of powers. More important than the coining of this phrase, the number and scope of such claims expanded radically during Eisenhower's presidency. Whereas Truman had claimed what amounted to executive privilege five times[6] and then only for reports prepared at his direction or involving national security investigations, Eisenhower asserted forty-five executive privilege claims, and his claims extended beyond individuals who communicated directly with the president to include all executive employees and all reports produced within the executive branch (whether from Cabinet departments or federal regulatory agencies).[7]

The greater deference toward the presidency during the 1950s was partially the result of an adverse reaction to McCarthyism. Contemporaries interpreted McCarthyism as confirming the risks and costs of a democratic politics; for them, a politics of exposure was harmful and irresponsible. In their reaction to McCarthyism, both liberals and conservatives came to support the need to shield the presidency from intensive congressional scrutiny. Thus, contemporary newspaper editorials uncritically defended President Eisenhower's May 17, 1954, claim of a right not to provide information that

McCarthy's committee had requested concerning specified contacts between Army counsel John Adams and the Eisenhower White House. (McCarthy had requested all oral and written contacts between the Army and the White House involving the administration's strategy of halting a legitimate congressional inquiry.) The *New York Times* and the *Washington Post* commended this decision and summarily dismissed McCarthy's protest of censorship. The *Post* qualified its praise, maintaining only that "President Eisenhower was abundantly right in protecting the confidential nature of executive conversation in this instance." The *Times*, in contrast, did not simply commend this particular use but accepted the claim as a general principle: "The committee has no more right to know the details of what went on in these inner Administration councils than the Administration would have the right to know what went on in an executive session of a Committee of Congress."[8] Neither newspaper considered Eisenhower's action a cover-up or as portending that the White House's ability to control information could reduce Congress's oversight function and thereby enable presidents to cover up abuses of power or corruption.

Liberal newspapers were not alone in failing to see the potential for abuse, or in their overreaction to McCarthyism. The liberal historian Walter Johnson characterized Senator McCarthy's 1954 request for the records of "privileged conversations in the White House" as a "flagrant encroachment on the executive" and contended that during 1953–54 the Wisconsin senator had "also tried to usurp the powers of the presidency." As late as the 1960s, moreover, even prominent critics of the Johnson and Nixon administrations' Vietnam policies, such as U.S. Senator William Fulbright and former Pentagon official Daniel Ellsberg, expressed strong reservations and a distinct ambivalence about the desirability of an open public debate over foreign policy. Fearing a McCarthyite upsurge, these critics of presidential unilateralism preferred that policy elites recognize error and cease to be bound by the irrational anti-Communist fears of the Cold War years. "National security" concerns had combined with "executive privilege" to narrow the scope of what had come to be viewed as the proper basis for conducting U.S. foreign policy.[9]

This deference to the presidency—and to presidential "national security" and "executive privilege" claims—began to break down during the course of the national debate over the Johnson administration's Vietnam War policy. Richard Nixon's presidency and the Watergate Affair dramatically increased more critical views of the presidency. Significantly, the initiative for this challenge derived as much from President Nixon's tactics as from the emergence of a different set of attitudes about the wisdom of this earlier deference.

When the Senate Select Committee on Presidential Campaign Activities (chaired by Senator Sam Ervin and known as either the Ervin or the Watergate committee) and the national news media began during the spring and summer of 1973 to unravel the scope of White House involvement in the Watergate cover-up, President Nixon sought to undercut these efforts and to defend his own questionable role in part by citing "national security" considerations.[10] During a March 21, 1973, conversation between Nixon and White House aides H. R. Haldeman and John Dean, for example, the president pointedly queried what could be done should it be revealed that the White House Plumbers had been involved in engineering the break-in to the office of Dr. Lewis Fielding. Dean responded: "You might put it on a national security basis." Haldeman and Nixon concurred. If other revelations occur, Nixon added, the proper response should be that "the whole thing was national security." Dean affirmed: "I think we could get by on that."[11]

This strategy proved to be counterproductive. The release of confidential White House documents and the tapes of Nixon's Oval Office conversations confirmed that "national security" was employed to silence the president's critics and preclude public disclosure of the administration's misdeeds. Nixon's attempt to exploit "national security" inadvertently increased public cynicism. No longer would the public, the Congress, or the media accept blindly and on faith presidential "national security" claims. This increased skepticism coincided with a refusal during 1973–74 to accept presidential "executive privilege" claims.

In early April 1974, for example, Attorney General Richard Kleindienst maintained that "in his discretion" the president had the constitutional authority to withhold information and prevent the testimony of any executive branch employee if he determined that such disclosure "would impair the proper exercise of his constitutional functions." At the same time that Kleindienst was affirming this expansive but theoretical rationale for the president's right to deny information to the Congress, the Nixon White House was consciously devising an elaborate strategy based on an "executive privilege" claim to contain the Ervin committee's investigation of the Watergate Affair. Nor was this simply private deliberation. On March 12, 1973, Nixon publicly announced his right to prevent past as well as present White House staff members from testifying before congressional committees. On May 3, 1973, the president further expanded this claimed power to include a presidential right to deny the appearance and testimony of White House aides before grand juries and even the FBI.

Compelled almost immediately by an adverse public reaction to backtrack from these positions, Nixon at first sought to limit the scope of permissible questioning by the Ervin committee. Later, following revelations that Oval Office conversations had been taped, Nixon refused to turn these tapes over to the Congress or to the federal grand jury investigating the Watergate Affair. Ultimately, in August 1974, the U.S. Supreme Court in *U.S. v. Nixon* rejected Nixon's claimed right to refuse to produce subpoenaed tapes on "executive privilege" grounds.[12] These tapes sealed Nixon's political fate. They unquestionably revealed that his involvement in the Watergate cover-up dated from as early as June 23, 1972, and contradicted sharply his claims of innocence and ignorance. The effect of their release, like the "national security" claim, increased public skepticism and cynicism about "executive privilege": "executive privilege" was less a right than an attempt to cover-up misdeeds and abuses of power.

By the end of 1974, the association of Richard Nixon's overtly political uses of "national security" and "executive privilege" contributed to a vastly different political climate and concurrently altered popular conceptions of the presidency. One consequence of this changed climate was congressional approval in November 1973 of the War Powers Act of 1973, in the process overriding a presidential veto of October 24, 1973. Presidential war-making powers were thereby restricted, as any decision to commit U.S. troops overseas required congressional approval within sixty days. A second consequence was congressional approval in November 1974, again over a presidential veto—this time on October 17, 1974, by Nixon's successor Gerald Ford—of a series of seventeen amendments to the Freedom of Information Act of 1966. Taking effect February 19, 1975, these amendments narrowed the exceptions accorded to federal agencies by the 1966 act and were based on the premises that executive secrecy was contrary to the national interest and that an informed citizenry was essential to the functioning of the American polity. The most important of these amendments authorized federal judges to review *in camera* "national security" classified information at the behest of a petitioner, and to rule whether this information should remain classified. No longer could federal agencies on their own authority classify information as "national security" and thereby restrict public knowledge of their activities.[13]

The immediate reactions to Nixon's abuses of power were not confined to the enactment of these legislative reforms. A number of books published between 1973 and 1976 focused on the abuses of power of Nixon's presidency. Directly or indirectly, these books called into question earlier uncritical tolerance of an independent, unilateral presidency. The most sophisticated of these, Arthur Schlesinger's *The Imperial Presidency*, invited a reassessment of the proper role and powers of the presidency.[14]

Because their analyses were a reaction to Richard Nixon's political style and personality and the unpopular Vietnam War, these studies suffered from a distinct myopia. Collectively, they suggested that Nixon's abuses were unique to his presidency and were thus aberrational. Professor Schlesinger alone traced the historical expansion of presidential power and the potential for abuse. Nonetheless, the essential thrust of Schlesinger's analysis was also that only Richard Nixon's distinctive politics and personality gave rise to the "imperial presidency." The exclusive focus on the Nixon presidency fortified the conviction that the abuses of power revealed in 1973 and 1974 were singular.

These studies were almost immediately dated by additional revelations. For the very political climate which had brought forth the proliferation of Nixon books was responsible for yet another congressional investigation—this time focusing on the intelligence community. The catalyst to this investigation stemmed from a December 22, 1974, *New York Times* article by reporter

Seymour Hersh. In it, Hersh reported that the CIA in violation of its legislative charter had conducted a "massive illegal domestic intelligence operation during the Nixon Administration against the anti-war movement and other dissident groups in the United States." At first, CIA officials and the Ford administration neither confirmed nor denied Hersh's story. On December 23, 1975, however, Ford directed Secretary of State Henry Kissinger to report "within a matter of days" on the accuracy of Hersh's allegations. Kissinger in turn ordered CIA Director William Colby to prepare such a report. Completed by the end of the month, the report confirmed the accuracy of these allegations, thereby negating any possibility of denying or ignoring them. Faced also with the prospect that the Senate Armed Services Committee would conduct public hearings, and reeling from the public impact of a series of other news stories alleging that these files had been destroyed by the CIA, Colby publicly confirmed Hersh's story in January 1975. Concurrently, to limit the scope of the inquiry into past abuses, on January 4, 1975, by Executive Order 11828 President Ford announced the appointment of a special presidential commission on the CIA, headed by Vice President Nelson Rockefeller. The Rockefeller commission's authority, however, was limited to investigating CIA domestic intelligence abuses.[15]

The Ervin Committee investigation and then the House Judiciary committee's inquiry into impeachment resolutions had publicized how the Nixon administration had sought to use federal intelligence agencies for political purposes. Now, the Hersh revelations were published simultaneously with other news stories detailing the FBI's abuses of power. A Justice Department report released in November 1974 by Attorney General William Saxbe detailed the FBI's COINTELPRO—a program to harass and discredit dissident organizations—and a January 1975 disclosure revealed that during the 1964 Democratic National Convention the FBI had had under surveillance and had reported to President Lyndon Johnson conversations and strategies of members of Congress, Robert Kennedy, and civil rights leaders. In February 1975, moreover, Attorney General Edward Levi publicly admitted that former FBI Director J. Edgar Hoover had retained secret files in his private office containing derogatory information on prominent personalities (including presidents and members of Congress) and on those who simply opposed the FBI or his leadership of the bureau. Other news stories of that same month reported that CIA Director Richard Helms had ordered a CIA official to withhold Watergate information and deny Justice Department access to a key witness and further that Helms had not been forthright during 1973 testimony before the Senate Foreign Relations Committee.[16]

These revelations in the post-Watergate atmosphere only increased congressional unwillingness to defer to executive authority or acquiesce in presidential efforts to minimize public disclosures about the federal intelligence agencies' policies and procedures. On January 21, 1975, Senator John Pastore introduced S. Res. 21 to establish a Senate select committee to investigate "intelligence activities carried out by or on behalf of the Federal Government" to determine the extent "if any" of "illegal, improper, or unethical activities" engaged in by *any* federal agency or persons acting "on or behalf of the Federal Government," and further:

(1) Whether the Central Intelligence Agency has conducted an illegal domestic intelligence operation in the United States.

(2) The conduct of domestic intelligence or counterintelligence operations against United States citizens by the Federal Bureau of Investigation or any other Federal agency.

(3) The origin and disposition of the so-called Huston Plan. . . .

(7) Nature and extent of executive branch oversight of all United States intelligence activities. . . .

(9) The extent to which United States intelligence agencies are governed by Executive orders, rules, or regulations either published or secret and the extent to which those Executive orders, rules, or regulations interpret, expand, or are in conflict with specific legislative authority.

(10) The violation or suspected violation of any State or Federal statute by any intelligence agency or by any person by or on behalf of any intelligence agency of the Federal Government including but not limited to surreptitious entries, surveillance, wiretaps, or eavesdropping, illegal opening of the United States mail, or the monitoring of United States mail.

The Senate approved S. Res. 21 on January 27, 1975.[17]

The scope of the Select Committee's mandate underscored the proponents' intent to ensure an intensive investigation of the intelligence community. Such an investigation would not have been possible during the 1950s and 1960s. Presidents and intelligence bureaucrats would then have refused to give congressional investigators access to the classified files of the various intelligence agencies. In the post-Watergate atmosphere, President Gerald Ford and the intelligence agencies found it politically difficult to refuse such committee requests for relevant files and documents. The administration, however, did not volunteer information. With some reluctance and after lengthy negotiations with senators and staff members, the Ford White House ultimately agreed to permit the Select Committee a tightly controlled and selected examination of what had been the closed records of the intelligence agencies, the National Security Council, and the White House's "national security" documents.[18]

The result was eye-opening. The committee learned, and its public hearings and reports publicized, the scope of the intelligence community's past abuses of power. The committee established that the intelligence agencies' abuses had not been confined to the Nixon years, although the investigation did confirm that the scope, process, and intent of the Nixon administration's abuses were atypical. Popular and congressional acceptance of presidential "national security" and "executive privilege" claims and the secrecy of White House and intelligence officials had made possible far-reaching abuses of power. The committee investigation disclosed another equally alarming abuse, resulting not from presidential direction but from the lack of presidential control or oversight. Secrecy had made it possible for intelligence officials to act on their own authority, and either not inform or misinform responsible executive officials.

The result was the creation of what one author has loosely characterized as "The American Police State" and another as "The Lawless State."[19] The power of executive branch officials to make policy in secret had at least encouraged, if not ensured, abuses. Since 1936 internal security bureaucrats, principally high-level FBI officials, holding alarmist views of internal security threats, and not required to justify publicly these conclusions, acted purposefully to advance their own political interests and to curb the potential influence of individuals or organizations whose political views they found abhorrent. Unknown to the American public, the actions of these officials had brought the nation a long way on the road to "1984." These internal security bureaucrats may not have established what can truly be described as a "police state." Their failure stemmed as much from the weakness of the American left as from their own self-restraint. In either case, very little solace can be derived from the fact that a police state had not become operational. In the crisis of these years, the American political system had failed. A system —based upon checks and balances and on the principle that power derived from law and was thereby defined and "reined in"—had not really worked during the Cold War years. No longer can Americans comfortably conclude that the source of abuses of power was aberrant—that is, the politics and style of Richard Nixon—and that the impeachment provided the necessary resolution. Clearly the problem is more radical, and its solution requires far-reaching institutional and value changes.

Chapter One

The Huston Plan

In early June 1973 during the course of its investigation into the Watergate
Affair, the Senate Select Committee on Presidential Campaign Activities (the
Ervin committee) publicized the Nixon administration's decision to formulate and then to implement the Huston Plan. Under this plan, existing restrictions on intelligence collection (whether the resort to break-ins, mail
intercepts, electronic surveillance, or the minimum age of campus informants) would be lifted and a special interagency committee created to ensure
White House direction to the intelligence community. *Milwaukee Journal*
political cartoonist Bill Sanders characterized this revelation: "1984 came a
little early this century." Sanders's cartoon did not represent the media's
response; their reaction to the Huston Plan in fact dramatized the distinctive
priorities of conservative and liberal political analysts. Most conservative
commentators either were silent, represented the plan as the work of certain
individuals, or justified the plan's proposed violations of civil liberties on
"national security" grounds. In contrast, most liberals viewed the plan as
bespeaking the Nixon administration's flagrant unconcern for the law, the
Constitution, and the right to dissent. If conservatives perceived no constitutional problem, liberals nonetheless viewed the issue narrowly as deriving
from Richard Nixon's paranoid fears of dissent and the ultraconservative
views of White House aide Tom Charles Huston.[1]

More intensive investigation of the Huston Plan confirmed, however, that
the liberals had not understood the magnitude of this constitutional crisis.
The Huston Plan was not the product of the personal character and paranoia
of particular men but capsulized the searing impact of the Cold War on national institutions and values. For the Huston Plan was the culmination
(though not the logical consequence) of Cold War "national security" developments which in effect had ensured independence and secrecy to presidents
and internal security bureaucrats.

In one sense, the Huston Plan derived directly from the secrecy shrouding
"national security" policy. Throughout the deliberations leading to the formulation, then implementation, and ultimately recall of the plan specifically
recommending utilization of "clearly illegal" activities, White House and
intelligence agency officials were solely concerned about the risks of public
disclosure. Accordingly, they devised procedures to foreclose public discovery. These included transmitting recommendations through highly secret
channels under the code COMINT,* ordering destruction of all draft copies

---

*An acronym for Communications Intelligence, this was a highly secret classifi-
cation for National Security Agency (NSA) reports.

after the formal plan had been drafted, stipulating that the directors of the intelligence agencies making the plan's specific recommendations sign only the president's copy of the report, and having White House aide Tom Charles Huston alone sign the authorization memorandum. The sole dissenter to the plan's recommendations, FBI Director J. Edgar Hoover, concluded only that the risks of exposure were too great. Ironically, Hoover's insistence on written authorization (thereby maximizing the prospect of public disclosure) was the primary reason for President Nixon's decision to recall the plan's formal authorization.

Secrecy also permitted the formulators of the plan to act insubordinately. The responsible leadership of the intelligence community—upon whose good faith and integrity the president was dependent—neither informed Nixon about ongoing programs nor discontinued these programs after his later recall order. Lower-level FBI officials and other intelligence agency heads also intentionally misinformed FBI Director Hoover about the specific nature and origins of key decisions.

Secrecy alone, however, had not created the opportunity for the plan. The specific catalyst had been Richard Nixon's election to the presidency in 1968. Blurring the distinction between dissent and disloyalty and insisting upon absolute security, Nixon like other Cold War presidents and internal security bureaucrats considered surveillance of dissident activities necessary and proper. Where this anti-Communist differed from earlier presidents was in his more expansive conception of disloyalty.[2] Since 1946 Nixon had consistently attempted to discredit his opponents by attempting to create popular doubts about their loyalty. This tactic was strengthened by recent political exigencies: the radicalization of increasing numbers of middle-class citizens and college students by the 1970s had threatened to undermine Richard Nixon's intent to expand U.S. involvement in the ongoing, but increasingly unpopular Vietnam War. Having consistently challenged the loyalty of antiwar critics since 1965, Nixon nonetheless recognized the limited potential of such charges of disloyalty. Moreover, this conservative politician had won the presidency in 1968 not so much on the loyalty issue as by his promise of peace overseas and "law and order" at home. To discredit the antiwar movement as subversive, therefore, required more than charges; evidence was needed.[3]

In early 1969 the Nixon White House turned to the intelligence community to document foreign direction to antiwar dissent, information which could be used to discredit liberal and radical critics of its "national security" policies.

Ironically, at the very time in 1970 that the Nixon administration was soliciting evidence of "Communist" influence or direction to the antiwar and civil rights movements, the intelligence community and administration officials had learned of South Korean intelligence officials' efforts to shape congressional policy, including offering bribes, lavish partying, and granting of honorary degrees to important congressmen. Nixon administration officials, however, were relatively unconcerned about these efforts to influence national policy. Indeed, the Justice Department did not even formally investigate these activities until 1973.[4]

Committed to centralizing decision-making and to ensuring effective presidential control over the sprawling federal bureaucracy, Nixon was particularly responsive to proposals which would enable the White House to direct and monitor closely the various intelligence agencies' activities. Intelligence bureaucrats who sparked the evolution of the Huston Plan recognized that the Nixon White House provided an unparalleled opportunity to resolve their principal political problem: namely, FBI Director Hoover's opposition either to reinstituting or expanding illegal intelligence-gathering activities. The FBI director's decisions of 1965, 1966, 1967, and early 1970—ordering the termination of break-ins, use of students as informers, and mail intercepts; significantly reducing the number of wiretaps; and refusing to service automatically specific NSA and CIA investigative requests—had proved frustrating to important internal security bureaucrats like Noel Gayler, Richard Helms, and William Sullivan. The Nixon administration's insistence on fuller information about the antiwar movement, accordingly, provided these bureaucrats with an opportunity to surmount the Hoover obstacle. Such information, intelligence officials argued, could be obtained only if the president authorized the intelligence agencies to expand their investigative activities. Such presidential authorization was doubly desirable. First, it would circumvent Hoover's restrictions on FBI investigative activities. Second, such authorization would reduce these bureaucrats' vulnerability—many of the activities recommended under the Huston Plan might have been employed as early as 1940 but had not been based on direct formal White House authorization. Discovery of these activities could embarrass and possibly discredit intelligence agency bureaucrats.

The plan proposed to expand, not initiate, intensive surveillance of dissident antiwar and civil rights activities. In 1969, the Nixon administration had inherited a number of ongoing reporting programs. These included regular FBI reports to the White House about the activities of dissident American organizations and prominent leaders and on the contacts of members of Congress and congressional staff members with foreign embassies; IRS tax investigations of targeted dissident Americans; regular CIA reports on foreign contacts/influence of prominent antiwar and civil rights organizations and leaders; and a National Security Agency (NSA) program wherein the international telecommunications of targeted organizations and individuals were intercepted. These programs continued after 1969, refined to ensure more rational collection and dissemination procedures. The Nixon White House recognized that some of these activities were illegal. For example, CIA Director Richard Helms indicated in a February 18, 1969, memorandum to the president's national security adviser Henry Kissinger, accompanying "a survey of student dissidence world wide as requested by the President":

In an effort to round-out our discussion of this subject, we have included a section on American students. This is an area not within the charter of this Agency, so I need not emphasize how extremely sensitive this makes this paper. Should anyone learn of its existence it would prove most embarrassing for all concerned.

To ensure against "embarrassment" the intelligence agencies devised elaborate file-keeping procedures. The National Security Agency disseminated its top secret reports without any NSA identification and instructed recipients either to destroy or return these reports to the agency within two weeks.[5]

The president and his key aides nonetheless remained dissatisfied with the considerable information forwarded by the intelligence community. The reports had not established foreign influence or direction, and as such were of limited political value. Accordingly, the Nixon White House pointedly complained about the quality of the intelligence product and insisted upon future reports confirming such foreign direction.

As early as April 1969 Nixon directed White House legal counsel John Ehrlichman to have the intelligence community prepare a report on foreign Communist support of campus demonstrations. To obtain this "evidence," the White House defined foreign influence as including mere contact, unsolicited advice, or association. Thus, in identical June 20, 1969, memorandums, White House aide Tom Charles Huston advised the CIA deputy director and the FBI director that "foreign Communist support" should be "liberally construed to include all activities by foreign Communists designed to encourage or assist revolutionary protest movements in the United States." On June 19, 1969, moreover, Huston had informed FBI Assistant Director William Sullivan of the president's interest in learning in "greater depth" the details of New Left activities and specifically "all information possibly relating to foreign influences and the financing of the New Left." Other members of the intelligence community were being contacted, Huston advised Sullivan, to "develop whatever materials they may have within their jurisdiction" to be presented to the president "for his use." When Huston earlier informed the CIA deputy director of the White House view that "present collection capabilities . . . may be inadequate," he recommended that the agency correct any gaps in the collection program resulting from "inadequate resources or a low priority of attention." Dissatisfaction with the adequacy of FBI collection methods also led Attorney General John Mitchell to arrange a July 25, 1969, meeting with CIA Director Richard Helms. Advising Helms of his decision to establish a Civil Disturbance Group (CDG) within the Department of Justice because the FBI did not provide the needed intelligence analysis on civil disturbances, Mitchell requested that the CIA investigate the adequacy of the FBI's collection efforts and also attempt to persuade Hoover to forward FBI material to the CDG.[6]

Tom Charles Huston had been assigned responsibility to coordinate the White House effort to increase the intelligence community's intelligence-gathering activities. Originally appointed an assistant to White House speech writer Pat Buchanan, Huston brought to this coordination assignment particular views about the "national security" problem confronting American society and the necessary means to combat it. A former president of the Young Americans for Freedom, the right-wing lawyer viewed left dissent as subversive, possessed a messianic view of America's Cold War mission, and believed that to safeguard internal security, individual liberties and constitutional rights must be restricted. Like other Cold War conservatives, Huston was a McCarthyite: for him, however, the "Holy War against Communism" in particular required deference to the intelligence community.[7]

One result of Huston's White House assignment would be his close relationship with FBI Assistant Director William Sullivan. Ideologically compatible, Huston was particularly responsive to Sullivan's complaints about the difficulties under which FBI intelligence officials operated. Unless existing restrictions on FBI intelligence gathering were removed or revised, Sullivan advised Huston, the bureau could not service the White House's demands. Finding a sympathetic respondent in Huston, Sullivan convinced the White House aide that this problem in turn required devising a strategy to neutralize FBI Director Hoover's possible opposition.

Since 1965, Sullivan and other internal security bureaucrats became increasingly frustrated over Hoover's unwillingness to countenance activities which had long been normal bureau practices (if nonetheless recognized as clearly illegal). The year 1965 was not without significance: despite having reached mandatory retirement age of seventy that year, Hoover was allowed to continue as director because of an executive order of President Lyndon Johnson. Keenly sensitive to the fragility of his tenure, after 1965 Hoover became concerned about the political impact of disclosures which might embarrass the bureau and thereby discredit his leadership. During the late 1960s political risks seemingly had increased.

In the midst of the Vietnam War, members of Congress, the media, and organized interest groups had become more skeptical about federal surveillance policies. Indeed, in 1965 and 1966, an investigation of IRS surveillance tactics initiated by the Subcommittee on Administrative Practices and Procedures of the Senate Judiciary Committee had caused considerable concern to FBI and Justice Department officials. These officials feared that the subcommittee's investigation might publicize similar FBI practices. In addition, a series of federal court rulings between 1965 and 1969 challenged existing federal and state wiretapping practices and authority. The U.S. Supreme Court, for one, repudiated expansive wiretapping claims (notably in the *Berger*, *Katz*, and *Alderman* cases); furthermore, during federal court trials (notably involving lobbyist Fred Black and the so-called Chicago Seven) the extent and nature of FBI electronic surveillance were disclosed. Then, in 1967, *Ramparts* magazine published an article indicating that the CIA since the 1940s had compromised the National Student Association (raising concerns about CIA practices, authority, and threats to academic freedom). Concurrently, in 1965–67, Attorneys General Nicholas Katzenbach and Ramsey Clark imposed stricter controls over FBI wiretapping and microphone surveillance—at the minimum requiring a full written justification for each FBI wiretap or bug authorization request. Reacting to these developments, Hoover decided either to restrict or terminate altogether certain FBI investigative activities. Accordingly, in 1965 and 1966, Hoover prohibited "domestic security" break-ins, mail intercepts and/or mail covers, and use of trash covers.* Furthermore, in 1966, the FBI director imposed a numerical ceiling on FBI wiretaps and in 1967 restricted FBI contacts on college campuses and imposed an age minimum of twenty-one for FBI campus informants. Hoover's restrictions caused considerable frustration for those FBI officials having administrative responsibility in the internal security area—notably, William Sullivan and Charles Brennan, the senior officials of the bureau's Domestic Intelligence Division.[8]

FBI bureaucrats, however, were not the only intelligence officials frustrated by Hoover's recent concern about political risks. CIA officials had also become gravely concerned about the FBI director's March 31, 1970, decision to restrict FBI assistance to the CIA. This decision, deriving from an incident involving University of Colorado history professor Thomas Riha,[9] had been reached in response to CIA Director Richard Helms' earlier letter of March 20, 1970. In that letter, Helms had in turn responded to the FBI director's proposed "reexamination" of FBI/CIA relations. Because of the Riha incident Sullivan had been assigned responsibility to review earlier cases where the CIA had criticized the bureau's alleged failure to cooperate in collecting intelligence. Completing this review for Hoover, Sullivan recommended that the bureau "forthrightly" demand that the CIA specify appropriate changes in existing practices.

Although Hoover affirmed his interest in close coordination and his decision to handle this "at a headquarters level in order to avoid administrative confusion and misunderstanding," in his March 31 letter to Helms he announced that he had designated Sullivan to meet with CIA representatives to discuss these matters. Hoover then detailed the restrictions which would control FBI investigative policy, thereby formally extending his earlier 1965 and 1966 prohibitions on FBI investigative activities to the FBI's responses to the investigative requests of other intelligence agencies. The FBI director pointedly observed:

> With regard to electronic surveillance and mail coverage, there is no question as to the frequent value of such operations in developing needed intelligence. On the other hand, the use of these measures in domestic investigations poses a number of problems which might not be encountered in similar operations abroad. There is widespread concern by the American public regarding the possible misuse of this type of coverage. Moreover, various legal considerations must be

---

*These referred to illegal entries into private residences or offices, opening letters or reading the exteriors of envelopes, or investigating the trash of targeted individuals or organizations.

borne in mind, including the impact such coverage may have on our numerous prosecutive responsibilities. The FBI's effectiveness has always depended in large measure on our capacity to retain the full confidence of the American people. The use of any investigative measures which infringe on traditional rights of privacy must therefore be scrutinized most carefully. Within this framework, however, I would be willing to consider any proposals your Agency may make.[10]

Hoover's revised electronic surveillance policy had already troubled those CIA officials who since 1966 had urged the FBI director to increase the number of FBI wiretaps on domestic organizations and American dissidents. In 1969, moreover, Hoover advised Helms of a new bureau policy: that whenever the FBI received CIA electronic surveillance requests he would refer them "directly to the Attorney General for approval." Hoover's more restrictive requirements had also frustrated NSA officials. In 1967, NSA officials Louis Tordella and Marshall Carter had unsuccessfully attempted to have Hoover relax restrictions on the installation of electronic surveillances. At first relenting, Hoover reconsidered and then informed these NSA officials that he would assist the NSA only if specifically ordered to do so by either the president or the attorney general. Hoover's unwillingness to authorize electronic surveillance on his own proved deeply frustrating to these CIA and NSA officials: neither the CIA nor the NSA would consider formally requesting the attorney general (or the president) to authorize recognizably illegal activities.[11]

Unknown to Huston, his pressures on the intelligence community to provide a better intelligence product created, in the words of NSA official Louis Tordella, "nothing less than a heaven-sent opportunity."[12] Cognizant of the illegality of many ongoing programs, intelligence officials nonetheless had conducted them on their own authority since the 1950s but had then devised filing procedures to preclude discovery. Both because of the lack of presidential direction and because of their illegality, these activities rendered intelligence officials vulnerable. Then, in 1970, the opportunity both to avert this risk and to bypass Hoover occurred. The delicacy of the political problem and the possibility that even Richard Nixon might hesitate to take this major step, however, required a carefully thought-out strategy. In great part this strategy rested on the naiveté and ideological convictions of conservative White House aide Huston. Moreover, although FBI Assistant Director Sullivan had discussed the problems of "excessive" constraints on FBI intelligence gathering with Huston since June 1969, he had not moved the discussion to an action level. FBI Director Hoover's March 1970 decision to restrict FBI contacts with the CIA and to designate Sullivan as the principal FBI representative during subsequent FBI/CIA discussions thereby provided the specific catalyst to the development of such a strategy.

On April 13, 1970, Sullivan and Donald Moore (inspector-in-charge of the bureau's Espionage Research Branch) met with James Angleton, the chief of the CIA's counterintelligence staff, and an unidentified member of Angleton's staff. In an April 14, 1970, memo to Hoover aide Cartha De Loach, Sullivan described this meeting as "exploratory in nature," aimed at "defining the scope and limitations" of subsequent discussions. The April 13 discussion, Sullivan continued, focused on two issues raised by Angleton: FBI electronic surveillance coverage and the holding of "periodic seminars to coordinate our information." Sullivan claimed to have conveyed Hoover's position on electronic surveillance limitations to these CIA officials, adding:

> I made the point that the Bureau had not received the necessary support in this area from responsible quarters; that in the past the Bureau had a substantial amount of coverage of this type in the interest of both our own counterintelligence responsibilities as well as the national security interest but that we had to retrench in recent years largely as a result of the lack of support for such operations.

Sullivan then advised De Loach that the CIA was considering Hoover's 1969 suggestion that the agency take up with the attorney general its request for electronic surveillance coverage. Such a decision, however, would involve "a whole new set of procedures and policy considerations which would have to be carefully considered," and the CIA "would probably have something specific for the Bureau to consider at a subsequent meeting." The CIA had no specific recommendations on the "seminar" proposal but "would be in touch with us when they have firmed up various proposals."[13]

Coinciding with these FBI/CIA discussions, on April 22, 1970, White House staff members (H. R. Haldeman, Egil Krogh, Alexander Butterfield, John Ehrlichman, and Huston) would meet in Haldeman's office to discuss how coordination between the White House staff and the intelligence community could be improved and "whether—because of the escalating level of the violence—something within the government further needed to be done." The participants decided to plan a May meeting to be attended by the president and the heads of the four intelligence agencies. The White House could then request the intelligence agencies to prepare a report detailing what could be done to deal with the growing radical movement. (Because of the Cambodian invasion, and the reaction it engendered, this meeting was rescheduled for June 5, 1970.) It had also been agreed that Huston would assume principal responsibility for internal security matters.[14]

The coincidence of the two April meetings proved crucial. For given Hoover's position, there could be no resolution of what high-level internal security bureaucrats Sullivan, Angleton, Helms, and Tordella considered to be the crucial problem: rescinding Hoover's recently imposed restrictions on FBI intelligence gathering. Sullivan's April 14 memorandum clearly had posed the issue: support from "responsible quarters" was required and "a whole new set of procedures and policy considerations" had to be formulated. The CIA would not follow Hoover's 1969 suggestion to approach the attorney general. This option remained as unattractive in 1970 as it had been in 1969—perhaps because Helms doubted that Attorney General Mitchell would challenge Hoover. Sullivan's contacts with Huston, however, provided another avenue to explore, and a more fruitful one given White House aides Ehrlichman's, Haldeman's, and Krogh's consistently expressed contempt concerning the quality of FBI intelligence activities. More sympathetic to the bureau than his associates, Huston had concluded that the "low quality" of FBI intelligence derived from the restraints Hoover had imposed on the bureau.[15] Thus, the importance of the mere decision of the White House staff to convene a meeting between the president and the heads of the intelligence agencies offered a "heaven-sent opportunity" for intelligence bureaucrats.

The delay in holding this planned meeting only further intensified White House concerns. The Cambodian invasion unleashed an emotional, widespread protest on the college campuses. To the obsessed and besieged White House conservatives, continuing Hoover's restrictions on FBI intelligence gathering was dangerous to the extreme.

The day before the June 5 meeting, President Nixon met with Hoover to request that the FBI director head the to-be-proposed *ad hoc* interagency intelligence committee. This committee, the president confided, would be assigned responsibility to prepare an intelligence report. Hoover agreed to serve as chairman and to appoint Sullivan to head the committee's staff subcommittee.

Huston had urged the president to establish such a committee; in reality, however, William Sullivan authored this suggestion. To ensure that the desired changes would be implemented, Huston had further convinced Nixon that Sullivan should head the subcommittee staff—as in all such operations the subcommittee staff and not the prestigious but burdened committee members would perform the actual drafting work. Huston had also prepared a "talking paper" for the president's use during his June 5 remarks to the heads of the intelligence community. Apart from one minor digression, Nixon would read from Huston's prepared script. Huston's "talking paper" stressed the "magnitude of the internal security problem we face today"—Nixon's basic concern. (Indeed during his oral delivery the president digressed from the paper only to comment on his recent conversation with Venezuelan president Calder. Calder, Nixon remarked, had expressed concern about the possible relationship between black militancy in the United States and unrest in the Caribbean.) Huston's paper then emphasized the need for greater knowledge about possible foreign influence on dissident activities and to "develop a plan which will enable us to curtail the illegal activities of those who are determined to destroy our society." Stressing the importance of good intelligence, the paper affirmed the administration's intent "to insure that every resource of the Federal government is being mobilized to halt these illegal activities." Then, and the transition to these points appeared logical and rather innocent, it continued:

Based on my review of the information we have been receiving at the White House, I am convinced that we are not allocating sufficient resources within the intelligence community to the collection of intelligence data on the activities of these revolutionary groups. We need more hard information. . . .

Consequently, I would like Dick Helms to designate the USIB [United States Intelligence Board] representatives from the FBI, CIA, NSA, DIA [Defense Intelligence Agency] and military services to serve on a special subcommittee to review the collection efforts of the intelligence community and to recommend to me additional steps which can be taken to strengthen our capabilities in this regard.

This subcommittee should work with Tom Huston. . . .

I would suggest that the FBI representative serve as chairman of the subcommittee.

Tom Huston can provide the subcommittee with additional information on the scope of the review which I have in mind.

. . . We need to insure that the fullest possible inter-agency cooperation is being realized and that all our resources are being utilized to gather the types of information which will enable us to halt the spread of this terrorism before it gets completely out of hand.[16]

Apparently, Huston's and Sullivan's well-thought-out strategy had worked. Hoover might have accepted the honorific chairmanship of the interagency committee; Sullivan would handle the day-by-day decisions (and thus the effective conduct of the assignment). The FBI assistant director quickly exploited this opportunity. Delegated by Hoover to invite the other representatives to meet in his office on June 8, 1970, in a June 5, 1970, memorandum to Hoover aide Cartha De Loach "for the record and for possible reference use by the Director," Sullivan detailed the president's June 5 decision to establish the interagency committee. This special committee's purpose, Sullivan maintained in his memorandum, would be:

coordinating a more effective intelligence gathering function as a joint effort on the part of the Bureau, Central Intelligence Agency (CIA), National Security Agency (NSA), and Defense Intelligence Agency (DIA) to insure that comprehensive information is being obtained for the President's use which will provide him with a worldwide picture of New Left and other subversive activities.

Hoover, Sullivan then reported, had directed the working committee to meet on June 9 and "instructed me to serve in his place at this meeting to insure that the instructions he issues to the committee [on June 8] are carried through in specific detail." This working committee would meet twice a week with the aim of completing a draft report by June 22, 1970. Its report would then be reviewed by the FBI director and the other intelligence officials prior to being presented to the president on July 1, 1970.

In another (June 6, 1970) memorandum, Sullivan advised De Loach, final arrangements had been made for the June 8 meeting. He had decided to invite Charles Brennan (chief of the bureau's Internal Security Section) to assist in preparing the bureau's "portion of the report on the New Left and related matters." Appending a prepared statement to his June 6 memorandum, Sullivan suggested that the FBI director might wish "to give consideration to" this statement in addition to whatever other remarks he "has in mind." Sullivan's statement emphasized the magnitude, complexity, and distinctiveness of the subversive threat then confronting American society and the undeniable "foreign links" to domestic "disorder and violence." Intermixed with these assertions, Sullivan's statement affirmed:

> The President made it abundantly clear that he expects us, as members of the intelligence community, to do more than we have been doing to bring the worldwide picture of these problems into better perspective for him.
>
> . . . It is through unity of action that we [the intelligence community] can tremendously increase our intelligence-gathering potential and, I am confident, obtain the answers the President wants.
>
> I am establishing a working committee to insure that we achieve the desired unity. It will be the job of the committee to (1) assess the overall nature of the problem as we know it today, (2) examine individually and together the respective resources of each Agency to insure full utilization of them for the benefit of all, and (3) devise coordinated procedures designed to penetrate the current nebulous areas of subversive activities here and abroad as they relate to our domestic problems.[17]

Despite careful advance planning, Sullivan's and Huston's well-orchestrated strategy nonetheless confronted the ubiquitous obstacle in the person of Hoover. The FBI director viewed this committee's purpose narrowly, as did the president; namely, to draft a report on foreign intelligence activities and on foreign direction to New Left and domestic dissident activities. Accordingly, when opening the June 8 meeting, Hoover reminded the participants of the president's dissatisfaction with the intelligence he had been provided and alarms about foreign links to domestic radicals. Ignoring Sullivan's prepared statement, the FBI director maintained that the president had requested "an historical summary" of domestic unrest. The interagency staff committee would have responsibility to draft this report, would be chaired by Sullivan, and would first meet on June 9. Hoover then asked if the other intelligence bureaucrats had anything to add. None did at first until Huston spoke. Hoover had misunderstood the president's intent, the White House aide claimed. The president had not requested an historical summary but a current and future assessment, a review of "intelligence gaps," and a summary of options for "operational changes." In addition, Huston emphasized, the president wanted the advantages and disadvantages of various "collection methods" clearly spelled out in the form of pros and cons with the president reserving the option of the final decision. Excepting Hoover, the other intelligence bureaucrats (from NSA, CIA, and DIA) supported Huston's interpretation of the president's instructions. This created a tense situation and the meeting ended abruptly.[18]

Cognizant of the potential problem which Hoover's June 8 position posed, and committed to establishing a paper record to underpin his position as chairman of the working staff committee, Sullivan wrote another memorandum to De Loach reporting on the same day the June 8 meeting. Hoover had advised the committee members, Sullivan reported, of the president's concern over subversive activities and expectation that the committee would "coordinate and plan so that the worldwide picture could be better brought into perspective for the President." Sullivan then recounted:

> In outlining the work of the Committee, the Director pointed out
> . . . (2) Each agency must explore the facilities which must and can
> be used in order to develop facts for a true intelligence picture. The
> Director noted the President mentioned restrictions which were hampering our intelligence operations and accordingly we should list for
> the President in detail such restraints and restrictions together with
> the pros and cons involved so that the President can make a decision
> as to which ones should be utilized. (3) . . .
> . . . During the discussion all agreed that the initial primary problem confronting the Committee was to concentrate upon methodology
> in intelligence collection. The Director stated . . . a detailed listing of
> all the items which are currently obstructing the FBI and other intelligence agencies in attaining their goals must be set out clearly with
> pros and cons so that the President is able to make a determination
> as to what he is willing to let us do.[19]

Hoover's narrower directive had been neatly sidestepped. Carefully formulated memorandums for the record would allow Sullivan to misinform Hoover while at the same time helping to formulate a report offering far-reaching changes. In effect, the procedure of submitting recommendations for the president's consideration, moreover, would provide the opportunity to revoke Hoover's earlier restrictions while also establishing formal presidential authorization for ongoing activities or their expansion. Not surprisingly, then, Sullivan and Huston would work closely in tandem in drafting the report: Sullivan identifying specific recommendations and the report's thrust and Huston pressuring the other staff members to follow Sullivan's lead or to specify precisely proposed changes.

The participants at the June 8 meeting decided to meet thereafter in CIA headquarters in Langley, Virginia, to ensure maximum secrecy and preclude public knowledge of this interagency effort. This decision to meet in Langley enabled Huston and Sullivan to coordinate their efforts more effectively.

Driving together to and from Langley, the White House aide and the FBI assistant director discussed common strategy and reactions.[20] At the first Langley meeting on June 9 the participants decided to adopt an extremely high-level classification—"Top Secret–Handle Via Comint Channels Only"—and to maintain a list of all persons who worked on the report or had knowledge of the interagency committee's work. Prior to the next meeting, members also agreed to prepare a "list of those restraints which they consider hamper their intelligence collection activities" and to detail these restraints' advantages and disadvantages. To meet the working group's responsibility "to define and assess the existing internal security threat," Huston proposed that the FBI prepare such a paper from the domestic standpoint and the CIA from the international standpoint.

At subsequent meetings little time or attention would be devoted to the report's "existing internal security threat" portion. The group's discussions instead centered almost exclusively on the "restraints" problem. Moreover, while Huston formally directed these deliberations (consistent with the outline he had prepared for the meeting stipulating that the "scope and direction of the review [by the subcommittee] will be determined by the White House member"), Sullivan in effect determined the thrust and content of the working group effort. Thus, after the various members had submitted the required "restraints papers" at the June 12 meeting, Huston praised "the FBI submission" which "was in the form he desired" and ordered the other members to "pattern" their papers "after the FBI submission." Sullivan was assigned responsibility at the June 18 meeting, moreover, to draft the proposed report. His draft would then be circulated to all members of the group "after which the recipients will attempt to obtain high-level concurrence within their respective agencies or departments."[21]

As Huston's outline had stipulated, the working group would not make specific recommendations. The group would list various options, and outline each option's pros and cons; the final decision would be left to the president. Huston's objective was not so much to allow the president to have the final say as to bypass Hoover. If the report had been presented as the interagency committee's recommendations (which the president would then approve or disapprove in part or in whole) the FBI director could then have insisted on major changes or deletions as conditions for his signature. He could not do this if the report merely listed options.

This was not a minor matter. For the draft report recommended sweeping changes in the intelligence community's investigative methods, would have provided the first formal presidential authorization for recognizably "clearly illegal" activities, and in effect some of the changes would have repudiated Hoover's post-1965 restraints. Recommended changes included: increasing the number of wiretaps and microphone surveillances, broadening NSA interceptions of the international communications of American citizens by not "allow[ing] the FBI to determine what the NSA should do in this area without regard to our own requirements," relaxing restrictions on mail covers and mail intercepts, modifying restrictions to permit selective use of break-ins against domestic organizations and individuals, lifting age and other restrictions to increase FBI informant coverage of campus and student-related groups, and establishing an interagency intelligence committee responsible for evaluating domestic intelligence information and preparing periodic intelligence reports for the president. This proposed interagency committee would include a White House representative who would have the authority to "coordinate intelligence originating within this committee."[22]

Because the principal motivation had been to undercut FBI Director Hoover's authority, and because the strategy adopted to achieve this result had been back-handed and indirect, the formal requirement that the working group submit its draft report to the interagency committee members prior to final submission to the president posed a potential obstacle. The Huston-Sullivan strategy of submitting options to the president was intended to confront the FBI director with a *fait accompli*. In a further effort to achieve this result, two additional tactics were adopted. First, Hoover's assent was not sought until after the other intelligence agency heads (CIA, NSA, and DIA) had been approached.[23] Second, Sullivan (who had been appointed to represent the FBI, and presumably the director's, interests) regularly reported to Hoover (through De Loach) on the working group's activities. Sullivan's memorandums, to say the least, neither accurately conveyed the thrust of the working group's activities nor the FBI assistant director's central role.

Thus, in a June 10, 1970, memorandum to De Loach reporting on the June 9 meeting, Sullivan appended a copy of Huston's outline to the working group detailing the president's purposes and objectives when establishing the interagency committee. In essence, Sullivan conveyed the impression that the working group was obligated to respond to the president's demands. The president desired not to be "told what the current problem is, but rather what the future problems will be and what must be done to counter them." At the meeting, Sullivan further reported: "Members discussed the restraints currently in effect which limit the community's ability to develop this necessary intelligence. In accordance with the President's instructions, the next meeting of the Working Subcommittee will consider all restraints restricting intelligence collection efforts across the board. . . ."[24]

Sullivan adopted the same strategy when reporting on the June 12 meeting. The working group agreed that the report to be submitted to the president should cover three areas—an assessment of the current internal security threat, a listing of current restraints "which deter the development of this type of information the President desires," and an evaluation of interagency coordination. Consistent with this portrayal of White House direction and pressure, Sullivan then claimed:

> The White House representative advised the restraints portion of the Committee report to the President should include, in addition to identifying the restraints and a listing of the pros and cons of modify-

ing the restraints, a brief paragraph allowing the President to indicate what action he desires to be taken. Specifically, this would provide the President the opportunity to indicate whether he desired the restraints to be continued, relaxed, or that he needed additional information upon which to make a decision. It was the sense of the Committee regarding the third portion of the report that a permanent operations committee was needed to coordinate operations, prepare estimates of potential violence during future demonstrations, and to develop new policies. The creation of such a committee was endorsed by the White House representative, who indicated such a committee would probably be desired by the President.[25]

Sullivan's June 19, 1970, memorandum on the June 18 meeting was even more dishonest than his earlier two memorandums—particularly because Sullivan had been designated to draft the proposed report and the bureau's Research Section had written the first draft which Sullivan would bring to the meeting without having first shown it to Hoover. Sullivan began this June 19 memorandum by noting how the groundwork for the final meeting had been laid at the two previous meetings and how at the third meeting "the members of the four intelligence organizations worked out the report. I received the impression that Admiral Noel Gaylor [sic] of National Security Agency may have been a moving force behind the creation of this committee. The [deleted] Program which we discontinued a few years ago was raised immediately and figured prominently in the discussion." Sullivan continued by again emphasizing Huston's central direction and further Huston's insistence that the report "had to be a working subcommittee report and any opinions, observations, conclusions or recommendations of individual agencies should not and could not be set forth with one exception." "The President," Sullivan then asserted, desired that each intelligence agency make "a definitive recommendation relative to creating a group or committee which could deal with operational problems and objectives." Having focused attention on the permanent coordinating committee issue, Sullivan noted that inevitably the four intelligence agencies would disagree and added: "In view of this it is probably fortunate that no member was permitted to make any decisions, recommendations, or conclusions, et cetera, in that the President reserves this right for himself only. Each controversial issue has been so set up in writing that the President may quickly and simply indicate whether he wants or does not want any changes made." "We are completing" the first draft of the report, Sullivan concluded his memorandum. When completed, this report would be submitted to Hoover "with a cover memorandum explaining the various issues involved."[26]

Sullivan submitted the completed draft along with a cover memorandum to another Hoover adviser, FBI Associate Director Clyde Tolson, on June 20. In this memorandum, Sullivan attempted to circumvent the report's difficult political problem: namely, its recommendations' intrusion upon Hoover's authority. To minimize Hoover's reaction, Sullivan attempted to focus the FBI director's attention on the permanent interagency coordinating committee recommendation. The "investigative restraints and limitations" section was again described as "in accordance with the President's request, with the pros and cons outlined and with no recommendations of any kind made by the committee." These recommendations, Sullivan conceded, adversely affected the bureau as well as the other agencies. Similarly representing the proposed creation of a permanent interagency committee as responsive to the president's request, Sullivan emphasized his disagreement "with the scope of this proposed committee" and with the concept of "combined preparation of intelligence estimates."

Having identified problem areas, Sullivan suggested that the director either could make no objections, could do so orally, or could in writing oppose relaxing investigative restraints and the "extensive scope and ramifications" of the proposed new committee. Sullivan offered four recommendations:

(1) That approval be given for the Bureau to include in the final committee report a statement opposing the relaxation of investigative restraints which affect the Bureau.

(2) That the Bureau take a position at Tuesday's [June 23] meeting of the working committee that it is opposed to a new committee of the scope described in the attached draft, but that we would not object to a committee limited to better coordination of specific intelligence operations or problems.

(3) That, in addition, the Director give consideration to expressing his objections verbally to the President.

(4) That, if the Director's schedule permits, final meeting of Director's committee take place in his office at 11 A.M., Thursday, June 25. At that time the Director can inquire if other committee members have any further comments and, if not, he can present them with a copy of the final report. (If the Director does not wish to present this report personally to the President, we will prepare appropriate transmittal letter for liaison to handle.)[27]

Sullivan's cover memorandum confirmed the delicacy of his position. He had sought to minimize Hoover's reaction by recommending either that the FBI director submit "a statement" or "verbally" protest to the president. Hoover would not be so cooperative and at first refused to sign the report unless the restraints section and the recommended permanent interagency committee proposals were eliminated. In his 1975 testimony before the Senate Select Committee on Intelligence Activities Sullivan maintained that Hoover had complained that in the past he had authorized these activities but that they were "becoming more and more dangerous, and we are apt to get caught." The attorney general or some high-ranking person in the White House, Sullivan recalled Hoover as stating, should henceforth assume this responsibility. Sullivan eventually convinced Hoover to list his specific objections in the form of footnotes to the report. The FBI director directed Sullivan to draft the footnotes. This Sullivan did.[28]

Hoover's footnotes did not raise objections of principle to the proposed changes. Emphasizing the risks involved, the FBI director wrote that he would not object if the other agencies employed these investigative techniques. Present electronic surveillance coverage was adequate, one Hoover footnote affirmed, adding that the FBI director "would not oppose other agencies seeking authority of the Attorney General for coverage required by them and thereafter instituting such coverage themselves." Supporting "legal mail coverage" providing "it is done on a carefully controlled and selective basis," another Hoover footnote opposed any "covert" mail coverage (i.e., mail opening) because this was illegal and because "information would leak out of the Post Office to the press" and seriously damage the intelligence community. Hoover objected outright to break-ins and opposed lifting "present" restrictions concerning campus informants claiming that the risks of "leaks to the press . . . would be damaging and . . . could result in charges that investigative agencies are interfering with academic freedom." Opposing the creation of a permanent interagency committee, Hoover nonetheless affirmed the bureau's willingness to prepare "periodic intelligence estimates."[29]

Hoover's footnoted objections to having the FBI conduct these activities, emphasis on practical problems, and affirmation of the illegality of some of the recommended changes threatened to undermine this interagency drafting effort. In effect, Hoover's footnoted objections raised anew what had been the major problem from the start: the FBI director's refusal to allow the FBI to conduct illegal activities beneficial to other intelligence agencies. Hoover's willingness to have other agencies perform these illegal activities only further complicated the problem—under Hoover's proposals other agencies would assume the risk for conducting illegal activities, would be doing so knowing of Hoover's footnoted objections that these activities were illegal, and knowing further that their doing so would clearly violate laws prohibiting their involvement in internal security investigations.

Not surprisingly, then, the other intelligence agency heads reacted bitterly to Hoover's footnotes. DIA Director General Donald Bennett and NSA Director Noel Gayler immediately phoned Huston to insist either that another meeting be convened to have Hoover remove the footnotes or that *they* be allowed to insert footnotes of explanation. The White House aide successfully dissuaded Bennett and Gayler from taking any action, informing them that he would fully outline their views in his cover memorandum to the president. It would also be better not to create any avoidable difficulties with Hoover. Bennett and Gayler agreed, and the final signing ceremony on June 25 proceeded fairly amicably. Hoover concluded that meeting by reminding the directors to destroy all working copies of the report.[30]

In his July 1970 cover memorandum submitting the interagency committee's final report to the president, to which the White House aide appended another memorandum offering specific recommendations and their rationale, Huston followed the course he had outlined in his telephone conversations with Bennett and Gayler. Huston's memorandums indirectly confirm that the stated rationale of listing pros and cons to allow the president to decide among various options had merely been a ploy to prevent Hoover from vetoing proposed changes in the FBI's investigative activities. In his cover memorandum and his memorandum listing the recommendations, the White House aide summarily disparaged Hoover's objections. In the process, whether intentionally or not, Huston misinformed Nixon about the nature of the effort resulting in this report—describing neither the background to Hoover's restrictions, his own and Sullivan's central role in formulating the report, nor how the intentional bypassing of Hoover inevitably ensured the FBI director's objections.

Huston dishonestly described his own participation as merely "keeping the committee on the target the President established" believing that the report "would be more accurate and the recommendations more helpful if the agencies were allowed wide latitude in expressing their opinions and working out arrangements which they felt met the President's requirements consistent with the resources and missions of the member agencies." From the start, Huston claimed, the FBI director had attempted to "divert the committee from operational problems and redirect its mandate to the preparation of another analysis of existing intelligence." Hoover's footnoted objections, Huston then asserted, were "inconsistent and frivolous," reflecting only a concern about personal embarrassment. With the exception of Hoover all the individuals involved in preparing the report (including FBI officials "who have day-to-day responsibilities for domestic intelligence operations") were dissatisfied with current restraints on intelligence-gathering operations and believed that "changes in operating procedures [should] be initiated at once." The intelligence community needed better direction and coordination, Huston argued, adding: "Unlike most of the bureaucracy, the intelligence community . . . [agrees], with the exception of Mr. Hoover, that effective coordination within the community is possible only if there is direction from the White House." Hoover was a "loyal trooper," Huston amazingly concluded, and would not hesitate to accede to any decision of the president. Huston thus urged that Nixon call Hoover in "for a stroking session" and then explain his decisions, thank the FBI director for his candid advice and past cooperation, and seek his future cooperation in implementing the decisions. Another meeting of the heads of all the intelligence agencies should be convened at which the president should announce his decisions. "An official memorandum setting forth the precise decisions of the President should be prepared so that there can be no misunderstanding," Huston advised. "We should also incorporate a review procedure which will enable us to ensure that the decisions are fully implemented."[31]

Huston seemed insensitive to the significance of the proposed recommendations. In the guise of ensuring greater efficiency in and more effective presidential direction to the intelligence community's investigative efforts,

Huston was recommending that Nixon directly and in writing authorize recognizably illegal activities. Nixon might have approved the plan (as he subsequently claimed) on the belief that "the procedures were consistent with those employed by prior administrations and had been found to be effective by the intelligence agencies."[32] This president's principal concerns, however, did not include legality.

Hoover's footnoted opposition, nonetheless, proved important—even though the FBI director had signed the final report. Hoover had gone on record disapproving and citing the illegality of the recommended changes in investigative procedures. After some delay, H. R. Haldeman informed Huston of the president's approval. The nature of Nixon's approval underscored Nixon's awareness of the delicacy of the situation. Significantly, Nixon acceded to none of his White House aide's proposed steps: that the president invite Hoover for a "stroking session," then invite heads of the intelligence agencies to a formal meeting announcing his decision, and (most important) issue a memorandum clearly outlining his approval and the recommended procedures. Haldeman advised Huston that the president had "approved" the recommendations but was too busy to meet again with Hoover and with the other intelligence agency heads and would not

> . . . follow the procedure you outlined . . . regarding implementation. He would prefer that the thing simply be put into motion on the basis of this approval.
>
> The formal official memorandum, of course, should be prepared and this should be the device by which to carry it out.
>
> I realize that this is contrary to your feeling as to the best way to get this done. If you feel very strongly that this procedure won't work you had better let me know and we'll take another stab at it. Otherwise let's go ahead.

Sensing no difficulty, Huston enthusiastically followed Haldeman's suggested *modus operandi* and drafted the suggested "official memorandum."[33]

Significantly, only Huston signed the July 23, 1970, "official" memorandum to the four intelligence chiefs which was issued neither as an executive order nor as a presidential directive. The various recommendations to lift restrictions or expand intelligence collection had been approved and were to be implemented. Huston's memorandum merely reported that "the President has carefully studied the Special Report of the Interagency Committee on Intelligence (Ad Hoc) and made the following decisions: . . ." Huston did not, however, specify explicit presidential agreement to the proposed method. The last two paragraphs of Huston's memo, moreover, asserted:

> The President has directed that each addressee submit a detailed report, due on September 1, 1970, on the steps taken to implement these decisions. Further such periodic reports will be requested as circumstances permit.

The President is aware that procedural problems may arise in the course of implementing these decisions. However, he is anxious that such problems be resolved with maximum speed and minimum misunderstanding. Any difficulties which may arise should be brought to my attention in order that an appropriate solution may be found and the President's directives implemented in a manner consistent with his objectives.[34]

Richard Nixon had astutely decided to have his politically naive, conservative White House aide assume formal responsibility for initiating this plan. Such a decision would ensure a degree of presidential deniability. Knowledge of the decision would be closely guarded—only those having "a need to know" were aware of the plan's existence and future communiqués would be transmitted by courier under the super-secret code COMINT. Not having personally ordered lifting these restrictions and because Huston's authorization memorandum had not denoted specific presidential knowledge or decisions, Richard Nixon had retained the option of denying having authorized any activity which might subsequently become publicly exposed.

Ultimately, this presidential decision had important consequences, particularly given the astuteness of that wily Washington bureaucrat J. Edgar Hoover. Whether or not he was distressed that his footnoted objections had been ignored, FBI Director Hoover correctly recognized that the manner by which the plan had been authorized placed all intelligence officials in an extremely vulnerable position. In essence, the intelligence agency heads were being asked to assume the burden of risk in the event of public disclosure of these proposed activities. Too shrewd to be so used, the FBI director immediately informed his ostensible superior, Attorney General John Mitchell, of Huston's July 23, 1970, "official" memorandum.

Hoover's briefing caught the attorney general by surprise. The attorney general had not known of the interagency committee's existence and deliberations, let alone Huston's July 23 memorandum or its June 25 final report. Whatever his reactions to the specific recommendations, the attorney general urged Hoover to "sit tight" until Mitchell discussed the matter with the president (then vacationing in San Clemente, California). Hoover did not sit tight. Returning to his office, the FBI director wrote a memorandum to the attorney general (dated July 27, 1970) to which he appended a copy of Huston's July 23, 1970, memorandum.

In his memorandum Hoover reviewed the history of the establishment of the interagency committee and the specific recommendations detailed in the June 25, 1970, report to the president. "As set out in the attached letter from Mr. Huston," the FBI director pointedly observed, "*it is noted that the President has directed* the relaxation of four investigative restraints directly affecting the responsibility of the FBI" (emphasis added). Citing these four restraints and his specific objections to each proposed change, Hoover concluded:

Despite my clear-cut and specific opposition to the lifting of the various investigative restraints . . . and to the creation of a permanent interagency committee in domestic intelligence, the FBI is prepared to implement the instructions of the White House at your direction. Of course, we would continue to seek your specific authorization, where appropriate, to utilize the various investigative techniques involved in individual cases.

I would appreciate a prompt expression of your views concerning this matter, noting the request set forth in Mr. Huston's letter that an interagency committee be constituted by August 1, 1970. We are taking no action to implement the instructions contained in Mr. Huston's letter pending your reply.[35]

Hoover's insistence on specific instructions and announcement of his intent to request authorization each time before instituting a break-in, mail intercept, expanded campus coverage, or electronic surveillance ultimately forced the president to reconsider his earlier authorization. In effect, the FBI director's proposed method would have undermined Nixon's strategy of deniability. Written requests for the attorney general's authorization combined with the July 27 memorandum's references that the investigative activities had been instituted at the president's direction would establish a record that the FBI was responding to White House orders and further would increase the risks that these illegal activities could be discovered.[36]

Not surprisingly, then, the Mitchell-Nixon conversation (of July 27 coincidentally) focused on the plan's political risks. Both the president and his attorney general agreed that these risks were greater than the anticipated benefits. Responding to a Senate Select Committee interrogatory concerning his July 27 meeting with Mitchell, the president claimed to have been surprised to learn of Hoover's disagreement and continued:

Mr. Mitchell informed me that it was Director Hoover's opinion that initiating a program which would permit several government intelligence agencies to utilize the investigative techniques outlined in the Committee's report would significantly increase the possibility of their public disclosure. Mr. Mitchell explained to me that Mr. Hoover believed that although each of the intelligence gathering methods outlined in the Committee's recommendations had been utilized by one or more previous Administrations, their sensitivity would likely generate media criticism if they were employed. Mr. Mitchell further informed me that it was his opinion that the risk of disclosure of the possible illegal actions . . . was greater than the possible benefit to be derived. Based upon this conversation with Attorney General Mitchell, I decided to revoke the approval originally extended to the Committee's recommendations.[37]

Forewarned by Sullivan that Hoover had met with Mitchell and that the attorney general would meet with the president, Huston was not surprised when Haldeman called to report on the Nixon/Mitchell meeting. The White House aide was angered, however, when informed that the president had rescinded Huston's authorization memorandum. Complying, Huston directed the White House Situation Room to have the intelligence chiefs return his July 23, 1970, "official" memorandum. On July 28, 1970, this was done.[38]

Huston was not resigned to this decision. On August 3, he urged Haldeman to convince the president to reconsider this recall decision and instead meet with the attorney general and the FBI director. Following a meeting with Haldeman, Huston concluded that Nixon would meet with Mitchell and Hoover. Accordingly, on August 5, 1970, he wrote Haldeman outlining a proper course of action. Agencies other than the FBI had an interest in the matter and all except Hoover had supported the option "selected by the President." "For your private information," Huston added, "so did all the members of Mr. Hoover's staff who worked on the report (he'd fire them if he knew this)." The White House was not getting "the type of hard intelligence we need," Huston observed; to obtain this intelligence, certain risks would have to be taken and these risks had been carefully considered during the deliberations leading to the report. Appealing to the President's vanity, Huston argued that Hoover must learn "who is President"; "the entire intelligence community knows that the President made a positive decision to go ahead and Hoover has now succeeded in forcing a review. If he gets his way it is going to look like he is more powerful than the President." Listing and then rebutting possible "specious" arguments which the attorney general or the FBI director might raise, Huston emphasized the gravity of the internal security problem and at the same time minimized the risks. Huston then dismissed Hoover's insistence upon written authorization: "This is up to the AG, but I would tell Hoover that he has been instructed to do them by the President and he is to do them on that authority. He needn't look for a scape goat. He has his authority from the President and he doesn't need a written memo from the AG. *To maintain security, we should avoid written communications in this area*" (emphasis added).[39]

The White House aide, however, had failed to understand political realities. Involved here were not illusions, images, or the desirability of maintaining secrecy but considerations of power. The FBI director had clearly conveyed his unwillingness to serve as the servant of the White House. Hoover had further signaled his intent to create a written record of prior approval and direction. As much as Nixon might have desired fuller information on his domestic critics he would not directly order the plan's proposed changes. Unlike his aide, moreover, the president had a keener sense of the constitutional risks involved when a president directly authorized intelligence officials to violate the law—laws were not simply obstacles to surmount but responsibilities to fulfill and respect. Again, unlike Huston, Nixon had never been a right-wing ideologue; for him anticommunism was principally a successful political tactic.

Ironically, FBI Director Hoover was not the only person kept in the dark during the formulation of the Huston Plan. The intelligence bureaucrats either had not fully informed or in some instances misinformed Huston, and thereby President Nixon as well, about ongoing programs. The Huston Plan recommendations were either to lift existing restrictions on illegal intelligence gathering or expand existing but inadequate internal security investigative authority. Intelligence agency bureaucrats FBI Assistant Director William Sullivan, CIA Counterintelligence Chief James Angleton, NSA Assistant Directors Benson Buffham and Louis Tordella clearly implied that certain ongoing intelligence activities had been terminated. Thus, the White House aide understood (as did the president in view of the final report's language) that FBI break-ins during domestic security investigations had been terminated in 1966. In fact, such break-ins continued after 1966. Although the CIA had conducted a mail cover/intercept program since 1952 and had provided the FBI with Xerox copies of documents obtained under this interception program since 1958, the final report unqualifiedly stated that "covert coverage [mail intercepts] has been discontinued while routine coverage [mail covers] has been reduced." Huston was briefed neither about the FBI's COINTEL-PROs initiated in 1956 nor about the CIA's CHAOS program initiated in 1967 (although in the case of CHAOS the president and senior National Security Council aides were fully knowledgeable). Lastly, neither Huston nor the president was informed about the NSA's ongoing "Watch List" program (code-named MINARET) also initiated in 1967. Thus, Huston recommended to the president: "Present interpretation should be broadened to permit and program for coverage by NSA of the communications of U.S. citizens using international facilities . . . NSA is currently doing so [monitoring international communications] on a restricted basis . . . it would be to our disadvantage to allow the FBI to determine what NSA should do in this area . . . ."[40]

Moreover, while initiated without prior presidential authorization or knowledge, MINARET, COINTELPRO, CHAOS, FBI domestic security break-ins, and the CIA's mail intercept programs* were not terminated following President Nixon's rescission decision. Instead, the CIA continued its mail intercept and CHAOS programs and the NSA its Watch List program until 1973 while the FBI did not terminate COINTELPRO until 1971 and continued to resort to break-ins as late as 1976. The heads of the various intelligence agencies interpreted Nixon's recall decision as the denial of formal presidential authorization and as an unsuccessful effort to circumvent FBI Director Hoover's restrictions on FBI investigative activities. NSA officials simply viewed Nixon's decision as a lost "heaven sent" opportunity to obtain explicit presidential approval and not a prohibition of any ongoing program. They also hoped that Hoover's 1966 ban on FBI break-ins might thereby be relaxed. Lifting this ban would have enabled the FBI to assist the NSA to fulfill its perceived mission.[41]

*These programs are discussed in detail in subsequent chapters.

Throughout, the intelligence community's underlying objective had been to exploit Nixon's and the White House's concern about New Left political activism and not to inform the president about the scope and nature of ongoing intelligence activities. Accordingly when FBI Director Hoover subsequently changed his mind about certain investigative procedures, these were unilaterally instituted. Thus, on September 4, 1970, Hoover lifted his 1967 restriction requiring security and racial informants to be twenty-one years old and authorized recruiting eighteen-year-olds. On October 29, 1970, the FBI director approved, moreover, expanding the FBI's "security investigative coverage of extremist elements" to include individuals and organizations who might not meet Security Index criteria "to determine whether they have a propensity for violence." Both changes were instituted without the president's or the attorney general's prior knowledge or authorization. In addition, in July 1971, in this case with the approval of the Department of Justice, the FBI reinstituted a "legal mail cover" program.[42]

Not knowing that they had been misinformed by the intelligence community about ongoing programs and further that these programs continued after the president rescinded the Huston Plan, White House personnel remained committed to the plan. Unwilling to challenge Hoover again on intelligence collection restrictions, Nixon administration officials at the least sought more effective interagency coordination. Accordingly, following a September 17, 1970, meeting between Attorney General John Mitchell and White House aide John Dean (who succeeded Huston as the aide having principal staff responsibility in the internal security area), a decision to create an interagency intelligence unit was to be implemented. Such a unit could ensure more effective coordination and provide appropriate direction to the "type of intelligence that should be immediately pursued by the various agencies." In a September 18, 1970, memorandum to the attorney general, Dean reported their agreement "that it would be inappropriate to have any blanket removal of restrictions; rather, the most appropriate procedure would be to decide on the type of intelligence we need, based on an assessment of the recommendations of this unit, and then to proceed to remove the restraints as necessary to obtain such intelligence." Aware of Hoover's earlier objection to an interagency committee, Dean thought it best that this unit be created through White House direction but added that "it is essential that you work this out with Hoover before I have any dealings with him directly."

Dean also recognized the committee's sensitivity. Accordingly, the White House aide stressed, "Serious consideration . . . [should] be given to the appropriate Justice Department cover for the domestic intelligence operation." The IDIU (the Interagency Domestic Intelligence Unit within the Department of Justice) should provide this "cover"; Dean then explained: "I believe it is generally felt that IDIU is already a far more extensive intelligence operation than has been mentioned publicly, and that the IDIU operation cover would eliminate the problem of discovering a new intelligence operation in the Department of Justice."[43]

After further discussions, such a unit, the Intelligence Evaluation Committee (IEC), was formally created. Even then the committee's role had not been finally determined. The membership of the committee, composed of representatives of the FBI, the CIA, White House aide John Dean, Assistant Attorney General (and head of the Internal Security Division) Robert Mardian, and Justice Sharpe, alone would formulate the IEC's goals.

In a December 4, 1970, memorandum to Attorney General Mitchell, Mardian reported on the IEC's first meeting of December 3, 1970. The members had agreed that the IEC would: (1) centralize all intelligence data; (2) evaluate the severity of the internal security problem; and (3) ascertain needed future responses. "This evaluation," Mardian advised, "would, if necessary, disclose the sufficiency of our present intelligence resources, as well as the priorities which the government should attach to the problem." Sensitive to the need for secrecy, the participants at the December 3 meeting agreed that "there be no discussion or communication of our activities" except among the participants, the heads of their agencies, the attorney general, and designated White House personnel. In the event of a leak, Mardian advised the attorney general, "the governmental response would simply be that the activities of the Committee were an attempt to upgrade the intelligence-gathering activities of the IDIU which had heretofore been made public and that Justice Sharpe had been employed as a consultant by the Attorney General to assist in that endeavor."[44]

This proposal almost immediately encountered Hoover's resistance. In a February 3, 1971, memorandum, the FBI director informed Mardian that for "manpower and budgetary" reasons the FBI would not provide personnel for the proposed permanent intelligence estimation staff. The bureau, however, would cooperate fully in "providing all relevant intelligence which might be of assistance to the Committee."[45]

Hoover's refusal was not challenged. The Nixon administration, nonetheless, decided to institute this committee, even without FBI personnel. Of necessity, the committee's functions were thus limited. The committee could not, for that reason, even consider recommending lifting restraints on existing intelligence activities. In time, however, the combination of the Senate Watergate Committee's public revelation of the IEC's existence and the limited value of this effort led the Nixon administration to dissolve it on June 11, 1973.[46]

An earlier unsigned memorandum to Attorney General Mitchell and White House aides H. R. Haldeman and John Ehrlichman, dated January 19, 1971, on Justice Department stationery purported to speak for all the IEC members. This memorandum recommended implementing the Huston Plan as "the starting point for an effective domestic intelligence operation." Because of the severity of the current internal security problem, the memorandum stressed, the IEC should meet on an *ad hoc* basis in White House aide John Dean's office. This January 19 memorandum specifically recommended that any deficiencies in intelligence should be called to the attention of the existing agencies and corrections should be made through the normal structure. If this fails to produce the requisite intelligence, it is the recommend [sic] that the questions raised by the Ad Hoc Committee Report [the Huston Plan] be re-examined, to determine how either partial or full implementation of the recommendations in that report might be accomplished.[47]

Whether Hoover's February 3, 1971, refusal to assign FBI personnel to the IEC was in response to this January 19, 1971, memorandum or to other factors, the Nixon administration again attempted to convince the FBI director that the Huston Plan recommendations should be implemented. On March 25, 1971, Attorney General Mitchell invited Hoover to a March 31, 1971, meeting with himself, CIA Director Helms, and NSA Director Gayler. Held instead on March 29, 1971, the meeting had been requested by Helms (in the words of Hoover's April 12, 1971, memorandum for the files) "for the purpose of discussing a broadening of operations, particularly of the very confidential type in covering intelligence both domestic and foreign." In his memorandum on this meeting, Hoover claimed:

> I stated to the Attorney General, Mr. Helms, and Admiral Gaylor [sic] that I was not at all enthusiastic about such an extension of operations insofar as the FBI was concerned in view of the hazards involved. The Attorney General stated that he thought before he could make any final decision in this matter, Mr. Helms should make an in-depth examination of exactly what he and Admiral Gaylor [sic] desired and then submit to the Attorney General and myself the results of this examination, and he, the Attorney General, would call another meeting of this particular group and make the decision as to what could or could not be done.
>
> Mr. Helms said he would take care of this very promptly.[48]

The CIA director did not act promptly. The shrewd FBI bureaucrat had once again stymied another circuitous effort to circumvent his recently instituted restrictions. Reaffirming his unwillingness to expand FBI intelligence-gathering activities, Hoover in essence counseled the CIA and NSA to assume the risks of conducting illegal activities. Mitchell's suggestion that the CIA director submit specific recommendations in writing was of no assistance —such a proposal required Helms to create a record that he had requested the attorney general's authorization of clearly illegal activities. This differed from the Huston Plan where the intelligence community seemingly was only responding to the White House's bidding.

While never permanently implemented, the Huston Plan nonetheless highlights one of the major institutional changes of the Cold War years: the emergence of a quasi-independent intelligence community. The priorities of this community were based on rather expansive conceptions of "national security" threats. Given popular and congressional acceptance of the need for secrecy and deference to presidential "executive privilege" claims, intelligence officials' authority was virtually limitless. Increasingly during these years, internal security bureaucrats were principally concerned about the risk of public exposure. To obviate disclosure, accordingly, they devised elaborate procedures. Ironically, this penchant for secrecy also made possible the very duplicity and chicanery predominating throughout the history of the Huston Plan.

The Huston Plan was not merely an abortive or atypical effort but starkly highlights the major institutional and value changes which had evolved during the Cold War years. While its initiative came only during Nixon's administration, the plan was the culmination of the relationships and priorities which since 1936 had determined the actions of the U.S. intelligence community. Encouraged by their earlier successes in obtaining presidential authorization or in minimizing risks and by their belief in the righteousness of their course, by 1970 internal security bureaucrats had concluded both that they were above the law and that their activities need not be confined to those expressly authorized by presidents or attorneys general. The ultimate irony of the Huston Plan, however, was that FBI officials Sullivan and Brennan in their deceptive attempt to bypass the FBI director duplicated the very means employed by Hoover since 1936 to obtain presidential authorization to expand FBI investigative activities.

Chapter Two
Emergency Detention Programs

The history of the Huston Plan involved an attempt of duplicity by high-level FBI officials to circumvent FBI Director Hoover's policies. The history of the emergency detention program, in contrast, reveals a more unified bureau leadership committed to shaping its policy and willing to ignore direct orders of one attorney general, misinform or not fully inform other attorneys general about ongoing FBI policies, and contravene the spirit and intent of congressional policy.

FBI officials succeeded in forging and sustaining an emergency detention program in part because they were able to conduct policy in a vacuum. The national security psychology of the World War II and Cold War years had created a political climate tolerant of the need for secrecy and restrictions on civil liberties. This program's history, moreover, highlights certain basic characteristics of federal surveillance policies after 1936: the ineffectiveness of executive supervision over the internal security bureaucracy; the indifference of federal officials, particularly within the FBI, to constitutional and legal principles; and the arrogance of FBI officials who either ignored, misinformed, or selectively informed responsible elected officials about bureau policies and procedures.

Throughout this period (1936–78), the sole legislation authorizing an emergency detention program was the Internal Security Act of 1950 (also known as the McCarran Act). Title II of this act specifically authorized the detention of "dangerous" individuals in the event of war, invasion, or insurrection "in and of a foreign enemy" and defined "dangerous" persons "as to whom there is reasonable ground to believe that such persons will engage in, or probably will conspire with others to engage in, acts of espionage or sabotage."[1] Civil libertarians justifiably were alarmed about this act's authorization to list "dangerous" individuals for apprehension purposes and criteria for defining dangerousness. Ironically, however, this congressionally mandated program reflected a more serious concern about due process and individual liberties than the emergency detention program independently formulated and implemented by internal security bureaucrats (within both the FBI and the Department of Justice).

FBI Director Hoover publicly alluded to a detention program during congressional testimony of 1939 and 1940. He had then implied that the bureau had merely developed contingency plans, thereby masking a more far-reaching and distinctly political effort. Thus, in 1939, when reporting his decision to reestablish a General Intelligence Division within the bureau, Hoover claimed that this division would simply compile "extensive indices of individuals, groups, and organizations, engaged in . . . subversive activities, in espionage activities, or any activities that are possibly detrimental to the internal security of the United States." Such indexing, the FBI director assured concerned congressmen, would be "extremely important and valuable in grave emergency" as this would enable the bureau to "identify individuals and groups who might be a source of grave danger to the security of this country." In 1940 Hoover embellished this earlier testimony. The FBI's "general intelligence index," he then affirmed, contained the names of persons "who may become potential enemies to our internal security, such as known espionage agents, known saboteurs, leading members of the Communist Party, and the [German American] bund."[2]

The program actually implemented by the bureau, however, differed strikingly in intent and in method of compilation. Thus, on September 2, 1939 (the day after the German invasion of Poland), all special agents in charge were required to prepare reports on "persons of German, Italian, and Communist sympathies," as well as other persons "whose interest may be directed primarily to the interest of some other nation than the United States," for listing on a Custodial Detention index. These individuals' names were to be derived from subscription lists of German, Italian, and Communist newspapers; membership in identified organizations; and informant and agent reports on meetings and demonstrations. Almost immediately, on December 6, 1939, Hoover expanded the listing criteria to include "both aliens and citizens of the United States, on whom there is information available that their presence at liberty in this country in time of war or national emergency would be dangerous to the public peace and the safety of the United States Government." Existing information about such individuals was incomplete; more intensive and "discreet" investigations were accordingly ordered. Aware of the absence of statutory authority and, further, of the possibility that these investigations could be effectively criticized because of their focus on legitimate political activity, Hoover accordingly counseled FBI field offices:

> The purpose should be entirely confidential and it should be handled in the same manner as any investigation for the purpose of determining if the individual involved has violated the Registration Act or is engaged in subversive activities. The color of authority under which these matters are handled is, of course, the Registration Act and, if necessary, inquiries as to the reason for the investigation should be answered by reference to the Registration Act requiring agents of foreign principals to register with the State Department.[3]

The standards adopted for listing "dangerous" or "potential dangerous" individuals were exceedingly broad. Two listing categories were outlined: (1) should be "apprehended and interned immediately" upon outbreak of war or (2) should be "watched carefully . . . because their previous activities indicate the possibility but not the probability" that they will harm the national interest.[4]

Lacking statutory authority, the FBI director's Custodial Detention program could not become operational without, at the least, the attorney general's knowledge and concurrence. Therefore, in June 1940, Hoover requested Attorney General Robert Jackson's policy guidance relative to "a suspect list of individuals whose arrest might be considered necessary in the event the United States becomes involved in war."[5] It is not clear whether or not Hoover had briefed Jackson that this program had been initiated in September 1939. Conceivably, Jackson might have concluded that Hoover was requesting authorization to initiate such a program.

In any event, the attorney general concurred in the need for a Custodial Detention index and further directed the head of the newly created Neutrality Laws Unit to review the names of the listed individuals. Not having anticipated that the department would insist on a supervisory role, the FBI director initially resisted this request. Arguing that the bureau's confidential sources might be compromised and "counter-espionage activities" adversely affected, Hoover insisted that department personnel assigned to conduct these reviews "be selected with a great deal of care" to ensure against leaks. The FBI director also demanded that individuals on the list not be prosecuted since this might publicly expose bureau informants.

After five months of very difficult FBI–Justice Department negotiations, on April 21, 1941, Assistant to the Attorney General M. F. McGuire formally ordered the FBI to transmit its "dossiers" to the now renamed Special War Policies Unit. Jackson, nonetheless, had made two concessions. First, no action would be taken against an individual if this "might interfere with sound investigative techniques"; second, the identity of confidential informants would not be disclosed "without the prior approval of the Bureau." The attorney general also outlined how this program would be implemented. Following a presidential proclamation, the attorney general would authorize warrants to arrest alien enemies. A specially established department committee, the Special War Policies Unit, would consider whether American citizens on the list "not subject to internment" should be prosecuted under the Smith Act of 1940* "or some other appropriate statute." In 1941, at least, FBI officials devised separate submission and listing procedures for recommendations involving prominent personalities—such as U.S. Congressman Vito Marcantonio.[6]

Had Attorney General Jackson briefed President Roosevelt at this time of his decision to accede to a preventive detention program? The proposed methods for implementing the program—relying on a presidential proclamation as opposed to seeking legislative authorization—would logically suggest that Jackson had done so. There is no record, however, of such a briefing.

---

*Although designed mainly to compel the registration of alien residents, the Smith Act of 1940 also made illegal advocacy of the overthrow of government by force or violence and authorized the deportation of any alien who "advises a change in the form of government of the United States" or who "engages in any way in domestic political agitation."

Conceivably the briefing had been done orally; conceivably the document(s) confirming this briefing and the president's assent remain classified. We cannot, however, dismiss the possibility that Roosevelt had not been briefed and that a preventive detention program had been exclusively initiated by the FBI director and the attorney general.

Jackson's successor as attorney general, Francis Biddle, did not share these apprehensions about internal security threats. Accordingly, in a July 16, 1943, memorandum to FBI Director Hoover and Assistant Attorney General Hugh Cox, Biddle concluded that "these individual danger classifications . . . serve no useful purpose." The detention of alien enemies was already handled by the Department of Justice's Alien Control Unit; this unit had found the bureau's classification procedures to be useless. "There is no statutory authorization or other present justification," the attorney general added, "for keeping a 'custodial detention' list of citizens. The Department fulfills its proper functions by investigating the activities of persons who may have violated the law. It is not aided in this work by classifying persons as to dangerousness." These classifications should not be used in the future, Biddle ordered; the files of individuals given such a "custodial detention" classification should henceforth include a card stipulating: "This classification is unreliable. It is hereby cancelled, and should not be used as a determination of dangerousness or of any other fact."[7]

FBI Director Hoover did not, however, comply with the intent of the attorney general's directive. In an August 14, 1943, letter (marked "personal attention strictly confidential") to all special agents in charge, Hoover merely changed the program's nomenclature, affirming that the "*character* of investigations of individuals (other than alien enemies) who may be dangerous or potentially dangerous to the public safety or internal security of the United States shall be 'Security Matter' and not 'Custodial Detention.' The phraseology, 'Custodial Detention,' shall no longer be used to designate the character of the investigation, *nor shall it be used for any purpose in reports or other communications*" (emphasis added). Almost in passing, the FBI director cited the attorney general's order that "the dangerousness classifications previously made by the Special Defense Unit and its successor, the Special War Policies Unit, be not used in the future for any purpose whatsoever."

Technically, Hoover had complied with Biddle's order. The attorney general had only ordered termination of a "custodial detention" classification and had not specifically prohibited investigations to compile a "Security Index" list of "dangerous" individuals. "Henceforth," Hoover advised FBI officials, "the cards known as Custodial Detention cards will be known and referred to as Security Index cards, and the list composed of such cards will be known as the Security Index." To ensure that the attorney general could not prohibit this activity, Hoover further directed: "The fact that the Security Index and Security Index Cards are prepared and maintained should be considered as strictly confidential, and should at no time be mentioned or alluded to in investigative reports, or discussed with agencies or individuals outside the Bureau other than duly qualified field representatives of the Office of Naval Intelligence and the Military Intelligence Service, and then only on a strictly confidential basis."[8]

Biddle's directive and acknowledgment that no statutory authority existed for a detention program, however, meant that this independently established "Security Index" program could not become operational. Only new legislation or another directive by a more sympathetic attorney general could provide the necessary authority. Such an opportunity occurred with the appointment of Tom Clark as Biddle's successor. (Nominated on June 15, 1945, Clark assumed duties on September 27, 1945.) In contrast to Biddle, Clark was less concerned about civil liberties or constitutional restrictions and held alarmist views on internal security threats. Consequently, intra-bureau consideration in 1946 of the need for a broader "security index" program soon led to an initiative directed to Truman's attorney general.

In a February 27, 1946, memo to FBI Director Hoover, FBI Assistant Director D. Milton Ladd emphasized that Communist allegiance to the Soviet Union and Communist control of key labor unions seriously endangered the internal security. To confront this danger, Ladd argued, more than the apprehension of "only" Communist party leaders or "more important figures" was required; the bureau should reestablish "the original policy of investigating all known members of the Communist Party" and prepare "security index cards on all members of the Party." Such a program posed certain difficulties, the central problem being "the necessity of finding legal authorization" to apprehend all Communists in the event of war. Enemy aliens could be interned, but there was no statutory authority to apprehend citizens. Ladd then recommended that the attorney general should be advised of the FBI's plans and the need for "a study as to the action which could be taken in the event of an emergency."[9]

Acceding to Ladd's advice, Hoover briefed Clark by memo on March 8, 1946. The FBI director did not then inform the attorney general that the FBI had an ongoing program in violation of Biddle's 1943 order. Hoover instead suggested the need for a new program and emphasized the seriousness of the Communist and Soviet espionage threat. Hoover then added, as if in passing, that the FBI was also "taking steps to list all members of the Communist Party and any others who would be dangerous in the event" of war or a break in diplomatic relations with the Soviet Union. American citizens might have to be detained during such a crisis; therefore a study should be initiated "to determine what legislation is available or should be sought to authorize effective action . . . in the event of a serious emergency."[10]

Hoover successfully convinced Clark to consider this proposal in part by dishonestly representing it as simply directed against "Communist Party activities and Soviet espionage." Significantly, the initial departmental response of July 17, 1946, was titled "Detention of Communists in the event of sudden difficulties with Russia." In this memo, department officials concluded that during an emergency martial law should be declared and writs of habeas corpus should be suspended.

Dissenting from this conclusion, bureau officials urged "statutory backing for detention" and broader standards to include "Communist sympathizers." In meetings with key departmental officials and in a long Hoover to Clark memo of September 5, 1946, FBI officials emphasized the serious threat posed by Communist sympathizers. Bureau officials listed the various fields —including organized labor, civil rights, political and governmental activities, and education—"not directly identified with the Communist Party" where Communists were "promoting Communist Party objectives and principles." Hoover particularly stressed the role of "persons holding important positions who have shown sympathy for Communist objectives and policies."[11]

Departmental personnel did not dissent from these broad standards though they did not concur that legislative authorization should be sought. Accordingly, the Security Index program continued, but now with responsible authorization and knowledge. In 1947, however, Hoover again objected to the department's plan to suspend the writ of habeas corpus during an emergency and reiterated the need for "appropriate legislation." Senior Justice Department officials again rejected this counsel (as quoted in a memo from Ladd to Hoover of January 22, 1948): "The present is no time to seek legislation. To ask for it would only bring on a loud and acrimonious discussion." Articulating rather cynical political values, these officials instead recommended initiating an educational campaign, in part by prosecuting Communist party leaders under the Smith Act and thereby proving the dangerousness of communism. In the event of a crisis, the president could proclaim an emergency and at that time seek congressional ratification.[12]

Again, we do not know whether the attorney general briefed the president about this tacit consent and, more specifically, the department's decision not to seek legislative authorization. By prosecuting the U.S. Communist party leaders under the Smith Act, the department did initiate an educational campaign to arouse public opinion "to the proposition that Communism is dangerous." A bureau memorandum records the department's concern that the courts might not sustain these indictments and conclusion that what was needed was "sufficient courage to withstand the courts . . . if they should act."[13]

Still dissenting from the department's assessment of the congressional mood, in a January 27, 1948, memo to Clark, Hoover affirmed that proposed legislation would "be adopted readily by Congress." Simultaneously, if not independently, on March 30, 1948, Secretary of Defense James Forrestal requested that the National Security Council urgently prepare a report "on the problems of our internal security, including the probable scope of the dangers, the strategy and strength of the subversive elements in the event of an emergency, and the proposed countermeasures." This NSC study was initiated (although its report was not submitted until 1949); however, the FBI director's political advice was again ignored. Instead, on August 3, 1948, the attorney general formally instituted a secret emergency detention program, the department's Portfolio. Three copies of this plan were prepared (two were retained by the bureau—one in Washington and the second in

Omaha—and the third by the attorney general). The department's Portfolio: (1) authorized an FBI Security Index of dangerous individuals; (2) ordered under a master warrant executed by the attorney general the apprehension of individuals listed on the Security Index at a time of "threatened invasion"; (3) suspended the writ of habeas corpus in such a situation; (4) authorized agents arresting such individuals to conduct searches and confiscate contraband; (5) permitted specially established Boards of Review to review cases of apprehended individuals within forty-five days after apprehension (these hearings would not be bound by rules of evidence); and (6) permitted apprehended individuals to appeal these boards' rulings only to the president. Indifferent to constitutional questions, the framers of this plan intended to secure *ex post facto* legislative authorization by immediately exploiting the crisis atmosphere following a declaration of war or national emergency. Accordingly, the department's Portfolio also included a draft president's Proclamation to be issued at such time and a draft Joint Resolution to be passed by the Congress supporting the president's Proclamation.[14]

Was Truman briefed about this 1948 program? Logically, it would appear that he had been. The program entailed far-reaching surveillance of American citizens who were not engaged in illegal activities. A decision to violate constitutional rights (for such surveillance lacked legal authority and could have a chilling effect on First Amendment rights) surely was sufficiently momentous to require the president's assent. Second, the decision not to seek formal legislative authorization but to base the program on a political strategy of *ex post facto* authorization seemingly required advance presidential knowledge and consent. Third, the timing of the program's initiation during the concluding months of Truman's term of office (and at a time when his election appeared in doubt) seemingly necessitated concurrence at the highest level of government.

There is no record that Truman had been briefed and formally authorized this program. Conceivably, the president was briefed and his assent obtained orally; conceivably also, the document(s) detailing this briefing and presidential assent remain classified. We cannot, however, dismiss the possibility that Truman had not been briefed and thus that this decision had been made independently by the attorney general.[15]

To expedite retrieval the FBI immediately began storing Security Index data on IBM cards. Moreover, beginning in October 1948, the bureau periodically forwarded the lists of persons included on the Security Index to the Department of Justice's Internal Security section. The procedures for implementing a preventive detention program were formalized on February 11, 1949, in an agreement between Secretary of Defense James Forrestal and Attorney General Tom Clark. The program's purpose, this agreement specified, was to ensure "maximum security with respect to the apprehension and detention of those persons who, in the event of war or other occasions upon which Presidential Proclamations, Executive Orders, and applicable statutes come into operation, are to be" detained, and the FBI was assigned responsibility for "investigating and apprehending" the persons to be detained.[16]

Apparently Secretary of Defense Forrestal had been briefed only that such an emergency detention program was being planned but had not yet been implemented. Either that or he failed to understand than an ongoing program existed; if he did so understand, he did not convey this knowledge to National Security Council staff members. For when preparing a draft report (NSC 20/4) on March 30, 1949, outlining "measures required to achieve U.S. objectives with respect to the USSR," the NSC staff endorsed the need to develop a program not knowing that one had already been instituted. That section of NSC 20/4 outlining internal security requirements, accordingly, stipulated:

(g) Readying a program for controlling the activities, in the event of a war-related emergency, of U.S. citizens and aliens who constitute threats to the nation's internal security, by apprehension and detention or by other appropriate measures, this program to provide the greatest practical procedural safeguards to the individual.[17]

NSC 20/4 would not become policy. During 1949 a lengthy debate ensued focusing as much on the National Security Council's initiative when assuming a policy-making role as on the council's specific recommendations. The Department of State led this challenge to the NSC's authority. State Department officials pointedly questioned some of NSC 20/4's specific assumptions about U.S. foreign policy. These officials, however, did not focus on the draft report's internal security recommendations. The comment of the Director of the State Department's Policy Planning staff, George Kennan, on these recommendations implied an understanding that these were recommendations for a future program. Kennan referred to these "plans for wartime controls over individuals and censorship" and further questioned whether the specific proposals to curb Soviet agents could be implemented "without the establishment of something resembling the Soviet iron curtain."[18]

This debate was finally resolved with the formal preparation, and submission to the president, of NSC 68 on April 14, 1950. That NSC paper focused almost exclusively on international security policy. The paper's internal security section had been considerably scaled down from the 1949 draft report and contained no reference to an emergency detention program. The only possible references to such a program conveyed the sense that such a program had yet to be developed: "(8) Development of internal security and civilian defense programs. (9) Improvement and intensification of intelligence activities."[19]

Then, in a September 13, 1949, memo to FBI Director Hoover, Peyton Ford, assistant to Attorney General J. Howard McGrath (appointed to succeed Tom Clark the month before), inquired as to "the standards upon which decisions are based to incorporate names in the Security Index or to remove them." Responding to this request on September 16, 1949, Hoover defined the criteria for listing an individual on the Security Index: membership in the Communist party or "similar ideological groups" and certain general activities. No individual was listed, Hoover emphasized, until fully investigated by the bureau.[20]

Whether because of McGrath's recent appointment as attorney general or because McGrath's predecessor had been ignorant of other FBI listing programs, Hoover did not inform McGrath that the FBI compiled other lists in addition to the Security Index. These included a "Comsab program" (concentrating on Communists with a potential for sabotage), a "Detcom program" (a "priority" list of individuals to be arrested), and a Communist Index (individuals about whom investigation did not "reflect sufficient disloyal information" but whom the bureau deemed to be "of interest to the internal security"). The existence of the Communist Index, Comsab, and Detcom programs was a closely guarded bureau secret. Indeed, in an October 19, 1949, letter to all special agents in charge, Hoover ordered that

> no mention must be made in any investigative report relating to the classifications of top functionaries and key figures, nor to the Detcom or Comsab Programs, nor to the Security Index or the Communist Index. These investigative procedures and administrative aids are confidential and should not be known to any outside agency.[21]

Unaware of this ongoing program, congressional proponents of Title II (the Emergency Detention Program) of the Internal Security Act of 1950 could not know that their legislative initiative would pose major policy problems for the bureau. For when Congress eventually legislated standards for the conduct of an emergency detention program, it would enact far more liberal and restrictive ones than those Attorney General Clark had formally authorized in August 1948. For example, under the 1950 act the writ of habeas corpus would not be suspended (as it had been under the Portfolio); detention was limited to individuals who since January 1, 1949, had been active in subversive organizations (individuals were included on the department's Portfolio's Security Index if they had at any time been actively engaged in subversive activities); apprehension was restricted to actual invasion, insurrection, or a declaration of war, and federal officials were required to obtain individual warrants which necessitated convincing federal judges that these individuals violated the law. The rights of individuals were protected by the further requirements that within forty-eight hours after apprehension or as soon as possible thereafter hearings were to be conducted, that these hearings would be based on rules of evidence, and that any U.S. Court of Appeals could review the decisions of these hearing boards.[22]

FBI officials almost immediately petitioned the Department of Justice. In a September 25, 1950, memorandum to the attorney general (two days after the act became law), Hoover specifically queried whether detention plans then in force would be affected by these provisions of Title II and whether the attorney general contemplated changing the ongoing program.[23]

On September 27, 1950, the FBI director formally met with the attorney general. Acknowledging receipt of his September 25 memorandum, McGrath informed Hoover that the ongoing detention program of August 3, 1948, should in no way be contravened by passage of the Internal Security Act. The bureau should proceed under this 1948 authorization. (An October 15, 1952, FBI memorandum from A. H. Belmont of the FBI Intelligence Division to D. M. Ladd reports that McGrath specifically instructed Hoover to disregard the McCarran Act and "proceed with the program as previously outlined.")

Assistant Attorney General James McInerney formally replied to Hoover's September 25 memorandum on October 9, 1950. Title II of the Internal Security Act was in conflict with the department's detention program, McInerney conceded. Should Title II remain in effect when a detention program became necessary, the department would introduce legislation repealing the 1950 act's detention provisions (and would submit these amendments along with the draft joint resolutions as provided under the August 3, 1948, plan). Many provisions of the Internal Security Act were "unworkable"; the department accordingly doubted that Title II would permanently supersede the department's Portfolio.[24]

McInerney's and McGrath's assurances, however, had not resolved the specific problem of differing detention standards. Thus, by memorandum of December 5, 1950, the FBI director specifically requested that the Department of Justice evaluate the FBI's Security Index listings. Responding on December 7, 1950, Deputy Attorney General Peyton Ford informed Hoover that the department lacked the necessary personnel to review all bureau Security Index listings. This posed no problem:

> In the event of occurrence of an emergency which requires the use of the detention program, all of the persons now or hereafter included by the Bureau on the Security Index should be considered subjects for immediate apprehension thus resolving any possible doubtful cases in favor of the Government in the interests of the national security.[25]

The deputy attorney general's instructions had not resolved the bureau's problem; they provided no alternative legal authority to the Internal Security Act's differing standards. The department might view these provisions as "unworkable"; they were law unless repealed. The act's more restrictive requirements, moreover, contravened the 1948 plan's standards and procedures in three areas. First, many of the 19,577 individuals listed on the bureau's Security Index did not meet the act's listing standards (i.e., active involvement in subversive activities after January 1, 1949). Second, the act limited the broad apprehension authority granted under the department's Portfolio by requiring individual warrants based on probable cause and by not specifically authorizing suspending the writ of habeas corpus and the right to search or confiscate contraband. Third, under the act the detention program was limited to situations of "actual" invasion (as opposed to the Portfolio's "threatened" invasion provision).

To ensure that "the Bureau would not be open to an allegation of using Police State tactics," FBI officials again requested Department of Justice review of each Security Index listing (excepting espionage subjects). Among those listed on this index were "prominent persons" whose apprehension "might cause the Bureau some embarrassment" and "result in considerable adverse publicity and criticism of the FBI." FBI Intelligence Division officials raised these questions at May 25, 1951, and May 31, 1951, conferences with Raymond Whearty, the head of the Justice Department's Criminal Division (until the internal security section was made a separate division in 1954 the head of the Criminal Division had supervisory authority over internal security matters). Whearty responded by asserting that the department considered the Internal Security Act unworkable and directed the bureau to continue to operate under the department's Portfolio. Attorneys in the department's Criminal Division, moreover, would review the FBI's Security Index listings. (When informed of this decision, Hoover queried, "What do our files show on these [Justice Department personnel]? Can't we get names of the attorneys making the reviews?")[26]

The FBI director's fears proved well founded. By 1951 Justice Department officials seemingly decided to comply with the 1950 act. Thus, in a June 1, 1951, memo to Hoover, Deputy Attorney General Peyton Ford directed revising Security Index standards "to conform more closely" with provisions of the Internal Security Act. This decision did not end the matter. High-level bureau personnel might have sought clarification as to what standards to follow; their principal objective, however, had been to obtain formal authorization to continue to list those persons the FBI deemed dangerous. Emphasizing the "wide disparity between FBI standards and those of the Department" in a June 28, 1951, memorandum the FBI director specifically complained that individuals could not be listed under the Internal Security Act (1) if it could not be proven that they were members of revolutionary groups, (2) if they were no longer involved in "current activity of a subversive nature," and (3) even if having associations or close affiliations "with individuals or organizations having a definite foreign interest or connection contrary and detrimental to the interests of the United States." Hoover demanded "a prompt resolution" of these disparate standards.[27]

The department did not respond promptly. Unwilling to permit this issue to rest, FBI Intelligence Division officials A. H. Belmont and F. J. Baumgardner again raised the standards issue at a March 14, 1952, conference with Whearty. When drafting Security Index standards, these officials observed, the department was apparently "interpreting" the Internal Security Act. From the bureau's standpoint, the department appeared to be "hedging" its previous stand basing apprehension on the department's Portfolio and not the Internal Security Act provisions. The attorney general must clearly outline how the bureau should proceed in planning an apprehension program; there should be no doubt that the FBI was operating under standards "specifically authorized" by the attorney general. The department's "broad interpretations" of the McCarran Act, moreover, might not stand up should an apprehension program have to be initiated. The head of the Criminal Division reassured these FBI officials that the Justice Department intended to proceed under the 1948 plan and added that in an emergency the proposed president's Proclamation would be issued and immediate congressional ratification sought. If by that time Title II would not have been amended, the Justice Department would seek repeal of these "unworkable" requirements in order to institute the department's program.[28]

Whearty's assurances could not resolve the bureau's dilemma, and the standards question surfaced again at a July 9, 1952, conference between Assistant Attorney General McInerney and FBI officials A. H. Belmont and C. E. Hennrich. These bureau officials demanded department approval of the FBI's Security Index listings. There was no problem, McInerney informed Belmont and Hennrich; pending the department's final decision as to applicable standards the bureau was already authorized to apprehend anyone on its Security Index. Belmont and Hennrich, nonetheless, reiterated their complaint, insisting upon the "Attorney General's specific approval of the standards under which we [the bureau] *are* operating" (emphasis added).[29]

Throughout this period (September 1950 through July 1952), responsible Department of Justice officials had refused to adopt a definite stance. They dismissed the Internal Security Act as unworkable and expressed their preference for the 1948 plan; they would not order the bureau either to comply with or to ignore the 1950 act. This ambivalence haunted the bureau: at times Justice Department officials had apparently decided to ignore the 1950 act; at other times these officials had concluded that the Internal Security Act could not be ignored.

An October 8, 1952, memorandum from Attorney General James McGranery to FBI Director Hoover reaffirming the department's intention to seek new emergency detention legislation, however, seemingly resolved this dilemma. Until amended, Title II of the Internal Security Act of 1950 would guide the administration's emergency detention program. Accordingly, McGranery wrote, the department would follow the 1950 act's standards when reviewing the FBI's Security Index listings.[30]

Unwilling to abide by this decision, on October 15, 1952, Hoover advised the attorney general of the problems this requirement would create for the FBI. The bureau's authority for its Security Index program had been based on the department's Portfolio instructions. The attorney general must specifically assure the FBI at this time that he intended to proceed under the department's Portfolio in any future emergency. Did the attorney general agree with the FBI's conceptions of the detention program and the Security Index standards outlined in Hoover's June 28, 1951, memorandum to Deputy Attorney General Ford the FBI director pointedly queried.

Hoover's October 15 memorandum precipitated a November 6, 1952, staff meeting of FBI intelligence officials and high-level Justice Department officials. The participants reached no final decision and agreed to study the matter further to determine whether to effect any changes.[31] Following this November 6 meeting, Hoover directed FBI Assistant Director D. M. Ladd to review the emergency detention program's history and to recommend appropriate action.

The bureau could operate "more efficiently" under the department's Portfolio than under the Internal Security Act's provisions, Ladd concluded in a November 13, 1952, memorandum. The FBI assistant director observed:

> There are contained among the 19,577 individuals listed in our Security Index the names of many persons whom we consider dangerous but who do not fall within the standards set forth in the Internal Security Act of 1950. If the Department should elect to proceed under this Act . . . many people who are now included in our Security Index as potentially dangerous to the internal security would necessarily have to be excluded therefrom.

The bureau could not wait until an emergency, Ladd added, to discover that the department had decided "that we would have to move against dangerous subversives under the Internal Security Act of 1950 rather than under the Department's Portfolio." The Internal Security Act seriously restricted the FBI's activities involving apprehension, securing warrants, right to search, conduct of hearings, and right of appeal. The department's Portfolio contained none of these restrictions. The FBI assistant director then concluded:

> While . . . I firmly believe that the internal security of the country could best be protected in the time of an emergency if we proceed under the plans set forth in the Department's Portfolio, I do not believe that it is desirable that the Bureau *go on record* with recommendations to the Department concerning this matter. . . . questions will be raised as to why it is necessary to proceed under a plan devised by the Department of Justice when there is a law on the statute books which ostensibly covers the purpose for which the Department's plan was set up to handle. . . .
>
> *Obviously the Department does not want to be placed in a position of having stated that it is not going to pay attention to the Internal Security Act of 1950.* They have hedged in this matter in the past and *it is to our interest* that we receive from them a positive expression of approval of *our concepts* of the Emergency Detention Program and *our concepts* of the standards for including individuals in the Security Index which is tantamount to scheduling these persons for apprehension. I believe that we should continue to call for a *positive statement* from the Department and that we should *under no circumstances make any commitments* regarding the desirability of proceeding under the Emergency Detention Program or under the Internal Security Act of 1950.[32] (emphasis added)

Should the FBI director agree with this strategy, Ladd submitted a draft memorandum to the attorney general for Hoover's signature detailing the bureau's position and requesting "a definite and clear cut answer." Hoover signed this memorandum on November 14, 1952, dissenting nonetheless from Ladd's recommendation against a specific bureau position: "While I have sent memo forward I do think we are hedging in not at least being on record as to what is best for the internal security of the country + then leaving it to Dept to decide whether to adopt it."[33]

The FBI officials' hesitancy stemmed only from political considerations, not disinterest: the harmfulness of going on record urging defiance of the will of Congress. Instead, the FBI sought to commit the Justice Department to this position. The department, however, refused to direct the bureau in writing to ignore the will of Congress; at the same time McGranery would not defy the FBI's demand to continue operating under the provisions of the 1948 plan.

Thus, in a November 25, 1952, "Top Secret" memorandum to Hoover, McGranery wrote:

> Reference is made to my memorandum of October 8, 1952, approving the standards used by your Bureau for the listing of names of individuals in the Security Index, and to your subsequent memorandum of October 15.
>
> Pursuant to the questions which you have raised in the latter memorandum, I wish to assure you that it is the Department's intention in the event of emergency to proceed under the program as outlined in the Department's Portfolio invoking the standards now used. This approval, of course, indicates agreement with your Bureau's concepts of the Detention Program and the Security Index standards as outlined in your memorandum of June 28, 1951 to former Deputy Attorney General [Ford].[34]

Interestingly, McGranery did not acknowledge, and thus directly respond to, Hoover's November 14 memorandum. The attorney general would not directly order the FBI to ignore legislatively mandated provisions. Administrative considerations, nonetheless, required some decision: the bureau needed to know which criteria were to be employed when compiling the Security Index. McGranery's memorandum, accordingly, merely outlined the standards for listing individuals. The other issues at hand were not directly addressed: whether to suspend the writ of habeas corpus, whether to base apprehension on general warrants or individual warrants showing probable cause, whether to conduct hearings according to rules of evidence, whether to permit individuals to appeal to the courts, and whether agents arresting such individuals could search and confiscate contraband. More importantly, McGranery had not formally ordered noncompliance with the Internal Security Act's emergency detention provisions; he simply declared the department's "intention" and represented this not as the department's exclusive decision but concurrence with the "Bureau's concepts" of the emergency detention program and Security Index standards.

Once again there is no record that McGranery briefed Truman about this 1952 decision to ignore legislatively mandated standards. Moreover, since McGranery had not been attorney general when the program had been initiated in 1948 or the department's Portfolio standards had been reaffirmed in 1950 he would not personally know whether the president had been briefed orally or in writing about these 1948 and 1950 decisions—unless still-classified FBI or Justice Department documents specified this.

Since his action constituted a conscious policy decision not to abide by congressionally mandated standards, McGranery's letter could not bind his successors. Following Dwight Eisenhower's 1952 election to the presidency, however, FBI Director Hoover briefed McGranery's successor, Herbert Brownell, about Security Index standards and apprehension procedures. (We do not know whether Hoover briefed Brownell fully about the department's Portfolio and whether President Eisenhower was in turn briefed. Either the briefings were oral or the relevant documents remain classified.) Responding to this briefing on April 27, 1953, Brownell authorized Hoover "to implement the apprehension and search and seizure provisions of this program immediately upon ascertaining that a major surprise attack upon Washington, D.C., has occurred. . . . all individuals listed in the Security Index [are to be apprehended] in the event that the . . . program is implemented prior to the completion of the review of the individual cases by the Criminal Division."[35]

Minutes of a June 11, 1954, Cabinet meeting suggest that the attorney general had at least been apprised of the Security Index standards' expansive nature. At this Cabinet meeting, Brownell reported that "many people" in government service were listed on the Security Index and had not as yet been suspended under the Eisenhower administration's federal employee security program. When reviewing federal employee security program cases, Cabinet officials should focus first on those personnel listed on the Security Index. President Eisenhower agreed with Brownell. Secretary of Agriculture Ezra Taft Benson then observed that he had recently suspended four attorneys who threatened to do something about this. Eisenhower interrupted to query: "Who were they going to go to—McCarthy?"[36]

Brownell's June 1954 report on the continued employment of individuals listed on the Security Index suggests that the administration viewed these cases as posing less a security than a political problem. Were it viewed strictly as a security matter, a more concerted effort would have been made to suspend these employees. The president's sarcastic response succinctly highlights the new administration's policy toward individual liberties and radical politics. During that same Cabinet meeting, the president sharply rebuked Secretary of Defense Charles Wilson for his department's handling of security dismissals. Citing the Navy Department's response to difficult security clearance cases of placing individuals under surveillance rather than dismissing them, Eisenhower chided: "Charlie, that's exactly what [Secretary of the Army] Stevens tried to do with Peress—dodge the issue." The President continued, "That just won't work. You have to face up to it and face up fast. There must be no more delays."[37]

Although we do not know how informed Brownell had been when he approved Security Index listings, we do know that between November 1952 and December 1954 the number of individuals listed on the Security Index increased from 19,577 to 26,174. In 1954, moreover, Brownell elevated the Internal Security section to the status of a division and authorized this newly created division to review the bureau's Security Index listings. Then, in December 1954, Brownell requested a briefing on the bureau's Security Index criteria. By a memo of December 23, 1954, the FBI director outlined the bureau's "general criteria" for Security Index listings. Following a January 1955 meeting between representatives of the bureau's Intelligence Division and the department's Internal Security Division, Hoover reported that "there was no area of disagreement between the Department and this Bureau on the criteria or concepts regarding dangerousness."[38]

Because Justice Department Internal Security officials no longer reviewed all FBI Security Index listings, in early 1955 bureau officials independently decided to revise Security Index criteria "to minimize the inevitable criticism of the [FBI's] dual role" both investigating and listing individuals. As a result, by July 30, 1958, the Security Index listings were reduced to 12,870. Individuals removed from the Security Index, however, were then incorporated on the bureau's independently established Communist Index. The rationale for this self-initiated decision was that such persons remained "potential threats and in case of an all-out emergency, their identities should be readily accessible to permit restudy of their cases."[39] Departmental officials were not briefed on this bureau decision to expand the Communist Index.

In a June 21, 1960, letter, moreover, Hoover advised special agents in charge (SACs) that henceforth the Communist Index would be renamed the Reserve Index and would be divided into two sections. Individuals on the Reserve Index, Hoover emphasized, "represent a greater potential threat in time of emergency than do others." Persons included in the first section, Section A:

> should receive priority consideration [and] should include those individuals whose subversive activities do not bring them within the Security Index criteria, but who, in a time of national emergency, are in a position to influence others against the national interest or are likely to furnish material financial aid to subversive elements due to their subversive associations and ideology.

Specifically included among Section A categories should be professors, labor union leaders and organizers, writers, newsmen and others in the mass media field, lawyers, doctors, "individuals who could potentially furnish material financial aid," and "other potentially influential persons on a local or national level." (Hoover specifically cited Norman Mailer and a college history professor who had praised the Soviet Union during one of his classes as examples of individuals to be listed in Section A.) Those remaining individuals formerly included on the Communist Index should be included in a second section, Section B.[40]

These procedures continued during the Kennedy years (although again there is no record that the president and/or the attorney general were fully briefed about this program's scope and nature). The only known briefings of Kennedy officials were Hoover's sketchy reference in a January 10, 1961, letter to Attorney General–designate Robert Kennedy (with copies to Dean Rusk and Byron White) and a vaguely worded FBI report on the status of internal security programs for the period July 1, 1960, through June 30, 1961, which Hoover submitted on July 25, 1961, to Special Assistant to the President McGeorge Bundy. The July 25 report vaguely described the emergency detention program but not the criteria for listing individuals. The department's Portfolio of 1948 was not even cited.

> The FBI maintains a current list of individuals, both citizens and aliens, to be considered for apprehension and detention, if necessary, in a period of emergency. . . . This list is kept current on a daily basis by the addition of new individuals whose activities make them potentially dangerous to the United States. . . . Included on the list of potentially dangerous individuals are nearly 200 persons who are engaged in pro-Castro Cuba activities or who sympathize strongly with such activities.[41]

Moreover, although intra-bureau memorandums of June 7, 1962, and December 11, 1962, reported that Security Index listings fell "within the emergency detention provisions in the Internal Security Act of 1950 as well as the emergency detention provisions of the Attorney General's Portfolio," there is no record that the Kennedy Justice Department had previously been briefed on this 1948 plan. Nor is there a record that Kennedy administration officials had been informed of the Reserve Index's existence.[42]

Whether or not the FBI was responding to a departmental initiative or to the new president Lyndon Johnson's request for a briefing on FBI internal security procedures, a December 9, 1963, FBI memorandum outlined how the Justice Department reviewed FBI Security Index listings. The department did not review individual cases "prior" to their listing on the Security Index, this memorandum reported; the bureau, however, furnished the department a monthly list of Security Index subjects for review purposes.[43] This memorandum did not record similar departmental reviews or monthly submissions covering the FBI's Reserve Index listings.

President Kennedy's assassination, however, had led the bureau's Intelligence Division personnel to recommend to the FBI director "a broadening of the factors which must be considered in evaluating an individual's dangerousness," given the fact that Lee Harvey Oswald had not been listed on the Security Index. Six additional criteria were enumerated; these were described as being "sufficiently elastic so that when applied with the necessary judgment the complex questions which arise can be resolved." Hoover concurred and in a December 17, 1963, letter advised special agents in charge that "the essential question" for initiating a security investigation on an individual was whether "the subject's activities are such as to depict him to be a *potential* danger to the national security of the United States in time of an emergency." Security Index criteria afforded "practical and workable guidelines . . . as to whether a subject represents a *potential* danger and are sufficiently elastic so that when applied with the necessary judgment, the complex questions . . . can be resolved" (emphasis added).[44]

Even this flexibility, however, proved insufficient. The rise of the unstructured and often anti-ideological New Left during the late 1960s challenged traditional FBI conceptions of dangerousness, conceptions wherein investigations and Security Index listings had been based on membership in established "subversive" or "revolutionary" organizations. In an April 2, 1968, letter to special agents in charge, the FBI director affirmed the New Left's subversive character and complained:

> The Bureau has recently noted that in many instances security investigations of these individuals [affiliated with the New Left movement who engage in violent or unlawful activities] are not being initiated. In some cases, subjects are not being recommended for inclusion on the Security Index merely because no membership in a basic revolutionary organization could be established. Since the new left is basically anarchist, many of the leading activists in it are not members of any basic revolutionary group . . . even if a subject's membership in a subversive organization cannot be proven, his inclusion on the Security Index may often be justified because of activities which establish his anarchistic tendencies. . . . a subject without any organizational affiliation can qualify for the Security Index by virtue of his public pronouncements and activities which establish his rejection of law and order and reveal him to be a potential threat to the security of the United States.[45]

The FBI director's decision to broaden Security Index criteria occurred at a time when the Justice Department was considering whether the emergency detention program should be revised to conform with the Internal Security Act—the first formal consideration since the 1950–53 period.

Responding to a presidential order to review the government's emergency plans, the Department of Justice on February 26, 1968, requested a conference with the FBI. There is no record that such a conference or conferences were held in February or March 1968. At an April 22, 1968, conference, however, FBI and Internal Security Division officials agreed that individuals should be apprehended and detained on the basis of "the provisions of the Emergency Detention Act" of 1950. The criteria ultimately approved none-

theless went beyond the 1950 statute and (in the words of an FBI memorandum reporting this presidential decision) constituted "an all encompass-
ing definition" of a dangerous person:

> . . . each person as to whom there is reasonable ground to believe
> that such person probably will engage in, or probably will conspire
> with others to engage in, acts of espionage and sabotage, including
> acts of terrorism or assassination and interference with or threat to
> the survival and effective operation of the national, state, and local
> governments and of the national defense effort.

Under this definition, individuals who participated in antiwar demonstrations
having the objective to disrupt governmental activities would qualify for a
Security Index listing.

The Justice Department nonetheless continued to review FBI Security
Index listings. On May 1, 1968, Hoover formally requested departmental
approval for the bureau's broader Security Index standards. Despite the department's June 17, 1968, response that the criteria were "under study,"
bureau officials on June 19, 1968, revised the FBI Manual and on June 21,
1968, issued new instructions to all FBI field offices. The Justice Department
formally responded only in September 1968, outlining the now modified
emergency detention program and rejecting the earlier policy of ignoring
the Internal Security Act's provisions for detention and hearings. Detained
individuals would "be entitled to a hearing at which time the evidence would
have to satisfy the standards of . . . the Emergency Detention Act [Title II
of Internal Security Act]." Compliance with the stipulated Internal Security
Act standards was not required; the department conceded the need for
"flexibility and discretion at the operating level in order to carry on an
effective surveillance program." These more "flexible" criteria included membership in revolutionary organizations within the last five years or front
organizations within the past three years and further:

> Investigation has developed information that an individual . . . has
> anarchistic or revolutionary beliefs and is likely to seize upon the
> opportunity presented by a national emergency to commit acts of
> espionage or sabotage, including acts of terrorism, assassination, or
> any interference with or threat to the survival and effective operation
> of the national, state and local governments and of the defense ef-
> fort.[46]

The FBI Manual was changed to comply with these revised criteria. In
late 1968, moreover, the FBI's New Left or black nationalist programs were
expanded.[47] Exploiting the flexibility of the September 1968 standards and
the inauguration of the security-obsessed Nixon administration, in March
1969 FBI Director Hoover reformulated the criteria for initiating security

investigations of New Left and civil rights activists. Hoover's more nebulous standards specified:

> It is not possible to formulate any hard-and-fast standards by which the dangerousness of individual members or affiliates of revolutionary organizations may be automatically measured because of manner revolutionary organizations function and great scope and variety of activities. Exercise sound judgment and discretion in evaluating importance and dangerousness of individual members or affiliates.

Five broad criteria were listed; one of these contained five subdivisions and three of the other four contained two subdivisions. This bureau directive then added:

> The above standards for institutions of investigations of individuals are not to be interpreted as all-inclusive. Where there is doubt an individual may be a current threat to the internal security of the nation, the question should be resolved in the interest of security and investigation conducted.[48]

These more flexible criteria and encouragement to use discretion did not resolve the concerns of FBI officials. At an October 29, 1970, executive conference Washington bureau officials[49] examined "whether the current situation demands intensification of certain security-type investigations." Three questions were considered: whether or not (1) to lift the existing moratorium on report writing and investigation of certain Security Index cases; (2) to expand investigations of extremists; and (3) to develop contacts against Soviet intelligence personnel. Lifting the moratorium, the conference minutes recorded, would require expanding investigations to verify the residences and employment of previously listed individuals. The activities of black student unions, college activists, the Students for a Democratic Society, and militant New Left organizations should be investigated, the conferees concluded, to determine their backgrounds, aims, and whether or not "they have a propensity for violence."[50]

This intra-bureau review of Security Index standards appeared irrelevant following congressional repeal on September 16, 1971, of Title II, the emergency detention provision of the McCarran Internal Security Act of 1950. (President Nixon signed this bill into law on September 25, 1971.) This congressional decision posed a serious dilemma. From 1950 through 1971, at least, the bureau's standards were responsive to congressional authorization of a detention program. After September 1971 this would no longer be the case: Congress had formally terminated such a program.

The bureau had not at first been concerned over the prospect of congressional repeal of the act's emergency detention provisions. Commenting on the introduction of such legislation, FBI officials concluded that should Title

II be repealed "the Government's inherent right to protect itself internally will continue to be safeguarded by the Bureau under its basic responsibility for protecting the Nation's internal security." When Title II was repealed, however, the head of the FBI's Intelligence Division Richard Cotter in a September 17, 1971, memorandum argued that the Security Index should be maintained: "the potential dangerousness of subversives is probably even greater now than before the repeal of the Act, since they no doubt feel safer now to conspire in the destruction of this country." Cotter nonetheless sought to protect the bureau from this decision's political consequences. The Justice Department, he counseled, should be consulted

> to determine if there is any manner in which the essence of the Security Index and emergency detention of dangerous individuals could be utilized under Presidential powers. . . . Some written authorization from the Attorney General [should be secured] not only to keep records which, in effect, represent a workable substitute for the Security Index, but also serves as a mandate for our continued investigation of subversive activity and related matters.[51]

The bureau's Office of Legal Counsel seriously appraised Cotter's recommendation. Repeal did not affect either the bureau's "basic investigative authority" or its right to carry "in its files an assessment of each principal subversive which would be sufficient to mark him for Government attention should need arise in a national emergency," FBI Assistant Director D. J. Dalbey, the head of the Legal Counsel Office, observed. Nonetheless, Dalbey urged Clyde Tolson, then the assistant to the FBI director, to request "a reassessment" from the attorney general "of our investigative and record-keeping authority concerning subversive matters." Such a request would "protect" the bureau if "some spokesman of the extreme left" claimed that Title II's repeal had undercut such investigative authority.[52]

Dalbey's recommendations were accepted. On September 30, 1971, FBI Director Hoover solicited Attorney General John Mitchell's views "concerning FBI authority to continue investigations of subversive activity covered, in part, by this Act [the repealed Title II]." All bureau planning "for emergency apprehension and detention" of those listed on its Security Index had been suspended. The bureau possessed other authority to investigate subversive activities (Hoover cited presidential directives of 1939, 1943, and 1950, and other statutes). The director contended:

> Likewise, we feel that the repeal of this Act does not limit the FBI's authority and responsibility to keep and maintain administrative records, including various indices, which may be necessary in fulfilling such responsibility and authority [to investigate "subversive activities and related matters"].
>   . . . We, therefore, feel that it is absolutely incumbent upon the FBI to continue investigations of those who pose a threat to the in-

ternal security of the country and to maintain an administrative index of such individuals as an essential part of our investigative responsibility.

The FBI director specifically solicited the attorney general's advice "at the earliest possible time": (1) whether the FBI should continue to investigate subversive activities; (2) "if you concur in our opinion that the repeal of the Emergency Detention Act does not prohibit or limit the FBI's authority to keep and maintain . . . an administrative index"; (3) if concurring that an administrative index should be maintained, whether the FBI should provide a copy of this list to the Department of Justice's Internal Security Division; and (4) what disposition should be made concerning the former emergency detention program's warrants and instructions.[53]

On October 22, 1971, Mitchell formally replied to Hoover's September 30 memorandum. The FBI's authority to investigate "subversive activities and related matters," the attorney general concurred, remained unaffected by repeal of the emergency detention title. Mitchell continued:

Furthermore, the repeal of the aforementioned Act does not alter or limit the FBI's authority and responsibility to record, file and index information secured pursuant to its statutory and Presidential authority. An FBI administrative index compiled and maintained to assist the Bureau in making readily retrievable and available the results of its investigations into subversive activities and related matters is not prohibited by the repeal of the Emergency Detention Act.

A copy of the administrative index lists need not be furnished to the Internal Security Division but only "a monthly memorandum reflecting the identity of government employees who by significant acts or membership in subversive organizations have demonstrated a propensity to commit acts inimical to our national security."[54]

Mitchell further conceded that the emergency detention "documents" had been "prepared on the basis of authority other than the Emergency Detention Act." The department was currently studying how to dispose of these instructions; Hoover would be informed when that decision was made. (Assistant Attorney General Robert Mardian ordered Hoover to destroy them on February 9, 1972.)[55]

By merely changing the program's nomenclature—this time with the attorney general's consent—Hoover once again succeeded in preserving the detention program. Because the attorney general would no longer review this new index's listings, FBI officials soon concluded that the FBI would "now [be] in a position to make a sole determination as to which individuals should be included in" an Administrative Index. This determination could be based "not on arrest and detention but on overall potential for committing acts inimical to the national defense interest." Membership in "old line revolutionary organizations" no longer need be established; bureau investigations could henceforth concentrate on the "new breed of subversive individual." The former Reserve Index would be amalgamated with the former Security Index, and this also meant that individuals ("teachers, writers, lawyers, etc.") "who are in a position to influence others to engage in acts inimical to the national defense or are likely to furnish financial aid or other assistance to revolutionary elements because of their sympathy, associations, or ideology" would henceforth be included on this renamed Administrative Index.[56]

FBI officials might not have justified the Administrative Index as providing the basis for an emergency detention program; nonetheless one FBI official privately conceded that the index could be "interpreted as a means to circumvent repeal of the Emergency Detention Act."[57] Mitchell's decision, moreover, had been reached at a departmental meeting wherein the participants agreed that an administrative index might prove helpful in the event of a military attack. The government could thereby quickly identify individuals who might threaten the national security (in the words of an FBI memo on this meeting) "so that investigation could be intensified and if necessary *the President could go to a joint session of Congress and ask for emergency legislation* permitting apprehension and detention of persons who threaten existence of the Government" (emphasis added).[58]

Apparently, the department had merely reaffirmed the strategy outlined in the department's Portfolio of August 3, 1948. This memo further suggests that the department recognized that the Administrative Index would not simply expedite investigations. Neither the FBI director nor the attorney general, however, were at all concerned that this action contravened congressional policy.

The changed national climate leading to congressional repeal of the emergency detention program, nonetheless, posed a potential political problem for the bureau. Certain bureau officials were deeply concerned about the altered political climate; in turn they began to question the FBI's investigative authority. The bureau's Intelligence Division soon concluded that the Administrative Index must be revised so that it could not be "interpreted as a means to circumvent repeal of the Emergency Detention Act." An intra-bureau study of August 1972 particularly emphasized the impossibility of publicly justifying the breadth and vagueness of Administrative Index (ADEX) standards as simply enabling the government to respond to serious internal security threats. ADEX, this study recommended, must be changed because "such broad terminology would leave us in a vulnerable position if our guidelines were to be scrutinized by disinterested Congressional committees, which has been threatened." Only those individuals should be listed on the ADEX, bureau investigator T. J. Smith concluded, "who represent an *actual danger now*" to the national security. Others identified as subversives should instead be included on separate "Extremist" and "Communist" indexes. "Neither of these indexes," Smith further claimed, "will constitute a program but will merely be a listing which will be computerized for ready retrieval at any time we need to quickly identify persons of this type who were involved in activity inimical to the national interest."[59] (Smith's rationale strikingly parallels the bureau's earlier rationale for the Communist Index, then for the Reserve Index, and later when modifying Security Index criteria.)

On September 18, 1972, Acting FBI Director L. Patrick Gray informed Attorney General Richard Kleindienst of the revised Administrative Index:

> Individuals, whether affiliated with organized groups or not, who have shown a willingness and capability of engaging in treason, rebellion, or insurrection, seditious conspiracy, sabotage, espionage, terrorism, guerrilla warfare, assassination of Government officials or leaders, or other acts which would result in interference with or a threat to the survival and effective operation of national, state, or local government.[60]

The internal security bureaucracy, however, could no longer make these decisions on their own. Bureau official T. J. Smith's August 1972 fears about the bureau's vulnerability if a disinterested congressional inquiry were initiated ceased to be merely hypothetical. A different political climate had evolved by 1973 following the highly publicized revelations of the Nixon administration's abuses of power.

Inevitably, then, in this post-Watergate atmosphere bureau officials became more concerned about political risks. As one result, in May–June 1973 they altered the existing ADEX program. Skeptical about the sufficiency of presidential directives, bureau officials sought to base new criteria on statutory authority. In a June 7, 1973, memorandum FBI Director Kelley advised all special agents in charge that the Administrative Index was to be considered "strictly an administrative device" and was to play no part "in investigative decisions or policies."[61]

Once this decision was reached it was but a small step to formal abolition of the Administrative Index. The decision to cease indexing individuals did not mean that the FBI and the Department of Justice had returned to the pre-1939 status quo. They had only decided to comply with a specifically mandated policy of Congress: repeal the emergency detention program. Both Justice Department and FBI officials, nonetheless, claimed the right to continue investigating groups which posed a "potential threat to the public safety" or which have a "potential" for violating specific statutes. A concern for public relations and not the law governed their policy responses. Thus, whereas these officials dramatically announced stringent restrictions in "domestic security" investigations in 1976, FBI agents' testimony in 1978 during a class action suit brought by the American Civil Liberties Union disclosed that FBI informers who had formerly been classified as "domestic security" informers were simply reclassified "foreign counterintelligence" personnel. The rationale for this was the still prevalent view of expansive presidential powers.

[W]ithout a broad range of intelligence information, the President and the departments and agencies of the Executive branch could not properly and adequately protect our nation's security and enforce the numerous statutes pertaining thereto . . . the Department, and in particular the Attorney General, must continue to be informed of those organizations that engage in violence which represent a potential threat to the public safety.[62]

Internal security bureaucrats might have abandoned a policy in 1976 derived from their notion of an unquestioned and unreviewable right to investigate and label individuals and organizations. These officials, nonetheless, continued to insist upon certain inherent powers, adding "potential threat to the public safety" to the "national security" specter as justification. The political situation of 1978 might differ from that of 1970, even more so from that of 1950, 1948, or 1939. But no important official publicly avowed the need to conform to those constitutional principles and constraints which had controlled pre-1936 national politics.

Chapter Three

Authorizing Political Surveillance

During a January 1976 interview, Bill Reed, executive assistant to FBI Director Clarence Kelley, pointedly queried: "Is the Constitution a suicide pact? Do we have to wait until the bomb goes off and people are killed or injured? Or can we act while the fuse is still sputtering?"[1] Reed's defensive comment was precipitated by the prospect that the recent debate over the FBI's political surveillance activities might result in reforms stringently limiting the bureau's investigative authority. His query about the Constitution's suicidal potential is troubling. The Founding Fathers would never have conceded that restricting federal investigative powers was possibly suicidal; instead they feared that federal officials would abuse power unless their authority was narrowly defined.

Federal officials had not always feared that the Constitution unduly restricted FBI investigative authority. Instead, Justice Department and FBI officials had consistently claimed that the bureau possessed the legal authority to conduct ongoing investigations of dissident political activities even when these activities might not violate federal law. During March 9, 1971, testimony before the Senate Subcommittee on Constitutional Rights, Assistant Attorney General William Rehnquist claimed that federal investigative authority derived from the president's "inherent" powers to "take Care that the Laws be faithfully executed." "Implicit in the duty of the President to oversee the faithful execution of the laws," Rehnquist argued, "is the power to investigate and prevent the violation of Federal law." If this authority had been abused at times, these were exceptions and did not confirm the inadequacy of executive oversight. "I think it quite likely," Rehnquist further posited, "that self-discipline on the part of the executive branch will provide an answer to virtually all of the legitimate complaints against excesses of information gathering. . . . isolated imperfections . . . should not be permitted to obscure the fundamental necessity and importance of Federal information gathering, or the genuinely high level of performance in this area by the organizations involved."[2] Echoing this optimistic view on October 7, 1971, when declining an invitation to permit FBI personnel to participate in a Princeton University conference on the FBI, FBI Director Hoover wrote Princeton Professor Duane Lockard testily: ". . . our investigative duties are not of our own choosing. They were delivered to us, with the requirement that we take all necessary action, by laws passed by the Congress and by rules and regulations laid down by the President and the Attorney General."[3]

Both Hoover and Rehnquist based federal investigative authority in part on the president's constitutional powers. Rehnquist's conception of expansive presidential powers need not concern us; the U.S. Supreme Court in

U.S. v. U.S. District Court (1972) and *U.S. v. Nixon* (1974) denied that presidents had such unlimited and unreviewable powers subject only to self-discipline.[4]

What, then, are the bases for the FBI's investigative authority? Not a national police, the FBI derives its authority exclusively from federal statutes or executive orders, and these limit FBI investigations to violations of federal laws. Why, then, has the FBI since the 1930s extensively investigated political activities and beliefs? Implied in Bill Reed's query about the bureau's proper preventive responsibility is the right to investigate "subversive activities and related matters." That phrase's meaning, however, constitutes the heart of the problem: no statute prohibits involvement in "subversive activities and related matters." Where, then, does the FBI derive this authority? From presidential directives, the bureau claims.

On July 23, 1970, Charles Brennan, then head of the FBI's Intelligence Division, advised the Scranton Commission on Campus Unrest that on September 6, 1939, President Franklin Roosevelt had directed the FBI to investigate "subversive activities" and that "within the framework of this executive order . . . basically the FBI over the years has tried to fulfill these responsibilities."[5]

FBI Assistant Director W. Raymond Wannall qualified this claim, however, during June 4 and 5, 1974, testimony before the House Committee on Internal Security. "The FBI interprets the September 6, 1939, directive as reaffirmed by subsequent directives," Wannall asserted, "as an instruction 'to take charge' and 'correlate' investigative work [relating to espionage, sabotage, subversive activities, and related matters], not as a grant of new or additional authority." Roosevelt's September 6, 1939, directive, Wannall continued, was viewed by the FBI "as an instruction that the FBI is to be the executive agency which will 'sift out' and 'correlate' security investigative matters as a clearinghouse." Wannall had not conceded that the FBI could not investigate "subversive activities." He based this authority instead on President Roosevelt's August 1936 oral directive "that investigations be made of subversive activities."

> Going back to the [September 6, 1939] directive, there is no reference in the first paragraph [of that directive] that the Attorney General had been requested by the President to instruct the FBI to take charge of subversive activities as such. But I think the [September 10, 1936] memorandum [describing the August 1936 decision] . . . is indicative of the basis for the statement in the third paragraph of the [September 6, 1939] directive requesting police officers, sheriffs, and all law enforcement officers promptly to turn over to the FBI information relating not only to espionage, counterespionage, sabotage, and violations of the neutrality laws, but subversive activities. . . . By its third paragraph, the directive of 1939 requested law enforcement officers to turn over to the FBI information relating to espionage, counterespionage, sabotage, subversive activities, and violations of the neu-

trality laws. By subsequent directives, we feel we were charged with the responsibility of correlating information regarding subversive activities. . . . It is our interpretation of subsection (d) of title 28, subpart P of the Code of Federal Regulations, that the Attorney General apparently has instructed the FBI to carry out the responsibilities which were imposed upon us by the directive of September 1939.[6]

In the absence of any description of the 1936 and 1939 directives, these quotes can only be confusing. They do establish that the bureau nonetheless based its authority to investigate "subversive activities and related matters," only on these presidential directives.

Did these directives provide such authority? Why, moreover, were they issued? Had President Roosevelt in 1936 in fact authorized the FBI to investigate "subversive activities"? A review of these questions supports two conclusions: (1) These directives did not formally authorize FBI investigations of "subversive activities and related matters." (2) By misinforming first Presidents Truman and Eisenhower and then Attorneys General Robert Kennedy, Nicholas Katzenbach, Ramsey Clark, and John Mitchell about Roosevelt's 1939 directive, FBI Director Hoover obtained tacit approval for ongoing FBI investigations of dissident activities.

At the outset, the scope of the program Roosevelt had authorized in 1936 cannot be definitely determined since our knowledge of this presidential directive derives exclusively from FBI sources. No unclassified White House document records the president's purposes and specific authorization. Roosevelt had orally conveyed this request to Hoover. Moreover, while one Hoover memorandum on the August 1936 meetings records the president's intent to file in the White House safe a handwritten memorandum detailing this authority, no such document has been found in either the Roosevelt Library at Hyde Park or the National Archives.

On August 24, 1936, Roosevelt and Hoover met privately in the White House, according to Hoover's memorandum on this conference, at the initiative of the president. Apparently, however, Roosevelt's invitation had not been self-initiated. For one, during this meeting Roosevelt commented on reports detailing the travel plans and activities of a Soviet consular official, Constantine Oumansky—reports that the president acquired either from the FBI or from military intelligence officials. In January 1936, moreover, Secretary of War George Dern had advised Attorney General Homer Cummings about the "definite indication" of foreign espionage in the United States and that "some [domestic] organizations would probably attempt to cripple our war effort [in an emergency] through sabotage." "A counterespionage service among civilians," should be established, Dern counseled the attorney general, "to prevent foreign espionage in the United States and to collect information so that in case of an emergency any persons intending to cripple our war effort by means of espionage or sabotage may be taken into custody."[7]

In any event, Hoover's memorandum reported that he began the meeting by recounting the extent of Communist control of, or Communist efforts to control, important trade unions (the West Coast Longshoremen, the United Mine Workers, and the Newspaper Guild), "the activities which have recently occurred with [sic] Governmental service inspired by Communists," and the Communist Internationale's directives to American Communists to "vote for President Roosevelt and against Governor [Alfred] Landon [the Republican presidential candidate] because of the fact that Governor Landon is opposed to class warfare." The anti–New Deal Catholic priest Charles Coughlin, Hoover further advised Roosevelt, had attempted to convince retired general Smedley Butler to "lead an expedition to Mexico"; Butler had also been approached by right-wing elements to lead an anti–New Deal coup.

Reacting to this report, the president allegedly expressed a desire for more systematic intelligence about "subversive activities in the United States, particularly Fascism and Communism," and for "a broad picture of the general movement and its activities as may affect the economic and political life of the country as a whole." Hoover claimed to have advised the president that "no governmental organization" currently compiled such "general intelligence information," that Communist party membership was not illegal, and that the FBI had "no specific authority to make such general investigations." Asked if he had any "suggestions . . . relative to this matter," Hoover advised Roosevelt that the FBI's appropriations authorization contained "a provision that it might investigate any matters referred to it by the Department of State and that if the State Department should ask us to conduct such an investigation we could do so under our present authority in the appropriation already granted."[8] Such an investigation, Roosevelt recommended, should be coordinated with the other military intelligence services. At Hoover's suggestion, another meeting—of the president, the FBI director, and Secretary of State Cordell Hull—was arranged for the next day.[9]

Again according to another Hoover memorandum, the president began the August 25 meeting by describing the Communist and Fascist movements as "international in scope and that Communism particularly was directed from Moscow, and that there had been certain indications that [Soviet consul] Oumansky, . . . was a leading figure in some of the activities in this country, so consequently it was a matter which fell within the scope of foreign affairs over which the State Department would have a right to request an inquiry to be made." Roosevelt apprised the secretary of state of his "desire" for a "survey" of "these conditions" and that "this survey could be made by the Department of Justice [i.e., the FBI] if the Secretary of State requested the Department to conduct the inquiry under the FBI Appropriations Act." "The matter . . . ," Roosevelt advised, should "be handled quite confidentially." When Hull concurred, Roosevelt directed Hoover to "speak to the Attorney General." Roosevelt and Hull further considered "the making of a protest, either formally or informally, to the Russian Government relative to its interference with [sic] affairs in this country."[10]

Clearly Roosevelt had directed the FBI to conduct a "general intelligence" operation and had not been unduly concerned about specific legal authorization. What, however, had been the president's purpose and the scope of his authorization?

Hoover's August 24 memorandum's reference to "subversive activities" does not aptly convey the president's more limited objective. Roosevelt had been concerned about the attempts by foreign agents to influence domestic affairs and how these foreign-directed efforts might affect the conduct of national politics. He had requested a "survey" to discover the relationship between domestic Communist and Fascist activities and the actions of foreign powers and/or agents; Roosevelt, however, had not authorized ongoing investigations focusing on domestic radicalism or "subversive activities." Roosevelt's and Hull's consideration of a formal protest to the Soviet Union, the president's directive that the FBI coordinate this "survey" with the military intelligence services and the State Department, his acceptance of Hoover's suggestion that the appropriations statute provided such authority, and his specific reference to Oumansky's leadership role—all confirm this limited purpose. A private FBI study of 1972 of the bureau's domestic investigative authority (in contrast to the October 28, 1975, analysis which the bureau prepared for the Senate Select Committee on Intelligence Activities) also ascribed the impetus behind this 1936 directive to "the concern for national security . . . [as] related to two international movements [communism and fascism]" and that "there was no national concern for indigenous anarchists or other groups designing the overthrow of this Government."[11]

Nonetheless, if Roosevelt's purposes were narrower, Hoover quickly exploited the latitude provided by this secret oral directive. Even prior to briefing Attorney General Cummings, required by the statute and by the president, he directed bureau personnel to begin planning an extensive surveillance program focusing on domestic political or trade union activities. In an August 28, 1936, memorandum to Hoover outlining how the information from these proposed investigations of "subversive activities" would be handled administratively, a Washington bureau official specified the "general [investigative] classifications." These included the maritime, steel, coal, clothing, garment and fur industries; federal governmental activities; the "newspaper field," educational institutions, and the armed forces; "general activities"; Communist and affiliated organizations, Fascists, anti-Fascist movements; and labor organizations' strike and other activities. Hoover commended this planning as a good beginning. Bureau officials instituted a broad surveillance and indexing program involving the extensive use of informers, daily reports on "major developments in every field" of subversive activities, and an elaborate filing system containing indexes and dossiers on "persons whose names appear prominently at the present time in the subversive circles." To compile these files, the FBI went beyond its agents and informers and acquired an extensive library of radical pamphlets, newspapers, and periodicals as well as quietly developing relations with conservative patriotic organizations, such as the American Legion.[12]

Hoover's September 5, 1936, letter to all special agents in charge and September 10, 1936, memorandum describing his briefing of the attorney general further ensured a far-reaching program that would focus on domestic radicalism. The letter (marked "personal and confidential") directed special agents in charge:

> The Bureau desires to obtain from all possible sources information concerning *subversive activities* conducted in the United States by Communists, Fascisti, *and representatives or advocates of other organizations or groups advocating the overthrow or replacement of the Government of the United States.* No investigation should be initiated into cases of this kind in the absence of specific authorization from the Bureau, but you should . . . immediately transmit to the Bureau *any information relating to subversive activities* on the part of *any* individual or organization, *regardless of the source from which this information is received.*[13] (Emphasis added)

Hoover's September 10 memorandum further reported:

> In talking with the Attorney General today *concerning the radical situation,* I informed him of the conference [sic] which I had on September 1, 1936 [sic], at which time the Secretary of State, at the President's suggestion, requested . . . investigation made of *subversive activities in this country,* including communism and fascism. I transmitted this request to the Attorney General, and the Attorney General *verbally* directed me to proceed with this investigation and to coordinate, as the President suggested, information upon these matters in the possession of the Military Intelligence Division, the Naval Intelligence Division, and the State Department. This, therefore, is the authority upon which to proceed in the conduct of this investigation, which should, of course, be handled in a most discrete and confidential manner.[14] (Emphasis added)

The disparity between Hoover's briefing of Attorney General Cummings and the intelligence program authorized by Roosevelt would have future policy consequences. For Cumming's and Roosevelt's conflicting understanding enabled the FBI director in 1938 to brief the attorney general fully and yet secure the president's approval for a substantively different "counterespionage" program.

In October 1938, Attorney General Cummings was appointed by the president to chair a committee "to inquire into the so-called espionage situation" and to report whether additional appropriations were needed for domestic intelligence. In turn, Cummings asked Hoover for recommendations. Roosevelt's concern over a possible scandal involving German espionage activities within the United States had precipitated this request. These activities had begun in 1935 and, after a lengthy investigation, resulted in the indictment of three individuals on February 26, 1938, and another eighteen on June 20, 1938. The delicacy of this case, and its possible effect on U.S.-German relations, underlay the administration decision to proceed cautiously. Whether or not to undercut this administration policy, Leon Turrou (the head of the FBI's New York field office in 1935 who had in 1938 resigned from the bureau) attempted during the late spring of 1938 to sell information about the investigation to the press. At a June 24, 1938, press conference, President Roosevelt decried Turrou's action and, to offset its impact, announced his decision to recommend increased appropriations for FBI counterespionage investigations.

Responding to this presidentially initiated review, in a lengthy memorandum to Cummings, Hoover outlined the "present purposes and scope" of FBI investigations. The FBI director specifically described the categories of files contained in the bureau's Intelligence Section as "dealing with various forms of activities of either a subversive or a so-called intelligence type" and as containing "approximately 2500 names . . . of the various types of individuals engaged in activities of Communism, Nazism, and various types of foreign espionage." Legislative authorization for these activities or their expansion should not be sought, the FBI director counseled:

> Such expansion . . . as may be desired and may become necessary can be covered, . . . under present provisions existing in the annual appropriations bill of the Federal Bureau of Investigation, . . . this provision is believed to be sufficiently broad to cover any expansion of the present intelligence and counter-espionage work which it may be deemed necessary to carry on.
>
> . . . Expansion of the present structure of intelligence work, . . . [must] be produced with the utmost degree of secrecy in order to avoid criticisms or objections which might be raised to such an expansion by either ill-informed persons or individuals having some ulterior motive. The word "espionage" has long been a word that has been repugnant to the American people and it is believed that the structure which is already in existence is much broader than espionage or counter-espionage, but covers in a true sense real intelligence values to the . . . Navy, the Army, and . . . the Department of Justice. Consequently, it would seem undesirable to seek only special legislation which would draw attention to the fact that it was proposed to develop a special counter-espionage drive of any great magnitude.

Hoover's reference to "subversive activities" and detailed description of FBI filing categories confirmed that FBI investigations focused on political activities and beliefs. When describing current investigations or the proposed expansion, however, Attorney General Cummings' October 20, 1938, cover letter to the president accompanying Hoover's memorandum did not use the phrase "subversive activities." Cummings referred only to the president's interest in the "so-called espionage situation." Whether he had read Hoover's memorandum closely, whether he had been influenced by his understanding of the September 10, 1936, briefing, or whether he merely responded to the Hoover memorandum's consistent reference to "espionage" given the fact that the president's concern over German espionage activities had precipitated this request, the attorney general offered a distinctively different description of ongoing FBI investigations and planned expansion.

Cummings' more limited description assumed crucial importance during a Roosevelt-Hoover meeting on November 2, 1938. In memorandums of November 1 and 7, 1938, the FBI director recorded having received two telephone calls from the president's secretary, Stephen Early, informing him of Roosevelt's desire for this meeting. Hoover then reported:

> The President advised me that he had this day . . . instructed [the director of the budget] to include in the Appropriation estimates $50,000 for Military Intelligence, $50,000 for Naval Intelligence, and $150,000 for the Federal Bureau of Investigation to handle counter-espionage activities. He stated that he had approved the plan which I had prepared and which had been sent to him by the Attorney General, except that he had not been able to grant the entire amount of money indicated as necessary [a $35,000 increase for each military service and a $300,000 increase for the FBI]. . . .

Had Roosevelt read only the attorney general's cover letter or had he also carefully reviewed the accompanying Hoover memorandum? Roosevelt's descriptive phrase "counter-espionage" (in light of his June 24 press conference comment) plus the considerably scaled-down appropriation recommendations, suggest that the president and the FBI director had two different programs in mind.[15]

Hoover's success, nonetheless, proved ephemeral. In March 1939, the FBI director became concerned about State Department efforts to coordinate domestic intelligence investigations—not an incidental matter since the statutory basis for FBI "counterespionage" investigations required the department's direction. In a March 16, 1939, memorandum to Attorney General Frank Murphy (Cummings's successor), Hoover submitted a copy of the bureau's 1938 program which he described as "intended to ascertain the identity of persons engaged in espionage, counter-espionage, and sabotage of a nature not within the specific provisions of prevailing statutes." Acknowledging that the existing program required the State Department's "specific authorization," Hoover feared that State would allow other federal agencies to conduct domestic investigations. Federal investigative agencies should accordingly be ordered to forward to the FBI, rather than to the State Department, information "relating to espionage and subversive activities." The confusion and violations of individual rights that had occurred in the

World War I period would thereby be avoided. Murphy concurred. The State Department's continued interest and Assistant Secretary of State George Messersmith's inauguration of a cumbersome committee system, however, would subvert an easy resolution of this matter.

At Hoover's urging, then, on June 17, 1939, Attorney General Murphy advised Roosevelt to abandon this interdepartmental committee and instead have the FBI and military intelligence services investigate "all espionage, counter-espionage, and sabotage matters." In a June 26, 1939, authorization memorandum, the president complied. His memorandum, however, limited these investigations to "espionage, counterespionage, and sabotage matters," "matters involving actually or potentially any espionage, counterespionage, or sabotage," or "data, information, or material that may come to their [the heads of all other investigative agencies] notice bearing directly or indirectly on espionage, counterespionage, or sabotage." Nowhere had the president cited "subversive activities"—this was not surprising since, when describing FBI investigations to the president and to Attorney General Murphy, Hoover and Cummings had only listed espionage, counterespionage, and sabotage. By shifting the authority for these investigations from the appropriations provision, moreover, the June 26 directive had confined FBI investigations (and those of the military intelligence services) to violations of federal statutes.[16]

FBI Director Hoover was not resigned to this restriction on FBI investigative authority and would quickly attempt to exploit the changed political situation created on September 1, 1939, with the German invasion of Poland. In a September 6, 1939, memorandum to Attorney General Murphy, the FBI director commented upon the creation of a special New York City police squad and the likelihood that private citizens would transmit information concerning sabotage to the New York City police. Indirectly recalling World War I vigilante activities, Hoover recommended at "the earliest possible moment" that Roosevelt "issue a statement or request addressed to all police officials in the United States and instructing them to turn over to the nearest representative of the Federal Bureau of Investigation any information obtained pertaining to espionage, counterespionage, sabotage, *subversive activities* and neutrality regulations" (emphasis added). Hoover submitted such a draft memorandum.

Upon receiving Hoover's recommendation and proposed presidential statement, Murphy conferred with FBI Assistant Director E. A. Tamm. The attorney general advised him, Tamm reported, that the president would issue "the order" that day requesting "all local law enforcement officials to *cooperate* with the FBI in the drive against espionage, sabotage, *subversive activities*, and violations of the neutrality laws" (emphasis added). In preparing the statement the attorney general tried to "make it as strong as possible" and based it on Hoover's memorandum. If responsive to Hoover's suggestion, nonetheless, Murphy either had a different conception of the program Hoover was recommending or supported a more limited authorization. The attorney general's letter to the president recommended only:

that matters *relating to espionage and sabotage* be handled in an effective, comprehensive and unified manner. To this end it is extremely desirable *informally to correlate* any information regarding these subjects that might be received or secured by state and local law enforcement agencies.[17] (Emphasis added)

President Roosevelt's directive of September 6, 1939, moreover, did not formally authorize FBI investigations of "subversive activities":

> The Attorney General has been requested by me to instruct the Federal Bureau of Investigation of the Department of Justice *to take charge of investigative work in matters relating to espionage, sabotage, and violations of the neutrality regulations.*
>
> This task must be conducted in a comprehensive and effective manner on a national basis, and all information must be carefully sifted out and correlated in order to avoid confusion and irresponsibility.
>
> To this end, I request all police officers, sheriffs, and other law enforcement officers in the United States promptly to *turn over to the nearest representative* of the Federal Bureau of Investigation *any information obtained by them relating to* espionage, sabotage, *subversive activities*, and violations of the neutrality laws.[18] (Emphasis added)

Issued in part to ensure the effective conduct and coordination of espionage investigations, Roosevelt's statement also was intended to avert sweeping, vigilante-type investigations focusing on dissident politics. A Murphy press conference held that same day to publicize the statement pointedly emphasized that purpose. The attorney general advised the press:

> Foreign agents and those engaged in espionage will no longer find this country a happy hunting ground for their activities. There will be no repetition of the confusion and laxity and indifference of twenty years ago.
>
> We have opened many new FBI offices throughout the land. Our men are well prepared and well trained. At the same time, if you want this work done in a reasonable and responsible way it must not turn into a witch hunt. We must do no wrong to any man.[19]

Roosevelt authorized the Bureau to perform two quite separate functions. The first paragraph of Roosevelt's September 6, 1939, statement affirmed the FBI's responsibility to take charge of specified investigations, and those enumerated (espionage, sabotage, and violations of the neutrality regulations) involved violations of particular statutes. The statement's last paragraph could properly be described as a recipient authorization. The FBI had been authorized not to investigate but to receive information about "subversive activities" from local law enforcement officials (to file or refer to the appropriate federal agency).

Attorney General Francis Biddle's September 25, 1942, order defining the duties of the various divisions of the Department of Justice and another Roosevelt statement of January 3, 1943, further confirm this limited purpose. Biddle's order identified the FBI's duties: to "investigate" criminal offenses against the United States and to act as a "clearing house" for information pertaining to "espionage, sabotage, and other subversive matters" required to "carry out" the September 6, 1939, directive.[20] Issued after the United States had formally entered World War II, Roosevelt's January 3, 1943, statement, moreover, merely specified:

> On September 6, 1939, I issued a directive providing that the Federal Bureau of Investigation of the Department of Justice should take charge of investigative work in matters relating to espionage, sabotage, and violations of the neutrality regulations, pointing out that the investigations must be conducted in a comprehensive manner, on a national basis and all information carefully sifted out and correlated in order to avoid confusion and irresponsibility. . . .
>
> I am again calling the attention of all enforcement officers to the request that they report all such information promptly to the nearest field representative of the Federal Bureau of Investigation, which is charged with the responsibility of correlating this material and referring matters which are under the jurisdiction of any other Federal agency with responsibilities in this field to the appropriate agency.
>
> I suggest that all patriotic organizations and individuals likewise report all such information relating to espionage and related matters to the Federal Bureau of Investigation in the same manner.[21]

Did Roosevelt's 1943 statement supersede that of 1939? The 1943 statement contained no reference to "subversive activities." Deletion of this phrase, moreover, conformed with Attorney General Biddle's order later that same year terminating the Custodial Detention program. In that July 16, 1943, order, Biddle would conclude that no statutory authority existed for listing individuals believed dangerous to the nation's security. The Justice Department's "proper" role, the attorney general further claimed, was limited to investigating "the activities of persons who may have violated the law."[22] In addition, Roosevelt's 1943 statement requested that "patriotic organizations and individuals" report to the FBI information "relating to espionage and related matters." This addition seems to be further evidence that the president's principal concern in issuing the statement had been to avert vigilante activities rather than to expand FBI investigative authority.

The absence of the phrase "subversive activities" from the 1943 directive complicated Hoover's position. During 1939, 1940, and 1941 congressional testimony on FBI authority and priorities the FBI director had consistently emphasized the limited duration of this FBI effort and had also pointedly cited Roosevelt's September 1939 directive's reference to "subversive activities." The FBI director might not have accurately conveyed the intent behind the president's statement; nonetheless, the phrase permitted him to cite it as formal authority.[23] Following issuance of the 1943 directive, Hoover could no longer claim such presidential authorization. The Delimitation Agreements of 1940 and 1942, concluded between the FBI and the military intelligence services—stipulating the FBI's responsibility to investigate citizens involved in "subversive activities"—moreover, did not provide this authority.[24] These agreements were based on Roosevelt's June 26, 1939, directive (and not the directive of September 6, 1939) and had been independently drafted by the intelligence community. Because neither Roosevelt's June 26, 1939, nor January 3, 1943, directives contained the phrase "subversive activities," the bureau could not claim presidential authorization to investigate such activities.

The wording of the September 6, 1939, directive and the absence of the phrase "subversive activities" from the January 3, 1943, directive provide insights into a later attempt to secure such authorization. On August 17, 1948, Attorney General Tom Clark (Biddle's successor) submitted a memorandum to President Harry Truman. To this memo, Clark appended a draft of "a statement concerning investigations in the internal security field," observing that this "appears to be the appropriate time for a third [statement]." If this Justice-proposed statement had been issued FBI investigations of "subversive activities" would have been directly authorized. When submitting this measure to the president, however, the attorney general implied that it merely reaffirmed Roosevelt's 1939 and 1943 directives. Why was a "third" statement needed?

By mid-August 1948 the nation was in the midst of an intensely partisan presidential campaign. During the first week of August, two Republican-controlled congressional committees (the House Committee on Un-American Activities and a Subcommittee of the Senate Committee on Expenditures in the Executive Departments) had initiated dramatic and widely publicized hearings. Through these hearings, conservative congressmen sought to create the impression that a serious internal security problem existed to which the Truman administration was indifferent. To defuse this Republican effort, the president publicly depicted these investigations as a "red herring" designed to divert public attention from the "reactionary" record of the Republican Eightieth Congress. At the same time, the White House began to draft presidential speeches and position papers establishing Truman's solid anti-Communist credentials and his critics' partisan irresponsibility.[25]

Clark's August 17 proposal indirectly sought to exploit the president's partisan objectives and perceived vulnerability. Seemingly the statement was no more than a request that interested citizens and law enforcement officials forward information relating to "subversive activities" to the FBI. This was the responsible and effective way of dealing with subversive threats. FBI Assistant Director D. Milton Ladd argued this point during a September 20, 1948, meeting with White House aide Stephen Spingarn. Ladd argued, as

Spingarn's memo of that Ladd-initiated meeting recorded, that the "purpose of the statement was to spike vigilante activity in the internal security area by private organizations and persons, making it clear that the FBI is the proper agency to handle such matters and that any information obtained on the subject should be reported promptly to that organization." By issuing this statement, the White House would also offer a striking contrast to the publicity-seeking and partisan efforts of its political adversaries. The statement Clark proposed, however, read:

> On September 6, 1939, and again on January 8, 1943, a Presidential directive was issued providing that the Federal Bureau of Investigation should take charge of investigative work in matters relating to espionage, sabotage, *subversive activities, and in similar matters.* It was requested that all law enforcement officers in the United States, and all patriotic organizations and individuals, promptly turn over to the Federal Bureau of Investigation any information concerning these matters.
>
> *The Federal Bureau of Investigation has fully carried out its responsibilities with respect to internal security of the United States under these directives.* The cooperation rendered to the Federal Bureau of Investigation in accordance with the directives has been of invaluable assistance to it.
>
> I wish to emphasize at this time that *these directives continue in full force and effect.*
>
> *Investigations in matters relating to the internal security* of the United States to be effective must be conducted in a comprehensive manner, on a national basis, *and by a single central agency. The Federal Bureau of Investigation is the agency designated for this purpose.* At this time again, I request that all information concerning any activities within the United States, its territories or possessions, *believed to be of a subversive nature,* be reported promptly to the nearest field representative of the Federal Bureau of Investigation.[26] (Emphasis added)

Upon close analysis, this statement was not so innocuous, nor was the FBI's interest merely to quash vigilante activities. Instead, the proposed statement *for the first time* would have included "subversive activities, and in similar matters" within the FBI's "take charge of investigations" authority. The statement's fourth paragraph, in addition, defined the FBI's responsibility as "the single central agency" empowered to receive information either "relating to the internal security" or "believed to be of a subversive nature." The wording of this fourth paragraph thereby constituted a formal and direct authorization.

Truman did not, however, issue the proposed statement in 1948; the press of the presidential campaign and the White House's decision to refer the proposal to the National Security Council (NSC) averted formal action.

Since April 1948, the NSC had been reviewing the internal security activities of all federal intelligence agencies. The NSC's objective had been to establish clear lines of authority, minimize overlap, and ensure effective coordination and cooperation among the various agencies.

Because the August 17, 1948, statement affirmed the FBI's central role in internal security matters, the White House decision to refer Clark's proposal to the NSC ensured against its issuance. Assigned responsibility to study the 1948 proposal, NSC Executive Secretary Admiral Sidney Souers first drafted an alternative statement. This draft reflected the NSC official's assumption that Roosevelt's September 6, 1939, directive had indeed authorized the FBI to take charge of "espionage, sabotage, and subversion" investigations. Souers merely deleted those provisions of Clark's August 17, 1948, draft defining the FBI as the "single central agency" having investigative responsibility "in matters relating to the internal security."[27]

Souer's alternative draft was not issued. Instead, the NSC continued to deliberate how best to coordinate internal security matters. An understanding between Secretary of Defense James Forrestal, Attorney General Clark, and FBI Director Hoover was finally reached on February 1, 1949. This agreement in turn was incorporated in a plan recommended to President Truman on March 22, 1949. Two committees were to be established within the NSC under the supervision of the NSC executive secretary to coordinate internal security activities—the IIC (Interdepartmental Intelligence Conference, headed by the FBI director and including the directors of the Army, Air Force, and Navy intelligence divisions) and the ICIS (Interdepartmental Committee on Internal Security, composed of representatives of the departments of Justice, State, and Treasury, and the military services). President Truman formally approved this recommendation on March 23, 1949.[28]

Subsequently, on July 18, 1949, the NSC issued formal charters specifying these committees' responsibilities. Under these charters, the IIC was authorized to "effect the coordination of all investigation of domestic espionage, counterespionage, sabotage, subversion, and other related intelligence matters affecting internal security."[29]

Interestingly, the IIC charter and the Delimitation Agreement of February 23, 1949, unknowingly assumed that the FBI already had authority to investigate subversive activities. In contrast, Hoover understood that these charters could not provide the needed investigative authority. Accordingly, acting then in his capacity as head of the IIC, on July 5, 1950, the FBI director renewed the 1948 strategy. A new presidential statement should be issued, Hoover recommended to the NSC, "*to bring up to date and clarify prior Presidential Directives* which were issued September 6, 1939, and January 8, 1943, outlining the responsibilities of the Federal Bureau of Investigation in connection with espionage, sabotage, *subversive activities and related matters*" (emphasis added). Such a request seemed innocent; its timing was also opportune. In the summer of 1950, political reasons made the Truman administration responsive to suggestions permitting it to proclaim its vigilant anticommunism and indirectly identify Senator Joseph McCarthy's efforts as partisan demagoguery.

Complementing Hoover's effort, on July 11, 1950, Attorney General J. Howard McGrath wrote White House Special Counsel Charles Murphy to urge the president to issue the proposed statement "at this time." McGrath enclosed a copy of the statement with his letter. Implying that this proposal reaffirmed Roosevelt's earlier directives, McGrath concluded that the "effect of issuing the statement now" would be "most helpful" and further would

> remind all agencies, patriotic organizations and individual citizens that the Federal Bureau of Investigation is charged with responsibility *for investigating* all matters pertaining to espionage, sabotage, *subversive activities and related matters,* and that it is also *the agency charged with the responsibility of being the central coordinating agency* for all information relating to the same matters. (Emphasis added)

Murphy did not forward McGrath's request to the president. Instead, White House aide George Elsey was assigned responsibility to study the matter. Neither contrasting the 1950 statement with those of 1939 and 1943 nor reviewing it in the light of the 1948 effort, Elsey focused exclusively on the fact that the NSC was then reviewing this recommendation and advised Murphy: "The Department of Justice should not have attempted an end run to the White House at a time when their proposal is in the NSC." McGrath's letter should be referred to the NSC for study and the council should report (to Murphy) when "ready to make a recommendation to the President." Elsey drafted such a memorandum to NSC executive secretary James Lay which Murphy signed on July 13, 1950.[30]

The minutes of the NSC's deliberations on the July 5 Hoover/IIC proposal remain classified; thus we do not know how seriously the recommendation was reviewed or what priorities governed NSC deliberations. Ultimately, however, the NSC recommended and on July 24, 1950, the president issued a modified version of the statement:

> On September 5, 1939, and January 8, 1943, a Presidential directive was issued providing that the Federal Bureau of Investigation of the Department of Justice should take charge of investigative work in matters relating to espionage, sabotage, subversive activities and related matters. It was pointed out that the investigations must be conducted in a comprehensive manner on a national basis and all information carefully sifted out and correlated in order to avoid confusion. I should like to again call the attention of all enforcement officers, both Federal and State, to the request that they report all information in the above enumerated fields promptly to the nearest field representative of the Federal Bureau of Investigation, which is charged with the responsibility of correlating this material and refer-

ring matters which are under the jurisdiction of any other Federal Agency with responsibilities in this field to the appropriate agency.

I suggest that all patriotic organizations and individuals likewise report all such information relating to espionage, sabotage and subversive activities to the Federal Bureau of Investigation in this same manner.[31]

Hoover's original proposal had been considerably modified. The bureau was authorized to coordinate and refer to the appropriate agency whatever information it received from law enforcement officers, patriotic organizations, and citizens. Apparently, however, the NSC either assumed that the bureau had or should have authority to investigate "subversive activities and related matters" (not having reviewed carefully the 1939 and 1943 directives and accepting Hoover's representation at face value).

The FBI and the Department of Justice quickly exploited this presidential statement (the FBI in a July 26, 1950, press release reissued by the Department of Justice on July 28, 1950). Attempting to heighten public anxieties about internal security threats and to emphasize the FBI's investigative responsibilities, the FBI's release enunciated an expansive view of subversion:

The forces which are most anxious to weaken our internal security are not always easy to identify. Communists have been trained in deceit and secretly work toward the day when they hope to replace our American way of life with a Communist dictatorship. They utilize cleverly camouflaged movements, such as some peace groups and civil rights organizations, to achieve their sinister purposes. While they as individuals are difficult to identify, the Communist Party line is clear. Its first concern is the advancement of Soviet Russia and the godless Communist cause. It is important to learn to know the enemies of the American way of life.[32]

Truman's July 24, 1950, statement raises two important questions: (1) Did he specifically authorize FBI investigations of "subversive activities"? (2) Was the review process representative of executive oversight over the bureau? Even if it is conceded that presidents have "inherent" powers to authorize investigations of "subversive activities and related matters," the 1950 directive's sole reference erroneously affirmed that this had been authorized by the earlier directives. The 1950 directive provided no independent formal authorization. The nature of NSC review and acceptance of the contention that the 1939 and 1943 directives had provided such authority, furthermore, indicates indifferent, if not sloppy, staff work and supervision.

Although the Truman White House was unaware that FBI investigations of "subversive activities" were not authorized by Roosevelt's earlier directives, FBI Director Hoover's knowledge of this fact led him to recognize the vulnerable status of the FBI's "subversive activities" investigative authority. The election of the conservative anti-Communist Eisenhower to the presidency in 1952 thereby provided both an opportunity and a dilemma for the bureau. The opportunity derived from the candidate's campaign pledge to institute more effective internal security procedures and possible dependence on Hoover for information about ongoing programs and authority. The dilemma stemmed from the possibility that the new administration might be more jealous of its prerogatives and careful in its oversight function. Developments in 1953 quickly established, however, that the Eisenhower administration's oversight of the bureau would be no more effective than Truman's.

As early as January 28, 1953, FBI Director Hoover sought to ensure that the Eisenhower administration accepted the bureau's authority to investigate "subversive activities." In a lengthy memorandum to Assistant to the President Sherman Adams, Hoover described the bureau's internal security responsibilities and authority. This "responsibility" went beyond "statutory" authority, the FBI director observed, and was based on presidential directives of 1939, 1943, and 1950 to "take charge of investigative work in matters relating to . . . subversive activities and related matters." To document this claim, Hoover appended to his January 28, 1953, memorandum only a copy of Truman's July 24, 1950, statement but not copies of the 1939 and 1943 statements.[33]

Then, on December 15, 1953, President Eisenhower issued another statement:

> On September 6, 1939, January 8, 1943, and July 24, 1950, Presidential Directives were issued requesting all enforcement officers, both Federal and State, to report promptly all information relating to espionage, sabotage, subversive activities and related matters to the nearest field representative of the Federal Bureau of Investigation.
>
> The Federal Bureau of Investigation is charged with investigating all violations of the Atomic Energy Act, . . . I am requesting that all enforcement officers, both Federal and State, report all information relating to violations of the Atomic Energy Act to the nearest field representative of the Federal Bureau of Investigation.
>
> I suggest that all patriotic organizations and individuals likewise report all such information to the Federal Bureau of Investigation in the same manner.[34]

This directive was released following a National Security Council meeting that same day which Hoover attended; the participants (including Attorney General Brownell and AEC Commissioner Lewis Strauss) seemingly understood this proposal as constituting part of a broader counterintelligence effort. FBI Director Hoover reminded the attorney general in a December 29, 1953, memorandum that "additional funds" for the FBI's "counterintelligence coverage" had been discussed at the meeting and that the president "wanted to have" the "additional counterintelligence coverage." The impetus to the December 15 NSC deliberation apparently came from Chairman Strauss's responsiveness to FBI suggestions "for improvement in AEC security." Since November 23, 1953, and more regularly after being informed on December 2, 1953, that Senator McCarthy might investigate the Oppenheimer matter, Strauss had frequent contacts with FBI officials (including three telephone conversations on December 15).

The minutes of the December 15 NSC meeting do not record that the December 15 presidential statement was either discussed or approved. As such, we cannot definitely ascertain why the administration decided to issue this statement and the extent of the president's (and the NSC's) knowledge of the nature and background to the 1939, 1943, and 1950 directives. The participants, who apparently had not been fully briefed, concluded that the proposal was part of a broader "counterintelligence" effort.[35]

Eisenhower's statement, moreover, differed from earlier presidential directives only because it cited FBI responsibility to investigate violations of the Atomic Energy Act of 1946. This citation was not a grant of new authority; the Atomic Energy Act already specified this was the bureau's responsibility.[36] Law enforcement officials and patriotic organizations and citizens were simply urged to refer to the FBI any information they gained concerning violations of the Atomic Energy Act.

What motivated this public appeal? On December 2, 1953, the president had been apprised that an FBI report raised serious questions about the security clearance status of atomic scientist J. Robert Oppenheimer (a consultant to the Atomic Energy Commission). This FBI report worried administration officials; Secretary of Defense Charles Wilson described it as "the worst one so far." Administration personnel feared that Senator McCarthy might exploit the Oppenheimer case to challenge the effectiveness of the Eisenhower administration's security procedures. On December 1, 1953, Atomic Energy Commission Chairman Lewis Strauss confided to Secretary of Defense Wilson his fear that Senator McCarthy "knows about [the Oppenheimer file] and might pull it on [the administration]." Strauss's fear was not groundless. Senator McCarthy had considered investigating the AEC in July 1953 and had then queried Hoover about Oppenheimer. Advising McCarthy not to proceed, Hoover informed the Wisconsin senator that FBI files on atomic energy matters would not be provided to McCarthy's committee (the Permanent Investigations Subcommittee of the Senate Committee on Government Operations). Following this meeting, Hoover concluded that he had successfully contained the Wisconsin senator.[37]

Eisenhower did not have such an extreme fear about McCarthy as Strauss did; he did conclude that the Oppenheimer case should be brought to the attorney general's attention. (Brownell also served as the president's political adviser.) This December 2, 1953, decision did not end the matter. At the time the administration was privately assessing how to deal with the Oppenheimer matter, its recent attempt to impugn President Truman's 1946 handling of FBI reports about Treasury Department official Harry Dexter White was the subject of a dramatic public debate.

The attorney general had purposefully resuscitated the White case in a November 6, 1953, Chicago speech, contrasting Truman's treatment of these

FBI reports with the Eisenhower administration's more effective internal security procedures and the increased authority granted to the FBI. Brownell's oblique charge of incompetence, if not disloyalty, led Truman to respond aggressively: the former president first defended his administration's disposition of the White case and then accused the Eisenhower administration of McCarthyism. To substantiate his charges, the attorney general, accompanied by FBI Director Hoover, would repeat them during testimony before the Senate Internal Security Subcommittee. Truman's attack on McCarthyism, moreover, led the Wisconsin senator in turn to demand equal radio and television time to respond to the former president. The Eisenhower White House, however, did not welcome McCarthy's response. The senator's speech, White House aide C. D. Jackson concluded, not only attacked Truman but declared a "war on Eisenhower" and challenged the president's leadership of the Republican party.[38]

McCarthy's speech simply brought to a head a long intra-administration debate over how best to respond to the Wisconsin senator. Some advisers had urged Eisenhower to challenge the senator directly; a policy of appeasing the Wisconsin senator, they argued, would wreck the Republican party and lead to defeat in the 1954 and 1956 elections. Rejecting this advice on December 2, the president would not "get into the gutter" with McCarthy.

That very night, however, Secretary of Defense Wilson informed the president of the Oppenheimer report and of Strauss's conviction that McCarthy might exploit this case. While he had then expressed a lack of concern about McCarthy, Eisenhower had not yet read the FBI's report on Oppenheimer, nor could he be certain that McCarthy would be unable to exploit the Oppenheimer case. The Wisconsin senator had already demonstrated his ability to obtain classified security information from administration sources—most dramatically revealed in his subcommittee's investigation of Army security procedures at Fort Monmouth, New Jersey, formally initiated in October 1953 (an investigation having possible atomic energy implications insofar as convicted atomic spy Julius Rosenberg had been employed there during World War II). Nor could the matter be considered on the basis of the quality of information contained in FBI security files: if released, even unsubstantiated allegations could create the public impression of a serious problem and/or of administration laxity. The easiest recourse then was to attempt to plug leaks and thereby reduce the controversial and independent Wisconsin senator's effectiveness. Eisenhower's December 15, 1953, directive had that purpose, and indirectly affirmed the 1950 interpretation of the 1939 and 1943 directives.[39]

Presidents might come and go but FBI Director Hoover remained. In view of how Hoover obtained presidential authorization for FBI "subversive activities" investigations in 1950 and 1953, the election of the liberal Kennedy administration at the least required the reaffirmation of this authority. Hoover did not, however, seek issuance of another presidential statement in 1961. If his method differed, Hoover's strategy had not changed: misinform the Kennedy administration about the September 6, 1939, Roosevelt directive. To minimize the prospect that the claimed presidential authorization would be carefully analyzed, the FBI director sought to slide it by responsible officials introducing it in the context of a purported description of the FBI's campaign against communism.

In a January 10, 1961, letter to Attorney General–designate Robert Kennedy (with copies to Secretary of State–designate Dean Rusk and Deputy Attorney General–designate Byron White), Hoover enclosed a memorandum "setting forth the over-all activities of the Communist Party, USA (CPUSA) and its threat to the internal security of the United States" and the bureau's "responsibilities in the internal security field and our counterattack against the CPUSA." Buried in this section of the memorandum, Hoover claimed:

> By Presidential Directive dated September 6, 1939, the FBI was designated as the civilian intelligence agency *principally responsible* for protecting the Nation's internal security. *Since that date, it has been the FBI's duty to investigate subversion* within the United States and to correlate all information relating to America's internal security and disseminate these data to interested Federal agencies.[40] (Emphasis added)

Moreover, in a July 25, 1961, letter to Special Assistant for National Security McGeorge Bundy ostensibly reporting on the status of the Interdepartmental Intelligence Conference's (IIC) internal security programs, FBI Director Hoover described both the IIC's charter and the Delimitations Agreement of 1949 between the FBI and the military intelligence services. These agreements had designated the FBI as the agency responsible for investigating and coordinating information relating to subversive activities. This investigative program's primary purpose, Hoover maintained, was "to counter the ever-increasing and continual threat from international communism and Soviet-bloc espionage and subversion."[41]

Then, on February 12, 1962, the FBI director requested Attorney General Robert Kennedy's guidance on policy concerning the unauthorized disclosure of classified information to the press. Hoover's memorandum remains classified and its full thrust cannot be ascertained. Attorney General Kennedy's May 9, 1962, response, however, selectively quoted from Hoover's February 12, 1962, memorandum to indicate department policy. Kennedy referred to three categories: "restricted data under the Atomic Energy Act," "leaks of classified defense information," and "data covered by paragraph 5, National Security Council Intelligence Directive Number 1." When discussing the defense leaks category, Hoover's February 12 memorandum had cited the espionage statute as authority for an FBI investigation and noted that the FBI advised the particular agency involved, submitting a report of this to the Internal Security Division of the Department of Justice. The attorney general responded to this paragraph, obviously citing the language of President Roosevelt's 1939 directive but not the 1950 or 1953 interpretations of that directive:

. . . In the light of the specific statutory responsibility assigned to the
FBI to investigate leaks of Restricted Data subject to the Atomic
Energy Act (42 USC 2271(6)) and the responsibility pursuant to a
directive issued by President Roosevelt on September 6, 1939, *reissued* by President Roosevelt January 8, 1943 and *reaffirmed* by
President Truman on July 24, 1950, "to take charge of investigative
work in matters relating to espionage, sabotage and violations of the
neutrality regulations." It is the opinion of the Department that while
cases involving leaks of classified defense information should be considered primarily matters to be handled by the agency which is responsible for safeguarding the information, it remains, however, the
responsibility of the Department to determine whether a specific set
of facts constitutes a violation of our criminal statutes.[42] (Emphasis
added)

Had Hoover cited the 1939, 1943, and 1950 directives as authority for
FBI investigations of "subversive activities" in his February 12 memorandum, the attorney general either had not caught this addition, refused to
accept this characterization of Roosevelt's directive, or had simply consulted
the 1939 directive when preparing his response. In any event, Kennedy's
memorandum implicitly denied this investigative authority, and particularly
Hoover's consistent misrepresentation of Roosevelt's 1939 directive. Nonetheless, Kennedy almost concurrently countermanded this position.

President Kennedy's faith in his brother's leadership and his own distinctive administrative priorities resulted in a June 1962 decision to assign
supervisory control over internal security matters to the attorney general.
(Under Eisenhower and Truman, the National Security Council had been
assigned this role.) Executed by NSC memorandum of June 9, 1962, the
president specified: "The continuing need for these committees and their
relationship to the Attorney General will be matters for the Attorney General to determine."[43]

Coinciding with this new supervisory assignment, on June 1, 1962, Attorney General Kennedy issued an order defining the FBI's investigative authority and responsibilities. The impetus to this order remains unknown, and
conceivably FBI Director Hoover had suggested its need. In any event,
Subpart P of this section of the Code of Federal Regulations essentially
affirmed Hoover's consistent misrepresentation of Roosevelt's 1939 directive:

Carry out Presidential directive of September 6, 1939, as reaffirmed
by Presidential directives of January 8, 1943, July 24, 1950, and December 15, 1953, designating the Federal Bureau of Investigation to
take charge of investigative work in matters relating to espionage,
sabotage, subversive activities, and related matters.[44]

This characterization of Roosevelt's directive is evident when Attorney
General Kennedy reissued the charter of the Interdepartmental Intelligence

Conference on March 5, 1964 (under his assigned internal security responsibilities). He directed the IIC to continue "the coordination of all investigation of domestic espionage, counterespionage, sabotage and subversion, and
other related intelligence matters affecting internal security." Kennedy's reauthorization memorandum further affirmed that this reissued charter neither
"modified" nor "affected" the previous "Presidential Directives" defining the
duties of the FBI and that the Delimitations Agreement of 1949 "shall remain in full force and effect."[45]

There is no available evidence that President Lyndon Johnson or his attorneys general either reviewed the 1939 directive independently or that FBI
Director Hoover again raised the matter. Having secured the incorporation
of his characterization of Roosevelt's 1939 directive in the Code of Federal
Regulations, conceivably Hoover saw no need to misinform the new president and his key advisers. Nonetheless, Hoover's annual reports on FBI
activities for 1964–68 specifically claimed that Roosevelt's 1939 directive
authorized FBI investigations of subversive activities. The 1964 report, for
one, noted:

> The FBI was charged with the primary responsibility for the protec-
> tion of the internal security of the United States by Presidential
> Directive on September 6, 1939. The scope of this authority includes
> investigations of espionage, sabotage, subversive activities and related
> matters as well as correlation and dissemination of intelligence data.[46]

The right-wing anticommunism of Richard Nixon, in contrast to previous
presidents, created a unique problem for Hoover. Rather than having to
manipulate the president to assign FBI investigative authority, the FBI director instead had to ward off a complicated administration attempt to
expand FBI investigations. Ironically, by 1970, Nixon administration personnel had concluded that the FBI director was unduly concerned about
legal and constitutional restrictions and had become soft toward subversives.[47] These pressures did mean, however, that Hoover had no difficulty
in 1969 and 1971 when seeking reaffirmation of his interpretation of Roosevelt's September 1939 directive.

Concerned over campus demonstrations and other civil rights and New
Left protest activities, the bureau in October 1968 initiated a "comprehensive study" to assess these movements' "dangerousness," "true nature,"
"worldwide ramifications . . . as well as their impact on the internal security
of the country." Receiving this completed report in early 1969, the Nixon
Justice Department's Internal Security Division did not question the bureau's
authority to conduct these investigations but prodded Hoover to extend
them. On February 18, 1969, Assistant Attorney General J. Walter Yeagley
directed the FBI to investigate "whether there is any underlying subversive
group giving illegal directions and guidance for the numerous campus disorders throughout the country." Yeagley, moreover, specifically suggested
"areas of particular interest for future investigative efforts."[48]

A different issue surfaced following congressional repeal of the emergency detention provision (Title II) of the Internal Security Act of 1950. Thereupon, on September 30, 1971, Hoover requested Attorney General Mitchell's approval to continue the bureau's Security Index program but under a new name.[49] The FBI director also sought Mitchell's authorization for continued FBI investigations of "subversive activities." Hoover did not then request issuance of an appropriate presidential directive—that tactic might prove too risky, despite the anticommunism of the Richard Nixon–John Mitchell administration. Instead, Hoover predictably misinformed Mitchell about Roosevelt's September 1939 directive:

> In addition to statutory authority . . . , we feel this authority for the FBI to conduct investigations of *subversive activity and related activity is clearly set forth in certain Presidential Directives.* . . . On September 6, 1939, the President issued a Directive as follows: "The Attorney General has been requested by me to instruct the Federal Bureau of Investigation of the Department of Justice to take charge of investigative* matters relating to espionage, sabotage, *subversive activities*† and violations of‡ neutrality regulations. . . ."
>
> On January 8, 1943, the President issued a Directive *reiterating* his previous Directive of September 6, 1939, and subsequently on July 24, 1950, the President issued a third Directive, *reiterating* previous Directives of September 6, 1939, and January 8, 1943, *and broadened the scope* of investigative activity by the FBI to include "subversive activities and *related matters*" [italics in original] as well as the specific matters involving espionage and sabotage. On December 15, 1953, the President issued *a statement in which he set forth the language contained in the combined Presidential Directives* dated September 6, 1939, January 8, 1943, and July 24, 1950, concerning the investigative responsibilities of the FBI in matters relating to "espionage, sabotage, subversive activities and related matters." . . .
>
> Based on interpretation of existing statutes and the language set forth in the various Presidential Directives cited above, we feel that the repeal of the Emergency Detention Act of 1950 *has not eroded the FBI's authority and responsibility to conduct investigation of subversive activities and related matters.* Likewise, we feel that the repeal of this Act *does not limit the FBI's authority and responsibility to keep and maintain administrative records, including various indices, which may be necessary in fulfilling such responsibility and authority.* (Emphasis added)

*Here Hoover deleted the phrase "work in" which had appeared in the 1939 directive.

†Here Hoover inserted the phrase "subversive activities" which had not appeared in the 1939 directive.

‡Here Hoover deleted the term "the" which had appeared in the 1939 directive.

Hoover then asked whether the attorney general concurred with this assessment of the FBI's authority and requested a reply "to the foregoing questions at the earliest possible time."[50]

At the least, the attorney general could expect that the FBI director had accurately paraphrased and quoted from these earlier presidential directives. Mitchell's unquestioning trust in Hoover's integrity, moreover, was wholly consistent with the executive branch's historical relationship with the FBI since Roosevelt's administration.

Accordingly, when replying on October 21, 1971, Attorney General Mitchell did not evaluate the authority granted by the various presidential directives. Mitchell merely "advised" Hoover that "the FBI's authority to investigate . . . subversive activities and related matters in accordance with its statutory responsibilities and the Presidential directives, cited in your memorandum, remains unaffected by the repeal of the Emergency Detention Act."[51]

Ironically, concurrent with Hoover's claim that presidential directives and statutes provided sufficient authority for FBI investigations of "subversive activities," FBI policies, procedures, and authority were undergoing closer scrutiny at a Princeton University conference. Held in October 1971, the Princeton conference offered an independent and searching review of the FBI.[52] In February 1971, moreover, the Subcommittee on Constitutional Rights of the Senate Judiciary Committee under the chairmanship of Sam Ervin, Jr., had initiated hearings on the impact of computers and data banks on the Bill of Rights. The focus of these hearings shifted in March 1971 to the Army's surveillance of antiwar and civil rights activities. For the first time during the Cold War years an important congressional committee had initiated a public examination of the authority for federal agencies' investigations of dissident activities.[53]

Then, on February 24, 1972, during confirmation hearings on his nomination to be attorney general, Richard Kleindienst expressed ignorance as to the bureau's guidelines for investigating individuals or groups. FBI investigations, Kleindienst conjectured, were "restricted to criminal conduct or the likelihood of criminal conduct." Apprised of Kleindienst's testimony, Hoover directed bureau personnel to prepare a "succinct memo to [Kleindienst] on our guidelines." Presented to the acting attorney general on February 25, this summary reported that the bureau investigated "any individual" who is "affiliated with or adheres to the principles of" an organization "which has as an objective" the violent overthrow of the government or "other criminal activity detrimental to the National Defense." FBI investigations were not confined to obtaining evidence for prosecution but also sought "intelligence data in order to have day-to-day appraisal of strength, dangerousness, and activities of the organization; and to keep the Department of Justice and other affected Government agencies advised." Such investigations of "subversive activities" which did not "often . . . clearly involve a specific section of a specific statute" were based on President Roosevelt's September 1939 directive "reiterated and broadened by subsequent Directives."[54] Like his predecessors, Kleindienst did not independently examine the validity of this claim.

Because of his long tenure and direct initiative in defining the FBI's investigative authority, J. Edgar Hoover's death on May 2, 1972, portended a possible problem. On May 3, 1972, President Nixon appointed an FBI outsider to be acting FBI director—Deputy Attorney General L. Patrick Gray. As one of his first official actions, Gray requested a review of the bureau's "authority" to conduct investigations "where there is no violation of law." Such a position paper, dated May 19, 1972, was prepared and submitted to Gray by FBI Assistant Director E. S. Miller, the head of the bureau's Intelligence Division. This paper enumerated the various presidential directives, executive orders, delimitation agreements, and general authorizations from attorneys general. Miller would withdraw this memorandum following a conference with Gray; a lengthier paper was completed after further study in July 1972.[55]

Ironically, Gray's request for this review precipitated a serious split within the Intelligence Division over the bureau's investigative authority. Some officials concluded that the FBI had "overstated our authority supposedly derived from Presidential directives" and accordingly should request "legal guidance and advice [of the attorney general] as to just how much authority we have or need." Other officials feared that reliance solely on statutory authority would "undermine" bureau policies. This latter view prevailed and the resultant July 31, 1972, position paper claimed that FBI political surveillance investigations could properly be based on the "concept" that their purpose was "to prevent a violation of a statute." The paper, however, questioned whether the FBI should rely on presidential authority, citing past instances of White House political uses of the bureau.

Following receipt of this position paper, Acting FBI Director Gray hesitated to seek policy guidance from the attorney general. Gray directed Washington bureau officials in August 1972 to indicate the FBI's "jurisdictional authority" for ordering investigations of particular cases "by citing the pertinent provision of the U.S. Code, *or other authority*" (emphasis added). These officials should report "whether or not an investigation was directed by DJ [Department of Justice], or we opened it without any request from DJ"; in the latter case the reasons for this independent action were to be cited.[56]

Gray's directive did not resolve the matter. The acting FBI director's ignominious resignation on April 27, 1973, and Clarence Kelley's appointment as FBI director only raised anew the issue of the FBI's political surveillance authority. The immediate impetus to this review derived from the more skeptical political climate created by the Senate Watergate Committee's revelations and the Senate Constitutional Rights Subcommittee's findings concerning Army surveillance activities. Senator Sam Ervin, who had headed both investigations and who had emerged as a respected authority on federal agencies' abuses of power, publicly demanded legislation prohibiting the Army from investigating dissident activities. Furthermore, at least according to a bureau memorandum, Ervin also supported legislation prohibiting the FBI "from investigating any person without that individual's consent, unless the Government has reason to believe that person has committed a crime or is about to commit a crime."

Responding to these political pressures, Washington bureau personnel began to consider what course the FBI should then pursue. After considerable internal discussion, on August 7, 1973, FBI Director Kelley submitted to Attorney General Elliot Richardson a memorandum outlining the "scope of FBI jurisdiction and authority in domestic intelligence investigations" and a draft executive order which Richardson was requested to submit to the White House "with a strong recommendation for approval."[57]

The FBI director's August 7 memorandum briefed the attorney general on the background to this report, citing the specific questions raised by congressional committees and public opinion leaders. This FBI study revealed, Kelley advised, that the bureau "publicly" based its authority on legislation, presidential directives, and instructions from the attorney general. Then, in the first admission that Roosevelt's 1939 directive provided no such authority, the bureau study concluded:

> In carefully analyzing the language of the first directive, dated September 6, 1939, and considering that the subsequent directives all are hinged on this one, we believe that there is a *misconception* as to the extent of jurisdiction or authority conveyed to the FBI by these directives. It appears that while the 1939 directive fixed responsibility on the FBI to handle espionage, sabotage, and neutrality matters, *it did not convey any authority or jurisdiction which the FBI did not already have from legislative enactments.* It is difficult to read into this directive or in any of those which followed any *authority* [italics in original] to conduct intelligence-type investigations which would or could not be conducted under an umbrella of legislative enactments.[58] (Emphasis added)

Despite the conclusion that these directives provided no such authority, Kelley nonetheless maintained that the bureau (1) had been directed to collect information from state, local, and federal law enforcement agencies and patriotic citizens and (2) had the responsibility to conduct "whatever investigations are necessary to determine if statutes relating to espionage, sabotage, insurrection or rebellion, sedition, seditious conspiracy, advocacy of overthrowing the Government, and other such crimes affecting the national security have been violated." The FBI director then maintained:

> . . . had there never been a single one of the Presidential directives in question the FBI would have conducted and will, through necessity, continue to conduct the same intelligence-type investigations as were conducted from 1939 to the present date. . . . *in order to counter the criticism and skepticism* of such individuals as Professor Elliff and

Senator Sam J. Ervin . . . an *up-to-date* Executive order should be issued clearly *establishing a need for* intelligence-type investigations, and *delineating a clear authority for* the FBI to conduct such investigations.[59] (Emphasis added)

This request, Kelley added, should not be construed as an admission that the FBI currently lacked authority to conduct such investigations. To the contrary; the FBI was merely "being realistic" recognizing the need to "update to fit 1973 needs" the "basic statutes" providing such authority. Citing bills recently introduced in the Congress to "spell out" the FBI's jurisdiction and authority, the FBI director then counseled Richardson:

> It would appear that the President would rather spell out *his own* requirements in an Executive order *instead of having Congress tell him what the FBI might do to help him fulfill his obligations and responsibilities* as President.
>
> The political climate of suspicion and distrust resulting from disclosures coming out of the Watergate hearings *could present an obstacle to getting any such Executive order signed in the immediate future.* However, the rationale is nevertheless valid and when scrutinized closely, the language in the Executive order *we hereinafter propose* establishes *definitive guidelines which have heretofore been unclear.*[60] (Emphasis added)

Not surprisingly, in view of the history of Hoover's uses of the 1939 directive, the FBI-recommended executive order explicitly authorized FBI political surveillance. In one sense, this order repeated the basic strategy that intelligence bureaucrats had employed in June–July 1970 to secure Nixon's assent to the Huston Plan. For the 1973-proposed executive order began by outlining the president's constitutional authority, responsibility to enforce the laws, defend the Constitution, and protect the nation from internal and external attacks and thus led up to his need for "intelligence information for appropriate decisions." The order specified:

> The Attorney General prepare and issue guidelines, conforming to the principles of the Constitution and the Bill of Rights, and outlining the necessary direction, coordination, and guidance of investigations to assure that the Federal Bureau of Investigation provides on a continuing basis intelligence information essential to the execution of laws pertaining to subversive activity and other such activity affecting the national security, domestic tranquility, and general welfare of the United States.[61]

Kelley was obviously interested more in securing authority than in clarity: the proposed executive order's authorization paragraph was so vague and all-encompassing that it would have ensured wide latitude and flexibility.

This, moreover, was Kelley's purpose, highlighted further by his memorandum's concluding comments:

> It would be folly to adopt an investigative policy based on the concept of investigation *only* when there is reason to believe a crime involving the national security *had been* committed [italics in original]. The FBI must obviously anticipate the crimes described above [terrorism, bombings, hijackings, killing of police officers]. We believe that in order for the Government to be in position to defend itself against revolutionary and terrorist efforts to destroy it, the FBI must have sufficient investigative authority to conduct intelligence-type investigations not normally associated with enforcement of the statutes. In other words we think the President has the inherent Executive power *to expand by further defining* the FBI's investigative authority. . . . Such *expanded* authority must be formally set forth in an Executive order and that this recommendation is responsive in the Attorney General's expressed interest in laying *more formal* guidelines to our work in areas where definition is not now clear.[62] (Emphasis added)

Further study was needed before any action could be taken on these recommendations, Richardson advised the FBI director on September 12, 1973.[63] President Nixon's October 20, 1973, dismissal of Special Prosecutor Archibald Cox, and Richardson's resultant resignation, however, deferred any immediate action. For different reasons, William Saxbe, Richardson's successor as attorney general, would also postpone acting on this recommendation, assigning priority instead to a departmental inquiry into the bureau's recently disclosed COINTELPRO.[64]

The Ford administration, however, did not have the luxury of postponement. Revelations of the abuses of power which led to President Nixon's August 1974 forced resignation had created a far different political climate. The Congress and the news media no longer uncritically tolerated either independent executive initiatives or the expansion of surveillance authority based on "national security" claims. Thus, when the Department of Justice released a revised version of its COINTELPRO report in November 1974, condemning certain bureau practices but defending most of the activities as "legitimate," the public was not mollified. Instead, the report on the FBI's COINTELPRO combined with recent press revelations about the CIA's CHAOS program and former FBI Director Hoover's retention of files on prominent personalities in his office precipitated demands for an intensive congressional investigation of the intelligence community. Accordingly, on January 21, 1975, Democratic Senator John Pastore introduced S. Res. 21 to establish a Select Committee on Intelligence Activities. The resolution was agreed to on January 27, 1975.

Throughout 1975, the Ford administration was forced on the defensive. For political reasons, the administration reluctantly complied with the Senate committee's requests for heretofore classified documents which in effect uncovered the scope of the FBI's past abuses of power. Recognizing the need for some corrective action and adopting the strategy outlined by FBI Director Kelley in his August 7, 1973, memorandum, on February 18, 1976, President Ford issued Executive Order 11905 intended to limit the intelligence agencies' investigate activities. Then on March 10, 1976, Attorney General Edward Levi issued a series of guidelines on FBI investigations. Levi's March 10 guidelines admittedly tightened existing rules, and were more stringent than those which Kelley had recommended in August 1973. These guidelines nonetheless provided considerable latitude and flexibility to the FBI and FBI officials immediately interpreted them as authorizing intelligence investigations of "subversives" (defined either as individuals who might attempt to overthrow the government in the future or who "use . . . force" to interfere with local and state government).[65]

Levi's "restrictions" would not preclude extensive FBI surveillance of dissident political activity (the "use of force" concept would have permitted FBI investigations of the civil rights and antiwar demonstrations of the 1960s which sought to effect political change by disrupting governmental activities). The July 27, 1977, congressional testimony of FBI Director Clarence Kelley and the March 1978 court testimony of FBI Associate Director James Adams confirm this. Responding to questions posed by American Civil Liberties Union attorneys during a class action suit alleging that FBI domestic security investigations violated their clients' civil rights, Adams admitted that as many as two-hundred-fifty informers who had originally been listed under the heading "domestic security" were merely reclassified "foreign counterintelligence" following issuance of Levi's 1976 guidelines. During his July 1977 congressional testimony, after initially maintaining that FBI domestic surveillance investigations had been terminated in April/May 1976, Kelley later qualified this assertion. He then contended that "domestic intelligence" investigations had been reduced to two hundred, and that twenty-two of these two hundred investigations involved organizations. These investigations were not predicated on statutory violations but on three criteria: "that activities *may be*, or are in fact, currently under way which will involve *violence*, the *potential* overthrow of the Government, and a violation of Federal law" (emphasis added).[66]

The history of FBI political surveillance authority indirectly raises serious questions about the effectiveness of executive order reforms. Whether political consideration or blind trust is the explanation, neither presidents nor attorneys general exercised meaningful oversight over the FBI since 1936. Not surprisingly, then, FBI Director Hoover unilaterally initiated a far-reaching program abusive of individual rights (COINTELPRO) and since 1939 volunteered political information to the White House or responded readily to White House requests for such information. During consideration of this program, FBI officials had not been concerned about legality or constitutionality. Their main consideration of legal or constitutional questions centered on how to devise a legal or constitutional rationale for a desired activity.

Chapter Four

Wiretaps, Mail Openings, and Break-Ins

In their highly politicized efforts to curb "subversive activities," internal security bureaucrats increasingly relied upon a number of investigative techniques—some clearly illegal, others of questionable legality. These officials were not troubled by legal or constitutional questions; results counted and, in any case, "national security" needs justified violating the law or the Constitution. Former FBI Assistant Director William Sullivan starkly affirmed these distorted priorities during November 1975 executive session testimony before the Senate Select Committee on Intelligence Activities:

> During the ten years that I was on the U.S. Intelligence Board, . . . never once did I hear any body, including myself, raise the question: "Is this course of action which we have agreed upon lawful, is it legal, is it ethical or moral?" We never gave any thought to this realm of reasoning, because we were just naturally pragmatists. The one thing we were concerned about was this: will this course of action work, will it get us what we want, will we reach the objective we desire to reach?[1]

During the 1940s and early 1950s, moreover, FBI, CIA, NSA, and Justice Department officials neither publicly nor privately justified particular investigative activities on constitutional grounds. Whether devising secretive filing procedures or relying upon a crisis atmosphere, they instead attempted to avert the external scrutiny which might have exposed illegal activities. The alteration of popular and congressional attitudes toward centralized power during the Cold War years, contributing to greater deference toward expansive presidential claims to "inherent" powers, encouraged these officials during the late 1950s and the 1960s to advance torturous constitutional justifications. These claims would be challenged in the mid-1970s by the more skeptical popular, press, and congressional attitudes in the aftermath of the Watergate Affair. Concerned congressmen and public leaders then demanded reforms to preclude future abuses of power by presidents or intelligence agency officials.

Electronic surveillance policy most dramatically highlights how national attitudes changed during the Cold War years, thereby contributing to a serious constitutional crisis. Throughout the 1936–78 period, the public consistently expressed concern about the Big Brother aspects of such surveillance. Despite this rhetorical concern, increasing numbers of informed citizens had nonetheless come to accept the need for wiretapping and bugging to counter subversive and criminal activities. Thus, whereas wiretapping was legislatively prohibited in 1934, by 1968 Congress authorized wiretaps under judicial controls during criminal investigations and recognized the president's (undefined) constitutional powers in the "national security" area. The "national security" exception was challenged only in the aftermath of the Watergate-related revelations. Even then, in 1978, executive branch and congressional leaders advocated a degree of presidential latitude and flexibility consistent with a president's (undefined) constitutional "national security" powers. What, then, is a "national security" wiretap?

Two March 22, 1976, news stories provide indirect answers to this question. These stories also raise additional questions about the changing meaning of the phrase "national security" and the uses of these surveillances. One reported FBI Director Clarence Kelley's speech to the Palm Beach (Fla.) Round Table advocating legislation to authorize the FBI to wiretap or bug "suspected" domestic terrorists for intelligence purposes. (By the 1970s, FBI officials cited terrorists as the principal internal security threat, in contrast to earlier citations of Communists and subversives.) The second reported former President Richard Nixon's deposition. A defendant in a suit brought by former National Security Council consultant Morton Halperin, the former president was responding to a series of questions involving his administration's illegal tapping of Halperin's phone during the years 1969–71. Some of these questions related to the political nature of FBI Director Hoover's reports to the Nixon White House based on these wiretaps. Lamely conceding that these were not "a proper subject for the FBI to be informing the White House on," Nixon further claimed that Hoover's reports listing the foreign policy advisers working for Democratic presidential aspirant Senator Muskie "was not requested as far as I know."[2]

In contrasting ways, the Kelley and Nixon statements capsulize the national security wiretap problem. FBI Director Kelley might have claimed that the bureau's legislative objective was to prevent imminent criminal acts —and thus had a crime prevention purpose. Reports of the Halperin taps confirm that the FBI had immediately forwarded political information to the Nixon White House which it had picked up incidental to "national security" electronic surveillance. It is immaterial whether this political reporting simply responded to presidential direction or whether it was an unsolicited attempt to assist the Nixon White House. Since the reports were dated variously December 29, 1969; May 4, 1970; June 23, 1970; and November 13, 1970; and since Halperin's home phone had been tapped from May 1969 until February 1971, over a year after the termination of his NSC consultantship, the president had the opportunity to order the termination either of Hoover's political reporting or of the Halperin tap. Suggestive of what was by then a common intelligence community practice, moreover, the records of this wiretap program were filed separately from the FBI's other "national security" wiretaps.

These March 1976 news stories further confirm that the debate over federal surveillance authority has heretofore been unduly confined to the constitutionality of electronic surveillance. At the same time, other important questions have not been explored: namely, whether executive branch officials effectively oversee the bureau or how information gained from electronic surveillance has been used. The result has been that our understanding of federal electronic surveillance policy and authority has been narrowly confined—and so too have been legislative policy debates and judicial decisions.

U.S. District Judge Augelli's October 13, 1970, decision in *U.S. v. Butenko* and the Department of Justice's September 1974 brief in another case, *Ivanov v. U.S.*, illustrate these points dramatically.

Denying defendant Butenko's claim that illegal governmental wiretapping entitled him to access to these taps' records, Judge Augelli concluded that government wiretapping neither had been an unreasonable search and seizure nor had violated Section 605 of the Federal Communications Act of 1934. (This section stipulated that "no person not being authorized by the sender shall intercept any [wire and radio] communication and divulge or publish the existence, contents, substance, purport, effect, or meaning of such intercepted communication to any person."[3]) Augelli based his interpretation of "reasonableness" on conclusions about the president's constitutional powers to gather foreign intelligence information and Congress's intent when enacting Section 605. Thus, the senior judge ruled:

> As stated earlier in this memorandum, the findings of this Court is that the surveillances were conducted solely for the purpose of gathering foreign intelligence information. In operating in this area, the President is exercising his power as Commander-in-Chief of our armed forces and as the Nation's sole organ in the field of foreign affairs to gather information he deems essential to protect the national security interest. That the Communications Act of 1934 was not intended to limit or interfere with the President's prerogative of obtaining foreign intelligence information is evident from a reading of Title III of the Omnibus Crime Control and Safe Streets Act of 1968, 18 U.S.C. #2511 (3) . . . .
>
> It thus appears that when Congress enacted Title III of the Omnibus Crime Control and Safe Streets Act, it expressly recognized the existence of the President's power to gather foreign intelligence information, and made it clear that Section 605 of the Communications Act of 1934 did not limit that power. As the Government points out, the Executive Branch has consistently taken the position that wiretapping for intelligence purposes did not violate Section 605. . . .[4]

In its September 1974 memorandum petitioning the U.S. Supreme Court for a writ of certiorari in the case of *Ivanov v. U.S.*, the government repeated Augelli's interpretation of Section 605:

> Prior to the 1968 amendment Section 605 provided that "[n]o person not being authorized by the sender shall intercept any communication and divulge or publish the existence, contents, substance, purport,

effect, or meaning of such intercepted communication to any person."
While no explicit exception to this provision is set forth in the statute, it is clear that Section 605 is not and was not concerned with
proscribing surveillances conducted for the purpose of gathering foreign intelligence information. There is nothing in the legislative history to indicate that Congress intended to prohibit wiretaps authorized
by the President or Attorney General for such foreign intelligence
purposes.[5]

Are these historical references accurate and sound? Unfortunately, they
are not. The Department of Justice's and Judge Augelli's contentions about
congressional intent were bad history, principally because they assumed that
congressional conceptions of presidential authority had remained static and
because they ignored the courts' changing interpretations of presidential
powers since 1937. In fact, congressional attitudes of the 1960s toward legislation recommended by executive officials to authorize "national security"
wiretaps have changed radically from the congressional position of the
1930s.[6]
Congress might have acceded to presidential claims to "inherent" powers
in the national security area during the Cold War years. Congress had not
always been so deferential. Extremely jealous of its prerogatives, the Congress of the 1930s and 1940s had sought through highly publicized hearings,
resolutions, bills, and constitutional amendments to restrict presidential foreign policy initiatives. Thus, while the government's memorandum (and the
Court of Appeals) correctly noted that no proponent of Section 605 had
expressed the intent to curb presidential foreign intelligence authority, it
does not follow that Congress implicitly recognized this authority. Congressional consideration of the Federal Communications Act of 1934, moreover,
coincided with enactment of other legislation (the Johnson Act of 1934 and
the Neutrality Acts of 1935, 1936, and 1937) and investigative hearings
(the 1934–37 Nye committee investigations of the munitions industry, private banking loans to belligerent powers, and the Wilson administration's
conduct of foreign policy). These provide a contrary contemporary record
of congressional conceptions of presidential authority, underscore Congress's
intent then to define precisely executive foreign policy authority, and confirm Congress's refusal to countenance inherent powers claims deriving from
responsibilities as "Commander-in-Chief and administrator of the nation's
foreign affairs."[7]
These differing congressional attitudes were also shared by the Supreme
Court of the 1930s. Despite the 1934 ban, the FBI had continued to wiretap
during the late 1930s. The bureau's use of wiretaps in a criminal case, *U.S.
v. Nardone*, brought this matter before the courts in 1937 and again in 1939.
In its briefs, the government did not distinguish between domestic crime and
foreign intelligence and did not claim the right to intercept communications
for merely intelligence purposes. Section 605's reference to "any person," the
government then argued, did not apply to federal investigative agents. The

Supreme Court rejected this reasoning and affirmed in 1937 that Section 605's ban applied to federal law enforcement officials and forbade in 1939 the divulgence or "derivative use" of intercepted telephone conversations. In striking contrast to Judge Augelli's interpretation of congressional unwillingness to limit executive powers, Justice Robert's 1937 majority opinion pointedly rejected the government's claim that the 1934 act did not apply to federal officials:

> Taken at face value the phrase "no person" comprehends federal agents, . . . It is urged that a construction be given the section which would exclude federal agents since it is improbable Congress intended to hamper and impede the activities of the government in the detection and punishment of crime. The answer is that the question is one of policy. Congress may have thought it less important that some offenders should go unwhipped than that officers should resort to methods deemed inconsistent with ethical standards and destructive of personal liberty.[8]

In response to the decisions of 1937 and 1939, Attorney General Robert Jackson, by Order No. 3343 of March 15, 1940, prohibited all FBI wiretapping. The attorney general's ban, however, did not long remain in force. Although the background to this decision is not known, on May 21, 1940, President Franklin Roosevelt directed Jackson:

> I have agreed with the broad purpose of the Supreme Court decision relating to wiretapping in investigations. The Court is undoubtedly sound both in regard to the use of evidence secured over tapped wires in the prosecution of citizens in criminal cases; and it is also right in its opinion that under ordinary and normal circumstances wiretapping by Government agents should not be carried out for the excellent reason that it is almost bound to lead to abuse of civil rights.
>
> However, I am convinced that the Supreme Court never intended any dictum in the particular case which it decided to apply to grave matters involving the defense of the nation.
>
> It is, of course, well known that certain other nations have been engaged in the organization of propaganda of so-called "fifth columns" in other countries and in preparation for sabotage, as well as in active sabotage.
>
> It is too late to do anything about it after sabotage, assassinations and "fifth column" activities are completed.
>
> You are, therefore, authorized and directed in such cases as you may approve, after investigation of the need in each case, to authorize the necessary investigating agents that they are at liberty to secure information by listening devices direct to the conversation or other communications of persons suspected of subversive activities against the Government of the United States, including suspected spies. You

are requested furthermore to limit these investigations so conducted to a minimum and to limit them insofar as possible to aliens.[9]

Authorizing the attorney general to approve "national defense" wiretaps, President Roosevelt did not then claim inherent presidential powers or that foreign intelligence investigations were exempted from the 1934 act's prohibitions. The President's directive was based on a narrow reading of the Supreme Court's rulings: the Court had not "intended" to prohibit such wiretaps when "the defense of the nation" was involved.[10] In addition, although his directive's language ranges from the general to the specific, wiretapping was limited to activities involving military or espionage threats. Roosevelt's reference to "persons suspected of subversive activities," moreover, had not directly authorized wiretaps of domestic radicals; the preceding language in paragraphs two, three, and four and of the authorization paragraph's final sentence qualify this phrase's meaning.[11]

Roosevelt's qualifying language in part explains Attorney General Tom Clark's 1946 recommendation to President Harry Truman to "reaffirm" this 1940 directive. Concerned about domestic radicalism—specifically the American Communist party's involvement in labor, civil rights, and legislative lobbying activities—Truman's conservative attorney general sought formal presidential authorization to wiretap "subversives." Yet, Clark did not recommend issuance of a revised directive specifically expanding the FBI's wiretapping authority to include investigations of "subversive activities." Rather, by quoting selectively from Roosevelt's 1940 directive, the attorney general in a July 17, 1946, letter informed the president:

Under date of May 21, 1940, President Franklin D. Roosevelt, in a memorandum addressed to Attorney General Jackson stated:

"You are therefore authorized and directed in such cases as you may approve, after investigation of the need in each case, to authorize the necessary investigating agents that they are at liberty to secure information by listening devices directed to the conversation or other communications of persons suspected of subversive activities against the Government of the United States, including suspected spies."

This directive was followed by Attorneys General Jackson and Biddle, and is currently being followed in this Department. I consider it appropriate to bring the subject to your attention at this time.

It seems to me in the present troubled period in international affairs, accompanied as it is by an increase in subversive activities here at home, it is as necessary as it was in 1940 to take the investigative measures referred to in President Roosevelt's memorandum. At the same time, the country is threatened by a very substantial increase in crime. While I am reluctant to suggest any use whatever of these special investigative measures in domestic cases, it seems imperative to use them in cases vitally affecting the domestic security, or where human life is in jeopardy.

As so modified, I believe the outstanding directive should be continued in force. If you concur in this policy, I should appreciate it if you would so indicate at the foot of this letter.

In my opinion, the measures proposed are within the authority of law, and I have in the files of the Department materials indicating to me that my two most recent predecessors as Attorney General would concur in this view.[12]

Beginning his letter by quoting from Roosevelt's 1940 directive, Clark conveyed the impression that approval was being sought for "investigative measures referred to in President Roosevelt's memorandum" modified only to permit wiretapping in criminal cases "vitally affecting the domestic security, or where human life is in jeopardy." Clark's selective quotation meant that Truman's approval would expand FBI wiretapping authority to include "subversive activities." For one, Clark's quote from Roosevelt's directive had deleted the authorization paragraph's final sentence—"You are requested furthermore to limit these investigations so conducted to a minimum and to limit them insofar as possible to aliens." Clark had also not cited the preceding paragraphs' references qualifying Roosevelt's authorization paragraph's "subversive activities" reference. These paragraphs referred to "sabotage," "active sabotage," and "sabotage, assassinations and 'fifth column' activities." Clark's selective quotation, accordingly, secured Truman's approval to extend FBI wiretapping to "subversive activities."

Significantly, in 1946 the attorney general did not claim that presidents had inherent powers to authorize "national security" wiretaps. Instead, he merely cited his two predecessors' conclusion that the Supreme Court had not prohibited wiretapping for investigative purposes. Absent a contrary Court ruling, investigative wiretapping was legal. The president had the responsibility to safeguard the national defense (a far more specific phrase than the more nebulous "national security" claim of the 1950s and 1960s) and the Court had not rejected this responsibility.

Clark's crafty bureaucratic maneuver (selective quotation and having the president sign a letter to be returned to the attorney general) successfully expanded FBI wiretapping authority, thereafter directed principally at domestic radicals. Ironically, because of the FBI's use of this authority in the Judith Coplon case, President Truman would become apprised of his attorney general's dishonesty.

An employee of the Department of Justice's alien registration section, Ms. Coplon was arrested on March 4, 1949, as she allegedly was about to deliver twenty-eight FBI documents to Valentin Gubitchev, a member of the Soviet Union's United Nations staff. Indicted in Washington, D.C., for unauthorized possession of these documents and in New York City for attempting to transmit them to Gubitchev, Ms. Coplon was tried in both cities. During the first (Washington) trial, Ms. Coplon's lawyers demanded that the full texts of the twenty-eight documents found in her handbag at the time of her arrest (and which she was accused of stealing) be introduced in evidence. Pressured by the FBI, the prosecution objected to this defense motion on "national security" grounds. Judge Albert Reeves overruled this objection holding that the government could not insist on the "national security" importance of the documents and then refuse to reveal their contents on "national security" grounds.

The released documents disclosed no national secrets, but proved deeply embarrassing to the FBI because they confirmed the highly political nature of FBI investigations. The documents disclosed that they did not investigate illegal or treasonous activities but focused on prominent New Deal liberals Edward Condon and David Niles, Hollywood actors Frederick March and Edward G. Robinson, supporters of Henry Wallace's 1948 Progressive party campaign, opponents of the House Committee on Un-American Activities, and the author of a master's thesis on the New Deal in New Zealand. The documents further revealed that information for fifteen of the twenty-eight reports had been acquired through wiretaps.

Defense attorneys, exploiting the wiretapping revelation, requested a pretrial hearing to ascertain whether the FBI had also tapped Ms. Coplon's phone. This motion should be rejected, U.S. Attorney John Kelly, Jr., contended: "I deem what he said regarding tapping of telephones to be primarily a fishing expedition which requires no answer." Judge Reeves concurred and Ms. Coplon's Washington trial proceeded without ascertaining whether the government's case had been based on illegal wiretapping.

Sylvester Ryan, the presiding judge in Ms. Coplon's second (New York) trial, was more responsive to the defense motion for a pretrial hearing. This six-week hearing established that forty FBI agents had tapped phones at Ms. Coplon's office and apartment and at her parents' Brooklyn home, and that these taps had been installed on January 6, 1949, and continued for two months after her arrest, thereby intercepting privileged conversations between Ms. Coplon and her attorneys.

These revelations raised at least two questions. First, had information gained through illegal FBI wiretapping led to Ms. Coplon's arrest and informed the government of the defense's trial strategy? Second, were responsible Department of Justice officials fully aware of FBI wiretapping? Had the FBI acted insubordinately and then sought to cover up illegal actions and insubordination? Could one rely on the integrity of FBI agents? This second series of questions was not idle speculation. For FBI agents (who had been present at the time) had not informed U.S. Attorney Kelly of his error when he righteously denied that the government had wiretapped Ms. Coplon during her Washington trial. Additionally, the FBI agent who initially claimed during the New York pretrial hearing "no previous knowledge" of wiretapping in the Coplon case had, in fact, routinely received the records of these interceptions and would later admit to having destroyed "quite a number" of the tapes. This last admission added a further dimension—contradicting earlier court testimony that the Coplon tap records had been destroyed "as a routine matter," FBI agents had destroyed these records pursuant to a bureau order "in view of the imminence of her trial."[13]

These revelations precipitated a vigorous protest. Assuming a leadership role in this criticism, the National Lawyers Guild demanded reforms to ensure against their recurrence. In June 20, 1949, and January 19, 1950, letters (the latter accompanied by a detailed analysis of the trial record) to President Truman, National Lawyers Guild president Clifford Durr sharply criticized FBI practices and demanded the appointment of a presidential commission "of outstanding citizens, including representatives of the national bar associations and civil liberties organizations, to undertake a comprehensive investigation into the operations and methods of the Federal Bureau of Investigation." When the president responded politely but evasively to Durr's first letter and totally ignored the second, the guild sought the support of prominent liberals (such as Joseph Rauh of the Americans for Democratic Action) who had greater respectability and greater leverage with the administration. Rauh would cooperate. In a February 24, 1950, speech, the prominent ADA official sharply condemned FBI practices and demanded that the president establish a special commission.[14]

FBI Director Hoover and high-level Justice Department officials attempted to defuse this and future criticisms and avert an independent investigation of the bureau by pursuing four independent but coordinated strategies.

First, to ensure against future embarrassment, on July 8, 1949, Hoover issued Bureau Bulletin No. 34. Thereafter, "facts and information which are considered of a nature not expedient to disseminate or would cause embarrassment to the Bureau, if distributed" were not to be included by agents in their investigative reports but on the reports' administrative page.[15] Normally, the administrative pages had been used to summarize major investigative findings and future investigative policy. This procedure for reporting "embarrassing" facts and information (such as illegal wiretaps, break-ins, investigations focusing on prominent personalities) on administrative pages would minimize the risks of court disclosure. Should judges in the future require release of FBI reports, the bureau could technically comply without releasing the administrative page.

Second, in a March 31, 1949, press release Attorney General Clark publicly denied that the bureau either had acted insubordinately or had wiretapped extensively. The FBI had wiretapped only "in limited [number of] cases with the express approval in each individual instance of the Attorney General. . . . There has been no new policy or procedure since the initial policy was stated by President Roosevelt and this has continued to be the Department's policy whenever the security of the nation is involved." Following the more dramatic New York trial revelations, J. Howard McGrath, Clark's successor as attorney general, offered the same defense on January 8, 1950: the attorney general strictly controlled FBI wiretapping. "There has been no new policy or procedure since . . . President Roosevelt." McGrath ominously added: "In view of the emergency which still prevails and the necessity of protecting the national security, I see no reason at the present time for any change."[16]

Third, because of the National Lawyers Guild's leadership role in this criticism, the FBI sought to influence the president's views on the guild and thereby reduce the likelihood that Truman would establish an independent commission. On December 1, 1949, and again on December 22, 1949, Hoover forwarded to McGrath reports detailing the guild's "subversive" activities and personnel. (These reports had been compiled in part from illegal wiretaps of the guild's Washington office and possibly from information obtained through break-ins.) The guild's objective, Hoover warned, was to subvert the internal security. McGrath forwarded Hoover's memorandums to the president; in a December 7, 1949, letter the attorney general also reported that the guild planned to release and to publicize extensively a report on FBI practices. Hoover had fully informed McGrath about the guild's progress in drafting and seeking support for this report. At the same time, FBI Assistant Director Louis Nichols worked with Lyle Wilson, the head of UPI's Washington bureau, to elicit a firm denial from Truman's press secretary that any investigation of the Bureau was contemplated.

This FBI/Justice lobbying effort succeeded. In a December 17, 1949, letter to McGrath, Truman commented that "there are a number of crackpots" in the National Lawyers Guild "who like very much to stir up trouble. I don't think there is any way to stop the report," Truman lamented, "and I would suggest that you handle it in the best possible manner when it comes out."[17]

Although the president had become convinced that the National Lawyers Guild's protest should be ignored, many liberals (and not only Rauh) nonetheless remained deeply concerned about FBI policies and procedures. The Coplon trial revelations heightened these concerns, which were not dissipated by McGrath's and Hoover's claims that FBI wiretapping derived from Roosevelt's 1940 directive. In its January 17, 1950, and February 22, 1950, editorials, for example, the *Washington Post* condemned FBI wiretapping as illegal, insisted that Congress thoroughly investigate "the extent to which the law has been violated and the courts of the United States hoodwinked by a Federal agency," and denied that any president could or even had authorized illegal wiretapping.[18]

Fourth, to undercut this protest and regain the initiative, Assistant Attorney General Peyton Ford urged Truman to release the text of Roosevelt's May 21, 1940, wiretapping directive. Doing so would rebut criticisms that the FBI had wiretapped without proper authority and would also "protect" the president; Truman's 1946 directive, for that reason, need not be made public. Before acting on this recommendation, White House aide George Elsey was assigned to advise the president on this matter.

Elsey contrasted Roosevelt's May 21, 1940, directive with Clark's July 17, 1946, letter. In a February 2, 1950, memorandum which he discussed personally with the president that day, Elsey explained how Clark had secured Truman's approval of "this new and broader language" by editing Roosevelt's 1940 directive. "The release of the Roosevelt memorandum," Elsey continued, would not "protect" Truman but "would result in additional criticism of the F.B.I. on the grounds that it is exceeding the authority granted to it by President Roosevelt. This would lead inevitably, I believe, to public reference to President Truman's broader directive." Elsey then urged the president to "consider rescinding his 1946 directive."

At this February 2 meeting Truman directed Elsey and Special Counsel to the President Charles Murphy to prepare a directive "which would cancel the current authorization for wiretapping by the F.B.I. and would return to the authorization granted by President Roosevelt in May 1940." The White House staff prepared such a draft "memorandum for the Attorney General." Dated February 7, 1950, it read:

> You are authorized, in such cases as you may expressly approve in writing after you have investigated and determined in each case that it is necessary to the interests of the national security, to author- ize investigative personnel of your Department to intercept, listen in, or record telephone communication in the investigation of the fol- lowing categories of cases only: cases involving the investigation of persons suspected of treason, espionage, sabotage, or subversive activ- ities directed against the United States.
>
> I desire that the foregoing authority be exercised only in those cases where the national security requires it, and that you establish appropriate measures of control to assure this result.[19]

Neither the February 7, 1950, draft nor a differently worded order re- scinding the 1946 directive were issued by the president—even though Tru- man had expressed such an intent upon learning how Clark had earlier obtained his approval. The 1946 letter was never canceled and constituted the basis for the FBI's "subversive activities" wiretapping authority until 1968.

Why didn't Truman rescind the 1946 letter? Even had he issued a secret executive order, Truman could not be sure that this restriction on FBI inves- tigative authority would not become publicly known. Had such a rescission order been leaked congressional conservatives undoubtedly would have de- nounced this hamstringing of the FBI as confirming the president's "softness toward communism." The conclusion that political expediency was the cru- cial factor in Truman's decision of 1950 is admittedly speculative. The president's failure to rescind the 1946 letter pointedly raises serious questions about the effectiveness of executive supervision over the FBI.[20]

The Coplon case had had further ramifications for federal surveillance policy. During the successful appeal of Ms. Coplon's Washington trial con- viction, defense attorneys cited the New York trial revelations of govern- mental illegality. The court ordered a new trial on the grounds that the trial judge had improperly withheld wiretap records from scrutiny by defense counsel, and these records were essential to determine whether or not these interceptions had aided prosecution of the case. The government's appeal of this ruling to the Supreme Court failed and Ms. Coplon eventually obtained her freedom.[21]

The Justice Department had suffered a substantial defeat in the Coplon case. The White House, if not the public, had been apprised of Attorney General Clark's 1946 method for obtaining President Truman's assent to expand FBI wiretapping authority. Having almost simultaneously learned about other Justice Department insubordination to secure congressional approval for an alien detention bill, the Truman White House in May 1950 attempted (abortively) to curb the department's internal security initiatives.[22]

In the aftermath of the Coplon case Justice Department officials responded in two diverse ways. First, exploiting the adverse reaction to the Court's rulings, they actively lobbied for legislation authorizing internal security wiretapping.[23] Second, Attorney General J. Howard McGrath outlined revised electronic surveillance procedures in a February 26, 1952, memorandum to Hoover:

> . . . The use of wire tapping is indispensable in intelligence coverage of matters relating to espionage, sabotage, and related security fields. Consequently, I do not intend to alter the existing policy that wire tapping surveillance should be used under the present highly restrictive basis and when specifically authorized by me.
>
> The use of microphone surveillance which does not involve a trespass would seem to be permissible under the present state of the law, . . . Such surveillances as involve trespass are in the area of the Fourth Amendment, and evidence so obtained and from leads so obtained is inadmissable.
>
> . . . please be advised that *I cannot authorize* the installation of a microphone *involving a trespass* under existing law.
>
> It is requested when any case is referred to the Department in which telephone, microphone, or other technical surveillances have been employed by the Bureau *or other Federal Agencies (when known)* that the Department be advised of the facts at the time this matter is first submitted.[24] (Italics in original)

McGrath's order did not substantively alter wiretapping policy; FBI officials were required only to inform Justice Department officials whenever wiretaps had been employed in cases forwarded to the department for possible prosecution. (Whether FBI officials complied with this order in view of Bureau Bulletin No. 34 cannot presently be ascertained.) McGrath's requirement would enable the department to weigh the risks of exposing illegal activity. The department could decide before seeking an indictment not to prosecute—thereby minimizing any embarrassment during trial proceedings—or prosecute only major cases. Microphone surveillance had not been explicitly banned, moreover—McGrath's order permitted the FBI director to authorize bugging on his own, contrary to the attorney general's ruling that this was illegal. In effect, the February 26 memorandum would compromise Hoover should FBI bugging ever be publicly disclosed.

In *Goldman v. U.S.*,[25] the Supreme Court in 1942 upheld the constitutionality of evidence obtained from microphone surveillances installed without physical trespass. That same year (although there might have been no connection with this ruling) FBI Director Hoover authorized an illegal break-in program but devised a sophisticated "Do Not File" procedure to ensure against disclosure. In 1944, moreover, Hoover posed a series of "hypothetical" questions to the Department of Justice. One of these involved the legality of microphone surveillance. Responding in a July 4, 1944, memorandum to Hoover, Assistant Attorney General Alexander Holtzoff misinterpreted the Court's *Goldman* decision: "Microphone surveillance is not equivalent to illegal search and seizure"; "evidence so obtained should be admissable" even where "an actual trespass is committed."[26]

By not informing the department that the FBI was already installing bugs, and instead presumably only seeking policy guidance, Hoover successfully obtained a department ruling without having formally requested authority to install such devices. This had important policy consequences. Insofar as President Roosevelt's May 1940 order had responded to Congress's prohibition only of wiretap interceptions, FBI officials concluded that Roosevelt's authorization requirement did not apply to microphone interceptions. Accordingly, Hoover never advised the attorney general of FBI microphone surveillances; these surveillances were not subject to the same controls or supervision as were wiretaps.[27]

This independent installation procedure was first challenged when Hoover informed McGrath on October 6, 1951, of FBI microphone policy. Whether the attorney general was preparing to submit electronic surveillance legislation to Congress or was reviewing electronic surveillance policy and practices, he then asked the FBI director the right questions. Hoover responded:

> As you are aware, this Bureau has also employed the use of microphone installations on a highly restrictive basis, chiefly to obtain intelligence information. The information obtained from microphones, as in the case of wiretaps, is not admissible in evidence. In certain instances, it has been possible to install microphones without trespass, as reflected by opinions rendered in the past by the Department on this subject matter. In these instances, the information obtained, of course, is treated as evidence and therefore is not regarded as purely intelligence information.
>
> As you know, in a number of instances it has not been possible to install microphones without trespass. In such instances the information received therefrom is of an intelligence nature only. Here again, as in the use of wiretaps, experience has shown us that intelligence information highly pertinent to the defense and welfare of this nation is derived through the use of microphones.

The FBI director demanded "a definite opinion from you [the attorney general]" whether the FBI should continue breaking-in to install microphones.[28]

McGrath apparently "did not know" or refused to acknowledge that he knew that the FBI illegally installed microphones. The attorney general, nonetheless, did not explicitly prohibit this practice. His February 1952 order instead merely affirmed that he could not "authorize the installation of a microphone involving a trespass under existing law." McGrath's February 1952 memorandum, however, meant that future FBI break-ins would be conducted in contravention of the attorney general's written conclusion that these practices were illegal. Formerly, the bureau could either rely on Holtzoff's 1944 memorandum and/or technically share responsibility by briefing department officials of such installations on a case by case basis.

Unwilling to assume total responsibility, Hoover formally informed bureau officials on March 4, 1952, that he would no longer approve microphone surveillances requests which would involve trespass. (This did not mean, however, that this practice stopped. Conceivably Hoover authorized a separate filing procedure for these requests—like the "Do Not File" procedure for break-ins—or orally approved future requests knowing that the FBI would be protected from discovery by the existence of this written prohibition.)

The FBI director, moreover, continued to pressure the Justice Department to approve such microphone installations to no avail; the department rejected another FBI request on April 10, 1952. The bureau may or may not have terminated the resort to break-ins—this cannot be ascertained since complete records of illegal entries were not kept. The FBI continued to install or monitor microphone surveillances, although the actual number in use declined from 75 in 1951 to 63 in 1952 and to 52 in 1953.[29]

Not resigned to McGrath's restriction, Hoover and other high-level Bureau officials almost immediately capitalized on the ignorance and anticommunism of the newly elected Eisenhower administration. Early in 1953, they recommended to officials in the Justice Department's Internal Security Section "a less restrictive interpretation of the law pertaining to microphone surveillance." Through a tortured interpretation of the Fourth Amendment, the department concurred: a break-in to install a microphone was not a search and seizure. Having won on this issue, the bureau in July sought the attorney general's advance approval for every such microphone surveillance on the premise that were a break-in ever discovered "it would precipitate adverse publicity in the press and result in embarrassment publicly, both to the Bureau and the Department." Then, on December 22, 1953, Assistant Attorney General Warren Olney III (the head of the Internal Security Section) formally approved "broaden[ed]" use of microphone surveillance. The department had not yet specifically authorized microphone surveillances "where the security of the country was at stake."[30]

The Eisenhower administration's receptivity to reinterpreting the ban of the Fourth Amendment, to "broadening" use of this technique, and its willingness to concede that break-ins to install microphones during emergencies might not "legally constitute trespass" offered hope to FBI officials. The opportunity to obtain explicit approval soon arrived: in a criminal case,

Irvine v. California, the U.S. Supreme Court ruled that evidence obtained from an illegally installed warrantless microphone was inadmissible and specifically condemned the gross abuse of privacy resulting when a bug had been installed in a bedroom.[31]

The Court's ruling had not addressed whether or not "national security" warrantless bugging that involved trespass was constitutional. Accordingly, Hoover wrote Brownell ostensibly seeking the attorney general's policy guidance and enclosing a proposed memorandum (drafted by FBI official Alan Belmont) authorizing the FBI to install microphones. We do not know what Hoover wrote or how he specifically phrased his memorandum to the attorney general. The Justice Department did review and revise Brownell's draft and on May 20, 1954, Brownell forwarded this revised memorandum to FBI Director Hoover. In effect this memorandum rescinded McGrath's 1952 ban and authorized extensive microphone surveillance of dissident political activists and foreign agents. The attorney general then ordered:

> . . . in some instances the use of microphone surveillance is the only possible way of uncovering the activities of espionage agents, possible saboteurs, and subversive persons. In such instances . . . the national interest requires that microphone surveillance be utilized by the Federal Bureau of Investigation. This use need not be limited to the development of evidence for prosecution. The FBI has an intelligence function in connection with internal security matters . . . The Department of Justice approves the use of microphone surveillance under these circumstances and for these purposes.
>
> I do not consider that the decision of the Supreme Court in *Irvine v. California*, supra, requires a different course. That case is readily distinguishable on its facts. . . . The Court's action is a clear indication of the need for discretion and intelligent restraint in the use of microphones by the FBI in all cases, including internal security matters. . . . It may appear, however, that important intelligence or evidence relating to matters connected with the national security can only be obtained by the installation of a microphone in a [bedroom]. It is my opinion that under such circumstances the installation is proper and not prohibited by the Supreme Court's decision in the *Irvine* case.
>
> . . . It is realized that not infrequently the question of trespass arises in connection with the installation of a microphone. The question of whether a trespass is actually involved and the second question of the effect of such a trespass upon the admissibility in court of the evidence thus obtained, . . . [pose problems which the Department will review] in each case in light of the practical necessities of investigation and of the national interest which must be protected. It is my opinion that the Department should adopt that interpretation which will permit microphone coverage by the FBI in a manner most conducive to our national interest. I recognize that for the FBI to

fulfill its important intelligence function, considerations of internal security and the national safety are paramount and, therefore, may compel the unrestricted use of this technique in the national interest.[32]

Brownell's lengthy memorandum leaves unanswered a number of questions. First, what information had Hoover provided since his briefing memorandum precipitated the attorney general's response? Second, given his memorandum's vague language what was the scope of Brownell's authorization? Did he wish to confine uses narrowly? Was the attorney general's prior approval required for each installation? Unqualified references recur throughout this memorandum to "subversive persons," the "national interest," "internal security," or the "national safety." What investigations were permitted under this language? In addition, had the attorney general (1) insisted on his advance approval for "the circumstances in each case" prior to installation of a microphone surveillance, (2) recognized the need for "the unrestricted use of this technique in the national interest," or (3) tacitly approved a "Do Not File" procedure permitting the FBI to install bugs without any reporting requirement to ensure that this illegal activity would not be vulnerable should the department prosecute and defense attorneys file disclosure motions? Apparently, Brownell's reference to "unrestricted use" related only to installing bugs in particular rooms (that being the issue raised in the *Irvine* case) and had not intended to allow the FBI director to authorize bugs without the attorney general's prior approval. The attorney general would later claim that he had never authorized the use of bugs "outside of the internal security area" and was "completely unaware" of instances wherein bugs had been installed by means of a break-in. In any event, the attorney general clearly authorized FBI microphone surveillance and recognized the serious legal and prosecuting problems involved—though Brownell did not allow legal or judicial considerations to control his decision. Brownell apparently hoped that secrecy could enable the government to continue to resort to illegal activities without risk—prosecution need not be abandoned or a case lost during trial.

The same questions which Brownell's May 1954 memorandum raise about the department's oversight over the bureau recur with the attorney general's response to Hoover's March 8, 1955, memorandum outlining bureau wiretapping authority. The attorney general's prior approval was required for FBI wiretapping in "cases vitally affecting the domestic security or where human life is in jeopardy." Hoover informed Brownell that this policy was based on Roosevelt's May 21, 1940, letter [*sic*] and Clark's July 17, 1946, memorandum [*sic*]. If the attorney general concluded that these statements provided insufficient authority, he "may want to present this matter to President Eisenhower to determine whether he holds the same view with respect to the policies of the Department of Justice with respect to wiretapping."[33]

Apparently, Hoover had not forwarded and the attorney general would not independently review the actual texts of the 1940 and 1946 directives.

In response, Brownell advised Hoover in a March 16, 1955, memorandum: "In view of the fact that I personally explained to the President, the Cabinet, the National Security Council and the Senate and House Judiciary Committees during 1954 the present policy and procedures on wiretaps, at which time I referred specifically to the authorization letter to the Attorney General from President F. D. Roosevelt, I do not think it necessary to reopen the matter at this time."[34] Hoover's reference to Clark's 1946 "memorandum" apparently left no impression on the attorney general; the FBI director apparently did not subsequently advise the attorney general that current wiretapping policy was based on this later directive. Significantly, during 1954 congressional testimony and other public speeches that year, the attorney general based FBI wiretapping authority only on Roosevelt's 1940 directive.

Brownell's 1954 and 1955 actions confirm the laxity of departmental oversight of the bureau. Not surprisingly, then, microphone surveillances had been employed by the bureau even before Brownell's formal authorization memorandum.[35] Brownell's order merely formally authorized an ongoing FBI practice. In addition, regardless of whether the attorney general had also intended to allow Hoover to authorize such surveillances on his own in every case, the FBI director so interpreted Brownell's May 20, 1954, memorandum.

John F. Kennedy's election to the presidency and the appointment of his brother, Robert Kennedy, as attorney general potentially threatened continuance of Hoover's independent authorization, though not the extensive use of electronic surveillance, since the new attorney general was a proponent of wiretapping. Hoover obtained Kennedy's approval of current FBI wiretapping practices, once again, by exploiting the newly appointed attorney general's ignorance of prior procedures, willingness to defer to the FBI's claimed authority, and belief that an effective internal security and criminal investigative program required extensive use of this technique.

The new attorney general formally abandoned the fiction that the department complied with the congressional ban on wiretapping (Section 605 of the Federal Communications Act of 1934) and with the Court's 1937 and 1939 rulings. Issuing Order No. 263–62 on March 13, 1962, Kennedy rescinded Attorney General Jackson's March 15, 1940, wiretapping ban.[36] In 1961, and again in 1962, moreover, Robert Kennedy proposed legislation to authorize electronic surveillance during "national security" and "criminal" investigations.[37]

Ostensibly to assist in the preparation of the attorney general's testimony before the Senate Subcommittee on Constitutional Rights, then holding hearings on the administration's proposed electronic surveillance bill, in a May 4, 1961, memorandum FBI Director Hoover wrote:

> Our policy on the use of microphone surveillance is based upon a memorandum from former Attorney General Herbert Brownell dated May 20, 1954, in which he approved the use of microphone surveil-

lance with or without trespass. In this memorandum, Mr. Brownell said in part:

"I recognize that for the FBI to fulfill its important intelligence function, considerations of internal security and the national safety are paramount and, therefore, may compel the unrestricted use of this technique in the national interest."

In the light of this policy, in the internal security field we are utilizing microphone surveillances on a restricted basis even though trespass is necessary to assist in uncovering the activities of Soviet intelligence agents and Communist Party leaders. In the interests of national safety, microphone surveillances are also utilized on a restricted basis even though trespass is necessary, in uncovering major criminal activities. . . .

There is no Federal legislation at the present time pertaining to the use of microphone surveillances. The passage of any restrictive legislation in this field would be a definite loss to our investigative operations, both in the internal security field and in our fight against the criminal elements.[38]

The FBI director was being disingenuous. First, Hoover forwarded this memorandum when the department officials were principally concerned about legislative strategy and thus while the FBI director technically informed the attorney general at the same time he successfully averted Kennedy's careful scrutiny and review of FBI policies and procedures. Second, the FBI director inaccurately described the bureau uses of the technique and Brownell's 1954 order. Wrenching the "national safety" reference out of context and by selective quotation, Hoover conveyed the impression that Brownell had authorized an extensive program to include criminal investigations. In fact, Brownell's order specifically focused on "national security" cases. Furthermore, the examples Hoover cited of such "national security" uses—"activities of Soviet intelligence agents and Communist Party leaders" —did not accurately portray the FBI's broader uses. The FBI had also bugged Communist sympathizers, a U.S. congressman under investigation because of his relations with the sugar lobby, and a "black separatist group." Failing to ascertain independently the scope and nature of his predecessor's authorization, the attorney general instead allowed Hoover to continue to approve bugs without his supervision. This procedure conformed with the attorney general's legislative strategy: he had concluded that legislative controls over bugging should be avoided. A July 6, 1966, FBI memorandum, moreover, tacitly confirms that Kennedy had not been advised that the bureau installed bugs in criminal investigations by means of break-ins.[39]

Kennedy's laxity emboldened Hoover to rely increasingly on bugs (which did not require the attorney general's prior authorization) as opposed to wiretaps (which did) for sensitive intelligence investigations. Thus, whereas the bureau had installed a total of 52 microphones during 1953 it increased the number of such installations to 99 in 1954, 102 in 1955, and an average of 72.6 for the remaining five years of the Eisenhower administration. During Robert Kennedy's roughly four-year attorney generalship, in contrast, the average annual number of installations reached 92.75. Those subject to FBI bugging without Kennedy's knowledge or approval included the Reverend Martin Luther King, Jr., a U.S. congressman, the Student Nonviolent Coordinating Committee, two "black separatist groups," one "black separatist functionary," and one "(white) racist organization."[40]

Administratively, the disparate authorization procedures for wiretaps and bugs were indefensible, the more so because installing bugs often required illegal trespass. Inevitably, then, the appointment of an attorney general more concerned about his own authority and responsibilities—if not about the law or civil liberties—would ensure tighter procedures and more effective oversight. Such a development occurred with Nicholas Katzenbach's appointment as attorney general; Ramsey Clark, Katzenbach's successor, instituted more far-reaching changes.

Two developments precipitated tighter administrative controls over wiretapping. The first derived from the political impact of hearings conducted by the Senate Subcommittee on Administrative Practice and Procedure, chaired by Senator Edward Long, into federal agencies' investigative techniques. The second derived from Acting Attorney General Katzenbach's discovery of illegal FBI electronic surveillance during the prosecution of an espionage case, *U.S. v. Baltch*, and a criminal case involving Fred B. Black, *Black v. U.S.*

Following inquiries of the FBI, on September 28, 1964, the U.S. attorney prosecuting the Baltch case denied in open court that the government had engaged in any illegal investigative activities. U.S. Attorney Hoey the next day reaffirmed that no leads had been secured from eavesdropping or other illegal activities. In fact, however, the FBI had both bugged the Baltchs' apartment and illegally opened their mail. (Informed about the bug on October 2, Katzenbach immediately directed Hoey to advise the court that his September 28 statement had been incorrect. Because of the case's complications the Justice Department would eventually decide to drop prosecution.) In the course of preparing a memorandum during the Black case, moreover, Justice Department officials became apprised of the absence of any formal authorization by attorneys general since Herbert Brownell for FBI microphone surveillance.[41]

From its inception, the Long committee inquiry gravely concerned FBI and Justice Department officials. Initially, this congressional investigation might have focused on IRS investigative and surveillance activities. In time, the subcommittee broadened its inquiry to include all federal investigative agencies, their record-keeping procedures, and their files on American citizens which might invade privacy rights. If fully answered, the Long Committee's questionnaire to federal agencies could have disclosed both the scope of the FBI's illegal activities (mail intercepts, wiretaps, bugs, and break-ins) and the FBI's separate file-keeping procedures (notably, the "Do Not File" procedure involving break-ins).

Accordingly, in February 1965 FBI officials secured White House cooperation to contain the subcommittee's inquiry. The strategy of emphasizing the need to avert public exposure of sensitive "national security" matters succeeded. At the time, "national security" appeals still commanded widespread support within the Congress. Combined White House and FBI efforts convinced Senator Long to exempt FBI activities from the subcommittee's public inquiry. Nonetheless, the possible impact of any embarrassing revelations on his continued tenure as FBI director led Hoover in 1965 and 1966 to prohibit certain FBI investigative techniques. Hoover's orders (1) limited wiretaps to internal security cases and occasional investigations involving possible loss of life, (2) discontinued altogether microphone surveillances, (3) terminated the bugging of the hotel rooms of Reverend Martin Luther King, Jr., and (4) terminated break-ins, trash covers, and mail covers.[42]

Katzenbach's restrictions were less substantive than those of Hoover. On March 30, 1965, the attorney general limited individual wiretap authorizations to six months after which his reauthorization was required and ordered that authorization requests be submitted in writing. The attorney general must also approve all microphone surveillances in advance which were limited to six month periods. In September 1966, Assistant Attorney General Fred Vinson ordered Hoover to "set up and maintain appropriate indices with respect to electronic surveillance and the materials derived therefrom."

In November 1966 Acting Attorney General Ramsey Clark further instructed all U.S. attorneys not to proceed with any investigation or case wherein evidence had been illegally obtained through electronic surveillance. U.S. attorneys were required to ascertain carefully whether any cases "now pending or hereafter received" posed potential electronic surveillance problems and then "immediately inform" Assistant Attorney General J. Walter Yeagley. The department could then initiate a further inquiry. Clark had sought to enable the Department of Justice to disclose in court all illegal wiretapping—repudiating the earlier departmental policy of not disclosing unless the tappers were caught or physical evidence of wiretapping had been discovered.

Then, on June 16, 1967, Clark, the newly appointed attorney general, required all federal agencies to institute "tight administrative control" to ensure that all electronic surveillance "will not be used in a manner in which it is illegal and that even legal use will be strictly controlled." The advance written approval of the attorney general was required for all microphone surveillance. Clark, however, permitted exceptions to these guidelines for investigations "directly related to the protection of the national security." There, he specified, "special problems with respect to the use of [bugs and wiretaps] in national security investigations shall continue to be taken up directly with the Attorney General in the light of existing stringent restrictions."[43]

Katzenbach's and Clark's orders established the first effective reviewing process for such uses. Their record-keeping requirements contributed to Hoover's 1966 decision to terminate or limit the use of wiretaps and bugs.

Creation of a fuller record would increase the risks of exposure of illegal FBI activities and conceivably might fully establish the scope of the FBI's uses. Between 1965 and 1966, then, FBI wiretaps declined from 233 to 174; the number of bugs from 67 to 10. Clark's more stringent procedures further reduced FBI wiretaps from 113 in 1967 to eighty-two in 1968 and the number of bugs declined to zero in 1967 and nine in 1968.[44]

Katzenbach's March 1965 order had not restricted FBI "national security" electronic surveillances. Nonetheless, on September 14, 1965, Hoover advised the attorney general that in the "present atmosphere" FBI uses of bugs would be "discontinue[d] completely," wiretaps would be "cut down," and "I am not requesting authority for any additional wiretaps."[45] Hoover had clearly created a record of termination or reduction of these techniques; further, any future initiative for their use was to come from outside the bureau. Whether Hoover actually terminated or reduced these uses cannot be ascertained. The only real changes might have been a more cautious attitude and new separate filing procedures.

Responding to Hoover's September 14 memorandum on September 27, 1965, Katzenbach authorized certain "emergency" exceptions to his March order's requirement that all uses of wiretaps and bugs obtain the attorney general's prior authorization. "At this time," Katzenbach stipulated, use of wiretaps and bugs requiring trespass should be "confined to the gathering of intelligence in national security matters." He further emphasized: "I see no need to curtail any such activities in the national security field." Conceding that there were "occasions" when it "would be appropriate" to use wiretaps or bugs "outside of the strict definition of national security (for example, organized crime)," Katzenbach nonetheless concluded that "in the light of the present atmosphere" such uses were inappropriate. The attorney general, however, adopted a more permissive policy toward installing bugs without trespass: "the Bureau should continue to use those techniques *in cases where* you believe it appropriate without further authorization from me."[46]

Clark's more substantive reforms proved, however, to be of limited duration. Cold War "national security" fears and a reaction to urban racial unrest and antiwar demonstrations combined in 1968 to impel congressional repudiation of the 1934 act's wiretapping ban. The Omnibus Crime Control and Safe Streets Act of 1968 permitted electronic surveillance during criminal investigations subject to a warrant requirement and established criminal penalties for failure to comply with these procedures or restrictions. Congressional deference toward presidential "national security" claims resulted in a major exception to the act's warrant requirement. Section 2511(3) specified:

> Nothing contained in this chapter or in section 605 of the Communications Act of 1934 (48 Stat. 1143, 47 U.S.C. 605) shall limit the constitutional powers of the President to take such measures as he deems necessary to protect the Nation against actual or potential attack or other hostile acts of a foreign power, to obtain foreign

intelligence information deemed essential to the security of the United States or to protect national security information against foreign intelligence activities. Nor shall anything contained in this chapter be deemed to limit the constitutional power of the President to take such measures as he deems necessary to protect the United States against the overthrow of the Government by force or other unlawful means, or against any other clear and present danger to the structure or existence of the Government.[47]

This vague, often meaningless language invited an expansive usage of electronic surveillance by the newly elected Nixon administration. Richard Nixon and his Attorney General John Mitchell were alarmed about internal security threats and believed that presidents had broad, unreviewable national security powers. Accordingly, they unhesitatingly instituted electronic surveillance of dissident political activities under Section 2511(3)'s clause exempting "national security" taps from the warrant requirement.[48]

The most controversial of these wiretap uses involved seventeen individuals—White House and National Security Council aides and four prominent Washington reporters—whom Nixon administration officials suspected had been responsible for leaking information about the president's 1969 decision to bomb Cambodia. The focus of these wiretaps and their duration —extending beyond the NSC tenure of at least two staff members—posed potentially serious political problems for the Nixon administration. To minimize the prospect of disclosure, these "national security" wiretap records were filed separately from the FBI's other national security wiretap records. Because of the "extreme sensitivity of the request from the White House," FBI Assistant Director William Sullivan was given custody of these wiretap records. In addition, other departmental wiretap authorization rules were not followed—namely, the requirement that the attorney general authorize and after ninety days reauthorize all wiretaps. Reports based on these taps were forwarded after 1970 to the president's principal domestic policy adviser, H. R. Haldeman (instead of as formerly to Henry Kissinger, the president's national security adviser).[49]

Even separate book-keeping procedures—which could preclude public disclosure in the event of possible court-ordered disclosure rulings—apparently did not completely assure Nixon administration officials. Thus, in July 1971, in the midst of his widening rift with FBI Director Hoover, FBI Assistant Director William Sullivan conferred at length with Assistant Attorney General Robert Mardian about the "possible abuses of the material." Having physical control over these tap records, Sullivan impressed upon Mardian their sensitivity and the possibility that Hoover "might use these tapes for the purpose of preserving his position as Director of the FBI." Flying immediately to California on July 12 to brief the president, Mardian soon returned to Washington and ordered Sullivan, apparently at Nixon's direction, to transfer these files to the safety of the White House. This decision was kept from Hoover who would only learn that the FBI no longer controlled these records after Sullivan resigned in September 1971. Attorney General Mitchell would then misinform Hoover that these wiretap records had been destroyed.[50]

Events in 1972, however, resulted in the Nixon administration's loss of the initiative. First, on June 19, 1972, the Supreme Court in *U.S. v. U.S. District Court* acknowledged the president's constitutional power to "protect our Government against those who would subvert or overthrow it by unlawful means." Presidents could not, however, authorize warrantless electronic surveillance of a domestic organization neither directly nor indirectly connected with a foreign power. "This case involves only the domestic aspects of national security," the Court emphasized. "We have expressed no opinion as to issues which may be involved with respect to activities of foreign powers or their agents." Rejecting the Nixon administration's expansive national security claims, the Supreme Court's ruling had, however, limited impact—particularly because it apparently conceded that the government could wiretap without warrant individuals having a "significant connection with a foreign power, its agents or agencies" and that "domestic security surveillance may involve different policy and practical considerations" than ordinary crime.[51]

Second, and ironically, the Court's ruling was announced three days after the arrest of the Watergate burglars. The so-called Watergate Affair would soon precipitate a major political crisis. Its significance derived in great part from the Nixon White House's response to this arrest by devising an elaborate strategy (1) to contain the FBI's investigation of this break-in and (2) to avert publicity about the 1969–71 White House activities of some of the individuals indicted for the break-in. When White House Counsel John W. Dean III decided to plea bargain in May–June 1973 and then to fully testify before the Senate Watergate Committee in June 1973, the political situation altered dramatically. Among his revelations of seamy Nixon White House activities, Dean disclosed the attempted implementation of the Huston Plan, the 1969 NSC wiretaps and the transference of these records to the White House in 1971, and the so-called Plumbers group activities.

To undercut the political impact of these disclosures and to regain the initiative, the Nixon White House adopted a two-prong strategy. On one level, the president in a series of public statements defended his administration's record, promised full disclosure, and emphasized the need for secrecy based on "executive privilege" and "national security" considerations. On a second level, the White House adopted what could be described as a "so's your old man" strategy: claiming that earlier presidents had employed wiretaps more extensively and in a more political manner.[52]

This strategy not only failed but proved counterproductive. A far different political climate had evolved—in part because Nixon's strategy increased popular fears about presidential powers and purposes and sensitized the public to the possibility of abuses of power by federal intelligence agencies. Measures—such as Senator Gaylord Nelson's bill introduced in 1971 to establish a joint congressional oversight committee to review the activities of federal intelligence agencies—which had earlier been ignored commanded greater attention and support. The Nixon administration's electronic surveillance practices also called into question Section 2511(3)'s "national security" electronic surveillance exception.

To close this loophole, in 1973 Senator Nelson introduced another bill requiring prior court authorization for "national security" electronic surveillance. This bill, S. 2820, was referred to the Subcommittee on Criminal Laws and Procedures of the Senate Judiciary Committee, chaired by Senator John McClellan. Unlike Nelson, McClellan did not support legislative restrictions on FBI electronic surveillance authority. Consequently, hearings were not even scheduled on Nelson's bill.

Stymied by this roadblock, Nelson (joined by Senator Sam Ervin) adopted a different strategy. On August 22, 1974, the two Democratic senators introduced an amendment to H.R. 15404, the State, Justice, Commerce and Judiciary Appropriations Act of 1974, stipulating that no monies could be expended for warrantless electronic surveillance. The Nelson-Ervin amendment's objective had been to compel consideration of S. 2820. This strategy succeeded. During floor debate on August 22, in return for Nelson's agreement to withdraw the amendment, Senator McClellan promised to schedule hearings that session on S. 2820.[53]

Hearings were held on October 1–3, 1974. Testifying on October 2, FBI Director Clarence Kelley and Attorney General William Saxbe opposed the proposed prior court authorization requirement for "national security" electronic surveillance. Kelley's testimony succinctly captures the internal security bureaucracy's continued reliance on a now somewhat refined "national security" rationale:

> Let me first take notice of the fact that the FBI has a vital mission to support the President in discharging certain constitutional mandates: his responsibility to formulate and to implement foreign policy, to maintain our Nation's defenses, to preserve the basic structure and existence of our Government from hostile acts by foreign powers or their agents.
>
> How do we do this? Essentially in two ways. First, the FBI provides the President with intelligence information essential to foreign policy planning and essential to those officials responsible for the national defense.
>
> If we can provide advance indicators of a dramatic diplomatic initiative by an adversary foreign power, our foreign policy planners are invaluably aided.
>
> If we can detect a spy, the interests of national defense are certainly well served.
>
> Second, we support presidential objectives by investigating violations of Federal statutes relating to the national security such as espionage, sabotage, and treason.[54]

In contrast to previous FBI justifications citing the threat of "subversive activities," Kelley's 1974 testimony emphasized "foreign intelligence" responsibilities and investigations of violations of federal statutes. Significantly, the non-prosecuting rationale then offered was founded on the equally nebulous "foreign intelligence" need—supplanting the by then discredited "national security" rationale. The examples Kelley cited of possible benefits, in addition, were either vague or unconvincing. For one, foreign embassy taps would hardly provide "advance indicators of a dramatic diplomatic initiative by an adversary power" unless that nation intentionally wanted to convey a signal to the U.S. government. Foreign diplomats, particularly of adversary powers, assume their phones are tapped.

Saxbe's successor as attorney general, Edward Levi, reaffirmed this position, although with greater sophistications. Sharply articulated in a June 29, 1975, letter to Senator Edward Kennedy, Levi claimed that "the Executive may conduct electronic surveillance in the interests of national security and foreign intelligence, and in the aid of his conduct of the nation's foreign affairs, without obtaining a judicial warrant."[55]

A rather moderate reform, Senator Nelson's bill would not have prohibited "foreign intelligence" electronic surveillance. S. 2820 simply required prior court authorization and thereby sought to minimize the political abuse of "national security" taps or bugs. In the wake first of the Watergate disclosures and then of the Senate Select Committee on Intelligence Activities' revelations about the federal intelligence agencies' extensive abuses of powers, the internal security bureaucracy's posture of defiance became politically untenable.

Attorney General Edward Levi at first responded to the changed political setting by tightening administrative guidelines for electronic surveillance.[56] Because this limited reform was clearly inadequate, in 1976 the attorney general abandoned his initial stance of studied disinterest or opposition to S. 2820. Following February–March 1976 negotiations with key senators and their principal staff aides, Levi advocated a considerably modified version of Nelson's bill. Senate liberals acquiesced to secure administration support. In return for accepting the court authorization principle Levi insisted upon retention of sections reaffirming expansive presidential national security claims. The more important revisions included a reaffirmation that the president's constitutional powers remained unaffected, another that the NSA's international interception activities were not regulated by this legislation, another that authorization was not specifically limited to violations or probable cause violations of federal statutes, another that vaguely referred to "actual or potential" attack, another that limited the court's role when reviewing executive certification of "foreign intelligence" information, and a further (reflecting the fears of the 1960s and 1970s) that included in the definition of a "foreign agent" a person directed by a foreign power or group engaged in "terrorism" (a reference as vague and potentially as susceptible to abuse as earlier references to "subversion" or "communism"). This measure, S. 3197, was introduced in the Senate on March 23, 1976. The attorney general's support dislodged this bill from McClellan's subcommittee, and resulted in the full Judiciary Committee's approval on June 16, 1976. During June 29 and 30 and July 1, 1976, in hearings conducted by the recently established Senate Select Committee on Intelligence, the bill received, however, a more critical airing.[57]

While the Select Committee had improved upon the administration-supported bill, broad exceptions, justified on "foreign intelligence" grounds, elicited considerable controversy and many liberals continued to oppose the amended S. 3197. As a condition for their support, they insisted upon further amendments. Ultimately, however, the committee's late action and the priority of the forthcoming political campaign precluded floor debate and its passage during the closing days of the 1976 session. Legislation either closing or restricting the "national security" loophole thus remained one of the more important issues confronting the next session of Congress and the newly elected Carter administration. The continued need for such legislation was highlighted by the new administration's actions in two court cases. In one, during a brief filed on May 23, 1978, in *Halperin* v. *Nixon et al.*, the Carter Justice Department argued that former Nixon administration officials should have been granted "absolute official immunity" from prosecution "since this case involves an evaluation by the President of the United States and his chief advisers as to the impact leaks of highly classified foreign affairs plans and discussions were having on vital foreign affairs initiatives." In the second case, involving the trial of former U.S. Information Agency employee Ronald Humphrey and a Vietnamese expatriate on the charge of spying for Vietnam, the Government claimed the right of a president on national security grounds to authorize warrantless electronic surveillances and to ignore the protections against illegal search and seizure embodied in the Fourth Amendment.[58]

In the same year Congress challenged corporate records of executive "national security" electronic surveillance. Congressman John Moss, chairman of the House Oversight and Investigations Subcommittee, subpoenaed American Telephone and Telegraph Company records of government national security wiretap requests. The Ford administration resisted this subpoena. The administration's action was the first assertion of "executive privilege" in regard to the records of a private corporation and was also based on broad "national security" claims: "compliance with the subpena [*sic*] would involve unacceptable risks of disclosure of extremely sensitive foreign intelligence and counterintelligence information and would be detrimental to the national defense and foreign policy of the US and damaging to the nation's security." After losing its appeal before Federal Judge Oliver Gasch, the subcommittee appealed to the U.S. Circuit Court. This court remanded the case back to Judge Gasch with the instruction that he seek to effect a settlement. The new Carter administration, if more flexible than Ford's in regard to "domestic intelligence" tap requests, proved as unyielding in the "foreign intelligence" area.[59]

The FBI had not been the only federal agency employing electronic surveillance. Military intelligence services had begun an electronic surveillance program as early as World War II to assist in defense planning, and had secretly formed a Signals Intelligence Service to intercept international radio communications. In addition, naval intelligence had arranged with RCA to secure copies of Japanese cable traffic to and from Hawaii.[60]

This program continued throughout World War II. As part of a wartime censorship program all international telegraph messages were screened by military censors at the offices of the three international telegraph companies (RCA Global, ITT World Communications, and Western Union International). Messages of "foreign intelligence" targets were then turned over to military intelligence. Because this practice was scheduled to end with the termination of the war, in August 1945 military intelligence officials approached these companies' officials to secure postwar access to foreign governmental messages disseminated through their facilities. Advised by their attorneys that this was illegal (violating Section 605 of the Federal Communications Act of 1934), these executives received Attorney General Clark's personal assurance that they would be protected from legal suit and that legislation legalizing this interception would be sought. When no legislative effort was attempted, company officials met with Secretary of Defense James Forrestal in 1947. Forrestal then assured those officials that the Truman administration would neither prosecute nor expose these activities. The secretary also claimed that this arrangement had been cleared with Attorney General Tom Clark and President Truman. When legislation had yet not been enacted, in 1949 these officials sought and obtained renewed assurances from Louis Johnson, Forrestal's successor as secretary of defense. Johnson again advised these officials that Truman and Clark had been consulted and had approved these arrangements. This program, code-named Operation SHAMROCK, was not terminated until congressional and press disclosure on March 15, 1975. There is no record, however, that after 1949 company officials sought similar assurances from government officials.[61]

Then, beginning in 1967 and extending into 1968, as part of a more general surveillance program directed at the antiwar and civil rights movements, the Army Security Agency* began to monitor radio transmissions within the United States. (The ASA's interceptions also contravened Section 605 of the Federal Communications Act of 1934 which prohibited the interception of "any radio communication.") Apparently less concerned over illegality than desirous of external authorization, on April 29, 1968, representatives from the Office of the Army Assistant Chief of Staff for Intelli-

---

*This agency had the assigned responsibility to intercept international communications for "foreign intelligence" purposes. Such interceptions could provide information essential to military defense planning. The ASA's mission, however, was broadly conceived to include information relating to foreign policy. The ASA's sophisticated technological capabilities enabled it to service domestic objectives as well.

gence sought a Federal Communications Commission opinion on such Army monitoring. Army officials, however, did not wait for a FCC response but continued these surveillance efforts. Finally responding on August 15, 1968, the FCC orally informed Army officials that such monitoring violated the 1934 act. The commission agreed, however, not to record its conclusion that such monitoring was "illegal" in writing; instead it replied that it could not provide "a positive answer" to the Army's request.

Army monitoring of domestic radio signals continued. On October 13, 1969, the Office of the Army Assistant Chief of Staff for Intelligence requested another legal opinion, this time of the Army judge advocate general. Colonel William Nichols of the Judge Advocate General Corps responded on October 20, 1969, that ASA's monitoring was probably illegal. This activity was still not terminated. The colonel's ruling, however, successfully aborted a proposal to formalize the ASA's role in the Army's civil disturbance program.

This monitoring program was not terminated until December 10, 1970, and then not because of any reaction to its illegality, which Army officials recognized all along, but rather to a concern over adverse publicity. On December 1, 1970, NBC News had publicly reported that ASA units had monitored civilian radio broadcasts during the 1968 Democratic National Convention.[62]

The ASA was not the only military agency conducting electronic surveillance. When President Tuman established the NSA by a "top secret" October 24, 1952, directive, he had two objectives: (1) to obtain foreign intelligence information essential to the national security and (2) to safeguard U.S. governmental communications. The NSA not only assumed operational control of Operation SHAMROCK but almost immediately began to intercept targeted overseas communications (including telephone calls and telegrams), in some cases intercepting messages between the United States and foreign countries. The NSA's sophisticated technological capabilities proved most seductive to internal security bureaucrats during the 1960s when they became keenly alarmed by the magnitude of domestic antiwar and civil rights dissent. These officials (notably in the FBI and the CIA) proposed that the NSA intercept the international communications of specially targeted American citizens and organizations.

At first, this interception program was directed at foreign activities. In the fall of 1967, however, this NSA interception effort shifted in focus. Responding to pressure from the Johnson White House and from the intelligence community (notably the Army assistant chief for intelligence and the FBI) the NSA began intercepting messages of targeted civil rights and antiwar activists. Recognizing the extremely sensitive nature of this interception program because American citizens were targeted, NSA officials devised separate filing procedures to ensure security. These included hand-delivering NSA-intercepted communications to the requesting agencies (military services, FBI, CIA, Secret Service). As NSA Director Lew Allen later testified, these reports were not "published as a normal product report but in a special series to limit distribution on a strict need-to-know basis." Unlike other NSA reports, these intercepted communications were classified "Top Secret," were not specifically identified as having been intercepted by the NSA, were disseminated "For Background Use Only," were not assigned a serial number, and were not filed with regular communications intelligence intercepts.[63]

The ongoing but informal program of targeting American citizens was formalized on July 1, 1969, under the code name MINARET. MINARET's formal charter prepared within the NSA stipulated:

> 1. MINARET(C) is established for the purpose of providing more restrictive control and security of sensitive information derived from communications as processed [deleted] which contain (a) information on foreign governments, organizations or individuals who are attempting to influence, coordinate or control U.S. organizations or individuals who may foment civil disturbances or otherwise undermine the national security of the U.S. (b) information on U.S. organizations or individuals who are engaged in activities which may result in civil disturbances or otherwise subvert the national security of the U.S. An equally important aspect of MINARET will be to restrict the knowledge that such information is being collected and processed by the National Security Agency.

Recognizing the adverse consequences of such a formal program, NSA officials sought to prevent adverse publicity (the NSA's charter only authorized interceptions of foreign communications) by requiring:

> 3. MINARET information will not be serialized, but will be identified for reference purposes by an assigned date/time. . . . Further, although MINARET will be handled as SIGINT [Signal Intelligence —the task and mission of the NSA] and distributed to SIGINT recipients, it will not . . . be identified with the National Security Agency.

In addition, those officials who received "MINARET information" were directed either to destroy or return these reports to the NSA within two weeks.[64]

Like other illegal programs, MINARET was terminated during the 1970s. Again the termination decision was not based on a concern for legality or constitutionality but rather the risk of public exposure and adverse political consequences. Three events in the summer and fall of 1973 altered the political context and thereby imperiled MINARET's continuance: first, the highly publicized hearings conducted by the Special Senate Committee investigating the Watergate break-in; second, the disclosure of the Huston Plan during these hearings; and third, in a complex interconnection, defense motions and court rulings during a federal trial, *U.S. v. Ayers.*

The change in political climate brought about by the Watergate hearings was expressed in an increased concern among key congressmen, the press, and the articulate public about federal agencies' violations of civil liberties.

These concerns were particularly intensified by the publication of the Huston Plan, recording presidential approval of recognized "clearly illegal" activities and the proposed expansion of the intelligence agencies' investigative authority. The simultaneous revelations of the activities of the so-called White House Plumbers (notably the break-in to the office of Daniel Ellsberg's psychiatrist) raised doubts whether the Huston Plan had been rescinded or whether the formal authorization memorandum had only been recalled.

Capitalizing on this climate of doubt and concern, and on documented evidence of identified federal agencies' actual or planned techniques, in June 1973 defense attorneys during the *U.S. v. Ayers* case involving leaders of the radical Weathermen organization filed a motion requesting disclosure of all illegal federal surveillance directed at their clients. The defense attorneys specified that their request included any acts of electronic surveillance, mail intercepts, break-ins, sabotage, espionage, and/or provocation conducted by the NSA, FBI, CIA, DIA, and the White House Plumbers. Federal Judge Damon Keith upheld this defense motion and on June 5, 1973, ordered the government to inform the court and defense counsel of such illegal activities by June 18. Keith's order followed the defense motion in specifying the activities and the agencies; included among these was any NSA electronic surveillance. On June 7, 1973, U.S. Attorney Will Ibershof queried whether the government had to comply fully with Keith's June 5 order. Later that month, Ibershof filed an affidavit affirming that the FBI had not engaged in illegal or other "unauthorized" activities. Confining the government's response to FBI activities, the U.S. attorney tersely added that the government did not "believe this a proper forum for a trial of government misconduct."

Judge Keith rejected this effort to ignore his June 5 order. On July 9 Keith ruled that the prosecution's June 25 response was "perfunctory." Stipulating in greater detail the information sought from the government, Keith directed that Ibershof "fully comply" with his June 5 order by September 4 "by filing sworn statements from a person or persons with full knowledge of the actions of each specified group or agency"—the NSA was among those specified. Keith also announced that evidentiary hearings on this matter would be held on September 24.

Unable to comply with the submission order's September 4 deadline (hearings would be delayed until September 12 because of Judge Keith's involvement with another case), U.S. Attorney Ralph Guy then requested a thirty-day extension. This extension, Guy explained, derived from Judge Keith's unusual requirement for affidavits from sensitive federal agencies not under Justice Department jurisdiction. On September 12, the U.S. attorney also informed the court that he wished to present an affidavit from an unspecified federal agency for the judge's *in camera* inspection. The interception cited therein, Guy maintained, involved a sensitive national security matter and did not affect this case's prosecution. If the judge should rule that this affidavit must be turned over to the defense, Guy requested return of the exhibit and "the [government's] liberty to exercise their option to dismiss the proceedings." After a brief exchange between Guy and defense attorney William

Goodman, Judge Keith granted the thirty-day extension, adding that this would be the "last continuance of this matter."

Unknown to the participants in this trial, the defense motion and Judge Keith's ruling threatened to disclose the NSA's sensitive MINARET program. Attempting to comply with Judge Keith's order, the Justice Department had first solicited the required affidavits from the various identified federal agencies. In response, NSA officials requested an August 28, 1973, meeting with Assistant Attorney General Henry Peterson (who headed the Criminal Division). Peterson was then informed for the first time that some of the defendants' international communications had been intercepted under the NSA Watch List program and that NSA officials pointedly opposed "any disclosure of this technique and program." On September 4, 1973, Peterson informed Attorney General Elliot Richardson of this program "of which we had no previous knowledge." Concurrently, in a September 7, 1973, memorandum to FBI Director Clarence Kelley, Peterson solicited a response by September 10 of "the extent of the FBI's practice of requesting information intercepted by the NSA concerning domestic organizations or persons for intelligence, prosecutorial, or any other purposes . . . [and] any comments which you may desire to make concerning the impact of the *Keith* [*U.S. v. U.S. District Court*] case [of June 19, 1972] upon such interceptions."

Kelley responded on September 10, 1973. The FBI had requested NSA intelligence "concerning organizations and individuals who are known to be involved in illegal and violent activities aimed at the destruction and overthrow of the United States Government." These interceptions were not, the FBI director claimed, "electronic surveillance information in the sense that was the heart of the *Keith* decision." Kelley elaborated:

> We do not believe that the NSA actually participated in any electronic surveillance, per se of the defendants for any other agency of the government, since under the procedures used by that agency they are unaware of the identity of any group or individual which might be included in the recovery of national security intelligence information.

On September 21, 1973, Peterson thereupon informed the attorney general of the number of names the FBI had submitted for the NSA's Watch List. The FBI (and Secret Service) should "cease and desist" requesting information from the NSA about specific individuals and organizations but the NSA should continue to forward information to the FBI and the Secret Service picked up "on its own initiative in pursuit of its foreign intelligence mission." Richardson concurred with these recommendations and on October 1, 1973, directed FBI Director Kelley (and the Secret Service director) to cease requesting information from the NSA obtained "by means of electronic surveillance." That same day, the attorney general advised NSA Director Lew Allen of the questionable legality of the Watch List activity in light of the *Keith* decision. The NSA should "immediately curtail the further dissemination" of Watch List information to the FBI and the Secret Service. "Relevant information acquired by [the NSA] in the routine pursuit of the collection of foreign intelligence information," Richardson added, could "continue" to be furnished to "appropriate" government agencies but not in "a matter that can only be considered one of domestic intelligence."

Richardson's and Peterson's deliberations coincided with NSA Director Allen's assessment of the possible consequences of the court's disclosure requirements. In a September 17, 1973, letter to FBI Director Kelley, the NSA director reaffirmed his agency's willingness to respond to future FBI information requests. Kelley should review the appropriateness of FBI Watch List entries and ascertain that the letter or spirit of the law was not violated. Principally concerned over the possible public disclosure of his agency's involvement, the NSA director wrote Kelley: "the need for proper handling of the list and related information has intensified, along with ever-increasing pressures for disclosure of sources by the Congress, the courts, and the press, and naturally I am concerned ultimately for the protection of highly vulnerable SIGINT sources."

Upon receiving Richardson's October 1 letter, Allen informed the attorney general on October 4 that he had "directed that no further information be disseminated to the FBI and Secret Service, pending advice on legal issues." These complicated exchanges, and not a clear order or decision, accordingly resulted in MINARET's official termination. In addition, despite having informed the court on October 4 of the receipt of all the requested affidavits and its desire that Judge Keith rule on the *in camera* submission question, on October 15, 1973, the government moved to dismiss the case without argument. Unwilling to risk an unfavorable ruling, the department had decided to drop prosecution. Inadvertently, then, *U.S. v. Ayres* had forced intelligence officials to terminate an ongoing illegal program.[65]

Also because fearful of disclosure, in 1966 FBI Director Hoover formally terminated an elaborately planned FBI break-in program to install bugs or obtain information such as organizational membership lists, minutes, and correspondence. While break-ins might have been conducted earlier on the basis of more informal, *ad hoc* authorization procedures, in 1942 FBI officials formally devised a sophisticated separate filing system to preclude the future discovery of this illegal practice. Operationally, FBI agents did not formally request permission to conduct break-ins in every instance until after having broken in. If the break-in was successful in obtaining valuable results, agents then formally requested Hoover's authorization stating that they were certain important information could be obtained; if unsuccessful no one would know about the effort.

Recognized as being clearly illegal, break-ins were nonetheless an invaluable technique for acquiring otherwise unobtainable information about domestic political activities, foreign intelligence, and espionage. FBI officials did not, however, inform responsible Justice Department officials (notably the attorney general) of this practice—except hypothetically in 1944 and in 1951, 1954, 1961, and 1964 when reporting having installed bugs that involved trespass. This separate filing system for break-in requests and authorization enabled high-level FBI officials to supervise (imperfectly, it turned out) the resort to this technique without having created a retrievable record which could lead to their discovery whether by law enforcement officials, the courts, the press, or congressional committees.

A July 19, 1966, memorandum from William Sullivan (then the head of the bureau's Domestic Intelligence Division) to FBI Assistant Director Cartha De Loach outlined these break-in authorization procedures. Sullivan's memo in part described:

> We do not obtain authorization for "black bag" jobs from outside the Bureau. Such a technique involves trespass and is clearly illegal; therefore, it would be impossible to obtain any legal sanction for it. . . .
>
> The present procedure followed in the use of this technique calls for the Special Agent in Charge of a field office to make his request for the use of the technique to the appropriate Assistant Director. The Special Agent in Charge must completely justify the need for the technique and at the same time assure that it can be safely used without any danger or embarrassment to the Bureau. The facts are incorporated in a memorandum which, in accordance with the Director's instructions, is sent to Mr. Tolson [Assistant to the FBI Director] or to the Director for approval. Subsequently this memorandum is filed in the Assistant Director's office under a "Do Not File" procedure.
>
> In the field the Special Agent in Charge prepares an informal memorandum showing that he obtained Bureau authority and this memorandum is filed in his safe until the next inspection by Bureau inspectors, at which time it is destroyed.

FBI officials confirmed in 1975 that Sullivan's 1966 memorandum accurately described the authorization and monitoring procedures for FBI break-ins employed since 1942. Former FBI Assistant Director Charles Brennan specifically explained the record-destruction advantages of the "Do Not File" procedure. Unlike other serialized bureau documents which could not be destroyed without this becoming obvious, break-in documents under the "Do Not File" procedure were filed separately and were not serialized. Those FBI agents in the bureau's organized crime section who conducted break-ins also filtered the information so obtained into FBI files by the device of "confidential sources." In addition, the "Do Not File" procedure enabled FBI officials both tightly to control the use of this technique and yet affirm in response to discovery motions during trial proceedings that a search of the bureau's files indicated no record of any illegal governmental activities (at least relating to break-ins).

In July 1966, however, FBI Director Hoover ordered that "no more such techniques must be used." Attorney General Katzenbach's decision to state (if indirectly) that the FBI had installed bugs involving trespass without the attorney general's formal authorization since Brownell's tenure further contributed to Hoover's July decision. Hoover's ban was less than total. First, Hoover had only banned the use of break-ins against domestic organizations and citizens, and not "foreign counterintelligence." More important, Hoover apparently had not banned break-ins but his earlier requirement that the FBI director specifically authorize each break-in. FBI field offices continued after July to request Hoover's authorization to conduct break-ins. In a January 6, 1967, memorandum to FBI Assistant Directors Clyde Tolson and Cartha De Loach, Hoover accordingly ordered:

> I note that requests are still being made by Bureau officials for the use of "black bag" techniques. I have previously indicated that I do not intend to approve any such requests in the future, and, consequently, no such recommendations should be submitted for approval of such matters. This practice, which includes also surreptitious entrances upon premises of any kind, will not meet with my approval in the future.

Had Hoover ordered termination of this practice in 1966? Had he in January 1967 qualified the July 1966 "no more such techniques must be used" reference to permit break-ins but on the sole authority of lower level FBI personnel (whether special agents in charge or FBI assistant directors)— though these officials would know that such actions contravened Hoover's written record of disapproval? In short, was Hoover concerned less that "black bag" jobs were illegal than that until 1966 he had authorized them in writing? Alternatively, had Hoover in 1966 and 1967 merely created a written record of his disapproval in the event that FBI break-ins were disclosed and had then authorized either a new filing system or a new procedure based on oral requests and oral authorization?

When the bureau's past practices became subject to intensive congressional scrutiny and FBI break-in policy became known outside the bureau during the 1970s, during a July 14, 1975, press conference at first FBI Director Clarence Kelley affirmed that FBI break-ins had been terminated in 1966. Other FBI officials reaffirmed this claim in testimony and in memorandums to the Senate Select Committee on Intelligence Activities and in press interviews.

In 1975 FBI officials might have convinced skeptical congressmen that the FBI had ceased breaking-in. The bureau soon suffered a more serious challenge as the result of a suit brought by the Socialist Workers party for damages suffered because of the FBI's infamous COINTELPRO. Trial proceedings involving this suit publicly disclosed in June–July 1976 that FBI break-ins continued after 1966 and as late as July 7, 1976. These disclosures, moreover, coincided with a Justice Department investigation of past FBI break-in practices. As one result, in 1977 the department presented information to a federal grand jury to indict FBI agents for having conducted illegal activities (including wiretaps, mail intercepts, and break-ins). FBI Director Kelley, however, in March 1977 wrote FBI agents to assure them that they would not be disciplined for pleading the Fifth Amendment if questioned about FBI break-ins.

By March 1978, only one FBI agent, John Kearney, who headed a special New York City FBI squad investigating radical activists, had been indicted. Press leaks in 1977, nonetheless, had disclosed that between 1971 and 1974 FBI agents had conducted break-ins extensively. Then, on April 10, 1978, Attorney General Bell announced the indictments of former Acting FBI Director L. Patrick Gray, former FBI Associate Director W. Mark Felt, and former FBI Assistant Director Edward Miller for authorizing break-ins. At the same time the prosecution of Kearney was dropped. Complicating this matter, during July 27, 1977, congressional testimony, FBI Director Clarence Kelley maintained that the staff of the Executive Conference had deceived him as to the termination of domestic security break-ins in 1966. (In contrast, during a pre-trial motion of May 1978, former FBI Assistant Director Edward Miller claimed that he had told Kelley of post-1966 break-ins in July 1973.)

Whether having orally authorized break-ins (contravening his written July 1966 ban) or desiring at the time to ensure the existence of a written record of his disapproval, in November 1971 FBI Director Hoover personally reviewed and then ordered the transfer of the July 19, 1966, Sullivan to De Loach memorandum (cited above and at the bottom of which Hoover had recorded his disapproval) from his Personal and Confidential Files to his Official and Confidential Files. By transferring this document Hoover ensured that an official record existed of his 1966 disapproval of "black bag" jobs. Why was Hoover so concerned in 1971?

During August 1977 grand jury testimony, former FBI Assistant Director William Sullivan claimed that in 1971 Hoover had verbally authorized the use of "any practical means" (which would include break-ins, illegal wiretaps, and mail openings) during FBI investigations of radical activists. Although self-serving, Sullivan's statements cannot be dismissed as baseless. Attorneys of former FBI agent Kearney and former FBI official Miller cited Sullivan's statement in their June 28, 1977, and May 22, 1978, briefs defending their discovery motions. In both motions, the attorneys claimed that their clients had been following orders. Miller also contended that former FBI Directors William Ruckelshaus and Clarence Kelley had learned of these break-ins in 1973. In addition, attorneys for Miller and former FBI Director L. Patrick Gray maintained that the resort to break-ins in this investigation was initiated in response to pressures from the Nixon White House "to use all means possible to stop terrorist activities." Conceivably these questions will be resolved during the forthcoming trial of these FBI officials.

Significantly, in the Justice Department's October 31, 1977 response to Kearney's June 28, 1977, brief, the U.S. attorneys did not challenge the accuracy of Sullivan's statement that Hoover had orally ordered break-ins in 1971. The government responded only that "a general order from the Director of the FBI to use 'any means necessary' in an investigation is hardly the fourth amendment equivalent of a warrant." Other FBI agents, moreover, claimed that break-ins and other illegal activities had been conducted under Hoover's (and his successor L. Patrick Gray's) oral orders.

The testimony of Attorney General Griffin Bell before the House Subcommittee on Government Information and Individual Rights on June 9, 1977, further complicates the resolution of this issue. Bell starkly admitted that he did not know whether FBI break-ins were "continuing . . . I would not have any way of knowing." The attorney general pledged, however, to develop a "fail-safe" system to preclude their recurrence. The core of this system was to be the requirement that any orders to commit illegal activities would have to be in writing—a tacit admission perhaps that post-1966 FBI break-ins had been conducted on the basis of oral orders. On April 21, 1978, moreover, Bell initiated an internal investigation of whether FBI officials had deliberately deceived congressional investigators during 1975 testimony on post-1966 FBI break-ins.[66]

The FBI relied on similar separate filing procedures to preclude discovery of other questionable activities. On April 11, 1940, FBI Director Hoover outlined new procedures to be employed when preparing memorandums for submission to Washington which were not to be retained and filed in the bureau's general files. Refined by other memorandums (of November 15, 1941, March 1, 1942, January 16, 1943, March 9, 1943, and November 9, 1944), this procedure required the submission of such memorandums on pink paper (later blue). In contrast, all white paper documents were given serial numbers for filing purposes. This pink paper procedure would minimize unnecessary paperwork. More importantly, it ensured that sensitive information could be submitted to bureau headquarters with the assurance that it would not be compromised or disclosed. Hoover's March 1, 1942, memorandum highlighted this purpose: pink paper should be used for memorandums "prepared solely for the benefit of the Director or other officials and eventually be returned to the dictator [of the memorandum] to be destroyed or retained in the Director's office."

For example, Hoover's "Official and Confidential" file on Alger Hiss contains three memorandums captioned "This memorandum is for administrative purposes to be destroyed after action is taken and not sent to files." Written by Hoover and sent to FBI officials Tolson, Tamm, Ladd, and Clegg, these memorandums reported the FBI director's suggestion to Secretary of State James Byrnes and to Attorney General Tom Clark to leak derogatory information about Alger Hiss to conservative congressmen in an effort to force Hiss to resign. The political sensitivity of this effort explains why Hoover adopted this filing procedure. Significantly, Hoover's "Official and Confidential" file on Hiss contains no memorandums from Clegg, Tamm, Ladd, or Tolson reporting their action on this 1946 proposal and further contains no memorandums reporting FBI agent Ed Hummer's role in leaking information to Father John Cronin in 1948 or the close contacts and leaks of FBI Assistant Director Louis Nichols to Congressman Richard Nixon throughout 1948. Under this filing procedure, such memorandums would not be retained in Hoover's files but would have been destroyed or returned to their sender.[67] Not surprisingly, then, as in the *Coplon* and *Baltch* cases, U.S. attorneys remained unaware of the bureau's illegal activities and the government's possible vulnerability to discovery motions.

FBI officials were concerned more about political embarrassment than illegality. This indifference to the law, all-too-common to the internal security bureaucracy, is confirmed by the FBI's and the CIA's initiation of a series of mail intercept programs. Beginning in 1940 and continuing until July 1966, the FBI instituted eight tightly controlled mail programs. Under these programs, mail of suspected espionage agents and of dissident political organizations and citizens was opened. FBI Director Hoover originally authorized these programs and telephonically ordered their termination without ever apprising the attorney general, the White House, or Post Office officials of these decisions. Political considerations once again influenced his decision to terminate this illegal activity. Because the investigative hearings initiated in 1965 by the Senate Subcommittee on Administrative Practice and Procedure under the chairmanship of Senator Edward Long threatened to expose FBI practices and embarrass the bureau, Hoover ordered:

> I don't see what all the excitement is about. I would have no hesitation in discontinuing all techniques—technical coverage, microphones, trash covers, mail covers, etc. While it might handicap us I doubt they are as valuable as some believe and none warrant FBI being used to justify them.[68]

Concerned exclusively that the FBI might be "used," Hoover did not hesitate to "use" the CIA. In 1952 the CIA had begun a mail program in New York City. Postal officials then understood that the agency would only record the names and addresses from envelopes of letters (a mail cover) between the United States and the Soviet Union to collect "foreign intelligence" information. Unknown to postal officials, the CIA almost immediately expanded the program's scope (numbers of letters and the countries involved) and nature (to include opening letters). Then in January 1958, FBI officials inquired "confidentially" of Post Office officials as to "the feasibility of covering outgoing correspondence from the U.S. to the U.S.S.R." These officials informed the FBI of what they understood to be the CIA's ongoing mail cover program. After a briefing by CIA officials (at which the FBI representatives did *not* advise the CIA of the bureau's own mail opening program), formal procedures were established in February 1958 whereby the FBI could request and receive information from this CIA mail opening project.

FBI officials effectively exploited this CIA project, outlining five sets of categories and ultimately identifying 286 individuals and organizations to be serviced by the CIA. The information culled proved to be of little espionage or counterespionage value (either to the FBI or the CIA); nonetheless the FBI obtained considerable information about dissident political activities. To ensure that the mail intercept source could not be compromised, the bureau devised yet another separate reporting procedure. By a November 26, 1962, memorandum FBI officials responsible for receiving information from the CIA's mail opening project were specifically admonished neither to disseminate this information outside the bureau nor to cite it in any investigative report. Copies of intercepted correspondence were not to be filed in the individual's case file (though cross-referencing permitted retrieval) but in a secure area separate from other FBI files. When FBI mail intercept programs were terminated in 1966, FBI officials neither informed the CIA of this decision nor terminated this relationship—the CIA's program involved no risk to the bureau. Further, when the CIA decided to terminate their by then risky mail program in 1973 and sought to ascertain the FBI's interest in assuming responsibility the bureau rejected the offer. At no time were FBI and CIA officials seriously troubled by these programs' illegality; their abiding concern was whether the program could be conducted without risking exposure and resultant political harm.[69]

The CIA's expansion of its mail project after 1955 and servicing of FBI requests after 1958 involved the agency in domestic spying—despite the 1947 National Security Act's formal prohibition that "the Agency shall have no police, subpoena, law enforcement powers or internal security functions." CIA officials' willingness to ignore this prohibition underscores the mind-set of the national security bureaucracy. Reviewing this mail program during the early 1960s because of concern about the possibility of congressional exposure, CIA officials concluded that the risks were acceptable and devised a strategy of denial. If illegal activities could be concealed, there was no reason to be troubled by illegality. This same mentality underlay the CIA's 1967 decisions to institute a series of far-reaching programs focusing on American citizens' dissident political activities, the so-called CHAOS, MERRIMAC, and RESISTANCE programs.

In their inception, these programs had limited and quasi-defensible purposes: to ascertain any foreign influence on domestic dissident organizations and demonstrations and to ensure the security of CIA installations and personnel. Almost immediately, these programs shifted to uncovering and submitting to the White House information about domestic dissent. Recipients of these reports during both Lyndon Johnson's and Richard Nixon's presidencies were pointedly admonished to safeguard the source of this information because of this program's "sensitivity" (i.e., illegality).

Recognizing these programs' illegality and concerned solely about embarrassment and the attendant political ramifications, CIA officials terminated them only when their continuance was too risky politically. Although low-level CIA personnel expressed concern as early as 1972 "over monitoring the political views and activities of Americans not known to be, or suspected of, being involved in espionage," high-level officials only ordered reducing the "intensity of attention to political dissidents." These programs were formally terminated in March 1974 and then only in response to the impact of the Senate Watergate Committee hearings. Because of the former CIA connections of the arrested participants, these hearings had raised serious questions about whether the CIA had been involved in the actual Watergate break-in. In time, the CIA's role in servicing the White House Plumbers and the public release of the Huston Plan raised additional questions about CIA practices and priorities.[70]

Illegal activities had not been the exception during the Cold War years. Whether sincerely believing that the national security required violations of the law or confident that political or judicial constraints could be circumvented because of their ability to maintain secrecy, internal security bureaucrats followed a higher calling. Richard Nixon's 1976 public claim to "sovereignty"[71]—that a president may order illegal activities "which, if undertaken by the sovereign in protection of the nation's security are lawful but which, undertaken by private persons, are not"—starkly expressed the prevailing political philosophy within the internal security bureaucracy. The sole deterrent was the risk of adverse publicity—and this risk was reduced by devising separate filing procedures, offering tortured constitutional interpretations, and relying on public, press, and congressional deference to "national security" or "executive privilege" claims.

The latitude of these arrogant bureaucrats was reduced only with the disillusionment with the presidency and the "national security" catchall in the aftermath of the Vietnam War and the Watergate Affair. Temporarily greater risks—and not these bureaucrats' "born again" concerns about legality—led to decisions to terminate many of these activities. The prospect remained, however, that with the receding of the passions of the 1970s, and the concomitant concern about secrecy and abuses of power, these practices could be resumed under more elaborate safeguards. A commitment to constitutionalism had not been restored during the political crisis of the 1970s. This was most dramatically revealed both in the efforts of conservatives (whether politicians, commentators, or internal security bureaucrats) during 1976–78 to preclude prosecution of FBI and CIA officials who in the recent past had either violated the law or committed perjury and in the Ford administration's 1976 decision not to prosecute CIA agents who had illegally opened the mail. In a press release announcing this decision not to prosecute, the Justice Department conceded that these activities "would be unlawful if undertaken today" but in the past had been based on the conviction that "in response to exigencies of national security, the president's constitutional powers to authorize collection of intelligence was of extremely broad scope."[72] Paradoxically, when offering this rationale, the department failed to recognize that the CIA's mail intercept program had never been authorized by Cold War presidents and thereby lacked even this highly questionable constitutional base.

Chapter Five
Political Counterintelligence

Having secured authorization to investigate "subversive activities" and having carefully devised procedures to preclude disclosure of questionable investigative activities, FBI officials no longer were principally concerned that politically motivated investigations could be effectively challenged. They, however, did not remain satisfied merely to compile extensive files and indexes on organizations and individuals targeted as threats to the nation's security. The FBI became a national political force committed to averting "potential subversion," and in time devised alternative extralegal measures to safeguard the "national security."

For one, their conservatism rendered FBI officials responsive to using politically information obtained through intensive investigations to discredit dissident activities. In addition, because much of this information either had been illegally obtained (whether through wiretaps, break-ins, or without specifiic legislative or executive authority) or involved no criminal activities, FBI officials possessed quantities of otherwise unusable data.

At first, such FBI political efforts were nonstructured, informal, and instituted on an *ad hoc* basis. On one level, the FBI voluntarily alerted White House officials to the "subversive" background of dissident groups and individuals. (This political effort is discussed in greater detail in the succeeding chapter.) FBI officials simultaneously sought to influence national policy by a conscious policy of leaks to "friendly" sources in the media, the Congress, or conservative organizations.

If these efforts dated from the early 1940s, the first attempt to formalize this response occurred in February 1946. On February 27, D. M. Ladd (head of the FBI's Intelligence Division) wrote FBI Director Hoover to recommend that the bureau influence "public opinion" by releasing "educational material" through "available channels." This effort, Ladd emphasized, could undermine Communist support in the labor unions, among prominent religious personalities and "liberal elements," and demonstrate "the basically Russian nature of the Communist Party in this country." The Catholic priest Father John Cronin was on recipient of this FBI informational program; given access to FBI files, Cronin used them to prepare reports in 1945 for the American Catholic bishops and in 1946 for the U.S. Chamber of Commerce. Radio commentator Walter Winchell and other conservative reporters as well as congressmen were other recipients of similar FBI leaks.[1]

In time, this FBI political effort was further refined. In addition to maintaining FBI records, the FBI's Crime Records Division was assigned other, political responsibilities. These included liaison with "friendly" congressmen, authors, and news reporters. By the 1960s the bureau developed a formally described Mass Media Program wherein derogatory information on prominent radicals was leaked to the news media. The Crime Records Division, moreover, helped draft speeches and/or letters for members of Congress and leaked information to conservative authors (like Don Whitehead) who in turn wrote books and articles either highly favorable toward the bureau or critical about bureau critics. Similarly, to further the bureau's liaison role, beginning in 1950 FBI agents were ordered to collect information first on candidates for Congress and then on prominent state political leaders—the resultant files included information about the individual's attitudes toward the bureau and personal background. Earlier, on his own initiative, FBI Director Hoover approached American Legion officials to develop a liaison relationship. Hoover proposed (and a November 1940 Legion conference concurred) that Legion members furnish confidential information to the FBI. Last, while not the Crime Records Division's exclusive responsibility, that division (as well as the bureau division having this assignment) serviced White House name check requests.[2]

These efforts to contain radicalism by leaking derogatory information about prominent radicals and organizations did not constitute the sole political activities of FBI officials. They also sought to reduce the ability of radical organizations to function effectively or to recruit new members. For a time, with the intensification of Cold War fears and the rise of McCarthyite politics, these informal efforts bore fruit. In 1948, for example, twelve Communist party leaders were indicted under the Smith Act of 1940. Then, under provisions of the McCarran Internal Security Act of 1950 and the Communist Control Act of 1954, Communist, Communist-front, and Communist-action organizations were required to register as foreign agents with the Subversive Activities Control Board and to label their publications as Communist propaganda. Beginning dramatically in 1947 and extending throughout the 1950s, moreover, through highly publicized hearings, congressional committees (notably the House Committee on Un-American Activities and the Senate Subcommittee on Internal Security) relied directly or indirectly on FBI investigative reports to expose Communist influence in the federal government, in the entertainment industry, in labor unions, and in public schools and universities. Last, FBI investigative reports were employed during the conduct of federal loyalty/security programs to raise doubts about the loyalty, and deny employment to, certain individuals. (The loyalty/security program is discussed in detail in chapter seven.)

The resultant litigation, loyalty/security program proceedings, and congressional hearings provided opportunities for effective utilization of FBI investigative findings. FBI investigative reports thereby served to popularize the conclusion of bureau officials that radicals were subversive, to sensitize the American public to the seriousness of the internal security threat, and concomitantly to discredit individuals and/or organizations active in radical politics. By the mid-1950s, however, and not because of a change in popular fears or executive branch policy, this political avenue appeared thwarted.

High-level FBI officials had always been deeply concerned about prosecuting activities. These concerns increased after 1947 as FBI officials became troubled by the effect of prosecution on the FBI's intelligence-gathering capabilities. For example, over one hundred FBI informants had had to be exposed during the various Smith Act trials and Subversive Activities Control Board proceedings. Then, in a series of important rulings in 1956 and 1957, the U.S. Supreme Court imposed major restrictions on uses of FBI reports, challenged the premise that individual liberties must be sacrificed to safeguard the national security, and thereby threatened to close what for FBI officials had been an effective means of propagandizing antiradical fears. The Court's decisions in effect reduced the scope of the Eisenhower security program, limited federal loyalty officials' ability to fire summarily individual employees, struck down state loyalty statutes, undercut the earlier *Dennis* ruling so that a Smith Act conviction now required the government to prove advocacy to commit violence, ordered the Subversive Activities Control Board* to reconsider its ruling that the U.S. Communist party must register as a Communist organization because of the "tainted" evidence on which this ruling had been based, held that state officials' summary dismissal of employees who took the Fifth Amendment violated due process, required that FBI reports on pretrial testimony of government witnesses be made available to defense attorneys during trial proceedings, and overturned House Committee on Un-American Activities contempt citations of a subpoenaed "unfriendly" witness on the ground that the committee's "question under inquiry" had not been made clear to the individual.[3]

These Court decisions ironically occurred simultaneously with an increased concern among FBI officials, in the aftermath of the successful Montgomery (Alabama) bus boycott of 1955, about the degree of Communist influence in the more militant civil rights movement, which threatened to disrupt Southern race relations and to transform national politics. Reflecting this conservative concern, FBI Director Hoover sent, in the spring of 1956, a series of reports to the White House alleging Communist influence and involvement in the civil rights movement. President Eisenhower responded by requesting that Hoover brief the Cabinet on the Southern racial situation. Hoover did so, emphasizing particularly the Communists' role in lobbying for civil rights objectives and the NAACP's plans to push for civil rights legislation. Following up on this effort, in 1957 the FBI prepared and disseminated to the military intelligence agencies a 137-page report on Communist influence and strategy toward the NAACP.[4]

Sensitive to the restrictions imposed by the Supreme Court's rulings on the uses of the bureau's investigative findings, still alarmed over the seriousness of the internal security problem, in August 1956 FBI officials devised a formal program to provide alternative means for containing Communists.

---

*The SACB had been created by the McCarran Internal Security Act of 1950 and had been assigned responsibility to enforce the act's registration provisions.

Having successfully averted meaningful executive oversight (whether by the president or the attorney general) either when formulating the Security Index program or when securing presidential authorization to investigate "subversive activities," FBI officials unilaterally instituted a so-called counterintelligence program to neutralize the U.S. Communist party—the first of a series of programs (captioned COINTELPROs). This COINTELPRO was initiated without the knowledge or authorization of either the attorney general or the president. Hoover's 1956 decision was unique not because the bureau began to "disrupt" radical organizations—the FBI had been doing that at least since 1941—but because it initiated a formal program based on written directives and responsive to the direct supervisory control of the FBI director. No longer willing simply to prosecute Communist officials, bureau officials had concluded by 1956 that more aggressive and extralegal techniques were essential and feasible.[5]

The memorandum formally instituting this program, dated August 28, 1956, sharply outlines the political nature of this decision. By August 1956 bureau officials no longer considered the Communist party an actual espionage or sabotage threat. Instead they were concerned about the Communist party's "influence over the masses, ability to create controversy leading to confusion and disunity, penetration of specific channels in American life where public opinion is molded, and espionage and sabotage potential." These officials' extreme anti-radicalism and elitism, in short, made them fearful that without effective counteraction the public might be unduly receptive to radical appeals. In a memorandum to FBI official L. V. Boardman, Alan Belmont (the head of the FBI's Internal Security Section) further highlighted these political objectives. The FBI had traditionally attempted to "foster factionalism" within the Communist party, Belmont wrote. Internal Communist party divisions resulting from developments at the Twentieth Party Congress of the Soviet Communist party and the disruptive impact of Smith Act prosecutions and Subversive Activities Control Board proceedings, however, provided an unparalleled opportunity for the bureau to "initiate on a broader scale than heretofore attempted, a counterintelligence program against the CP." Belmont then enumerated recommended FBI-initiated "disruptive" efforts and concluded: "The Internal Security Section is giving this program continuous thought and attention and we are remaining alert for situations which might afford additional opportunities for further disruption of the CP, USA." This COINTELPRO-Communist party was expanded in March 1960 and then in October 1963 to prevent Communist infiltration of mass organizations varying from the NAACP to Boy Scout troops. Significantly, under this expansion the program's focus shifted from party members to non-Communist groups or individuals whom FBI officials suspected might be susceptible to Communist influence.[6]

The highly political nature of COINTELPRO activities as well as the fact that this program had been initiated without the knowledge of responsible administration officials necessitated procedures to ensure against public knowledge and, in addition, to control whatever information high-level administration officials received about this program. Prior to instituting a COINTELPRO-activity, FBI agents were required to secure advance approval (whether from FBI Director Hoover directly, FBI Assistant Director Clyde Tolson, or the head of the Intelligence Division) and to specify proposed safeguards that would preclude public knowledge of the FBI's involvement in these approved activities. A memorandum authorizing the initiation of a later COINTELPRO pointedly articulated this concern: "under no circumstance should the existence of the program be made known outside the Bureau and appropriate within-office security should be afforded to sensitive operations and techniques considered under the program." Such control procedures (similar to 1942 Do Not File procedures for break-ins and the 1940–44 pink slip/blue slip procedure used by FBI officials for "sensitive" information forwarded to FBI Director Hoover) indicates the FBI officials' sole concern: not illegality but political embarrassment and/or political harm.[7]

On May 8, 1958, FBI Director Hoover ostensibly informed Eisenhower administration officials of this COINTELPRO-Communist party. Having precluded independent knowledge of this program outside the bureau, Hoover could volunteer whatever information he deemed appropriate. Hoover's May 8, 1958, letters advising Attorney General William Rogers and Special Assistant to the President Robert Cutler that in August 1956 the FBI had initiated a program "designed to promote disruption within the ranks of the Community Party," carefully confined administration knowledge about this COINTELPRO. Specific FBI activities were listed, including the use of informants to provoke "acrimonious debates" and anonymous mailings to ensure "disillusionment and defection" and increase "factionalism" among party members. Beyond citing the use of informants and mailings, however, Hoover had not fully informed the Eisenhower White House about other more questionable FBI COINTELPRO activities.[8]

Neither Rogers nor Cutler pressed Hoover for further details about this program. In addition, Hoover, on November 8, 1958, briefed the Eisenhower Cabinet about the FBI's COINTELPRO-Communist party. (We do not know why Hoover had been invited to do so. The considerable time lag between the FBI director's May letters and this November briefing suggests that the two were not related. Hoover's briefing and the booklet he distributed at the November Cabinet meeting that focused on Soviet espionage activities further suggest that the catalyst stemmed from administration concerns about Soviet activities.) The briefing did not accurately portray the nature and thrust of FBI officials' objectives. The "top secret" booklet (which was collected at the end of the meeting) was intended to illustrate his remarks (in the words of the Cabinet minutes) "regarding Russian intentions, intelligence techniques and our counterintelligence activities." Hoover's oral remarks specifically cited double agents, scientific developments such as micro-dots, and the increased number of passport requests by "known Communist supporters." Seven FBI programs were described in the thirty-six-page booklet, identified as being "part of [FBI] counterintelligence operations" and "specific answers to specific problems which have arisen within the FBI's investigative jurisdiction." The first six programs related directly to espionage; the seventh described the FBI's COINTELPRO:

> To counteract a resurgence of Communist Party influence in the United States, we have a seventh program designed to intensify any confusion and dissatisfaction among its members. During the past few years, this program has been most effective. Selective informants were briefed and trained to raise controversial issues within the Party. In the process, many were able to advance themselves to higher positions. The Internal Revenue Service was furnished the names and addresses of Party functionaries who had been active in the underground apparatus. Based on this information, investigations were instituted in 262 possible income tax evasion cases. Anticommunist literature and simulated Party documents were mailed anonymously to carefully chosen members.[9]

Although the briefing book accurately conveyed some of the FBI's CO-INTELPRO activities, Hoover had ostensibly informed the administration without having in fact done so. First, the FBI director had introduced this COINTELPRO in the context of counterespionage activities. Both Hoover's oral report and the FBI booklet only briefly cited the COINTELPRO and directly tied it with espionage programs. Moreover, Cabinet officials had not had the opportunity to read the booklet carefully in advance of the meeting and thereby appreciate this seventh program's distinctiveness. Although Hoover had technically briefed the Cabinet, what he understood and what Cabinet officials were led to understand about this program would remain widely divergent. The Cabinet minutes, if brief (as were all Eisenhower Cabinet minutes), are eloquent testimony to this fact. Significantly, there is no record that Hoover was queried about this program's authority—whether legislative or executive—and whether the identified activities were legal or permissible. This does not confirm necessarily that the Cabinet had neither read nor understood pages 35–36 of the FBI booklet—constitutional and legal questions might simply not have troubled the conservative Eisenhower Cabinet.

By identical January 10, 1961, letters to Secretary of State–designate Dean Rusk, Attorney General–designate Robert Kennedy, and Deputy Attorney General–designate Byron White, FBI Director Hoover similarly informed high-level Kennedy administration officials about the ongoing COINTEL-PRO–Communist party. Hoover appended a memorandum to these letters outlining Communist party activities and the FBI's internal security responsibilities "and our counterattack against the CPUSA."

Hoover began by bleakly depicting the U.S. Communist party's subversive goals and the gravity of communism's "threat to the internal security of the United States." After outlining FBI investigative responsibilities and authority, the FBI director enumerated the FBI's "many-pronged" "counterattack" against the party and some of the FBI's "more effective programs":

penetration of the Party at all levels with security informants; *use of various techniques to keep the Party off balance and disillusion individual communists concerning communist ideology*; investigation of every known member of the CPUSA in order to determine whether he should be detained in the event of a national emergency; and gathering evidence to be used in prosecutions of communists and communist organizations. (Emphasis added)

The FBI director more precisely reported:

> As an adjunct to our regular investigative operations, *we carry on a carefully planned program of counterattack* against the CPUSA which keeps it off balance. *Our primary purpose is to bring about disillusionment* on the part of individual members which is carried on from both inside and outside the Party organizations. . . .
>
> In certain instances *we have been successful in preventing communists from seizing control of legitimate mass organizations and have discredited others* who were secretly operating inside such organizations.[10] (Emphasis added)

Hoover's memorandum apprised the attorney general–designate of the FBI's COINTELPRO–Communist party. To the individual currently knowledgeable about the COINTELPROs, the emphasized language can be interpreted as fully informative. Can we conclude, however, that Robert Kennedy understood what the FBI was doing? Hoover's language is both vague and cryptic; his references to what clearly constituted harassment were insufficiently descriptive and imprecise and were enveloped by more specific language either alarmingly describing Communist subversion or enumerating the FBI's legal authority and responsibilities. As in 1958, FBI Director Hoover technically informed his superiors about this COINTELPRO without having provided the information essential for an independent judgment. Kennedy, moreover, had not been informed that this program had been unilaterally instituted by Hoover without the attorney general's prior consent. This does not exonerate the attorney general; clearly he had failed to insist upon additional information about these activities and their authority. Nonetheless, when the Kennedy White House formally requested a later briefing on all "internal security programs," Hoover's July 25, 1961, description of the FBI's "investigative programs" did not list the COINTELPRO's disruptive activities.[11]

Hoover's and other high-level FBI officials' concern about the political activities of another radical organization—in this case, the Socialist Workers party (SWP)—resulted in yet another COINTELPRO, again initiated without the attorney general's prior knowledge or authorization. What particularly exercised Hoover, as his October 12, 1961 letter to all special agents in charge announcing this new "disruptive program" highlights, was the SWP's radical politics:

The Socialist Workers Party (SWP) has, over the past several years, been openly espousing its line on a local and national basis through running candidates for public office and strongly directing and/or supporting such causes as Castro's Cuba and integration problems arising in the South. The SWP has also been in frequent contact with international Trotskyite groups stopping short of open and direct contact with these groups.

Outlining this COINTELPRO's "educational" purpose, Hoover emphasized the need to "alert the public to the fact that the SWP is not just another socialist group but follows the revolutionary principles of Marx, Lenin and Engels as interpreted by Leon Trotsky." This was not to be a crash program; "only carefully thought-out operations with the widest possible effect and benefit to the nation should be submitted." After careful evaluation, this program might subsequently be expanded.[12]

While these FBI COINTELPROs (Communist party and Socialist Workers party) had been unilaterally initiated, the COINTELPRO–White Hate groups were indirectly responsive to Johnson administration pressures. Disturbed by the spread of the Ku Klux Klan activities throughout the South, in early 1964 Attorney General Robert Kennedy sent a team of Justice Department lawyers to Mississippi. Based on this team's report and his own findings, in a memorandum prepared by Assistant Attorney General Burke Marshall in June 1964 proposed that the FBI should be encouraged "to develop its own procedures for the collection of intelligence" and

consideration should be given by the Federal Bureau of Investigation to new procedures for identification of individuals who may be or have been involved in acts of terrorism, and to the possible participation in such acts by law enforcement officials or at least their toleration of terrorist activity. . . .

The unique difficulty . . . is in gathering information on fundamentally lawless activities which have the sanction of local law enforcement agencies, political officials and a substantial segment of the white population. The techniques followed in the use of specially trained special assignment agents in the infiltration of Communist groups should be of value. If you [Johnson] approve, it might be desirable to take up with the Bureau the possibility of developing a similar effort to meet this problem.[13]

Concurrently, President Johnson dispatched former CIA Director Allen Dulles to investigate the disappearance of three civil rights workers in Mississippi (involved in a nationally publicized voter registration project). In his report to the president, Dulles recommended substantially increasing the number of FBI agents in Mississippi to help "control the terrorist activities."[14]

Whether because of Dulles's or Marshall's recommendations (or both), the president subsequently directed Hoover (according to Don Whitehead's sympathetic study of the FBI) "to put people after the Klan and study it from one county to the next. I want the FBI to have the best intelligence possible to check on the activities of these people."[15]

White House and Justice Department officials might have wanted the FBI to intensify investigations of the Klan; bureau officials moved beyond this limited effort. In July 1964 Hoover first transferred supervision of investigations of the Klan and other white supremacist groups from the General Investigative Division to the Domestic Intelligence Division. Among the reasons advanced for this transfer were the Domestic Intelligence Division's "wide experience" in "the penetration of subversive organizations through informants, anonymous sources, sophisticated microphone and technical surveillance, interview programs of highly specialized nature, etc." In addition, the head of the Domestic Intelligence Division argued, his division "would be in a position to launch a disruptive counterintelligence program against the Klan and other hate groups with the same effectiveness that they are now doing insofar as the Communist Party is concerned." This recommendation was supported by the head of the FBI's Inspection Division and ultimately was approved by FBI Director Hoover.[16]

Concurrently, on July 30, 1964, Hoover directed the Domestic Intelligence Division to study whether to initiate a counterintelligence program aimed at "hate groups." On August 27, 1964, the Domestic Intelligence Division recommended the immediate initiation of "a hard-hitting, closely supervised, coordinated counterintelligence program to expose, disrupt and otherwise neutralize the Ku Klux Klan (KKK) and specified other hate groups." Hoover concurred and, in a letter of September 2, 1964, advised all special agents in charge:

> The activities of these groups [the Klan and other white supremacist organizations] must be followed on a continuous basis so we may take advantage of all opportunities for counterintelligence and also inspire action in instances where circumstances warrant. The devious maneuvers and duplicity of these groups must be exposed to public scrutiny through the cooperation of reliable news media sources, both locally and [in Washington]. We must frustrate any effort of the groups to consolidate their forces or to recruit new or youthful adherents. In every instance, consideration should be given to disrupting the organized activity of these groups and no opportunity should be missed to capitalize upon organizational and personal conflicts of their leadership.

Whether Hoover was more sensitive to the illegality of the FBI's expanded COINTELPRO efforts or concerned about this program's possible impact upon the bureau's relations with Southern law enforcement officials and political leaders, in contrast to his earlier COINTELPRO authorization letters, he pointedly emphasized the need for secrecy:

> In instances where a reliable and cooperative news media representative or other source outside the Bureau is to be contacted or utilized in connection with a proposed counterintelligence operation, it will be incumbent upon the recommending office to furnish assurances the source will not reveal the Bureau's interest or betray our confidence. . . . You are cautioned that the nature of this new endeavor is such that under no circumstances should the existence of the program be made known outside the Bureau and appropriate within-office security should be afforded this sensitive operation.[17]

Indirectly responsive to White House and Justice Department pressures, FBI Director Hoover later independently briefed Attorneys General Nicholas Katzenbach (in 1965), Ramsey Clark (in 1967), and John Mitchell (in 1969) and White House aide Marvin Watson (in 1965) about this COINTELPRO. Having only sought an intensification of FBI investigations of the Klan, Johnson administration officials had no independent knowledge of the general nature of the FBI's COINTELPROs (Mitchell was inadequately briefed about an ongoing program). Neither the Johnson nor the Nixon administrations apparently fully appreciated Hoover's briefing memorandums. Hoover's memorandums, moreover, focused on legitimate and legal FBI investigative activities and his descriptions of FBI "disruption" tactics were sketchy and incomplete.

Hoover began his September 2, 1965, memorandum to Attorney General Nicholas Katzenbach (captioned "Penetration and disruption of Klan organizations—racial matters"), for example, by recounting how the FBI's successful high-level "penetration" of the Klan had helped solve "a number of cases involving racial violence in the South," contributed to the recovery of stolen weapons and ammunition, without public knowledge "forestall[ed] violence in certain racially explosive areas," and FBI informants and sources were obtaining "up-to-date intelligence data concerning racial matters." Then, in a glancing reference to the FBI's COINTELPRO, the FBI director added:

> We also are seizing every opportunity to disrupt the activities of Klan organizations. Typical is the manner in which we exposed and thwarted a "kick back" scheme a Klan group was using in one southern state to help finance its activities. One member of the group was selling insurance to other Klan members and would deposit a generous portion of the premium refunds in the Klan treasury. As a result of the action we took, the insurance company learned of the scheme and cancelled all the policies held by Klan members, thereby cutting off a sizeable source of revenue which had been used to finance Klan activities.[18]

Hoover's September 2, 1965, memorandum (a copy of which was sent to Special Assistant to the President Marvin Watson) was disingenuous. Although recounting one incident of "disruption," it was vague as to method and did not cite representative COINTELPRO activities—identified activities, moreover, would not elicit a questioning response from the attorney general. Whether or not Attorney General Katzenbach read this memorandum carefully and fully understood the nature and extent of the FBI's anti-Klan activities, his September 3, 1965, response is at least revealing of Justice Department supervision of the bureau. Captioning his memorandum as responding to "Your memorandum of September 2, regarding penetration and disruption of Klan Organizations," Katzenbach either had not understood these disruption tactics or intentionally refused to acknowledge having been briefed about questionable "disruptive" activities:

> I have been aware in a general way of the accomplishments of the Bureau in the area of Klan penetration, but I appreciate having the benefit of detailed information on this subject, and I hope you will continue to keep me up to date on it.
>
> May I take this opportunity to congratulate you on the development of your informant system in the Klan organizations *and on the results* you have obtained through it. It is unfortunate that the value of these activities would in most cases be lost if too extensive publicity were given to them; however, perhaps at some point it may be possible to place these achievements on the public record, so that the Bureau can receive its due credit.[19] (Emphasis added)

During December 3, 1975, testimony before the Senate Select Committee on Intelligence Activities, the former attorney general pointedly denied having been briefed by this memorandum. The bureau, Katzenbach maintained, frequently "used terms of art, or euphemisms, without informing the Attorney General that they were terms of art."[20]

Katzenbach's December 1975 testimony cannot, however, be dismissed as a self-serving attempt to escape responsibility. Annual FBI reports of 1964, 1965, 1966, 1967, and 1968, which Hoover forwarded to the White House and to the attorney general, contain a lengthy section detailing the FBI's specifically designated "counterintelligence" programs. These reports described legitimate criminal investigations and did not even slightly hint that the FBI sought to "expose, disrupt and otherwise neutralize" organizations as diverse as the Communist party, the Socialist Workers party, or the Klan (and, after 1967 and 1968, Black Nationalist and New Left organizations). The annual reports conveyed a narrow, literal definition of counterintelligence. In addition, when Klan leaders complained to FBI and Post Office officials in 1967 about a possible mail fraud involving a faked letter actually prepared by the bureau under this COINTELPRO, FBI officials approached the Chief Postal Inspector's office in Washington to ascertain contemplated action on this complaint. Informed that the matter had been referred to the Justice Department's Criminal Division, FBI officials did not brief Justice or Post Office officials that FBI agents authored this faked letter. When the Criminal Division concluded that no investigation was warranted, Washington bureau officials then directed the local FBI field office to prepare a second phony letter.[21]

FBI Director Hoover's briefing of Attorney General Ramsey Clark paralleled that of Katzenbach. Hoover advised the attorney general on December 19, 1967, that the lengthy attached memorandum (with a copy to Deputy Attorney General Warren Christopher) captioned "Ku Klux Klan investigations FBI accomplishments" had been prepared in response to Clark's conversation with FBI Assistant Director Cartha De Loach "concerning FBI coverage and penetration" of the Klan. Much of this information was already a matter of public record, the FBI director conceded; his memorandum also cited "matters dealing with extremely sensitive operations of this Bureau and it is suggested that this be handled on a strict need-to-know basis." The memorandum summarized the Klan's history and present status, outlined FBI investigative authority, detailed FBI investigations of the more important Klan cases, and described the FBI informant program and what Hoover captioned as "special projects." This "special projects" section vaguely described the FBI's COINTELPRO.

Hoover specifically recounted a number of COINTELPRO projects. These included efforts to remove Klan officials; disseminating information within Klan units to discredit the leadership, provoke scandal, and reduce the Klan's effectiveness; disseminating information to local police officials to ensure prosecution of Klan officials under local law; identifying those state troopers who were Klan members to state authorities; and selectively interviewing Klan members to "cause disillusionment of the members and disruption of the organization." Hoover's references might have been lengthy and descriptive. Nonetheless, they did have distinct law enforcement purposes, and no single incident had been cited wherein the FBI had disseminated information to the media, attempted to deny Klan members private employment, or tried to break up marriages. Hoover's description, for example, of the FBI's "special projects" in Virginia specified:

> In the fall of 1965 the United Klans of America began an intensive organizational effort in the State of Virginia. We immediately began an all-out effort to penetrate the Virginia Klan, contain its growth, and deter violence. Working closely with local and state authorities we were able to disseminate information on contemplated cross burnings. Several arrests were made. . . .
>
> . . . We provided the Governor [in December 1966] with information regarding Klan activities in his state. As a result, Governor [Mills] Godwin pressed for more effective enforcements of Virginia cross burning laws, and publically [sic] repudiated the Ku Klux Klan. . . .
>
> In May, 1966, we learned of Klan plans to "arrange an accident" for [name deleted] a civil rights worker working in the State of Vir-

ginia. We advised [deleted] and local authorities of the plot against her life and alerted our informants to follow the plot closely. To this date, the Klan has taken no action against [deleted]. This is just one of many examples of our notifying authorities and intended victims of racial violence in order that they could take appropriate protective measures.[22]

During his December 3, 1975, testimony before the Senate Select Committee on Intelligence Activities, Clark also denied knowledge of the existence, scope, or purpose of the COINTELPRO-White Hate groups. When pressed as to his response to the December 19, 1967, memorandum, in a frank admission of the carelessness of the Justice Department's oversight of the FBI, the former attorney general affirmed: "Did they [the words describing the "special projects"] put me on notice? No. Why? I either did not read them, or if I read them, didn't read them carefully. . . . So I guess I think I didn't read this. I think perhaps I had asked for it for someone else, and either bucked it on to them or I never saw it."[23]

FBI Director Hoover also briefed Attorney General John Mitchell on September 17, 1969 (with copies to the deputy attorney general, and the assistant attorneys general in charge of the Criminal, Internal Security, and Civil Rights Divisions). In his one-page letter captioned "Investigation of Klan organizations–Racial Matters (Klan)," Hoover recounted the "significant progress we have recently made in our investigation of the Ku Klux Klan." "During the last several months [implying quite recent efforts although the COINTELPRO-White Hate groups had been initiated in 1964], the FBI director reported, "while various national and state leaders of the United Klan of America remain in prison, we have attempted to negate the activities of the temporary leaders of the Ku Klux Klan." The only "negation" activity Hoover cited was the "careful use and instruction of selected racial informants" to "initiate a split within the United Klans of America." The FBI director then promised to devote "full attention to our responsibilities in an effort to accomplish the maximum possible neutralization of the Klan."[24]

In 1967 the COINTELPRO–White Hate groups investigations were expanded to obtain "details concerning [Klan or other white supremacist organizations'] rallies [and] demonstrations" and in 1968 to include information about groups "known to sponsor demonstrations against integration and . . . bussing." In 1969 FBI coverage was broadened to include "full details concerning the speeches made at the rallies or demonstrations, as well as the identities of the speakers." Beginning in 1971, not only were persons with a "potential for violence" investigated but anyone "who in judgment of SAC should be subject of investigation due to extremist activities." This reporting requirement virtually granted special agents in charge of FBI field offices unlimited discretion to investigate dissident activities.[25]

Simultaneously, FBI investigations of civil rights and black nationalist organizations intensified in 1964, partly in response to White House pressure.

Following the outbreak of the first urban racial riots during the summer of 1964, President Johnson directed the FBI to investigate their origins and extent. As civil rights organizations became more active and militant, and as racial riots recurred in 1965 in other urban centers, the FBI in early 1965 and again in 1966 intensified investigations of "General Racial Matters." FBI investigations then focused on "black nationalist groups," "hate-type organizations" with a "propensity for violence and civil disorder," and "militant" black leaders and personalities active in planning demonstrations, rallies, or marches in the North or the South. At the same time, in June 1964, earlier FBI investigative efforts were refined and a "special desk" in the Domestic Intelligence Division was established to supervise an "intensifiication of the investigation of communist influence in racial matters."[26]

When these FBI investigations could not confirm either Communist control of and direction to civil rights activities or militant black leaders' violations of federal law, in August 25, 1967, FBI Director Hoover ordered twenty-three special agents in charge to institute another COINTELPRO–Black Nationalist–Hate groups. Again, this COINTELPRO's purpose was clearly political: "to expose, disrupt, misdirect, discredit, or otherwise neutralize the activities of black nationalist, hate-type organizations and groupings, their leadership, spokesmen, membership, and supporters, and to counter their propensity for violence and civil disorder." Hoover directed the agents to investigate these organizations on "a continuous basis"; to exploit "all opportunities for counterintelligence" "enthusiastic[ally] and imaginative[ly]," and specifically ordered:

> The pernicious background of such groups, their duplicity, and devious maneuvers must be exposed to public scrutiny where such publicity will have a neutralizing effect. Efforts of the various groups to consolidate their forces or to recruit new or youthful adherents must be frustrated.[27]

Concerned about the "tremendous increase in black nationalist activity, and the approach of the summer," on February 29, 1968, FBI official George Moore recommended extending this COINTELPRO to all forty-one FBI field offices (and not simply the twenty-three offices then conducting the program). Such an expansion was needed "to prevent the coalition of militant black nationalist groups, prevent the rise of a leader who might unify and electrify these violence-prone elements, prevent these militants from gaining respectability and prevent the growth of these groups among America's youth." On March 4, 1968, FBI Director Hoover concurred in this recommendation. He directed special agents to develop procedures, report back how they were handling this assignment, and submit a progress letter every ninety days "summarizing counterintelligence operations proposed during the period, operations effected, and tangible results." Once again the FBI director emphasized: "Each operation must be designed to protect the Bureau's interest so that there is no possibility of embarrassment to the

Bureau. Beyond this the Bureau will give every possible consideration to your proposals."[28]

Black organizations not formerly prominent in civil rights activities or only recently organized had not been specifically cited under the August 25, 1967, or March 4, 1968, authorization letters. Individuals already on the FBI's list of Key Black Extremists (which included leaders of the Black Panther party) were, however, targeted. Soon concerned about the dramatic rise and appeal of the Black Panthers during the late 1960s, on November 25, 1968, Hoover ordered "imaginative and hard-hitting intelligence measures aimed at crippling" the Black Panther party and, on January 30, 1969, directed additional FBI field offices to expand this aim.[29]

Quite independently of these FBI efforts to discredit and limit the appeal of black civil rights organizations, the Department of Justice solicited additional information on black organizations or leaders who might have been conspiring to "plan, promote or aggravate riot activity." This intensified investigative effort was formally authorized on September 14, 1967, by Attorney General Ramsey Clark and was based on specific statutory authority. To refine this effort and to utilize effectively the obtained intelligence, the attorney general on December 18, 1967, specifically created an interdivision intelligence unit within the Department of Justice having the limited responsibility "for reviewing and reducing to quickly retrievable form all information that may come to this Department relating to organizations and individuals throughout the country who may play a role, whether purposefully or not, either in instigating or spreading civil disorders, or in preventing or checking them."[30] If Clark's purpose was prosecutive and not political, his authorization nonetheless provided cover for an already ongoing unilateral FBI program.

The 1960s was a decade of protest. College students as well as civil rights organizations were in the forefront of this protest. Beginning first by challenging arbitrary university requirements, college students soon moved to support civil rights objectives and then to radical politics, in reaction to the Vietnam War. Amorphous and nonideological, the student left (the so-called New Left) had limited connections and associations with traditional radical organizations. The appeal of the New Left, moreover, was not necessarily radical, deriving as well from moral convictions, an activist opposition to an increasingly unpopular war, and the policies and style of President Lyndon Johnson. Not surprisingly, FBI investigations of the New Left began by seeking whether to ascertain Communist or subversive influence and then whether to include student activists on the Security Index. As early as April 28, 1965, Hoover directed FBI officials to prepare a memorandum "with emphasis upon the communist influence" within the antiwar movement "so that it can be used publicly by prominent officials of the Administration whom the President intends to send in [sic] various parts of the country to speak on the Vietnam situation." Ultimately, the bureau's inability to confirm Communist control over the New Left, thereby discrediting campus radicalism, provided the impetus to establish the COINTELPRO–New Left.

The specific catalyst for this decision was a demonstration led by radical students on the Columbia University campus. FBI officials viewed this demonstration, like others on college campuses, as "a direct challenge to law and order and a substantial threat to the stability of society in general." Appalled by university officials' refusal to call in the local police, thereby effectively "tying the hands of law enforcement officials," and alarmed by the "era of disruption and violence" sweeping the nation "caused to a large extent" by the New Left, Domestic Intelligence Division officials Charles Brennan and William Sullivan on May 9, 1968, recommended the "immediate enactment" of a COINTELPRO "to neutralize the New Left and Key Activists . . . who are the driving forces behind the New Left." Brennan affirmed: "The purpose of this program is to expose, disrupt and otherwise neutralize the activities of this group and persons connected with it. It is hoped that with this new program their violent and illegal activities may be reduced if not curtailed."

FBI Director Hoover formally concurred on May 10, 1968, and solicited suggestions from all FBI field offices for "counterintelligence action against the New Left." After analyzing these replies, on October 28, 1968, Hoover authorized the COINTELPRO-New Left. Particular projects to be initiated included drafting anonymous letters and disseminating derogatory information to cooperative press contacts and "friendly news media." "Be alert for opportunities to confuse and disrupt New Left activities by misinformation. . . ." FBI officials were again urged: "You are reminded that no counterintelligence action is to be taken without Bureau approval. Insure that this Program is assigned to an Agent with an excellent knowledge of both New Left groups and individuals. It must be approached with imagination and enthusiasm if it is to be successful."[31]

Lacking external authorization (either in law, executive orders, or presidential directives) and clearly political, Hoover required his or a designated representative's advance approval for each proposed COINTELPRO project and further emphasized the need to forestall public knowledge of the project's existence and the bureau's involvement, and established a centralized reviewing system. Ironically, these carefully devised safeguards, particularly the requirement that proposed projects be submitted and receive formal authorization in writing, rendered the COINTELPRO vulnerable should the sanctity of FBI files be compromised.

On March 8, 1971, an activist antiwar group (the Citizens' Commission to Investigate the FBI) broke into the FBI's Media (Pennsylvania) resident agency office and stole approximately one thousand FBI documents. In subsequent weeks, this group selectively released carefully screened documents to members of Congress, individual journalists, and organizations identified in the pilfered documents as having been targeted by the FBI. These documents partially revealed investigative techniques, priorities, and the scope of the FBI's secret police activities. These included: surveillance of anti-war and black activist groups on college campuses, intelligence-gathering in black neighborhoods, and attempts to harass New Left activists. More important, one of the fourteen FBI documents released to the *Washington Post* was captioned COINTELPRO-New Left. This September 16, 1970, document recommended intensified FBI interviewing of dissidents so that this "will enhance the paranoia endemic in these circles and will further serve to get the point across there is an FBI agent behind every mailbox."[32] Release of these documents threatened to imperil COINTELPRO's continuance: should additional documents be pilfered from FBI offices revealing the scope and political nature of FBI COINTELPRO activities the integrity and authority of the FBI and its director could be severely undermined. (Hoover had reached mandatory retirement age in 1965 but had been allowed to continue as FBI director by an executive order of President Johnson.)

Although the Media documents confirmed the political biases of FBI investigations and hinted at COINTELPRO's existence (the captioned September 16, 1970, document), neither the Nixon White House nor Attorney General John Mitchell advocated an investigation of bureau practices and their legality. To the contrary. On March 23, 1971, Attorney General Mitchell warned that publication of these documents (which other Justice Department sources certified had been stolen from the FBI's Media office) could endanger national security and the lives of some federal agents. Before issuing this plea, Mitchell admitted to having considered seeking a court order restraining publication. The next day, however, Justice Department officials assumed the offensive and charged that the by-then released fourteen documents were among one thousand which had been stolen from the FBI office and that those responsible for this raid and dissemination had carefully selected documents to create an unwarranted impression of FBI illegality and irresponsibility. "Actually," one Department of Justice official affirmed, "a full examination of the stolen documents reveals the FBI showed restraint rather than overzealousness."

The next month (on April 14, 1971), Senators Gaylord Nelson and Edmund Muskie released copies of still other FBI reports disclosing FBI surveillance of Earth Day activities. Senator Nelson, moreover, demanded creation of a special commission to investigate domestic intelligence-gathering and surveillance activities. The Nixon White House responded by dismissing these charges as unfounded, "blatantly political," and intended to create the false impression that the FBI was spying on law-abiding citizens. Not Earth Day activities but persons known to foment violence had been under surveillance, Mitchell claimed. "One reason the FBI is the most respected investigative agency in the world," the attorney general affirmed, "is that it has steadfastly remained apart from politics and political activity, and has concerned itself solely with threats against national security and violations of federal law." The administration, moreover, was not the bureau's sole defender. Democratic Senate majority leader Mike Mansfield similarly dismissed criticisms of the FBI as "more noise than substance"; Mansfield strongly implied that he opposed a congressional investigation of the FBI.[33]

Although the Nixon administration and the congressional leadership might have disdained to investigate FBI practices, release of the Media documents precipitated two internal FBI decisions. Within four months of the raid, FBI Director Hoover ordered the closing of 103 of the FBI's resident agencies; rules governing which papers and files would be kept in residence agencies were tightened and more strictly enforced. In addition, intricate alarm systems were installed in resident agencies not housed in well-guarded and secure buildings. Second, various COINTELPROs were formally terminated on April 28, 1971.

In an April 27, 1971, memorandum to William Sullivan (the head of the Domestic Intelligence Division), Charles Brennan recommended discontinuing COINTELPRO in order "to afford additional security to our sensitive techniques and operations." Brennan never alluded directly to the Media documents; his concern derived, however, less from COINTELPRO's illegality than the FBI director's requirement that all recommended COINTELPRO activities be submitted and authorized in writing by Washington headquarters. Brennan accordingly counseled:

> These program involve a variety of sensitive intelligence techniques and disruptive activities which are afforded close supervision at the Seat of Government [a bureau phrase for Washington headquarters]. They have been carefully supervised with all actions being afforded prior Bureau approval and an effort has been made to avoid engaging in harassment. Although successful over the years, it is felt they should now be discontinued for security reasons because of their sensitivity.
>
> In exceptional instances where counterintelligence action is warranted, it will be considered on a highly selective individual basis with tight procedures to insure absolute security.

FBI Director Hoover concurred. On April 28, 1971, he ordered the immediate discontinuance of the various COINTELPROs but added:

> In exceptional instances where it is considered counterintelligence action is warranted, recommendations should be submitted to the Bureau under the individual case caption to which it pertains. These recommendations will be considered on an individual basis.
>
> You are reminded prior Bureau authority is required before initiating any activity of a counterintelligence nature.[34]

The decision to terminate COINTELPRO was not then a decision to terminate COINTELPRO-type activities. The Media raid had confirmed that future raids on FBI field offices could compromise FBI investigative activities. COINTELPRO's vulnerability, in fact, stemmed from Hoover's earlier requirements (1) that every proposal be submitted for his approval and (2) that field offices submit follow-up reports. In April 1971, Hoover had simply ordered discontinuance of a formal, and for that reason vulnerable, program. In the future such activities could still be instituted *ad hoc*.

The Senate Select Committee on Intelligence Activities investigation of COINTELPRO, moreover, uncovered at least three COINTELPRO-type operations conducted after Hoover's April 28, 1971, termination order. The committee obtained information concerning two of these operations from the FBI; the third program (which involved the leaking of derogatory information about Daniel Ellsberg's lawyer to Ray McHugh, the chief of Copley News Service's Washington bureau) had been independently uncovered by the committee staff. In the Senate Select Committee report on COINTEL-PRO staff counsel Barbara Banoff concluded:

> The Committee has not been able to determine with any greater precision the extent to which COINTELPRO may be continuing. Any proposals to initiate COINTELPRO-type action would be filed under the individual case caption. The Bureau has over 500,000 case files, and each one would have to be searched. In this context, it should be noted that a Bureau search of all field office COINTELPRO files [in 1975] revealed the existence of five operations in addition to those known to the [Assistant Attorney General Henry] Petersen committee [which was directed in 1974 to prepare a report on the FBI's COIN-TELPRO]. A search of all investigative files might be similarly productive.[35]

The bureau's interest in limiting its vulnerability proved to be politically astute—though not because the Nixon administration or the congressional leadership was willing to investigate the FBI. (Senator Nelson's 1971 resolution to create a joint congressional oversight committee died in committee. Reintroduced in 1973, 1974, and 1975, the resolution was seriously considered only after the dramatic revelations of the federal intelligence agencies' abuses of power were publicized in 1975 and 1976 by the Senate Select Committee on Intelligence Activities. Responding to the impact of these revelations, in May 1976 the Senate approved a resolution to establish a Senate Select Committee on Intelligence.) Rather, the FBI's COINTELPROs were uncovered, because of a suit brought by NBC correspondent Carl Stern.

On March 20, 1972, Stern wrote Attorney General Richard Kleindienst requesting "any document which (i) authorized the establishment and maintenance of Cointelpro–New Left, (ii) terminated such program, and (iii) ordered or authorized any change in the purpose, scope or nature of such program." On January 13, 1973, the attorney general denied Stern's request. The NBC reporter then brought suit under the Freedom of Information Act of 1966 in the U.S. District Court for the District of Columbia. During the subsequent trial, the Justice Department (among other responses) contended that the court "lacks jurisdiction over the subject matter of the complaint". The department further had the right to withhold the requested documents by virtue of Freedom of Information Act exemptions (arguing that release of these documents would reveal instructions "on the manner in which the

FBI conducts investigations" and would thereby substantially impair the effective operation of the FBI).

On July 16, 1973, U.S. District Judge Barrington Parker ordered the government to submit the requested documents to the court by July 24, 1973, for *in camera* inspection. The Justice Department complied. After reviewing the documents, on September 25, 1973, Judge Parker ordered their release to Stern. The Justice Department first appealed this ruling on October 20, 1973, reconsidering this decision, but then, on December 6, 1973, announced it would not appeal the judge's order.

That same day Acting Attorney General Robert Bork released two documents to Stern—one dated May 10, 1968, announcing the initiation, and the other dated April 28, 1971, the termination, of the COINTELPRO–New Left. These releases publicly compromised three other FBI COINTELPROs. On March 7, 1974, the NBC reporter received seven additional documents concerning FBI COINTELPROs involving the Socialist Workers party, White Hate groups, and Black Nationalist–Hate groups (but inexplicably not the COINTELPRO–Communist party).[36]

Stern's suit had forced Justice Department officials at least to initiate an investigation of FBI practices and procedures. The Department of Justice at the time had been reviewing FBI Director Clarence Kelley's proposal that the president issue an executive order directing the FBI to "expand by further defining the FBI's investigative authority to enable it to develop advance information" about "terrorist and revolutionaries who seek to overthrow or destroy the Government."[37] In December 1973, however, Acting Attorney General Robert Bork convinced Attorney General-designate William Saxbe to delay action on Kelley's proposal and instead to investigate the FBI's COINTELPRO practices. Saxbe concurred and Assistant Attorney General Henry Petersen was assigned responsibility to conduct this inquiry. When informed of this committee's formation, FBI Director Kelley urged Bork to exclude the FBI's "extremely sensitive foreign intelligence collection techniques" from the department's review. These, Kelley warned, were handled within the bureau "on a strictly need-to-know basis" and should not be included in a study "which will be beyond the control of the FBI."[38]

Still unwilling to exercise administrative responsibility over the FBI, the Department of Justice concurred in Kelley's suggestion. In addition, Petersen at first demurred to accept responsibility to conduct the investigation. FBI Director Kelley, the Assistant Attorney General instead suggested, should "undertake this responsibility." Replying that Kelley was extremely busy and did not "know what was going on over there either," Saxbe requested that Petersen conduct this inquiry "for both of us." Claiming ignorance as to where information could be obtained, Petersen accordingly requested the FBI to prepare summaries; these would be "spot checked" for "accuracy" by representatives from the Justice Department's Criminal Division." These FBI summaries were brief and rather bland. By not seeking direct access to the bureau's raw files, moreover, the Petersen committee could not learn either the reasons why agents had proposed and FBI Director Hoover had approved particular projects, or how these particular activities had been implemented.

The Senate Select Committee investigation into the raw files eventually disclosed the extremely misleading nature of these FBI summaries when contrasting one FBI summary with the approved FBI COINTELPRO project. The FBI summary reported: "It was recommended that an anonymous letter be mailed to the leader of the Blackstone Rangers, a black extremist organization in Chicago. The letter would hopefully drive a wedge between the Blackstone Rangers and the Black Panther Party. The anonymous letter would indicate that the Black Panther Party in Chicago blamed the leader of the Blackstone Rangers for blocking their programs." In fact, the proposed project was more ambitious and far less incidental. The recommendation emphasized that the Blackstone Rangers were prone to "violent type activity, shouting, and the like" and accordingly that an anonymous letter should be sent to a Blackstone Rangers leader stating that "the Panthers blame you for blocking their thing and there's supposed to be a hit out for you." This anonymous letter "may intensify the degree of animosity between the two groups" and "lead to reprisals against [the Black Panther party] leadership."

In addition, although criticizing "isolated instances" for practices "abhorrent in a free society" and "a small number of instances" where programs "involved what we consider today to be improper activities," the Petersen committee report nonetheless affirmed that most programs "were legitimate" and "were entirely proper and appropriate law enforcement procedures." The report enumerated these "entirely proper and appropriate" procedures:

> notifying other Government authorities of civil and criminal violations of group members; interviewing such group members; disseminating public source material on such individuals and groups to media representatives; encouraging informants to argue against the use of violence by such groups; and issuing general public comment on the activities, policies and objectives of such groups through testimony at legislative hearings and in other formal reports.

Conceding that certain FBI COINTELPRO proposals violated the law, the Petersen committee nonetheless recommended against a criminal investigation:

> any decision as to whether prosecution should be undertaken must also take into account several other important factors which bear upon the events in question. These factors are: first, the historical context in which the programs were conceived and executed by the Bureau in response to public and even Congressional demands for action to neutralize the self-proclaimed revolutionary aims and violence prone activities of extremist groups which posed a threat to the peace and tranquility of our cities in the mid and late sixties; second, the fact that each of the COINTELPRO programs were personally approved and supported by the late Director of the FBI; and third,

the fact that the interference with First Amendment rights resulting from individual implemented program actions were insubstantial.

Rather than prosecution, the attorney general should publicly release the committee's report. (Saxbe complied with this recommendation and during November 20, 1974, testimony before the House Subcommittee on Civil and Constitutional Rights released the full report—portions of the report had been made public in April 1974.) The Petersen committee also recommended issuance of a directive prohibiting the FBI

> from instituting any counterintelligence program such as COINTEL-PRO without [the attorney general's] prior knowledge and approval. Specifically, this directive should make it unmistakably clear that no disruptive action should be taken by the FBI in connection with its investigative responsibilities involving domestic based organizations, except those which are sanctioned by rule of law, procedure, or judicially recognized and accepted police practices, and which are not in violation of state or federal law.[39]

Attorney General Saxbe issued no such directive. In November 1975, however, Saxbe's successor, Edward Levi, established a departmental committee to develop new FBI "guidelines." This committee proposed a series of "preventive action" guidelines. Under one of these, the FBI would have been authorized to take "nonviolent emergency measures" to "obstruct or prevent" the use of force or violence upon the attorney general's specific finding that there was "probable cause to believe that violence is imminent and cannot be prevented by arrest." Because of congressional opposition and because of recognition that this proposal would not have prevented the recurrence of COINTELPRO-type activities, Attorney General Levi was eventually forced to abandon this proposal when formally issuing Justice Department guidelines on March 10, 1976.[40].

Justice Department efforts to minimize COINTELPRO activities—whether claiming that violations of First Amendment rights were "insubstantial" or that most projects were legitimate—did not accurately reflect their thrust and nature. First, many of the activities the Petersen committee report listed as being "entirely proper and appropriate law enforcement procedures" scarcely warrant this characterization. Second, the FBI's purposes for leaking derogatory information to the media about targeted individuals or organizations were purely political. Third, even when forwarding information to local and state authorities concerning planned or actual violations of local and state laws, the FBI had secured this information without prior investigative authority. Fourth, many of the bureau's contacts with public officials either constituted harassment or were intended to deny targeted individuals public employment.

COINTELPRO activities included sending anonymous, scurrilous, and false letters to break up marriages, to sow internal dissension within organizations, or to inform public and private employers of the political activities and organizational membership of radical individuals. Other CO-INTELPRO activities included efforts to provoke violence, prevent the election of radicals to public office, prevent dissidents from speaking or holding meetings, and prevent targeted individuals or organizations from publishing and disseminating their views. In addition, the Justice Department's own review of the FBI's COINTELPRO files led Attorney General Edward Levi to announce on April 1, 1976, the department's decision to send notification letters to individuals who might have been harmed by, or who remained ignorant that they had earlier been the target of, FBI COINTELPRO activities. By July 1977, 282 such notifications letters had been sent.[41]

Neither innocent nor benign, FBI COINTELPRO activities confirmed the FBI's consciously political efforts to undermine political movements which bureau officials found abhorrent. The FBI, moreover, had not merely responded to public, congressional, or executive pressure. FBI officials had unilaterally initiated the various COINTELPROs without the prior knowledge and consent of responsible leaders either in the Congress or the executive branch. Furthermore, elaborate procedures had been devised to ensure against the attorney general's, the Congress's, and the public's knowledge of those activities. This program was formally terminated, it should also be emphasized, only when the COINTELPROs' secrecy was compromised in 1971. The nature of the activities conducted under the various COINTELPROs, the quest to ensure secrecy, and the far-reaching abuses of power confirmed the extent to which the FBI had become a law unto itself, had successfully precluded meaningful external oversight, and had based investigations on political considerations.

Chapter Six
Political Uses of Surveillance

During the years 1940–75, federal investigative activities were not confined to "national security" matters. FBI, CIA, NSA, and IRS surveillance efforts were also based upon conservative goals and, furthermore, were responsive to the partisan interests of incumbent administrations. Increasingly after 1939 detailed information was forwarded to the White House about the strategies of the presidents' political adversaries' in legislative, convention, public opinion, congressional or presidential lobbying matters. These reports might not have determined legislative or election results; they did compromise First Amendment rights. Organizations under surveillance ranged from the radical to the ultraconservative, and included the John Birch Society, the U.S. Communist party, the Southern Christian Leadership Conference, the Nation of Islam, the International Council of Christian Churches, the Progressive party, and the National Lawyers Guild. Among the individuals were 1948 Progressive party presidential candidate Henry Wallace, Mrs. Eleanor Roosevelt, U.S. Supreme Court Justice William Douglas, financier Bernard Baruch, 1964 Republican presidential candidate Barry Goldwater, Republican adviser Anna Chenault, U.S. Senators Joseph McCarthy, J. William Fulbright, and Wayne Morse, CBS television correspondent Daniel Schorr, and Democratic presidential aspirant Edmund Muskie's campaign advisers Morton Halperin and Anthony Lake.[1]

A paramount explanation for the intelligence agencies' political role is the distorting impact of the Cold War. Obsessed over the possibility or foreign-directed espionage and subversion, increasingly after 1945 congressional and public opinion leaders accepted the expansion of the FBI's, CIA's, and NSA's surveillance role. These leaders also concluded that the intelligence agencies could fulfill their important mission only if accorded wide latitude and assured of secrecy.

Public opinion and congressional leaders had expected, however, that internal security bureaucrats would operate within acceptable "national security" boundaries. That these officials would report to the White House on dissident political activities had not been anticipated. The absence of external controls ensuring accountability allowed, if not encouraged, internal security bureaucrats to assume this intelligence function. Having devised relatively fail-safe filing procedures, intelligence officials complied with White House requests or unsolicitedly forwarded political intelligence information to the White House.

Former constitutional constraints no longer operated effectively. On the one hand, no president after Franklin Roosevelt spurned the opportunity to obtain invaluable political intelligence. On the other hand, convinced that the national interest required violating the Constitution or the laws, internal security bureaucrats increasingly were less concerned about legal restraint.

The FBI's role in providing political intelligence to the White House began in 1940 during Franklin Roosevelt's administration. The FBI could assume such a role because of a series of decisions Hoover had made during the years 1936–41 to expand FBI investigative activities and develop particular files. These included investigations of Fascist and Communist activities pursuant to President Roosevelt's 1936 order and then Hoover's September 1939 order that FBI field offices investigate persons of German, Italian, and Communist "sympathies" and any other persons "whose interests may be directed primarily to the interest of some other nation than the United States." Hoover identified the targets of the 1939-ordered investigations as including members and officers of Communist, German, and Italian societies "whether they be of a fraternal character or of some other nature"; subscribers to German, Italian, Communist foreign-language, and any other newspapers with "notorious" nationalist sympathies; and members of any other groups "which might have pronounced Nationalistic tendencies." One month later, Hoover ordered FBI field offices to initiate confidential investigations of "various so-called radical and fascist organizations" to identify their leading personnel, purposes, aims, and the "part they are likely to play at a time of national crisis." Hoover extended this order in June 1940 to include additional information on individuals to be used to compile a (custodial detention) list of "Communistic, Fascist, Nazi, or other nationalist background."[2] Then, in an October 1, 1941, "informative memorandum—not to be sent to Files Section," the FBI director informed bureau officials of his decision to maintain a "confidential file" in the office of the then Assistant-to-the-Director Louis Nichols. This file, Hoover advised, would "be restricted to items of a more or less personal nature of the Director's and items which I might have occasion to call for from time to time such as memoranda to the Department [of Justice] on the Dies Committee, etc." In this memo, Hoover also acknowledged the existence "presently" of another "confidential file" initiated during the 1920s and maintained in the office of his personal secretary, Helen Gandy, "in which are kept various and sundry items believed inadvisable to be included in the general files of the Bureau." Both these confidential files would enable the FBI director to influence official policy, key political leaders, and, through carefully orchestrated press leaks, public opinion.[3]

To safeguard the bureau's interests and preclude discovery of the FBI's intelligence role, the FBI director concurrently devised separate filing procedures based on the rationale creating the Gandy and Nichols files. Normally, field office reports to FBI Washington headquarters were serialized and could thus be compromised during court proceedings. To preclude serialization of these and other sensitive reports, in 1940, and in additional, refining memorandums of 1941–44, the FBI director advised bureau officials of special filing procedures to permit destruction of these reports by not creating a record of their existence. In 1949 and 1962, Hoover later extended these separate filing requirements to information reported by FBI agents which might be "potentially embarrassing" to the bureau or which might disclose illegal investigative activities.[4]

These separate filing procedures and investigative programs thereby enabled the FBI director to influence presidential policy. Hoover's political efforts, however, predated the formulation of these procedures. In 1937, for example, the FBI director advised Attorney General Homer Cummings and President Roosevelt about two radical projects. One involved a planned pilgrimage to Washington organized by the American Youth Congress (which Hoover characterized as strongly Communistic) to lobby for legislation benefiting American youth. The second involved the Communist party's role in Workers Alliance plans (a radical labor organization) to organize nationwide demonstrations protesting the plight of the unemployed and to lobby Congress in support of federal relief programs.[5]

Whether or not President Roosevelt was aware of the extent of the FBI's political surveillance activities instituted first in 1936 and then radically expanded in 1939 and 1940, he was aware that the FBI investigated foreign direction to domestic Fascist and Communist organizations and thereby could retrieve information at least identifying those individuals who had associations with foreign agents. Such FBI investigative findings could service the president's policy interests.

Convinced that then-dominant neutralist sentiment (which had resulted in congressional enactment of the Neutrality Acts of 1935–37) was unrealistic, President Roosevelt had consciously sought since 1937 to alter public and congressional opinion. The outbreak of World War II in September 1939 further increased the president's efforts to move the nation to support a more activist, anti-Axis role. Such a role, however, ran counter to the dominant sentiment. In 1940, nonetheless, Roosevelt supported such potentially controversial policy measures as increased defense appropriations and the destroyer-bases deal with Great Britain. These presidential actions were sharply denounced by a number of influential public and congressional leaders—including Charles Beard, John Flynn, Robert Maynard Hutchins, Norman Thomas, Robert Taft, Hiram Johnson, Robert McCormick, Oswald Villard, Congressman Vito Marcantonio and Charles Lindbergh. This varied group of critics—including individuals whose political philosophies ranged from radical to conservative—would eventually organize the America First Committee to challenge the administration's increasingly interventionist policies. A predominantly conservative organization, the America First Committee was dominated by individuals who had consistently denounced Roosevelt's New Deal policies and the strengthening of the office of the presidency. Though its general political influence was limited, the committee's foreign policy criticisms did command widespread popular support and could thereby frustrate attainment of the president's foreign policy objectives.[6]

This concern led the president to approach Hoover. On May 18, 21, 23, 29, and 31, 1940, Stephen Early (secretary to the president) forwarded to the FBI director lists of individuals who had sent telegrams criticizing President Roosevelt's national defense address. "It was the President's idea," Early wrote, "that you [Hoover] might like to go over these, noting the names and addresses of the senders." Early forwarded another list to Hoover on June 17, 1940, of those who had sent telegrams approving Colonel Charles Lindbergh's criticisms of the president's foreign policy. Hoover returned both sets of telegrams on May 25 and August 20, 1940, "with comment, and reports." The president might only have asked Hoover to list these individuals; nonetheless, he did not chastise Hoover for compiling reports. Instead, on June 12, 1940, Roosevelt directed White House aide Edwin Watson "to prepare a nice letter to Edgar Hoover thanking him for all the reports on investigations he has made and tell him I appreciate the fine job he is doing." Watson prepared and sent this letter to Hoover on June 14, 1940. The FBI responded to other White House requests of 1941 for information concerning critics of the proposed Lend Lease Bill. To meet this demand, the FBI did not then simply check its files for derogatory information, but conducted an intensive investigation including the use of wiretaps, bugs, and physical surveillances.[7]

In addition, in 1941, Hoover ordered and forwarded to the White House a comprehensive report on the activities of the administration's right-wing critics—specifically, the Christian Front and Mobilizers, the American Destiny party, the American Nationalist party, and the America First Committee. The activities of the League for Fair Play (a New York group) were detailed: the League furnished "speakers to Rotary and Kiwanis Clubs and to schools and colleges." Other FBI reports described Communist political activities—including efforts to influence the NAACP. In November 1941, Hoover requested and obtained Attorney General Francis Biddle's approval to wiretap the Los Angeles Chamber of Commerce, even though Hoover conceded there was "no record of espionage at this time."[8]

The FBI's political reporting to the White House did not cease in 1942 with formal U.S. involvement in World War II. Some of the subjects of these reports were loyal administration personnel Donald Nelson, Harry Hopkins, Sumner Welles, and Thomas Corcoran; the conservative nationalistic Polish American Congress; the left-oriented American Polish Labor Council; the NAACP; the independent liberal Independent Voters of Illinois (IVI); a Bronx (New York) child care center "apparently dominated and run" by Communists; and various so-called Communist-Front groups. A December 29, 1944, Chicago field office report on the IVI illustrates the emphasis of these reports. The IVI, the Chicago field office reported, had been formed to develop "neighborhood political units to help in the reelection of President Roosevelt and the election of progressive congressmen. . . . IVI sought to help elect those candidates who would favor fighting inflation, oppose race and class discrimination, favor international cooperation, support a 'full employment program,' oppose Fascism, etc." Attorney General Francis Biddle has also written that Hoover frequently shared "his extraordinarily broad knowledge of the intimate details of what my associates in the Cabinet did and said, of their likes and dislikes, their weaknesses and associations." This characterization of FBI reports was reiterated by Budget Director Harold Smith. Reporting a discussion he had with President Truman on May 11, 1945, Smith recounted Truman's opposition "to set up a gestapo" and "I then indicated that I thought it was not altogether appropriate to be spending Federal funds [to construct a special FBI building] merely to satisfy curiosity concerning the sex life of Washington bureaucrats and members of Congress."

The Office of Strategic Services (OSS) also investigated and reported on the activities of the American Slav Congress, leaders of the Polish-American community, and representatives from the Polish government-in-exile (in London) during World War II. These reports detailed how these individuals/ organizations attempted to influence public and congressional opinion concerning the administration's policy toward postwar Poland.[9] If begun to ascertain foreign efforts to influence U.S. foreign policy, OSS investigations soon spilled over to how concerned American citizens attempted to affect foreign policy decisions.

Roosevelt's death in April 1945 terminated an extremely intimate but informal relationship between himself and the FBI director. Hoover's political reporting, moreover, did not cease with Roosevelt's death. As early as April 23, 1945, Harry Vaughan (military aide to the president) acknowledged receipt of one such FBI report, affirmed that the president had read it "with much interest," and reported that Truman felt "that future communications along that line would be of considerable interest whenever, in your [Hoover's] opinion, they are necessary."[10] While the contents of this particular communication are not known, the president's positive response encouraged Hoover to continue to submit fairly regular political reports to the Truman White House (through either Vaughan or other presidential aides— Matthew Connelly, Sidney Souers, George Allen).

On May 23, 1945, for example, the FBI director informed White House aides E. D. McKim and Harry Vaughan of the activities of a high executive official. One of these reports included "transcripts of telephone conversations between [the official] and [U.S. Supreme Court] Justice Felix Frankfurter and between [the official] and [nationally syndicated columnist] Drew Pearson." Between June 1945 and May 1948, moreover, the FBI wiretapped and regularly reported to Harry Vaughan the activities of a former Roosevelt White House aide, Thomas Corcoran. Attorney General Tom Clark authorized this wiretap. FBI documents recorded that Clark had conveyed President Truman's "particular concern" about Corcoran's activities "and his associates" and desire for "a very thorough investigation" so that "steps might be taken, if possible, to see that such activities did not interfere with the proper administration of government."[11]

Hoover's regular reports to the Truman White House on a variety of dissident organizations and individuals can be divided into two categories. The first, which is clearly partisan and can be characterized as political intelligence, describes the strategies of the administration's critics (principally on the left, although right-wing individuals were also covered). The second highlights the FBI director's conservative political objective to discredit dissident activities.

A March 31, 1948, Hoover letter, for example, recounted a recent conversation between Tilford Dudley (assistant director of the CIO's Political Action Committee) and Chester Bowles (former OPA director, a leading liberal Democrat, and an ADA founder). CIO President Philip Murray had confided to Dudley his interest that the ADA assume an active pre-convention role. Dudley preferred drafting Dwight Eisenhower for the Democratic presidential nomination. Bowles concurred, "If we're going to try to remove him (the informant stated that Bowles referred to President Truman), we'd better get all the help we can." Murray opposed direct CIO involvement in this effort, preferring that the initiative come from people like Dudley and Bowles with labor helping later. Bowles emphasized that Murray, UAW President Walter Reuther, and PAC Director Jack Kroll nonetheless must oppose Truman publicly and at the same time express continued support for the Democratic party. "Alone" such a stance "would almost be enough to kill President Truman's chances."[12]

In addition, Hoover advised the White House of: (1) the Communist party's decision to support Henry Wallace's third party effort, (2) Communist party officials' October 1946 conclusion that a third party would succeed that year in New York State and nationally in 1948, and (3) the Socialist Workers party's decision to run their own candidate in 1948 rather than support Wallace's third party bid. Hoover also forwarded a photostatic copy of an October 11, 1947, report outlining the decisions of West Coast Democrats for Henry Wallace. In June 1947 he outlined the strategy of the Progressive Citizens of America to elect delegates to the forthcoming Democratic National Convention in order to have a major voice on policy and thereby either effect Wallace's nomination as vice-president or to the Cabinet. Should these efforts fail, the Progressive Citizens planned to bolt the convention and form a third party to elect Wallace president.[13]

An imminent sugar scandal might be "very embarrassing to the Democratic Administration," Hoover wrote on June 25, 1947. On January 27, 1950, he detailed how certain newspaper reporters planned a publicity campaign outlining organized gambling's connection with corrupt politicians. These news stories "will be critical of the Attorney General and will include information relating to his supposed association and contacts with members of the underworld, particularly in Kansas City, Missouri, and with the President's supposed association with these individuals and their contributions to the President's campaign."[14] Republican Congressman Alvin O'Konski, Hoover reported on June 18, 1947, planned to deliver a speech attacking Assistant Secretary of State Spruille Braden and the administration's Argentine policy. Then, on February 20, 1951, Hoover advised the White House that Senate Internal Security Subcommittee staff members, Senator Joseph McCarthy, McCarthy aide J. B. Matthews, and Hearst newspaper columnists George Sokolsky and Westbrook Pegler had obtained and intended to use politically the files of the Institute of Pacific Relations.[15]

In other reports, Hoover questioned the integrity and loyalty of recently fired Secretary of Commerce Henry Wallace and of Bureau of Standards Director Edward Condon; described how the Federation of Atomic Scientists and prominent radicals sought to effect David Lilienthal's confirmation as chairman of the Atomic Energy Commission; reported nuclear physicist J. Robert Oppenheimer's indiscreet comments; and outlined the anti-HUAC plans of the National Council of Arts, Sciences and Professions (an organization, Hoover claimed, having Communist sympathizers as officers and members).[16]

Hoover, moreover, detailed the plans of a variety of dissident organizations ranging from the Communist party, the Joint Anti-Fascist Refugee Committee, the National Committee to Win the Peace, the American Cab Drivers Association for Discharged Veterans, the National Association for the Advancement of Colored People, the Jewish War Veterans and other national Jewish organizations, the National Lawyers Guild, the Political Action Committee, and the Independent Citizens Committee of the Arts, Sciences and Professions. Citing no treasonous or illegal activities, Hoover's reports merely described attempts to influence either public opinion, presidential policy, or congressional legislative decisions. Even Hoover's reports on the Communist party concerned legislative efforts. "You will recall," Hoover advised Vaughan on December 4, 1947, "that the information was previously supplied to you indicating the Communist Party was planning to use certain pressure tactics in an effort to have certain measures passed during the present session of Congress." Then on January 5, 1946, Hoover wrote that "the National Board of the Communist Party has instructed all Communist Party districts throughout the country to in turn instruct every Party leader in the trade unions and all Party functionaries in the trade union movement 'to stir up among the rank and file of the workers of the country a feeling of revolt against the Truman anti-labor, anti-strike plan.' " A December 23, 1948, letter capsulizes Hoover's reports on non-Communist organizations: the National Lawyers Guild was promoting a conference between Bartley Crum and the president "to persuade the President to intervene with Democratic leaders to take steps to abolish the House Committee on Un-American Activities."[17]

The FBI director was particularly exercised about labor militancy in 1945–46. Labor unrest, Hoover charged, resulted from Communist influence within the organized labor movement. Yet Hoover's specific examples were quite innocent, disclosing only the heightened militancy of a labor movement insistent on improving wages and working conditions. Hoover also reported extensively on the plans of non-Communist leaders and unions.[18]

Hoover volunteered all these reports; none had been specifically solicited by the White House. Apparently, the FBI director sought to ingratiate himself, and the bureau, with the White House, and also to influence official policy by smearing leftist efforts as "subversive" or communistic. In addition, Hoover's reports encouraged the White House to use or to consider employing the bureau to further its own political interests.

One such effort involved Harold Ickes. In February 1946 Ickes dramatically resigned as secretary of the interior protesting President Truman's January 1946 decision to appoint Edwin Pauley under secretary of the navy. Pauley would play politics with offshore oil reserves, Ickes claimed, an important criticism given the naval under secretary's responsibility for oil policy. Learning that Ickes might have "a possible connection" with a gas company interested in acquiring the Big Inch Pipe Line, later that year, on December 4, 1946, White House officials requested FBI confirmation. A search of FBI files revealed no such affiliation, Hoover reported on December 6, 1946. "Mr. Ickes has been very friendly with Mr. Thomas C. Corcoran," the FBI director continued, "who reportedly is in the process of organizing a gas company for the purpose of submitting bids for the procurement of the Big Inch Pipe Line. . . . during the initial stages of this company's formation, Mr. Ickes was proposed for consideration as a director."[19]

During the 1948 presidential campaign, moreover, the White House seriously considered employing the FBI to ascertain the authenticity of certain Cardenas-Wallace letters. (On July 14, 1948, the *New York Times* reported that former Mexican President Lazaro Cardenas in an apparently unsolicited letter had lauded Wallace's candidacy as offering hope to Latin America and to the world that World War III could be prevented. The *Times* also reported Wallace's reply.) On August 25, 1948, White House aide George Elsey advised Special Counsel to the President Clark Clifford (Truman's principal campaign adviser) that "so far as [Assistant Attorney General Peyton Ford] has been able to ascertain, the Department of Justice has never been requested by the White House to ascertain [these letters'] validity." Should such a request be "now made" Justice could not provide "any useful information." The FBI "does not operate in Mexico, and . . . it would be highly hazardous for numerous obvious political reasons for the FBI to attempt to ascertain from Mr. Wallace's intimate associates whether he wrote a letter printed over his name." Although the CIA had agents in Mexico Elsey doubted "the wisdom of requesting that organization to ascertain the validity of these letters."[20]

FBI political activities were not confined to volunteering information to the White House. On February 27, 1946, FBI Intelligence Division Chief D. Milton Ladd proposed that the FBI release "educational material" through "available channels" to influence "public opinion." By so acting, the FBI could anticipate and thereby counteract the "flood of propaganda from Leftist and so-called Liberal sources . . . in the event of extensive arrests of Communists" should the United States go to war with the Soviet Union. Communist support among "labor unions," "persons prominent in religious circles," and "the Liberal elements" must be undermined and "the basically Russian nature of the Communist Party in this country" demonstrated. The FBI Executives Conference approved this recommendation. While the scope of FBI "educational" activities cannot be fully ascertained, certain of them have been disclosed. In June 1947, conservative Republican Senator Bourke Hickenlooper quoted from FBI dossiers to denounce the loyalty of twenty-four Atomic Energy Commission employees. This subversive problem, Hickenlooper argued, raised questions about the desirability of vesting control over atomic energy to civilians. (Hickenlooper had opposed transferring military control over atomic research to civilian officials.) In addition, in 1948 Father John Cronin, a Catholic priest, served as an intermediary between FBI agent Ed Hummer and Republican Congressman Richard Nixon and forwarded on a daily basis to the congressman the latest results of the FBI's investigation of Alger Hiss. (In his memoirs, Nixon obliquely confirms Cronin's account of Hummer's helpful role.) During prosecution of the Hiss case, moreover, FBI agents secretly investigated the tax returns of a Hiss defense expert and during an interview with Hiss's stepson Timothy Hobson FBI agents revealed their knowledge of Hobson's homosexual activities in an effort to deter him from testifying during the trial. As part of a broader effort to discredit Hiss, in 1946 FBI Director Hoover independently leaked to conservative congressmen and reporters, and urged Secretary of State James Byrnes to "contact several key men in the House and Senate" and advise them of derogatory information about Hiss. During 1948, moreover, FBI Assistant Director Louis Nichols, and other Bureau officials, developed a very close working relationship with HUAC. A December 9, 1948, FBI memorandum records a December 8, 1948, conversation between Nixon and several FBI agents at which the congressman "voluntarily stated . . . that he had worked very close [sic] with the Bureau and with [FBI Assistant Director Louis] Nichols during this past year on this matter." Indeed, these relations were so close that immediately after learning on December 2, 1948, that Chambers claimed to have additional documents, Nixon telephoned Nichols and (as recorded in a December 2, 1948, memorandum) "specifically urged that we [the FBI] not tell the Attorney General that we were told of this information as the Attorney General undoubtedly would try to make it impossible for the Committee [HUAC] to get the documents. [Nixon] also asked that the Bureau not look for the documents." Nichols continued by reporting that Nixon's strategy was to exploit the documents during December 18, 1948, HUAC hearings and that his purpose in calling "was merely to apprise the Bureau so that the FBI would not be caught off base." Hoover agreed with the recommendation and directed Nichols: "Do so—let me know result."[21]

FBI investigative findings, moreover, were not episodically leaked to the media. FBI officials instead consciously cultivated the news media. Cognizant of the potential political vulnerability of these leaks, FBI officials identified "friendly" media sources who would both keep this relationship confidential and support the bureau's interests. Conservative *Chicago Tribune* correspondent Walter Trohan benefited directly from this relationship. The FBI provided Trohan with classified information from bureau files, and Trohan soon developed a close friendship with Hoover, who later pointedly complimented the *Tribune* reporter for articles defending the bureau, "alerting Americans to the real issues we have got to face up to," and criticizing the New Left.

Other favored reporters—Jimmy Ward, Frederick Woltman, Gene Strul, Walter Winchell, Paul Harvey, Ray McHugh, Thomas Lubenow, Lyle Wilson, Ralph de Toledano, Karl Hess, George Sokolsky, Ed Montgomery, Charles McHarry—were leaked derogatory information about prominent radicals, the National Lawyers Guild, the New Left, the Nation of Islam, the Black Panthers, and the Socialist Workers party.

In addition, FBI officials in the Crime Records Division began in January 1940 to compile a "not to contact list" of "those individuals known to be hostile to the Bureau." Hoover specifically ordered on January 4, 1950, that "each name" on the list (including the historian Henry Steele Commager, "personnel of CBS," and former Secretary of the Interior Harold Ickes) "should be the subject of a memo."[22]

In another program instituted in 1950, FBI agents compiled "summary memorandums" on all "newly elected" U.S. congressmen. (This FBI coverage was extended in 1960 to nonincumbent gubernatorial and state attorney general candidates.) Information for these memorandums was acquired from "public sources" and "any other information that [field offices in that congressional district or state] had in their files." When this program was publicly compromised, FBI officials then claimed that these memorandums had been compiled for "liaison" purposes in order to "sell" hostile U.S. congressmen on "liking the FBI." This information enabled FBI officials to know and thereby assist its congressional friends. Former FBI Assistant Director William Sullivan, moreover, disputed this explanation. Whenever derogatory information about a member of Congress or his family was obtained, Sullivan maintained, that congressman was visited by an FBI agent. Advised that derogatory information had been incidentally acquired during the course of another FBI investigation, the congressman would be assured that this information would be closely guarded. In its effect, Sullivan observed, this FBI visit forewarned the congressman not to challenge the bureau.[23]

The FBI's political reporting was further refined during Eisenhower's administration. Briefing Assistant to the President Sherman Adams on FBI investigative procedures and authority on January 27, 1953, the FBI director thereafter forwarded FBI reports to Special Assistants to the President Dillon Anderson, Robert Cutler, Gordon Gray, and Secretary to the President Thomas Stephens.

A vast number of these reports could be characterized as political intelligence; they described how a variety of groups or individuals sought to influence national policy or challenge administration positions. Thus, Hoover advised the Eisenhower White House of the purely political or social contacts of Bernard Baruch (November 7, 1955), Mrs. Eleanor Roosevelt (February 13, 1958), U.S. Supreme Court Justice William Douglas (April 21 and 27, 1953), and a deputy assistant to the president (June 6, 1958). On April 11, 1958, Hoover forwarded FBI files on thirteen individuals (including Norman Thomas, Linus Pauling, and Bertrand Russell) who had brought suit to stop nuclear testing and on April 21, 1955, the advance text of a speech of a prominent labor leader. The White House was also advised of the role of the United Auto Workers at a NAACP conference (March 5, 1956), the decision of two New Jersey congressmen to sign a civil rights petition to the attorney general (March 7, 1956), the plans of the NAACP Leadership Conference on Civil Rights to ascertain certain U.S. senators' views on civil rights (March 5, 1956) and what resulted from these contacts (March 6, 1956), and Mrs. Eleanor Roosevelt's planned reception for the head of a civil rights organization (February 13, 1958). Hoover also forwarded to AEC officials information obtained through a bug of the office of nuclear scientist J. Robert Oppenheimer (whose security clearance was under review) including privileged conversations between the scientist and his attorney.[24]

Liberals and radicals were not the sole targets of FBI intelligence reports which were apparently responsive to White House requests. Because the Eisenhower administration's foreign policy and loyalty procedures were sharply criticized by right-wing extremist groups, Hoover submitted reports on the political activities of Gerald L. K. Smith, the Christian Nationalist Crusade, Carl McIntyre, the International Council of Christian Churches, Robert Welch, and the John Birch Society. FBI documents specifically record that during the 1950s the FBI collected and forwarded to the White House information on the John Birch Society because of the society's "scurrilous attacks on President Eisenhower and other high Government officials."[25]

The Eisenhower administration took Hoover's reports seriously; particularly because they comported with its conservative anti-Communist conception of expansive internal security threats. In contrast to the procedures followed during Truman's tenure, Hoover's reports were forwarded to those White House aides (Gordon Gray and Robert Cutler) serving as liaison with the National Security Council. Moreover, the administration devised formal procedures to ensure consideration and appropriate action on these reports.

During the Eisenhower years, FBI officials refined and extended their earlier efforts to influence official policy and public opinion. A broad program was initiated during the 1950s to collect information on dissident activities under the code name COMINFIL (or Communist Infiltration). Information obtained through these investigations was regularly forwarded to the White House. Covering "the entire spectrum of the social and labor movement" (including youth, women, legislative, civil rights, agricultural policy, and political activities), this program was justified as "fortify[ing]" the government against "subversive pressures." The steady decline in Communist membership and influence did not result in COMINFIL's termination.

Hoover's 1956 attempt to smear the civil rights movement exemplifies his conservative objective to equate dissident politics with subversive activities. On February 1, 1956, the FBI director advised National Security Council Executive Secretary J. Patrick Coyne of his willingness to brief the Cabinet on communism and the civil rights movement. Hoover followed up on this suggestion and in early March submitted a series of reports to the White House describing Communist influence and the NAACP's Senate lobbying efforts. Hoover's efforts were rewarded; on March 6, 1956, the FBI director was invited to brief the Cabinet on Communist "influence" in the civil rights movement. Hoover recounted the NAACP's legislative strategy and the activities of Southern governors and U.S. congressmen opposed to integration. Appealing obliquely to the administration's partisan interests, the director emphasized that "the Communist Party plans to use [an NAACP-sponsored] conference to embarrass the Administration and Dixiecrats who have supported it, by forcing the Administration to take a stand on civil rights legislation, with the present Congress. The Party hopes through a rift to affect the 1956 elections."[26]

FBI practices were not simply defensive. In 1960, as in their 1949 report on the National Lawyers Guild, FBI officials attempted to discredit criticism of the bureau's civil rights record. The specific target of the bureau's ire was the Knoxville (Tennessee) Area Human Relations Council. Responding to the council's accusation that the bureau practiced racial discrimination, FBI officials conducted name checks on the council's board of directors. The results of this investigation, including derogatory highly personal and political information, were forwarded to Attorney General William Rogers on May 25, 1960.[27]

FBI Director Hoover's ready access to the White House and ability to bypass the attorney general could not continue unmodified during the Kennedy years. The brother of the president, the new attorney general had also served as John Kennedy's campaign director in 1958 and 1960. As early as February 13, 1961, moreover, the attorney general apprised White House aides of his intent "to keep abreast of any contacts between the White House staff and his Department." "Any" meetings of White House aides with representatives of the department "will go through the Attorney General first." Second, under President Kennedy's reorganization of the NSC, Cabinet officials would coordinate all national security matters with other departments or agencies. By National Security Council Action Memorandum 161 of June 9, 1962, the attorney general was specifically assigned "primary" responsibility in the internal security area, including supervision of the Interdepartmental Intelligence Conference (IIC) and the Interdepartmental Committee on Internal Security (ICIS). (Both the IIC and the ICIS had formerly been under the supervision of the National Security Council staff.) On August 17, 1962, Robert Kennedy informed department and agency heads that all IIC and ICIS reports or recommendations "will now be directed to me as Attorney General."[28]

Ever the astute bureaucrat, Hoover adapted quickly to this altered circumstance and diverted his lines of communication through the attorney general. The FBI director, moreover, sought to sustain his political influence by a policy of educating the attorney general. Thus, in a January 10, 1961, letter to the attorney general-designate ostensibly outlining the FBI's responsibilities and mission, he once again employed the Communist bogey tactic to sustain FBI influence over national policy: alarmingly warning of the "overall activities of the Communist Party, USA (CPUSA) and its threat to the internal security of the United States."[29] Hoover's subsequent reports (dating at least from February 1961) to the Justice Department and the White House continually reiterated this theme, emphasizing particularly the subversiveness of elements of the civil rights movement and groups critical of the administration's Cuban policy. Initially, Hoover's reports troubled administration officials who were concerned only over how to respond to this information.[30]

Continuing to be solicitous to the White House, the FBI director was more sensitive to the delicacy of this reporting relationship. (Partisan information could not be volunteered through the attorney general—were Hoover to have done so the attorney general would have been compelled to consider the scope and intent of FBI investigative efforts.) In contrast to the Truman and Eisenhower years, accordingly, Hoover scaled down the FBI's political reporting.

The FBI director also sought to deter a more assertive administration role by indirectly suggesting the extent of FBI files. Thus, Hoover volunteered to the attorney general (on February 10, 1961) a summary of FBI file materials on a prominent entertainer having close ties with the president, (on February 6, 1961) background information on a woman who had told an Italian newspaper she had once been engaged to marry John Kennedy, (on February 8, 1961) background information on a woman who claimed that the president's daughter would enroll in her nursery school, and (on November 20, 1963) information from a bureau "source" regarding a group's plans to publish allegations about the president's personal life.[31]

At the same time, Hoover acted to service White House needs; for one, intensifying FBI coverage of right-wing organizations between 1960 and 1963—a practice begun during Eisenhower's administration. In January 1963, Hoover instructed all SACs how to categorize "Klan-type and hate-type organizations." Revealing a distinctive sensitivity to the limits of the bureau's investigative authority and to the political conservatism of FBI agents, Hoover requested full information on "the formation and identities" of " 'rightist or extremist' groups." The FBI director admonished:

> You are reminded that anticommunism should not militate against checking on a group if it is engaged in unlawful activities in violation of Federal statutes over which the Bureau has investigative jurisdiction.
>
> Investigations of groups in this field whose activities are not in violation of any statutes over which the Bureau has jurisdiction are not to be conducted without specific Bureau authority. A request for authority to investigate such a group should include the basis for your recommendations regarding violation.

The administration's concern to contain the political right had sharply increased following conservative leaders' virulent attacks on the Kennedy administration's support of desegregation (and civil rights in general), foreign policy decisions, and dismissal of Otto Otepka as the Department of State's chief security officer.* President Kennedy, indeed, singled out "right-wing extremist groups" as early as November 16, 1961. Queried during a November 29, 1961, press conference about the "sizable financial contributions to the sort of right-wing extremist groups you criticized last week," Kennedy observed that the government could not act so long as these contributions were within the law and were not intended to divert taxable income to nontaxable purposes. The president then added that "I'm sure the Internal Revenue Service examines that."

Whether or not intended as a subtle suggestion, Kennedy's statement was immediately acted upon by IRS Assistant Commissioner (Compliance Division) William Loeb. In a November 30, 1961, memo, Loeb called Audit Division Director Dean Barron's attention to the president's remark and ordered him to secure from IRS attorney Mitchell Rogovin a list of organizations to be examined for possible tax liability. Rogovin complied and forwarded a partial list of eighteen organizations which *Newsweek* and *Time* had publicly identified in December 4 and 8, 1961, news stories. The Fair Play for Cuba Committee (the leading left-wing critic of the Kennedy administration's Cuban policy) was added to this list on January 18, 1962. As one result, six large corporate taxpayers who allegedly were financial backers of New York and San Francisco extremist groups were tax-audited by the IRS in March 1962. Three large New York and San Francisco extremist groups were also targeted, in part because they "appear to be the largest and most publicized groups." Rogovin forwarded another list of eighteen "left of center" organizations to the Audit Division the next month, which he had obtained from the FBI.

This program was not simply an independent IRS effort to further the administration's partisan objectives. A March 1962 letter, for one, indicates that Attorney General Robert Kennedy had been formally briefed about this program and that Special Assistant to the Attorney General John Seigenthaler had previously expressed interest in the tax status of right-wing groups. In addition, President Kennedy showed confidential IRS records on some business leaders to at least one journalist.

In 1963 the White House received status reports on this IRS program. Expressing renewed interest in targeting left-wing and right-wing organizations, the president then emphasized the desirability of quick investigative action in view of scheduled (January 19, 1964) congressional hearings. An October 1, 1963, deadline was set at a series of meetings of IRS, White House, and Justice Department officials. A list of twenty-four organizations was prepared—nineteen of which were categorized as right-wing. Significantly, when White House interest waned following President Kennedy's assassination, the IRS's examination of the tax-exempt status of organizations targeted because of their ideological orientation and the FBI's investigations of right-wing extremist groups decreased in intensity.[32]

*The Otepka dismissal is discussed in greater detail in chapter seven.

Already disturbed by the large steel corporations' decision to raise steel prices in the wake of recent wage contract settlements, the Kennedy administration learned through news stories that Bethlehem Steel Company president Edmund Merkin had advised Bethlehem stockholders that a price increase was not needed to cover the wage settlement. On April 11, 1962, Attorney General Robert Kennedy requested that the FBI interview Merkin and the three (Associated Press, *Wall Street Journal*, and *Wilmington (Delaware) Evening Journal*) reporters who had filed this story to ascertain the facts. The results of this investigation were needed for a White House meeting the next day. The FBI complied; interviewing these individuals either late at night or early the next morning.[33]

The Kennedy administration's secrecy and "national security" concerns resulted in other requests for FBI investigations. Suspecting that a *Newsweek* article about U.S. planning in Germany had been based on classified information, President Kennedy directed the attorney general to ascertain the source of the leak. Robert Kennedy in turn informed Hoover of this presidential concern on June 27, 1961. Immediately initiating an investigation, the FBI established that the offensive article had been written by Lloyd Norman and, without the attorney general's prior authorization, wiretapped the reporter's residence. (Informed of the tap on June 28, the attorney general formally approved it on June 30. The tap was discontinued on July 3, when Norman left on vacation.) The resultant investigation, ironically, failed to prove that Norman had obtained classified information. Indeed, the FBI officials concluded that an intelligent reporter could have written the article without such access.[34]

New York Times military correspondent Hanson Baldwin's July 1962 article about Soviet missile systems again led the administration to conclude that classified information had been leaked. The FBI director was once again approached. The FBI then wiretapped Baldwin's and his secretary's residences (the reporter on June 28, 1962, and his secretary on June 27, 1962) without the attorney general's prior authorization (in the case of the secretary even advance knowledge). Subsequently authorized, the wiretaps continued until August without disclosing any leaks.[35]

Arguably, these taps were instituted for "national security" reasons. To accept this rationale, however, involves acceptance of the administration's right to control the flow of information to the public and thereby to determine the parameters and timing of the debate over U.S. foreign policy. While we do not know what information the FBI forwarded to the White House as the result of these "unproductive" taps, at least one other FBI wiretapping project which Attorney General Kennedy authorized proved politically beneficial to the Kennedy administration.

In February 1961, U.S. intelligence officials learned that officials of a foreign government "intensely desired passage of a sugar bill," then under consideration by the U.S. Congress, containing quotas favorable to their country. Because the administration was employing economic leverage to pressure that government to institute democratic reforms, it was keenly sensitive to the policy ramifications of congressional approval of quotas favorable to that government. At the same time, FBI officials informed the administration that this foreign government's representatives unlawfully might have paid or provided gifts to influence certain congressmen and Agriculture Department officials. In response, on February 16, 1961, Attorney General Robert Kennedy authorized FBI wiretaps on three Agriculture Department officials, the secretary to House Agricultural Committee Chairman Harold Cooley, and a lobbyist registered as a foreign agent of this government. On his own authority, Hoover instructed the New York field office to bug Representative Cooley's hotel room upon learning that the influential legislator was to meet representatives of this foreign government in New York City in mid-February 1961.

The FBI investigation uncovered possibly unlawful efforts to influence legislation but no evidence of payoffs. FBI investigative reports to the White House also contained purely political information. Such information included that the lobbyist was "working on the Senate and has the Republicans all lined up," had seen two "additional" members of the House Agriculture Committee, and had concluded that one opposed his position and the other was neutral and possibly supportive; and that Representative Cooley "had been fighting over the Rules Committee and this had interfered with his attempt to 'organize.' "

Whether or not this investigative program's purpose had not been merely political, the wiretaps were terminated when the Senate passed the administration-supported bill. (This measure granted to the president discretionary authority to deny quotas to countries for foreign policy reasons.) An FBI memo of April 14, 1961, on a meeting between Attorney General Kennedy and Courtney Evans (FBI liaison with the attorney general) quotes Kennedy as commenting that "now the law was passed he did not feel there was justification for continuing this extensive investigation." Another (December 22, 1966) intra-FBI assessment concluded that the taps "undoubtedly . . . contributed heavily to the Administration's success" in securing passage of desired legislation. This evaulation comported with the White House's contemporary appraisal. In a June 23, 1962, memorandum to McGeorge Bundy (the president's national security adviser) and to Myer Feldman (a key White House aide), CIA analyst William Brubeck reported the reaction of the foreign government: "The action taken by the House of Representatives in passing the House Agricultural Committee bill (the Cooley bill) has created a furor in the [deleted foreign country]." That country's officials were disturbed that the legislation "would be disastrous" to their country's "economy."

Accordingly, when advised by the FBI in June 1962 that representatives of this same foreign government might again seek to influence congressional sugar quota deliberations, Attorney General Kennedy authorized the FBI to tap five foreign establishments, the offices of Surrey & Karasik (a Washington, D.C. law firm representing that foreign country), and the residence of the House Agriculture Committee clerk.[36]

FBI officials did not simply respond to White House investigative requests but continued in their efforts to shape national policy. These officials regularly forwarded to the president and the attorney general information obtained through the bureau's COMINFIL program about radical and dissident political activities (detailing efforts to influence policy).[37]

Following the April 17, 1961, Bay of Pigs invasion, on April 27, 1961, Hoover specifically ordered all special agents in charge to report on all pro- and anti-Castro activities which might lead to violence or revealed foreign influence. These reports were then forwarded to the White House. Hoover's concern was not simply to prevent violence; the FBI director pointedly protested that the Fair Play for Cuba Committee had demonstrated "the capacity of a nationality group organization to mobilize its efforts in such a situation so as to arrange demonstrations and *influence public opinion*" (emphasis added).[38]

This attempt to smear dissident political movements as subversive extended beyond the debate on foreign policy. In a July 25, 1961, report to the president's National Security Adviser McGeorge Bundy—titled "Status of Internal Security Programs"—Hoover claimed that the Communist party had "attempted" to exploit "racial disturbances" in the South and had "endeavored" to "pressure" various government officials "through the press, labor unions, and student groups."[39]

These concerns intensified as civil rights organizations (notably the Southern Christian Leadership Conference, SCLC) succeeded in dramatizing the plight of Southern blacks and the more abhorrent features of segregation. Hoover depicted efforts to break down segregationist barriers as essentially subversive as early as 1956 and on September 20, 1957, ordered FBI agents: "In the absence of any indication that the Communist Party has attempted, or is attempting, to infiltrate this organization [the SCLC], you should conduct no investigation in this matter. However, in view of the stated purpose of this organization, you should remain alert for public source information concerning it in connection with the racial situation."[40]

Public source information had not sufficed to establish a Communist link; accordingly in October 1962 Hoover ordered a COMINFIL investigation of the SCLC and its president, Martin Luther King, Jr. Even these investigations failed to develop such hard evidence. To avert any challenge to the FBI's authority for these investigations, the FBI director regularly advised the various attorneys general of Communist efforts to influence Reverend King and the SCLC. Even before instituting this COMINFIL investigation the FBI had (in March 1960) listed Reverend King on its Reserve Index. King was included on the Reserve Index despite the bureau's conclusion that it lacked evidence "on which to base a security matter inquiry." Like others on the FBI director's independently established Reserve Index, King's major sin derived from his prominence, his ability to influence public opinion, and his holding political views to the left of the FBI director. Hoover's frustration over King's influence and respectability in time led to a July 27, 1962, order that FBI field offices search their files for "subversive" information about King and submit this information to the bureau in Washington in reports "suitable for dissemination."[41]

Information about the radical activities of two of King's advisers was uncovered and was immediately transmitted to the attorney general. (Conservative reporters, congressmen, and state officials soon learned this information; whether their knowledge was acquired independent of or through the FBI cannot presently be ascertained.) Emphasizing these advisers' Communist background, Hoover's reports created a real dilemma for the administration. Because the charges were serious, the administration could not ignore them; not responding could prove to be politically harmful insofar as the civil rights movement was already attacked as being communistic. Whether or not they were the recipients of FBI information, Southern segregationists (most notably Mississippi Governor Ross Barnett and Alabama Governor George Wallace) widely publicized charges about Reverend King's subversive associations.

Political considerations partially explain administration officials' hesitancy to challenge either the highly political nature of FBI reporting on King or the breadth of FBI investigations. Significantly, FBI reports went beyond allegations of Communist influence and described Reverend King's plans, activities, and strategy to pressure the administration to implement desegregation. And when civil rights organizations criticized FBI racial practices, the FBI responded by attempting to discredit these groups. For example, FBI officials first dismissed a November 1962 Southern Regional Council report criticizing bureau practices as slanted and biased and then instituted a search of FBI files for derogatory information about the report's author.

The FBI's effort to discredit King and the civil rights movement reached a crescendo in August 1963. That month FBI Director Hoover submitted a detailed report to the attorney general repeating the subversive charge and disparaging King's moral character. This report and the bureau's more general effort to challenge King's loyalty and morals eventually forced the attorney general to authorize in October 1963 FBI wiretaps on the civil rights leader's office and residence. Kennedy had considered ordering a wiretap in July 1963; but questions about the risk (particularly the harmful reaction to discovery) had then contributed to his decision not to authorize the tap.

At the same time, when assessing how to respond to the forthcoming March on Washington civil rights demonstration, on August 23, 1963, the FBI's Domestic Intelligence Division prepared a lengthy report summarizing the bureau's extensive investigations of the March. There was no evidence that Communists "actually initiated" or "controlled" the March; Communists, however, did participate. The next day, the Domestic Intelligence Division submitted a lengthier, sixty-seven–page seport to Hoover. This report essentially concluded that extensive Communist party "efforts" to exploit the discontents of black Americans had heretofore been an "obvious failure." Responding sharply to this conclusion challenging his own political biases, the FBI director sarcastically cited earlier reports that Cuban leader Fidel

Castro and his followers were not Communists. The ever-sensitive Intelligence Division bureaucrats quickly grasped this signal. In a series of reports, summarized best by an August 30, 1963, observation that "the Director is correct," these FBI officials rejected their earlier conclusions and described Reverend King as "the most dangerous Negro of the future in this Nation from the standpoint of communism, the Negro, and national security." It would be "unrealistic," the Intelligence Division officials now concluded, to "limit ourselves" to "legalistic proofs or definitely conclusive evidence" that the Communist party wielded "substantial influence over Negroes which one day could become decisive."

The quest for evidence to confirm a preordained conclusion ensured an intensive FBI investigation of King and the civil rights movement in general. Committed to proving that the civil rights movement threatened the national security, these conservative bureaucrats also sought derogatory personal information about King which could then be used to discredit the respected civil rights leader. This effort was formally recommended in January 1964; FBI Assistant Director William Sullivan then proposed that the "true facts" about King's activities and character should be leaked "at some propitious point in the future." On the one hand, in widely publicized April 1964 testimony before a House Appropriations Subcommittee, Hoover charged that "Communist influence" in the "Negro movement" was "vitally important." On the other hand, in November 1964 high-level FBI officials offered personally damaging information about Reverend King to the news media—this even included transcripts of the tapes of the FBI's electronic surveillance of King's home and hotel rooms. FBI memorandums, moreover, confirm that these bugs were planted in King's hotel rooms for the express purpose of obtaining personal information which could then be disseminated through the news media.

FBI officials also attempted to influence press reporting on the civil rights leader. In November 1964 a board chairman with whom FBI officials had good contact was approached to ensure that his magazine not publish an article favorable to King. In addition, FBI officials (1) in March 1967 prepared and distributed press conference questions to "friendly" journalists, (2) in May 1965 gave "background" information to at least one wire service, and (3) in May 1967 discussed plans on how to sabotage King's political campaign should the civil rights leader decide to run for national office.[42]

Ironically, the FBI's intensive surveillance of King resulted more from fortuitous circumstances than a conscious policy decision. Exploiting Attorney General Brownell's vague directive but without his prior authorization, since 1954 the FBI installed microphones. Robert Kennedy did not alter this procedure; indeed, his supervision of FBI bugging practices was even looser. When approving the King wiretap in October 1963, Kennedy required that this authority be evaluated after thirty days. The assassination of the attorney general's brother, the president, sidetracked this evaluation. If the attorney general had forgotten this October stipulation, Hoover did not remind him, nor did the FBI director seek the attorney general's further advice or direction. Kennedy's successor as attorney general, Nicholas Katzenbach, only learned of the FBI's microphone surveillance of King in mid-1965 when devising procedures to ensure tighter supervision over FBI electronic surveillance.

The attempt to discredit King had not been a personal vendetta of Hoover's. King's criticisms of FBI practices admittedly explain the intensity of Hoover's and other FBI officials' animosity toward the civil rights leader. Their principal concern about King in fact stemmed from political conservatism. For Hoover and other senior FBI officials, King's reliance on demonstrations to challenge segregation laws and traditions, use of extralegal methods to effect change, and successes either when motivating Southern blacks to adopt a more activist stance or when compelling Northern liberal leaders to support civil rights legislation confirmed the civil rights leaders' subversive proclivities and dangerousness to the national security.[43]

In effect FBI officials defined subversion in political terms: adherence to dissident/radical politics, willingness to challenge the status quo, support for disruptive change. Although not identifying all dissenters with communism, FBI officials, nonetheless, advocated investigating any individual to ascertain the extent (if any) of Communist influence. These were not fact-finding investigations but attempts to prove Communist direction and disseminate this information to the White House or "friendly" sources in the media or the Congress. Should such information not be acquired, further investigations would then be justified on the premise that Communists supported or might seek to influence these movements. These political objectives explain the similarity in both the methods and objectives of the FBI's formal COINTELPROs and the FBI's harassment and attempts to discredit King.[44]

This quest to link dissent with communism, not surprisingly, determined how internal security bureaucrats responded to the campus and non-campus unrest precipitated by the Johnson administration's decision to escalate U.S. involvement in the Vietnam civil war. FBI field offices were ordered as early as August 17, 1965, to intensify investigations of college "subversive activity," particularly the teach-in movement. Then, when public protest intensified, FBI agents were instructed to ascertain the possible "subversive backgrounds" of any individual associated with so-called free universities. FBI officials also initiated a formal investigative program, code-named VIDEM, to ascertain Communist influence on Vietnam demonstrations. Beginning on March 26, 1968, FBI field offices were required to forward all information pertaining to demonstrations "for immediate dissemination to the White House and other interested Government agencies, followed by . . . routine dissemination to the intelligence community."[45]

FBI activities were not confined to compiling reports for executive officials. In November 1965, the FBI San Francisco office anonymously mailed fifty copies of an article, "Rabbi in Vietnam Says Withdrawal Not the Answer," to "convince" members of the Vietnam Day Committee "of the correctness of U.S. foreign policy in Vietnam." Earlier that year, FBI officials leaked FBI file material on Communist efforts to "subvert" the administration's

Vietnam policy to conservative congressmen and actually prepared a speech for one congressman and then helped disseminate this speech to presidents of American universities and private corporations. On June 1, 1967, moreover, the FBI's Chicago field office proposed that a possible "Peace Party" ticket in the 1968 election be disrupted by "effectively tabbing as communists or as communist-backed the more hysterical opponents of the President on the Vietnam question in the midst of the presidential campaign would be a real boon to Mr. Johnson." To effect this political objective, on May 22, 1968, all FBI field offices were ordered to forward information to FBI headquarters "on a continuing basis" for "prompt . . . dissemination to the news media . . . to discredit the New Left movement." The information sought included New Leftists' political associations, Communist links, and personal life. "Every avenue of possible embarrassment," Hoover counseled, "must be vigorously and enthusiastically explored."[46]

Given their conservative anticommunism, FBI officials not surprisingly readily responded to White House requests for information about the administration's critics and independently sought to equate antiwar dissent with subversion. On April 27, 1965, CIA Director John McCone forwarded a report to President Johnson's Special Assistant for National Security, McGeorge Bundy, stating that the Chinese and the North Vietnamese believed that continuance of antiwar dissent within the United States might necessitate that the U.S. withdraw troops from Vietnam. In turn, Bundy solicited information from FBI Director Hoover concerning the Communists' role in criticizing the administration's Vietnam policy. That same day Hoover forwarded to the White House various columnists' press clippings attributing antiwar agitation to the Communists. (Undoubtedly, some of these news stories had been based on FBI leaks.) At an April 28 meeting with Hoover, President Johnson thanked the FBI director for the clippings, reaffirmed his concern over anti-Vietnam criticism, and (according to Hoover's memo of this meeting) claimed that Communists "no doubt" were "behind the disturbance." The president then requested, Hoover's memo continued, that the FBI director "brief at least two Senators and two Congressmen, preferably one of each Party, on the [anti-Vietnam] demonstrations so that they might in turn not only make speeches upon the floor of Congress but also publicly." The FBI director agreed and further informed the president that the Students for a Democratic Society ("largely infiltrated by communists and which has been moving into the civil rights situation which we know has large communist influence") planned to hold demonstrations in eighty-five cities from May 3 to May 9, 1965.

Immediately after this meeting, senior FBI officials were ordered to prepare a memorandum on the SDS which could "be used publicly by prominent officials of the Administration whom the President intends to send in various parts of the country to speak on the Vietnam situation." Without precluding "a good strong memorandum," care should be taken, the FBI director emphasized, so that "there will be nothing to uncover our informal coverage." FBI officials complied, and that same day submitted the requested memorandum to Bundy. At the same time, bureau coverage of SDS and other antiwar critics intensified and later that month and early the next month FBI officials briefed sympathetic congressmen.[47]

FBI Director Hoover also complied with other White House requests. The bureau conducted name checks on individuals who had signed telegrams criticizing the administration's Vietnam policy or who had written letters reprinted in the *Congressional Record* commending U.S. Senator Wayne Morse's criticism of the president's Vietnam policy. Hoover forwarded reports on the Committee for a SANE Nuclear Policy, why antiwar demonstrations were able to demonstrate during the president's speaking engagements, and on the author of a play critical of the president. The FBI responded to even more politically sensitive White House requests and prepared a "blind memorandum" (disguising the bureau's involvement) on seven U.S. senators who in 1967 criticized the president's decision to resume bombing of North Vietnam. Forwarding whatever derogatory information the FBI had in its files concerning these senators, FBI Director Hoover attempted to prove (in the language of a May 1967 memorandum to presidential aide Marvin Watson) that "the Communist Party and other organizations are continuing their efforts to force the United States to change its present policy toward Vietnam."[48]

In contrast to criticism of the Korean War, Vietnam War dissent was not confined to an uninfluential radical minority or to conservatives insisting upon a more militant anti-Communist policy and included respected liberal congressmen. As their impact increased, these congressional dissenters soon shifted from delivering speeches on the floor of the Congress to attempting to influence public opinion through televised hearings on the administration's Vietnam policy. The White House responded emotionally to this more powerful political dissent. Desiring to employ what had heretofore been a successful political ploy of equating dissent with disloyalty, the Johnson White House sought to confirm its liberal critics' "subversive" origins or associations.

In February 1966, White House officials requested that the FBI monitor the televised hearings of the Senate Committee on Foreign Relations and then draft a memorandum ascertaining whether Senator William Fulbright and other Senate critics "were receiving information from Communists." On February 24, 1966, Hoover wrote White House aide Marvin Watson and enclosed a memorandum "in response to your request" "which sets out the Communist Party line concerning some of the issues raised during the Senate Foreign Relations Committee hearings on U.S. policy in Vietnam." Senators Fulbright's and Morse's statements were correlated with either those of Communist leaders or Communist party publications. There was no indication, Hoover conceded, that the Communist party "or any other subversive groups" furnished materials to the senators and thereby prompted their statements.

Having failed to document Communist influence, the president sought alternative confirmation. During a March 14, 1966, meeting with FBI Assistant Director Cartha De Loach (personal liaison between the bureau and the White House), Johnson requested that the bureau "constantly keep abreast of the actions of representatives of [specified foreign officials] in making contacts with Senators and Congressmen and any citizens of a prominent nature. The President stated he strongly felt that much of this protest concerning his Vietnam policy, particularly the hearings in the Senate, had been generated by [certain foreign officials]."

Relying on the bureau's "national security" electronic surveillance of targeted foreign embassies, on March 22, 1967, FBI officials submitted to the White House a sixty-seven–page chronological survey of the contacts of U.S. senators, congressmen, and congressional staff members with these embassies during the period July 1, 1965, through March 17, 1966. A second survey of congressional (members and staff) contacts with these embassies was prepared and submitted to the White House on May 13, 1966. Thereafter until January 1969, biweekly additions were regularly prepared and transmitted to the White House.[49]

To confirm the "subversive" character of antiwar dissent, federal intelligence agencies also radically expanded their surveillance activities. In August 1967 President Johnson directed the CIA "to find out [the] extent to which Soviets, Chicoms [Chinese Communists] and Cubans are exploiting our domestic problems in terms of espionage and subversion." Johnson repeated this request in November 1967, motivated then by the October 1967 Pentagon demonstrations. Although the president had requested a study of the "International Connections of the U.S. Peace Movement," the CIA instead instituted a far-reaching program, Operation CHAOS, focusing on domestic organizations (in clear violation of the CIA's legislative charter which prohibited any "internal security" role). CIA Director Richard Helms from the start ordered CIA agents to secure information on the "illegal and subversive" connection between U.S. activists and "communist, communist front, or other anti-American and foreign [sic] elements abroad. Such connections might range from casual contacts based merely on mutual interest to closely controlled channels for party directives."[50]

These initial CIA investigations failed, however, to confirm espionage and foreign direction. Accordingly, to further the president's (and the agency's) political objectives, CIA investigations sought to establish mutual interest or mere contact between dissidents and foreign government. Not "foreign elements abroad" but citizen activists within the United States were the focus of these investigations. Because of the illegality of these investigations, CIA operatives were cautioned to safeguard this project's "high sensitivity."

Supplementing the CIA's and the FBI's domestic surveillance activities of the 1960s, the Army also began investigating domestic dissent. This Army surveillance effort initially had begun developing intelligence which might prove helpful should U.S. troops be assigned to handle racial conflict in the South. Following the outbreak in 1965 of Northern urban racial riots and then the use of federal troops during the 1967 and 1968 riots, this Army intelligence effort expanded. Responding also to the increase in antiwar dis-

sent and reflecting the military intelligence community's conservative political biases, in November 1967 the Army chief of staff formally approved
"continuous counterintelligence investigations" to obtain information on the
"civil rights movement," the "influence" of "subversive personalities, groups
or organizations" "on urban populations" in promoting civil disturbances,
and on "dissident elements" and the "anti-Vietnam/anti-draft movement."
In February 1968 Army investigations further expanded to include "prominent persons" either "friendly" with or "sympathetic" toward leaders of
disturbances or who held similar attitudes toward distrubances.[51]

Intelligence bureaucrats sought evidence to confirm their preconceived
equation of dissent with disloyalty and, in this sense, were committed to
implementing a sophisticated McCarthyite politics. These politically inspired
investigations could not succeed, and not simply because the Vietnam War
had become increasingly unpopular and "national security" contentions had
commanded less deference in the vastly different political atmosphere of the
1960s. For one, their obsessive anticommunism isolated intelligence officials
from current realities; the crude repetition of "the Communists are coming"
charges during the late 1960s not only carried less weight but proved counterproductive. Furthermore, and ironically, unlike an earlier generation of radicals the youthful dissidents of the 1960s were less vulnerable to such taint in
part because of the effective decimation of the Old Left by the purges of the
late 1940s and 1950s. Most New Left leaders had had no opportunity to
associate with Communists or to develop foreign connections as had their
Popular Front counterparts of the 1930s and 1940s.

The Johnson White House's uses of the intelligence community were not
confined to the Vietnam War debate. Both before and after 1965, for example, the White House requested and FBI officials conducted name checks
on authors of books critical of the Warren Commission Report, prominent
newsmen (including NBC commentator David Brinkley, AP reporter Peter
Arnett, nationally syndicated columnist Joseph Kraft, *Life* magazine Washington bureau chief Richard Stolley, *Chicago Daily News* Washington bureau
chief Peter Lisagor, and *Washington Post* executive Ben Gilbert), Treasury
and Justice Department officials responsible for wiring a witness during an
investigation of former Johnson aide Bobby Baker, the Senior Citizens
Golden Ring Council, those invited to Lynda Bird Johnson's Student Committee, and presidential scholars. Because of the political sensitivity of these
requests, in March 1967 White House aide Marvin Watson advised Cartha
De Loach, the FBI's liaison with the White House, that in the future "he
and the President" wanted Hoover to address all such reports to a lower
level White House staff member. Watson apprised De Loach of the "reason
for this change": this staff member "did not have the direct connection with
the President that he [Watson] had and, consequently, people who saw such
communications would not suspicion [*sic*] that Watson or the President had
requested such information or were instructed in such information." When
requesting an FBI investigation of those officials responsible for wiring Bobby
Baker (and specifically whether they had any connection with Robert Ken-

nedy), White House aides warned De Loach that the president wanted no
written record of this request. De Loach ignored this condition, believing
that "any instructions we received from the White House should be a matter
of record."[52]

Politically inspired investigations, however, were a two-way street. On
April 19, 1965, FBI Director Hoover requested Attorney General Katzenbach's authorization to wiretap the editor of an anti-Communist newsletter. Information about FBI loyalty/security investigations might have been
leaked, Hoover advised Katzenbach, and publication of this "classified information" constituted "a danger to the internal security of the United States."
The attorney general approved this and Hoover's June 7, 1965, request to
wiretap a Washington attorney with whom this editor was in close contact.[53]
The most blatant political use of the FBI, however, occurred during the
1964 general election campaign.

In June 1964 FBI officials on their own initiative established a special
desk within the Domestic Intelligence Division to supervise "the intensification of communist influence in racial matters." Because civil rights was
the "primary domestic issue on the political front today," F. J. Baumgardner
(chief of the bureau's Internal Security Section) rationalized, the bureau
should be able to respond to requests from "both sides" in the Senate debate
over the Civil Rights Bill of 1964 concerning "communist penetration into
the racial movement." FBI Director Hoover endorsed Baumgardner's recommendation, affirming further that the FBI must "stay ahead" owing to "the
complex political situation in an election year where civil rights and social
disturbances will play a key role in campaign efforts and possibly election
results."[54]

This conviction about the civil rights movement's subversive character
partially explains FBI officials' willingness to accede to an administration
request that the FBI cover the Democratic National Convention in Atlantic
City, New Jersey. Ostensibly, the White House was requesting FBI assistance
of the Secret Service to preclude civil disruption of the convention. Cartha
De Loach would head a thirty-man FBI squad at the convention. Relying on
either agent or informant infiltration of the principal civil rights organizations, electronic surveillance of key civil rights leaders (a wiretap of Reverend Martin Luther King's hotel room and a bug of the headquarters of
the Student Non-Violent Coordinating Committee), or agents posing as reporters, this FBI squad intensively covered the civil rights movement and
kept "the White House fully apprised of all major developments during the
Convention's course."

The reports of this FBI squad were not confined, however, to civil disturbances. A key political issue, and one threatening to undercut the president's convention strategy of retaining the civil rights movement's support
without unduly antagonizing Southern political leaders, involved the convention voting and representational status of the Mississippi Freedom Democratic Party (MFDP). Civil rights leaders sought to ensure the seating of
MFDP on the grounds of the regular Mississippi delegation's election impro-

prieties and the MFDP's loyalty to the national ticket. From De Loach's reports, the White House acquired privileged insights into MFDP supporters' strategy and tactics. Thus, De Loach advised the White House that civil rights leaders were prepared "off the record" to compromise; identified the delegates or personalities whom civil rights leaders were courting; emphasized the need to control admissions into the convention hall to prevent MFDP delegates from displacing regular Mississippi Democrats completely; and outlined how the civil rights leaders' planned to ensure White House neutrality in the contest involving the MFDP. Not surprisingly, the White House (in the language of one De Loach memorandum) "considered this [information] of prime importance." The FBI squad also kept Robert Kennedy under close surveillance, reporting the former attorney general's contacts with civil rights leader Martin Luther King, Jr.[55]

FBI officials' responsiveness to President Johnson's political requests went beyond this special squad. Apparently responding to the arrest of White House aide Walter Jenkins for a homosexual act, on October 26, 1964, White House aide Bill Moyers requested a special FBI file check of Republican presidential candidate Barry Goldwater's Senate staff employees. FBI officials used the U.S. Senate telephone directory as a guide, identified fifteen Goldwater staff members, checked these names against bureau files, and uncovered derogatory information on two. This information was hand-delivered by De Loach to the White House on October 28 along with a letter that FBI files contained no derogatory information on the other thirteen.[56]

This helpfulness precipitated a 1968 initiative (emanating not from noncandidate President Johnson's office but from candidate Vice President Hubert Humphrey's). The intensification of antiwar dissent had contributed to deep division within the Democratic party symbolized best by the antiwar liberals' support for Senators Eugene McCarthy's and Robert Kennedy's presidential candidacies. At first, the objectives of these Democratic liberals had been to raise the Vietnam issue in the campaign and to prevent Lyndon Johnson's renomination. The president's dramatic March 1968 announcement complicated this strategy and also paved the way for Humphrey's candidacy. Disdaining the primaries and an open debate over the Vietnam War, Humphrey instead relied on the support of established party leaders and the White House's power and influence. This campaign strategy in effect intensified already deep political divisions, inevitably ensuring a tumultuous convention. As well, many liberal and radical groups already planned to attend the Chicago Democratic National Convention; the liberals seeking to demonstrate their opposition to President Johnson's Vietnam policy and the radicals hoping also to disrupt convention proceedings.

Apprised of the FBI's Atlantic City effort by Marvin Watson (then postmaster general but formerly Johnson's principal White House aide), Bill Connell (Vice President Humphrey's executive assistant) telephoned Hoover on August 7, 1968. FBI Associate Director Cartha De Loach took Connell's phone call owing to the fact that Hoover was out of town. "Some time ago," Connell informed De Loach, Johnson had advised Humphrey of the FBI's special squad at the 1964 convention. "The President allegedly told the Vice President," De Loach's memorandum to Hoover on this call recorded, "the FBI had been of great service to him and he had been given considerable information on a timely basis throughout the entire convention." Connell wanted to discuss this matter personally with Hoover and hoped "the [FBI] Director would extend to him [Humphrey] the same service during the forthcoming Democratic National Convention in Chicago." Advising Connell that Hoover would return to Washington the next week, De Loach also assured Humphrey's assistant that the FBI's "Chicago Office is well prepared to gather intelligence and pass such intelligence on to appropriate authorities during the convention." De Loach recommended against sending a special squad to Chicago "which would entail considerable funds." The executive assistant to the vice-president should be told, De Loach advised Hoover, that "full preparations have been made by the [FBI] Chicago Office to handle the matter of passing intelligence to the Vice President and his aides" and that a special squad was unnecessary.

Having advised De Loach of his intent to call Hoover, Connell did so on August 15. As Hoover's memo of the conversation recorded, Connell stated "that he had talked to the Vice President about the team I [Hoover] sent into the convention area in 1964 that was so helpful . . . [Connell] was hoping perhaps I might be able to do the same thing for the Vice President out in Chicago and have my men directly in contact with him (Connell)." Hoover advised Connell that Marlin Johnson, the special agent in charge of the Chicago office, had already been contacted and that Connell should convey to him whatever "assistance" he desired which the Chicago SAC "will take care of." Hoover immediately briefed Marlin Johnson on this (Connell's) request for "an operation similar to what we did down at Atlantic City at the last Democratic Convention when Mr. [Lyndon] Johnson was running for renomination. I [Hoover] explained that he [Connell] would like to have us furnish the same type of information and be in contact with him, Connell, on any so-called intelligence we might get." Hoover continued: "We are not going to get into anything political but anything of extreme action or violence-contaminated we want to let Connell know." Stressing the need for thorough coverage, Hoover reported having again contacted Attorney General Ramsey Clark "about his failure to approve wire taps out there [Chicago] but I didn't think it will have any effect but that we want to cover it as well as we can."[57]

Hoover's criteria for distinguishing between "anything political" and "anything of extreme action or violence-contaminated" are not clear. The FBI director seemed apprehensive only that the bureau was being formally asked to perform a clearly partisan function. Given his direct knowledge of the 1964 operation, De Loach's memorandums suggest that the distinction in any event was not sharp. FBI officials, moreover, might not have serviced candidate Humphrey's political interests in 1968; this failure stemmed not from intent but from the reforms instituted by Attorney General Nicholas Katzenbach in 1965 (and further clarified by Attorney General Ramsey Clark in 1967) requiring the attorney general's prior authorization for all FBI wiretap and microphone installations.

Hoover's concluding cryptic comment referred to quite independent March/April/June 1968 requests that the attorney general authorize a wiretap on the National Mobilization Office for Demonstrations at the National Democratic Convention. When recommending this wiretap to the FBI director, FBI Domestic Intelligence Division officials Charles Brennan and William Sullivan advised Hoover on March 8, 1968, that the Mobilization Committee had rented an office to be used "in connection with activities aimed at influencing the course of the [Chicago] National Democratic Convention . . . [and] to disrupt the Convention." A wiretap, Brennan and Sullivan emphasized, would "enable us to furnish the appropriate Government officials with the plans of those groups which will try to embarrass or even inflict bodily harm on the President or other high Government officials."

When submitting the wiretap request on March 11, 1968, Hoover notified the attorney general that a leader of the Students for a Democratic Society had rented the targeted office, that a series of meetings had been held at this office to discuss the committee's plans for the convention, and that Communist party members attended these meetings and agreed to subsidize this office. Because this office was to be the "focal point" for demonstration and disruption efforts, a wiretap on this office would "provide extremely valuable information regarding the plans of these groups to disrupt the National Democratic Convention," furnish advance notice of "any possible activity" endangering "the safety of the President or other high Government officials," "greatly enhance" bureau coverage, "and could possibly forewarn of their [these groups] future activity that may be detrimental to the Government's interests." Attorney General Clark rejected this request. "At this time," Clark advised Hoover on March 12, 1968, "there has not been an adequate demonstration of a direct threat to the national security. Should further evidence be secured of such a threat, or re-evaluation desired, please resubmit." "Other investigative activities," the attorney general added, "should be undertaken to provide intelligence necessary to the protection of the national interest."

Domestic Intelligence officials were encouraged to resubmit this wiretap request by the attorney general's expressed willingness to reconsider. Disagreeing that there "has not been" an adequate demonstration of a national security threat, in a March 21, 1968, memorandum Brennan cited the announced plans of "various new left, civil rights, and subversive organizations" (the SDS, the Communist party, and the National Mobilization Committee were identified) to stage "massive demonstrations" at the convention. "There appears to be enough evidence that these demonstrations will represent a substantial threat to the national security," Brennan added. Hoover approved. Acknowledging Clark's reason for his earlier denial—"there has not been an adequate demonstration of a direct threat to the national security"—in a March 22, 1968, memorandum Hoover cited FBI-developed information "to date" that "a massive effort is being made by various new left groups, civil rights organizations and subversive organizations" to mobilize 200,000 to 500,00 demonstrators "with the objective of disrupting the Convention and forcing the Government to utilize Federal troops to contain the demonstrators." Hoover stressed the SDS's, the Communist party's, and the National Mobilization Committee's participation and earlier involvement in the October 1967 Pentagon demonstration. A wiretap, the FBI director reaffirmed, "would provide information regarding the plans and activities of the key organizers of these demonstrations which cannot be obtained from any other source."

Clark did not even respond to this request. Not dissuaded, on April 24, 1968, Hoover submitted another follow-up memorandum. A wiretap would enable the bureau to "fulfill its responsibilities in this important area of our work." The FBI director requested a response "as promptly as possible." Again the attorney general did not respond.

Still not dissuaded by the attorney general's obvious opposition, on June 6, 1968, Domestic Intelligence Division officials Brennan and Sullivan urged resubmission. Martin Luther King's and Robert Kennedy's assassinations confirmed "the ugly atmosphere of discontent" pervading "the American political scene today"; "extremist elements" might resort to violence to publicize their "causes and achieve their objectives at the convention." The bureau's intelligence responsibilities could not be fulfilled without wiretapping; the attorney general's "delay" in "acting on" this request was clearly "inexcusable." Hoover reiterated these arguments in his June 7, 1968, authorization request: "it is absolutely essential that we utilize every means at our disposal to effect this coverage needed to enable us to keep the intelligence community advised of the day-to-day plans and activities of these dissident groups. . . . I would be derelict if I did not express my concern over the delay encountered in connection with [this] request for a telephone surveillance. This delay has unquestionably caused a loss of valuable intelligence information in a most critical area of our operations." Once again, Clark did not respond to this politically motivated request.[58] As one by-product, the bureau could not forward to the White House in 1968 the political intelligence it had provided in 1964.

Demonstrations did occur at the Democratic National Convention, and the Chicago police brutally contained one of these. Incensed by critical press comments of "undue force" and the likely increase of charges of police brutality, on August 28, 1968, Hoover ordered the Chicago special agent in charge to obtain and promptly submit to FBI headquarters "all possible evidence that would disprove these charges." The head of the Chicago field office was ordered to "consider measures by which cooperative news media may be used to counteract these allegations." No steps should be taken, however, without "Bureau authority." Hoover's political objectives were clearly set forth in his letter's concluding paragraph:

Once again, the liberal press and the bleeding hearts and the forces on the left are taking advantage of the situation in Chicago surrounding the Democratic National Convention to attack the police and organized law enforcement agencies. When actual evidence of police brutality is not available, it can be expected that these elements will stretch the truth, and even manufacture incidents to indict law enforcement agencies. We should be mindful of this situation and develop all possible evidence to expose this activity and to refute these false allegations.

Committed to shaping public opinion and disproving "false allegations," on September 3, 1968, Hoover ordered all special agents in charge (and not only the Chicago SAC) to debrief all sources who had covered the convention and "collect all possible information regarding provocations of police by demonstrators [at the Chicago convention] and the reaction of police thereto." Emphasizing the "urgent need of this information," Hoover demanded a response by September 4.[59]

Hoover's concerns about the undesirability of dissent were not singular. President Johnson suspected that prominent American conservatives in combination with South Vietnamese officials were subverting his efforts to negotiate a peace settlement in Vietnam in the hope that Richard Nixon's election to the presidency would result in a harder U.S. negotiating stance. Through J. Bromley Smith, executive secretary of the National Security Council, he directed FBI Director Hoover on October 30, 1968, to institute physical surveillance of Mrs. Chennault and on October 29, 1968, to wiretap the South Vietnamese embassy and institute physical surveillance of South Vietnamese officials. (A conservative Republican, Mrs. Chennault had good contacts with South Vietnamese officials.) The wiretap request was approved by the attorney general on the same day it was submitted, October 29. FBI officials never requested Clark's authorization to wiretap Mrs. Chennault (perhaps suspecting that the attorney general would deny this request as he had their earlier requests to wiretap the Mobilization Committee's office). Records produced from these electronic and physical surveillances were forwarded directly to Smith at the White House but not to the attorney general. If intended to uncover "foreign intelligence" information, the South Vietnamese embassy wiretap also provided information on Mrs. Chennault's activities. An October 30, 1968, FBI memorandum conceded the political sensitivity of this project: "It was widely known that she was involved in Republican political circles and, if it became known that the FBI was surveilling [sic] her this would put us in a most untenable and embarrassing position." Accordingly, special filing procedures were devised to "protect and secure" this surveillance against discovery and preclude any adverse affect on the presidential election race.

On November 13, 1968, at President Johnson's request, the FBI checked Albuquerque, New Mexico, toll call telephone records to ascertain whether

Republican vice-presidential candidate Spiro Agnew had called Mrs. Chennault or the South Vietnamese embassy on November 2, 1968. (There was
no record of such calls.) Again at the White House's request, the bureau
verified candidate Agnew's Albuquerque arrival and departure times.[60]

Surely an attempt to postpone peace negotiations so that a new Administration could institute a different foreign policy line can hardly be considered a "national security" matter, it was comparable more to the Republican
senatorial effort of 1968 to deny President Johnson's right to replace U.S.
Supreme Court Chief Justice Earl Warren. The Johnson administration's
Vietnam policy had emerged as a crucial issue in the 1968 presidential campaign. Conservative as well as liberal and radical candidates then forcefully
challenged Johnson's policy decisions and advocated alternative courses.
Although Republican candidate Richard Nixon never clearly defined his
position—claiming to have a secret plan to end the Vietnam war which
he refused to outline ostensibly to avoid complicating President Johnson's
negotiation efforts—consistently since 1965 he had condemned the Johnson
administration's "soft" policy toward North Vietnam and indecisive conduct
of the war. Not without reason, South Vietnamese officials could well conclude that their cause would be better advanced if Nixon were elected.
(In 1948, the Chinese Nationalists had similarly counted on the victory of
another Republican presidential candidate, Thomas Dewey.)

Elected president in 1968 partially because his "law and order" campaign
theme effectively exploited widespread public antipathy to antiwar and civil
rights dissent, Richard Nixon also inherited the legacies of White House
political uses of the intelligence community and, reciprocally, of the independent political initiatives of internal security bureaucrats. Nonetheless,
Nixon was not a prisoner of the past, but an enthusiastic proponent. While
president, his actions might not have differed substantively from those of
his predecessors. For a variety of reasons (notably, his commitment to
exploiting the "internal security" issue, his expansive "national security"
conceptions, and his penchant for centralized, decision-making), this
conservative anti-Communist moved well beyond their precedent in his rationalization of existing procedures, specifically employing the intelligence
community for partisan objectives, or in his use of White House staff and
specially hired functionaries (rather than the FBI, CIA, or NSA) to perform
specific surveillance tasks. The more important changes instituted by Nixon,
accordingly, were administrative in nature, intended to increase the more
efficient use of the federal intelligence bureaucracy.

For one, on November 26, 1969, all special agents in charge (SACs) were
briefed on a newly instituted program—code-named "Inlet." Refining an
ongoing practice (as described by a February 2, 1973, bureau memorandum)
wherein the FBI had regularly "furnished various presidents and attorneys
general important intelligence matters on an individual basis," Inlet "consoli-
date[d] this information into one document" to provide the president and
attorney general "high-level intelligence data in the internal security field . . .

on a continuous basis." By formalizing and centralizing an earlier, *ad hoc* program, Inlet ensured a steady flow of political information to the Nixon White House and thereby permitted quicker action. The breadth of the information contained in these letters was outlined in Hoover's order that SACs forward all "information obtained in connection with our investigations which has the qualities of importance and timeliness necessary to secure the President's interest and to provide him with meaningful intelligence for his guidance." The FBI director enumerated the "suggested types of information (not all inclusive)": "security related" information; current or pending internal security cases; intelligence trends; foreign intelligence; and, (5) " 'inside' information concerning demonstrations, disorders or other civil disruptions which is of more than local signficance; (6) items with an unusual twist or concerning prominent personalities which may be of special interest to the President or the Attorney General." These instructions should be implemented "immediately." "It is absolutely essential," Hoover ominously warned, "that a steady flow of quality intelligence data be received. . . . Your submissions will be closely followed at the Bureau to insure this matter is receiving proper emphasis and attention."

Improvement in the bureau's communications capabilities in time enabled FBI field offices to teletype intelligence data directly to the White House. After 1969, FBI officials also compiled a series of special reports summarizing "extremist activities," their objective being to draw the White House's attention to these FBI submissions. For both technological and policy reasons, Acting FBI Director W. Mark Felt advised all FBI field offices on December 26, 1972, that "the 'Inlet' program has, for all practical purposes, been rendered obsolete." Termination of Inlet, however, Felt added, "does not relieve the responsibility of all offices to be alert for the intelligence data specified in referenced letters and to submit this information in a timely manner by teletype and in a form suitable for dissemination."[61]

During the three years of the Inlet programs between 1969 and 1972, the White House received reports detailing its political adversaries' strategies, planned activities, and background. The FBI reported on the activities of prominent personalities (a newsman, an entertainer, New Left professors, SCLC president Ralph Abernathy, ADA chairman Joseph Duffy, and anti-Nixon film producer Emil D'Antonio) and of dissident organizations (opponents of the antiballistic missile system and of a business corporation's war production policies, the women's liberation movement, conferences sponsored by church and civil liberties groups on amnesty for Vietnam veterans, and the 1970 Earth Day rally). Mistakingly interpreting a White House name check request, the FBI instead initiated a full background investigation of CBS correspondent Daniel Schorr. (When this investigation became publicly known, the White House falsely claimed that Schorr had been under consideration for an executive appointment.) On July 27, 1970, in response to White House aide Larry Higby's request, the FBI resumed reporting on congressional contacts (staff and congressmen) with foreign embassies. Ironically, the initiative for this resumption (FBI documents record) came from Senator Henry Jackson's complaint to the president about "an increase in [foreign nation] interest on Capitol Hill."

The FBI also advised the White House of the activities of the Reverend Carl McIntyre's right-wing American Christian Action Council after this conservative group began to criticize the Nixon administration's policies. (When forwarding its report on May 25, 1972, Acting FBI Director W. Mark Felt claimed that the American Christian Action Council fell within FBI/Secret Service guidelines on groups "potentially dangerous because of background, emotional instability or activity in groups engaged in activities inimical to the U.S.") The bureau's criterion for reaching this conclusion was decidedly political; the only activities of the council which were reported were its plans to demonstrate, enter law suits in school busing cases, oppose "Nixon's China trip," and support "public school prayer" constitutional amendments.[62]

The formulation of the Huston Plan also derived from the administration's desire to centralize power in the White House and to red-bait its critics.[63]

Partly responding to these White House pressures and partly to second-level FBI Domestic Intelligence Division and Inspection Division officials' desires, FBI domestic surveillance programs were concurrently intensified. For one, in September 1970, FBI Director Hoover rescinded his 1967 order requiring that FBI informants be at least twenty-one years old. Hoover also authorized more intensified investigations of the pro-Cuban Venceremos Brigade, the Students for a Democratic Society, the Black Student Union, black nationalist organizations, and antiwar activists associated with Father Philip Berrigan. Hoover specifically ordered Domestic Intelligence Division officials to exploit fully present "unparalleled opportunities" and expand domestic surveillance:

> You should bear in mind that the attitudes and instructions expressed by the President, the Director, and many of the legislators in Congress, have been to curtail the militant actions and violent activities on the part of a significant group of young people in the United States today. The thinking of the Supreme Court of the United States with its several recent changes may be along the lines of suppressing the activities of those who openly espouse the overthrow of democratic authority in the United States. In addition the Internal Security Division of the Department of Justice has been specifically enlarged and strengthened to deal with these matters.[64]

Nixon administration officials also attempted to rationalize Internal Revenue Service procedures for targeting individuals and organizations for tax audits. Responding to pressures both from the Permanent Investigations Subcommittee of the Senate Committee on Governmental Operations and from Nixon administration personnel, on June 25, 1969, IRS officials established a special division (the Special Service Staff—SSS). Not empowered to initiate tax audit investigations, the SSS could ensure that field investigations concentrate disproportionately on "dissident" and "extremist" individuals and organizations (whom it was able to identify through information obtained from the FBI, the CIA, and the Internal Security Division of the Department of Justice). IRS Commissioner Russell Thrower outlined this effort's rationale in a June 16, 1969, memo for the files: "The President has expressed . . . great concern over the fact that tax-exempt funds may be supporting activist groups engaged in stimulating riots both on the campus and within our inner cities." To ensure that this message was understood, White House aide Tom Charles Huston advised Roger Barth, an assistant to the IRS commissioner, that the "president is anxious to see some positive action taken against these organizations which are violating existing regulations, and I [Huston] have assured him [Nixon] that I will keep him advised of the efforts that are presently underway."

The SSS first gathered and analyzed information on anti-Nixon groups and individuals to ascertain if a tax issue were involved and then forwarded this information to the field offices for appropriate action. Some eight thousand individuals and three thousand organizations were targeted, including the Ford Foundation, the National Urban League, Common Cause, the John Birch Society, Senators Charles Goodell and Ernest Gruening, and syndicated columnists Joseph Alsop and Jimmy Breslin. An unsigned July 24, 1969, IRS memorandum conceded this project's political sensitivity and the need to confine knowledge of it to those who "need to know": "We certainly must not open the door to widespread notoriety that would embarrass the Administration or any elected officials. This is one of the reasons why we are not publicizing this Committee except as such publicity may be necessary within the Service."[65]

Because of its commitment to obtain derogatory information about its domestic critics, the Nixon White House also encouraged CIA officials in February 1969 to expand the CIA's recognizably illegal surveillance of domestic political activities. CIA Director Helms conceded illegality in his February 18, 1969, report to Nixon's national security adviser Henry Kissinger:

> In an effort to round out our discussion of this subject [youthful dissent and the sources of its support], we have included a section on American students. This is an area not within the charter of this Agency, so I need not emphasize how extremely sensitive this makes the paper. Should anyone learn of its existence it would prove most embarrassing for all concerned.

The White House responded to this admission of illegality by requesting additional information from the CIA, information which could confirm foreign control over domestic dissident groups. When the agency could not prove foreign Communist support for the antiwar movement, White House aide

Tom Charles Huston on June 20, 1969, urged the CIA deputy director to continue these investigations but under a revised definition of foreign control—"support" should be "liberally construed" to include Communist "encouragement."[66]

Indifferent to the law and committed to centralizing decision-making, the Nixon White House no longer relied exclusively on the FBI for political investigations. Instead, White House aides recruited their own investigative personnel who were paid through unexpended 1968 Nixon campaign funds. In June 1969, White House aide John Ehrlichman directed John Caulfield and John Ragan* to wiretap nationally syndicated columnist Joseph Kraft's Washington, D.C. residence. The decision to wiretap Kraft ostensibly derived from the president's concern about leaks of classified information to the media. Ehrlichman's White House investigative squad in time conducted a number of other politically motivated investigations. Among them were Senator Edward Kennedy's involvement in the Chappaquiddick incident, another 1971 investigation of the Massachusetts senator, and investigations of Senator Edmund Muskie, his New York State campaign manager, *Newsday* reporter Robert Greene, and more generally of prominent Democrats. When liberal Republican Paul McCloskey challenged Nixon for the Republican presidential nomination in 1972, Caulfield and Ulasewicz were assigned responsibility to monitor McCloskey's New Hampshire primary efforts. Posing as a reporter, Ulasewicz uncovered information about the McCloskey campaign's financial support, appeal to students, and general organization. These reports were forwarded to Attorney General John Mitchell on December 6, 1971 (at the time Mitchell had not resigned from the attorney generalship to assume formal direction of Nixon's campaign effort).[67]

The Ehrlichman squad did not constitute the Nixon White House's sole venture into the field of intelligence. In July 1971 another investigative group, again funded out of unexpended campaign funds, was established. The specific impetus to this decision stemmed from Nixon officials' dissatisfaction with the FBI investigation of Daniel Ellsberg's role in releasing the classified Pentagon Papers to the press. Although the bureau's investigation into the criminal charges had been thorough, it had not uncovered (at least to the satisfaction of White House aides) sufficient derogatory information which could be used to discredit Ellsberg's activities. Housed in the White House under the direction of Egil Krogh, the so-called Plumbers group relied on the contacts of White House aides E. Howard Hunt and G. Gordon

---

*A former New York City policeman, Caulfield had been appointed to the White House staff in March 1969 to serve as liaison with law enforcement agencies. His principal responsibility, however, became to conduct secret investigations at Ehrlichman's direction. A former FBI electronic surveillance expert, Ragan had been employed as a security consultant during Nixon's 1968 campaign and continued to serve as a consultant to the White House staff. Caulfield also recruited another New York City policeman, Anthony Ulasewicz, for this White House squad.

Liddy with the Cuban-American community to recruit experienced personnel to conduct a break-in of the office of Ellsberg's California psychiatrist, Dr. Lewis Fielding.[68]

At the request of the Nixon administration, the FBI instituted surveillance of columnist Joseph Kraft, possibly supplementing that directed by John Ehrlichman. Following Kraft's departure for Europe, on instructions from FBI Director Hoover and White House aide John Ehrlichman, FBI Assistant Director William Sullivan went to Paris to closely observe the columnist's activities and arranged for a French security agency to bug Kraft's hotel room. Reports based on these surveillances were sent directly to Hoover between July 3 and July 7, 1969, but because of their political sensitivity—under the bureau's Do Not File procedure—they were neither serialized nor filed with other bureau documents. As such, Sullivan's reports were rendered irretrievable through a normal file search. (In July 1971 Sullivan delivered these reports to Assistant Attorney General Robert Mardian along with other sensitive documents pertaining to FBI investigations for the Nixon White House.) The FBI once again investigated Kraft from November 5 through December 12, 1969.[69]

The Kraft surveillance was based on partisan considerations although not in the sense that information was sought on the administration's political adversaries. Committed to controlling the flow of information to the public, Nixon White House officials were motivated to ensure secrecy in their conduct of foreign policy (and particularly involving the administration's Indo-Chinese military and political initiatives). This quest for secrecy was partly predicated on "national security" considerations—disclosure could complicate, if not frustrate, delicate negotiations. These officials also feared that a public debate could undermine specific tactics and/or strategies.

In early 1969, the Nixon administration began bombing North Vietnamese supply lines and positions in Cambodia. Given the Cambodian government's formal neutrality and the strong domestic opposition (particularly in the Congress and the liberal press) to any further escalation of the Vietnam War, this bombing decision entailed major political risks. Elaborate procedures, devised to ensure secrecy, included falsifying military reports by identifying these bombing raids as having occurred over Vietnam and false information or testimony by administration officials responding to specific congressional inquiries. Despite these elaborate precautions, however, in a May 9, 1969, byline story *New York Times* Pentagon reporter William Beecher wrote that "according to Nixon administration sources" American B-52 bombers had raided several Vietcong and North Vietnamese supply dumps and base camps in Cambodia. The Cambodian government had not protested these raids, Beecher further claimed, but was cooperating with American and South Vietnamese military officials.[70]

Incensed by this revelation, the president's national security adviser Henry Kissinger telephoned FBI Director Hoover that morning to request that the bureau (according to Hoover's memorandum on that call) "make a major effort to find out where [the Beecher story] came from." Twice more that day, Kissinger telephoned Hoover to request that additional Beecher stories be investigated and that this investigation should be handled discreetly "so no stories will get out." On the basis of preliminary FBI inquiries, Hoover that afternoon informed Kissinger that national security aide Morton Halperin could have leaked this information to Beecher. Halperin, Hoover reported, "knew Beecher and that he [Hoover] considered [Halperin] a part of the Harvard clique and, of course, of the Kennedy era." Hoover's memorandum continued: "Dr. Kissinger said he appreciated this very much and he hoped I would follow it up as far as we can take it and they will destroy whoever did this if we find him, no matter where he is."

Whether the White House or the Bureau suggested wiretapping and whether individuals were targeted at Kissinger's or Hoover's initiative remain in dispute. In 1969, Nixon was aware of Kennedy administration wiretaps of newsmen to uncover leaks of "national security" information and of the Johnson administration's political use of the FBI. (The White House transcripts of Oval Office conversations disclose that when John Dean reported this information to the president in 1973, having learned of some of these activities from former FBI Assistant Director William Sullivan, President Nixon evinced no surprise. More than likely, Nixon had been briefed about those FBI activities by Hoover in 1969.) Indisputably, the White House pressured Hoover to discover the source of this leak, emphasized the seriousness of the matter, and ordered Hoover to "follow it up as far as we can take it."[71]

If Nixon had any reservations about wiretapping his own aides (and this is doubtful), his knowledge of these earlier precedents convinced him that such surveillance was legitimate. Attempting at a later August 22, 1973, press conference to undercut the sharp protests precipitated by disclosures of these taps, he cited the Kennedy wiretaps and, tongue in cheek, commented, "I think they were perfectly justified and I'm sure that President Kennedy and his brother, Robert Kennedy, would never have authorized them, unless he thought they were in the national interest."

The FBI eventually wiretapped seventeen individuals—seven National Security Council staff members (Morton Halperin, Anthony Lake, Winston Lord, Helmut Sonnenfeldt, Daniel Davidson, Richard Moose, and Richard Sneider), three Defense and State Department employees (Richard Pedersen, William H. Sullivan, and Robert Pursley), three White House aides (William Safire, John Sears, James McLane), and four Washington reporters (Beecher, *New York Times* reporter Hedrick Smith, *London Sunday Times* reporter Henry Brandon, and CBS correspondent Marvin Kalb). The Halperin tap was installed on May 9, three others on May 12, and the other thirteen taps between May 20, 1969, and December 14, 1970.

An expansive "national security" conception might have underlaid the original decision to tap Halperin and other national security aides.[72] Almost immediately, however, White House officials recognized these wiretaps' political sensitivity. In striking contrast to the Kennedy wiretaps (in part undoubtedly because of 1965 and 1967 administrative procedures governing wiretapping), precautions were taken to preclude discovery of this electronic surveillance. These wiretap records were not filed with other "national security" wiretaps and were not listed on the FBI's ELSUR Index. In addition, other Justice Department rules were not followed: the requirement that the attorney general either approve all wiretaps or reauthorize any tap extending beyond ninety days. Kissinger's national security aide Alexander Haig might later deny having formally ordered that no record be maintained of this surveillance. Haig then admitted "making very clearly [the point] . . . the extreme sensitivity of this thing, and the avoidance of unnecessary paperwork, which would make this program subject to compromise."

Having forwarded political information to the White House since 1940, FBI officials not surprisingly exploited these taps to apprise the Nixon White House of significant political developments. Hoover's reports advised the White House on various congressmen's legislative positions on questions of interest to the administration, the administration's congressional and Democratic critics' proposed speeches and articles, one NSC consultant's intention to resign "to work with Senator Fulbright (D-Arkansas) in opposing the war," and highly personal information about the seventeen individuals and their families (including mental difficulties and sexual activities). In at least one instance the White House acted on the basis of intelligence acquired from these taps. On December 12, 1969, Hoover reported former Secretary of Defense Clark Clifford's plans to write a magazine article criticizing President Nixon's Vietnam policy. "We are in a position to counteract this article in any number of ways," White House aide Jeb Magruder advised White House aides H. R. Haldeman and John Ehrlichman on January 15, 1970. In turn, Ehrlichman stressed to Haldeman: "This is the kind of early warning we need more of—your game planners are now in an excellent position to map anticipatory action." Haldeman concurred, adding: "I agree with John's point. Let's get going."

Providing otherwise unobtainable political intelligence, the wiretaps were continued well beyond their original purpose of ascertaining the source(s) of the leak. Thus, the tap on Halperin was not discontinued even after FBI Assistant Director William Sullivan reported on July 8, 1969: "Nothing has come to light that is of significance from the standpoint of the leak in question." Halperin's phone continued to be tapped even after he left the NSC staff (and thereby had no access to classified documents) and joined Democratic presidential aspirant Senator Edmund Muskie's staff. This tap (and another on National Security Council aide Anthony Lake who also joined Muskie's campaign staff) provided valuable political intelligence. For example, the FBI reported on December 22, 1970, that former President Lyndon "Johnson would not back Senator Muskie for the Presidency as he intended to stay out of politics." Not surprisingly, then, these wiretap reports ceased being sent to Henry Kissinger after July 1970 and instead were forwarded to the president's chief White House adviser H. R. Haldeman. When Sullivan later advised Assistant Attorney General Robert Mardian (and Mardian in turn advised Nixon) that FBI Director Hoover might use these tap records to blackmail the president, Mardian was ordered to hand-deliver these records immediately to the White House for safe-keeping purposes.[73]

The same political considerations which had led to the decisions to wiretap these seventeen individuals and then to isolate these wiretap records from other "national security" wiretap files also applied to a wiretap on Charles Radford II. A navy yeoman assigned as staff assistant to the Joint Chiefs of Staff, Radford was suspected of having leaked classified information to syndicated columnist Jack Anderson. (Anderson had described a private Nixon-Kissinger conversation in a December 1971 article.) As a result of the Radford tap, other State and Defense Department employees would be wiretapped and the purpose of this surveillance soon acquired another rationale: to establish how Pentagon officials had acquired highly classified National Security Council documents. The Radford tap records were also filed separately from other FBI records. A February 20, 1973, FBI memorandum specifically stated: "Our records [on this Radford tap] have been kept completely isolated from other FBI records, and there are no indices whatsoever relating to this project." Bureau officials' responses to the Supreme Court's June 19, 1972, ruling (in *U.S. v. U.S. District Court*) that warrantless "domestic security" wiretaps were unconstitutional particularly highlights this wiretap's special character. The Radford tap, a subsequent June 14, 1973, FBI memorandum reported, was not discontinued on June 19, 1972, "as others falling under the *Keith* [a reference to *U.S. v. U.S. District Court*] rule had been, since we were waiting for a decision from the White House." This tap was terminated on June 20, 1972, when the advice from the White House was received.[74]

Although authorization was more easily obtained during Nixon's presidency, FBI officials, as they had earlier, sought authority to wiretap dissident organizations and individuals. These included the Jewish Defense League headquarters (the league opposed Soviet treatment of Jewish citizens, and its activities could adversely affect the Nixon administration's efforts to normalize U.S.-Soviet relations), the Washington offices of the New Mobilization Committee to End the War in Vietnam (the committee had assumed a leadership role in organizing an anti-Vietnam War demonstration), black nationalist organizations, and a New Left organization (in part because its members intended to "take the radical politics they learned on the campus and spread them among factory workers").[75]

From Franklin Roosevelt's to Richard Nixon's administrations, and spanning thirty-five years, then, the FBI unhesitatingly forwarded political intelligence information to the White House. The vast majority of these reports might have been unsolicited; nonetheless, no president ordered Hoover to cease submitting these reports. Nor did FBI Director Hoover merely service unstintingly the incumbent administration's political needs. Hoover's reporting, rather, was based on the conservative political purpose of discrediting dissident and radical politics; in this sense, the criteria governing FBI (but also CIA, IRS, and military intelligence) investigations were ideological and not partisan.[76] For one, Hoover sought to ensure an adverse White House reaction (if not hostility) to liberal or radical efforts. Those few instances when Hoover reported on conservative organizations or individuals involved nonrespectable, extremist fringe groups whose activities challenged accepted national norms. FBI officials might not have always shaped official policy and public opinion. The very attempt to do so constituted an abuse of power.

Secrecy, the attendant deference to "national security" claims and the acceptance of "executive privilege" permitted had enabled internal security bureaucrats to resort to actions which at the time could not have been justified on their merits and indirectly paved the way for the abuses of power and abandonment of constitutional principles that became the hallmark of Richard Nixon's presidency.

Chapter Seven

Loyalty and Security Programs

Authorized explicitly by presidents since 1940, federal employee loyalty/ security programs were based on the premise that federal employment was a privilege and not a right. Their ostensible purposes, moreover, were to avert espionage, sabotage, or "subversion" by denying disloyal or "potentially" disloyal persons federal employment—otherwise government secrets might be stolen or the "national security" compromised.

On the face, these loyalty/security programs appear reasonable and their intent responsible. In fact, however, they were based on standards and administered in a manner greatly exceeding legitimate purposes. The standards for ascertaining disloyalty, loyalty, or suitability (the very language of successive presidential directives of 1947, 1951, and 1953) were vague to the extreme. Investigations, moreover, were not confined to applicants or incumbent employees—the Civil Service Commission, the FBI, the CIA, and the NSA also maintained extensive files on American citizens on the premise that at some future date these individuals might apply for federal employment. The FBI in particular exploited its investigative responsibility under these programs to initiate far-ranging investigations of dissident organizations. Furthermore, because dismissal under these programs was based not on overt actions confirming disloyalty but suspicion deriving from the individual's political associations, activities, or beliefs, a so-called attorney general's list of "subversive" organizations was devised. Established ostensibly to assist these officials responsible for administering the loyalty/security programs, this "subversive" organization list was almost immediately publicly released and was employed by conservative congressmen, right-wing organizations, private corporations, and state and local governments as a litmus test for judging the loyalty of particular individuals. As a result, after the 1940s, prominent entertainers were blacklisted, individuals were denied employment by private corporations or public schools, and the loyalty of federal employees was challenged publicly during congressional hearings.[1] Last, ambitious politicians—most notably Senator Joseph McCarthy—somehow obtained the FBI investigative files compiled under this program— which contained innuendo and rumor—and then used them to "prove" administration laxity toward a serious internal security problem.

The federal loyalty/security programs, in effect, profoundly influenced national politics by seemingly confirming the existence of a serious internal security problem and indirectly legitimizing a rather crude form of red-baiting. After 1947, American politics moved sharply to the right, although the nature of Cold War conservatism differed substantively from traditional conservatism. Cold War conservatives then supported statist controls over individual liberties and extensive political surveillance. Similarly, to establish their vigilant anticommunism American liberals qualified their traditional commitment to individual liberties.

When initiated in 1940, however, federal loyalty procedures were relatively constrained. Convinced that a formal program was needed to safeguard the internal security, the Roosevelt administration nonetheless was committed to precluding loyalty investigations into legitimate political and trade union activities and basing dismissal or denial of clearance on politically inspired charges. These attempts to formulate a loyalty program which safeguarded both individual liberties and the national security, moreover, brought the administration into conflict with conservative anti-Communists (whether congressmen or FBI bureaucrats) who instead urged the dismissal of controversial, activist federal employees.

Since 1938, the House Special Committee on Un-American Activities (HUAC) often crudely red-baited left-liberal and radical federal employees and trade unionists as Communists or Communist sympathizers. Dismayed that the Roosevelt administration did not dismiss those federal employees whom the committee had identified as belonging to the left-wing American League for Peace and Democracy, in 1940 HUAC Chairman Martin Dies first accused Attorney General Robert Jackson of endorsing Communist organizations and then in March 1941 demanded that the president discharge all persons active in organizations controlled by foreign powers.

This conservative assault was not confined to hearings and public charges. When approving the Emergency Relief Act in 1939, Congress also prohibited compensating anyone advocating "or who is a member of an organization that advocates the overthrow of the Government of the United States through force or violence." This provision was extended by the Congress that same year through the Hatch Act to all federal employees; Navy and War Department officials were also authorized through military appropriation legislation to dismiss summarily suspect employees. Then in the Justice Department Appropriations Act of June 28, 1941, Congress appropriated $100,000 to enable the FBI to investigate all federal employees who were "members of subversive organizations." Escalating the attack, in 1941 HUAC Chairman Dies forwarded to the attorney general the names of 1,121 federal employees whom he accused of being subversive. Later in 1943 Dies demanded the dismissal of thirty-nine "suspect" federal employees. Dies's 1943 effort partially succeeded. The House that year directed an appropriations subcommittee to investigate all charges of federal employee "subversive tendencies." This subcommittee eventually recommended that no money be spent for the salaries of three federal employees.

Concerned about fifth column activities, having already authorized an investigative program to ascertain foreign involvement in domestic Fascist and Communist activities, neither the president nor responsible administration officials challenged these legislative requirements. On the one hand, through Circular No. 222 of June 20, 1940, the Civil Service Commission interpreted the Hatch Act ban to apply to members of "the Communist

Party, the German Bund, or any other Communist, Nazi or Fascist organizations" and advised agency heads to terminate such individuals' employment under Civil Service Rule 12. In 1942, these standards were stiffened when the Civil Service Commission issued a regulation disqualifying anyone about whom there was "a reasonable doubt as to his loyalty to the Government of the United States." The number of Civil Service agents investigating federal employees also expanded from 80 in 1940 to 755 in 1944; and eventually 273,500 individuals were investigated (only 1,180, however, were found ineligible). The commission's "reasonable doubt as to loyalty" criterion, moreover, inevitably ensured that this program would focus on political activities. This political orientation became so serious that in November 1943 Civil Service investigators were cautioned not to ask applicants whether they read radical periodicals, attended racially integrated meetings, or belonged to the American Civil Liberties Union. "You are not investigating," the commission admonished, "whether his views are orthodox or do not conform with those of the majority of the people." Agents nonetheless continued to focus on dissident political activities and beliefs.

The Roosevelt administration's policies sharply contrasted with those of the Civil Service Commission. Far more sensitive to the partisan motivation behind congressional loyalty policy, the president in August 1940 sought to confine federal employee loyalty investigations by requiring that they be made "only upon request of the appropriate Department or Agency." This limitation, however, was not long sustained; on October 21, 1941, Attorney General Francis Biddle directed the FBI to investigate whenever it received an appropriate complaint. The bureau's resulting report was to be referred to the employee's agency without any recommendation and the recipient agency must report what actions had been taken and the reasons.

Biddle's October 1941 requirement created major administrative problems —many federal agencies and departments lacked the experienced personnel necessary for evaluating FBI reports. In April 1942, accordingly, Biddle created an Interdepartmental Committee to assist agency/department heads requesting assistance in evaluating FBI reports. The committee's advice need not be accepted; and the committee could only consider the Hatch Act's prohibitions on organizational membership or personal advocacy of revolution. In addition, federal department and agency heads were advised (1) to base dismissal rulings on reliable evidence and not mere suspicion and (2) to devise procedures ensuring a fair hearing to accused employees.[2]

Because of these restrictions, the Roosevelt program provided no necessary precedent for Cold War loyalty/security programs. First it was not a permanent program, although the Hatch Act and subsequent congressional measures required compliance with these legislative standards. More important, the Roosevelt administration's dismissal procedures required evidence and the FBI was confined to a servicing, not policy-making role. These attempts to preclude abuses and a politically motivated program were soon abandoned.

The catalyst to this abandonment derived from three events of 1945–46 seemingly confirming a serious internal security problem. First a June 1945 FBI raid of the offices and homes of individuals associated with *Amerasia*, a left-wing periodical on Far Eastern affairs, uncovered reams of classified State, Navy, and OSS documents. Second, the FBI testimony of Elizabeth Bentley enabled FBI Director Hoover to secure the attorney general's authorization to investigate (including use of wiretaps) certain federal employees and leak derogatory information to conservatives in Congress and in the media. Then, on June 27, 1946, a Canadian Royal Commission published a report detailing the operation of a Soviet espionage ring in wartime Canada. Based on a lead provided by a defector from the Soviet Embassy staff, the Canadian investigation confirmed that those Canadians who had joined the Communist party out of concern for social reform were susceptible to recruitment as espionage agents for the Soviet Union. The Royal Commission thereby recommended additional security measures "to prevent the infiltration into positions of trust under the Government of persons likely to commit" espionage.[3]

Influenced by these three events, a subcommittee of the House Committee on the Civil Service initiated hearings on July 10, 1946. The authority for these hearings derived from an earlier House resolution, H.R. 66 of January 8, 1941, to "make such investigation as it may deem proper with respect to employee loyalty and employment policies and practices in the Government." Having heard testimony from various federal security officials, the subcommittee hastily terminated this hearing and issued its report on July 25, 1946. Stressing that lack of time precluded the necessary exhaustive survey, the subcommittee, nonetheless, concluded that existing procedures were inadequate. All applicants for federal employment should be thoroughly investigated and fingerprinted. A committee composed of representatives from the State, Justice, War, Navy, and Treasury departments and from the Civil Service Commission should also be established to "make a study of existing laws or the adequacy of existing legislation" and recommend to the next Congress "a complete and unified program that will give adequate protection to our Government against individuals whose primary loyalty is to governments other than our own."[4]

Armed with this report, the chairman of the parent committee (Congressman Jennings Randolph), Attorney General Tom Clark, Civil Service Commissioner Arthur Flemming (and his successor Harry Mitchell), and indirectly FBI Director J. Edgar Hoover pressured President Truman to establish such a commission. To ensure a sympathetic commission, Hoover specifically urged Attorney General Clark to select A. Devitt Vanech as the department's representative on such a commission. President Truman, however, did not implement the commission that summer or fall. Until the November 1946 congressional elections, Truman simply kept the proposal under study.[5]

Following the Republicans' sweeping congressional victory, however, Truman acted on these recommendations and on November 25, 1946, established a Temporary Commission on Employee Loyalty. No longer could Truman ignore the possibility that to discredit the New Deal the Republican-controlled Eightieth Congress might initiate a partisan loyalty investigation. Throughout 1946, conservative congressmen—notably Senators James Eastland and Kenneth Wherry and Representatives Edward Cox, Richard Wigglesworth, John Rankin, George Dondero, and Louis Rabant—had pointedly challenged the loyalty of federal employees (and had acquired information directly or indirectly from FBI files).

The commission was to examine whether existing security procedures adequately protected the government from "disloyal or subversive" employees, evaluate whether any agency (or agencies) should be given responsibility for proscribing and/or supervising the implementation of new security procedures, and report its recommendations to the president by no later than February 1, 1947. Acceding to his conservative attorney general's suggestion (and unknowingly FBI Director Hoover's), the president appointed Vanech to chair the commission and selected the other commission members from executive departments having investigative divisions.[6]

The wording of Truman's executive order, the commission's composition, and Commission Chairman Vanech's letters to all department/agency heads requesting recommendations and advice delineated the parameters of this investigation.[7] At issue was not whether a loyalty program was needed; that had already been decided. The sole issue was how to ensure an effective but fairly administered program. The timing of his appointment of the commission as well as the February 1, 1947, reporting deadline further underlined Truman's desire to avert congressional action and thereby undermine partisan Republican efforts to exploit the anti-Communist issue.

Commission members nonetheless divided sharply on the nature of the proposed loyalty program. On the one hand, the intelligence agencies (the FBI, the military services, and Justice) recommended a far-reaching program focusing principally on political activities and beliefs; on the other, State and Treasury Department representatives advocated a program focusing more narrowly on overt activities. FBI Director Hoover's letter to the commission emphasizing the seriousness and the potential dangers posed by the employment of a "subversive or disloyal person" pointedly illustrated the intelligence agencies' political orientation. For Hoover, the problem derived from the ability of "subversives" to influence "the formation of policies of the United States Government either domestic or foreign" to favor another foreign country or weaken the United States, to influence the "execution of foreign or domestic policies," to spread within his/her agency "propaganda" favorable to a foreign country "in such a way as to influence other personnel of the agency and the expression of such propaganda to non-employees in such a way as to create an impression of official sanction to such propaganda," and to recruit "either federal workers or non-Government employees" for membership in a "subversive or disloyal group."

FBI officials, at the same time, sought to contain the scope of the commission's investigation and refused commission members Royall, Goodrich,

Foley, and Sullivan specific information supporting the bureau's contentions (1) that a substantial number of federal employees were disloyal and (2) that the Communist party "had established a separate group for infiltration of the government." Hoover's principal concern, moreover, was to avert disclosure of the FBI's questionable techniques—notably illegal wiretaps, security index programs and politically-inspired investigations. Pressed specifically about "the approximate number of names in subversive files . . . whether the Bureau had a file of names of persons who could be picked up in the event of war with Russia," and the bureau's criteria for placing an individual on such a list, FBI Assistant Director D. Milton Ladd would not answer. "This matter was not within the scope of the Commission." Dissatisfied with these non-responses, commission members requested Hoover's personal appearance and prepared a list of questions that they intended to pose to the FBI director. Hoover did not appear. Instead, Attorney General Clark testified during an executive session at which no minutes were taken. The attorney general supplemented his own earlier testimony before the commission, submitting a memorandum admitting that the number of subversive federal employees had "not yet reached serious proportions." Clark added, however, that the possibility of "even one disloyal person" securing government employment constituted a "serious threat."

Not only did bureau officials successfully avoid documenting their charges; the bureau also undercut the efforts of commission members efforts to minimize the FBI's future investigative role. These members had proposed that exclusive investigation responsibility for the program be assigned to either the employing department/agency or the Civil Service Commission and that investigative agencies should provide full information to departmental/agency hearing boards. In memorandums to the attorney general, the FBI director demanded that an early draft of the proposed executive order be amended. Requiring investigative agencies to make available to all agency/department heads "all investigative materials and information," Hoover complained, would reveal the identity of the bureau's informants and "our techniques, including among others, technical surveillances [wiretaps] which are authorized by you." Hoover also objected to the draft order's authorization that the Civil Service Commission provide investigative assistance to those agencies or departments lacking their own investigative services. The Civil Service Commission should investigate applicants and assist agencies and departments, Hoover conceded. Nonetheless, consistent with the FBI's "responsibilities under the provisions of the Hatch Act," the order should clearly specify "that the FBI should alone have the continuing responsibility" to investigate federal employees' subversive activities.

Knowing of the FBI's vulnerability to exposure (whether its use of wiretaps or security index program), Clark supported the need for confidentiality of FBI sources and programs. And because Justice Department representatives David Edelstein and Joseph Duggan drafted the final report, not surprisingly Hoover's objections were adopted. This deference to the FBI, moreover, had earlier led commission members to recommend a loyalty program even though their inquiry had not acquired hard evidence of a serious loyalty problem. The final report accordingly conceded:

> While the Commission believes that the employment of disloyal or subversive persons presents more than a speculative threat to our system of government, it is unable, based on the facts presented to it, to state with any degree of certainty how far-reaching that threat is. Certainly, the recent Canadian Espionage exposé, the Communist Party Line activities of some of the leaders and some of the members of a government employee organization, and current disclosures of disloyal employees provide sufficient evidence to convince a fair minded person that a threat exists.

President Truman acceded to these recommendations and on March 22, 1947, instituted a federal employee loyalty program. When defining the program's procedures and priorities, Truman's Executive Order 9835 indirectly authorized FBI investigations into subversive activities, accepted the principle of confidentiality which thereby enabled the bureau exclusively to evaluate the quality of information concerning incumbent or applicant employee loyalty, and further ensured that loyalty reports contained mere gossip, rumors, and political charges.[8]

The final report's language, however, also comported with the original recommendations—that is, minimizing the FBI's investigative and supervisory role.[9] Inevitably, then, FBI officials challenged these provisions: first during preparation of appropriation allocations to administer the loyalty program and later in response to departmental/agency requests for FBI investigative reports. In time, two additional issues emerged: whether to revise the dismissal standard and whether to authorize the Loyalty Review Board (established as the supervisory agency for this program) to impose uniform standards and recommend employee dismissal.

In memorandums to the attorney general of March 19 and 28, 1947 (both before and after issuance of the executive order), FBI Director Hoover challenged the order's discretionary language. Agency and department heads seemingly had been granted final authority to initiate investigations and to determine whether to dismiss individuals; the FBI's function was limited to servicing these requests. FBI investigative findings should be mandatorily used and broader investigative criteria were needed. The order's language affirming each department's or agency's responsibility "for the loyalty investigation of any of its employees whenever it is deemed necessary," Hoover protested, infringed upon the bureau's Hatch Act responsibilities. The FBI director elaborated:

> Upon an agency's ascertaining that one of its employees allegedly belonged to an organization advocating the overthrow of the constitutional form of our government, this information should be immediately made available to the FBI in order that an investigation under

the provisions of the Hatch Act can be made. It should not be a
question for the discretion of the agency head to determine the necessity for conducting such an investigation. In my memorandum of
January 29, 1947, I suggested that it should be made clear that the
FBI should alone have the continuing responsibility to inquire into
cases involving alleged subversive activities on the part of Federal
employees so as to insure that we may properly discharge our duties
in conducting these investigations under the Hatch Act.[10]

Denied exclusive investigative authority under the loyalty program (in part
because certain commission members suspected the FBI's political biases),
the FBI, nonetheless, capitalized on the Hatch Act's legislative requirements.
Hoover's effort succeeded. The attorney general for one pressed Hoover's
demand at the Cabinet level. After some initial vacillation, President Truman acceded to this position.

This Cabinet decision did not resolve the matter. The investigative responsibility issue again surfaced during the Bureau of the Budget's March 27
hearings on appropriation allocations to administer the newly authorized
loyalty program. FBI representatives then emphasized the bureau's responsibility to investigate all government employees. The Civil Service Commission challenged this position observing further that other agencies who had
helped formulate the loyalty program had not been invited to this March
27 hearing and that the FBI position contravened the order's clear intent.
Following this meeting Hoover assumed the offensive. On the one hand, the
FBI director claimed that the FBI's investigative authority rested on the
Hatch Act and "a wider concomitant jurisdiction predicated upon the Presidential Directive [of September 6, 1939] establishing the Bureau as the
agency to coordinate and direct all internal security investigations involving
civilians." Then referring to the Civil Service's claimed authority to "full,
complete, entire and exclusive responsibility for conducting all investigations
of Government employees about whose loyalty there is any question whatsoever," Hoover expressed the bureau's willingness "to withdraw from this
field of investigation rather than to engage in a tug of war with the Civil
Service Commission over the investigative jurisdiction of subversive employees of the Federal Government." The bureau's appropriations requests,
Hoover added, had been based on the assumption that the FBI had been
directed to investigate subversive employees by the Hatch Act, an unspecified directive of the attorney general, Roosevelt's 1939 directive, and the
Temporary Commission's report. He then added, "Of course, if the Civil
Service Commission challenges the Bureau's jurisdiction and will accept
the responsibility for the performance of this work, I will withdraw the estimates which I have submitted."[11]

Hoover had no intention to retire quietly from the scene; instead, he appealed to the attorney general by resuscitating the "national security" theme.
Submitting its appropriation estimates to the Bureau of the Budget, the FBI
projected that there were "not more than 4,000 Communists in the Govern-

ment." (Significantly the bureau had not proferred this sizable figure during testimony before the Temporary Commission; FBI officials at no time offered evidence to support this contention.) Then in April 3 and 5, 1947, memorandums to the attorney general, ostensibly seeking clarification of the bureau's responsibility under the loyalty program, the FBI director stressed (1) the confusion created by the executive order, (2) the many inquiries to the bureau made under the order, and (3) in the absence of clear authority and additional appropriations "compliance with the requests being made to this Bureau would ultimately result in a breakdown of the proper coverage of the Communist Party activities by this Bureau."[12]

Unwilling to press the matter, Civil Service's first response was that the FBI's position required amending the executive order. When responding to the copy forwarded to it of Civil Service Commission President Mitchell's letter protesting the Budget Bureau's March 27 position on the FBI, the Treasury Department did not endorse this timidity. Having served as Treasury representative on the Temporary Commission's working subcommittee, Stephen Spingarn was assigned to review this matter. The FBI's position contravened the commission report's and the executive order's language and intent, Spingarn protested, observing further that the FBI's budgetary request was "fantastic unless the FBI plans to make full field investigations of everyone in the Government service who reads the New Republic or P.M." Such far-reaching investigations had been rejected by the Temporary Commission; full field investigations had been limited to cases where there was substantial evidence of the employees' disloyalty. Querying whether this was fully understood "at top levels," Spingarn urged serious assessment of the FBI's action.[13]

Whether encouraged by the Treasury Department's skepticism or having become convinced of the merits of its position, on April 25, 1947, Civil Service Commissioners Harry Mitchell and Frances Perkins appealed directly to the president and specifically challenged the Bureau of the Budget's proposed appropriation allocations. The Budget Bureau's workload and appropriations estimates ensured that all loyalty investigations would be conducted by the FBI; this contravened the "spirit" of the Temporary Commission report and the "letter" of the executive order. Mitchell and Perkins then observed that after the order had been promulgated the FBI claimed authority to investigate only all incumbent employees under the Hatch Act; the president had agreed with this "as the FBI had already made investigations of many of these." "Now the FBI insists that it is its duty to also investigate probational employees named to positions subject to investigation by the Commission, and the Budget approves." Because seventy percent of all applicant employees were appointed subject to later investigations, under Budget's position the Civil Service "would be investigating a proportionately smaller number of cases than it has in the past." Other members of the Loyalty Commission were concerned as well. The commissioners requested a presidential appointment before the Budget Bureau finally approved appropriations. Upon receipt of the letter, the president directed Budget Bureau Director James Webb to "prepare an answer" and also ordered a White House staff study. Articulating his concerns to White House legal counsel Clark Clifford, the president expressed strong "anti-FBI" sentiments, sided with Civil Service Commissioners Mitchell and Perkins, and wanted to "hold FBI down, afraid of 'Gestapo.' "14

Assigned this investigative responsibility, White House aide George Elsey concluded that if the FBI were allowed to investigate all federal employees the intent of the Temporary Commission and the language of the executive order would be contravened. Such investigations would undoubtedly tarnish the reputations of innocent employees. Paradoxically, Elsey and Clifford then urged the president to concur with the Budget Bureau's proposed appropriation figures for pragmatic reasons: the FBI could better conduct such investigations because it possessed personnel, capability to infiltrate, and already extensively covered suspect organizations. Offering a torturous (and, as subsequent history confirmed, misplaced and erroneous) conception of threats to individual liberties, Clifford wrote the president on May 7, 1947:

> I am fully cognizant of the dangers to our Civil Rights which we face in the matter of loyalty investigations, and I share your feelings of concern. It is precisely because of the dangers involved that I believe that the F.B.I. is a better agency than Civil Service to conduct loyalty investigations for new employees; the more highly trained, organized and administered an agency is, the higher should be its standards. . . . The only justification for the program of employee investigations is the discovery and dismissal of disloyal elements within the government. I believe that the F.B.I. is better qualified to ferret out such persons than is the as yet non-existent group of Civil Service investigators.15

Elsey's and Clifford's belief that efficiency minimized abuse and their hope that FBI investigations would be tightly disciplined and professional neutralized (1) their recognition that Budget allocations contravened the president's executive order and (2) their fear of a program tarnishing "with suspicion" the reputations of "innocent" employees. Eventually a hollow compromise was reached to comply with the explicit language (but not the spirit) of the Temporary Commission recommendations and the executive order: the Civil Service Commission had responsibility for all applicant employee loyalty investigations but could request that the FBI conduct them.

FBI Director Hoover did not accept this *pro forma* deference to the Civil Service Commission's sensibilities. Writing to Attorney General Clark on May 12, 1947, Hoover feared that because of the "words employed confusion may still exist as to the jurisdiction of this Bureau." The FBI director insisted upon "immediate clarification" "clearly defining" which agency should handle these investigations. Directed to investigate Hoover's complaint, Assistant Attorney General A. Devitt Vanech thereafter advised White House aide Clifford that the administration would be politically vulnerable during congressional appropriation hearings were it not made clear that the FBI was fully responsible for all loyalty investigations. Reporting

Vanech's advice to the president, Clifford recommended altering either the budget estimates or their rationale. Significantly, while concurring with this assessment, Truman also observed pointedly: "But J. Edgar will in all probability get this backward looking Congress to give him what he wants. It's dangerous." The Truman administration was clearly unwilling to invest any political capital to ensure a restrained, less political program.[16]

The FBI director acted quickly to ensure full FBI control over the program's investigative phase and operational standards. Thus, on May 21, 1947, Hoover advised the attorney general that in "an increasing number of instances" federal agencies had failed to report to the FBI information concerning violations of the Hatch Act (i.e., federal employees' membership in Nazi or Communist organizations). The FBI had the responsibility to conduct all loyalty investigations "or charges" of disloyalty; "it appears necessary that at this time the attention of the various government agencies be directed to our investigative jurisdiction." Hoover attached to this memo "a suggested text for such a letter to the various agencies." Attorney General Clark unhesitatingly directed departmental officials to draft a letter "along this line."[17]

Hoover next pressed the attorney general to ensure the confidentiality of FBI sources to block any efforts (already proposed by the Interior and Treasury departments) whereby attorneys of accused employees would be permitted to cross-examine individuals who had made derogatory statements about their clients. Unless assured of confidentiality, individuals might hesitate to provide information to the bureau; the position of FBI informants might thereby be compromised.[18]

Hoover's recommendation followed an earlier (April 25, 1947) memorandum to Clark reporting the considerable number of requests for FBI data relating to federal employees. "It is undesirable at this time to distribute information concerning government employees promiscuously to every government department which makes any type of request," Hoover emphasized; until this matter was clarified such requests would be declined. At issue, here, was the executive order's requirement: "At the request of the head of any department or agency of the Executive Branch an investigative agency shall make available to such head, personally, all investigative material and information collected by the investigative agency concerning any employee or prospective employee."[19]

Again, the attorney general complied. Issuing Order No. 3464, Supplement No. 4 on July 8, 1947, Clark stipulated that unless first cleared by the attorney general no information obtained from FBI sources would be disseminated outside the Justice Department. Then, when discussing whether to permit defense attorneys to confront hostile witnesses during loyalty hearings, FBI Director Hoover advised the Loyalty Review Board that the FBI would not cooperate "unless the facts received in confidence by the FBI's investigation can be kept entirely confidential at all times and under all conditions."[20]

The attorney general's order and the FBI director's action were immediately challenged. Writing to White House aide Clark Clifford on December

29, 1947, Assistant Secretary of the Interior C. Girard Davidson queried why court procedures permitting defense attorneys to interrogate hostile witnesses could not also be allowed during loyalty hearings. An accused employee could then confront his detractors and test the government's evidence. Whenever the FBI refused either to disclose its sources or to permit its informants to testify, Davidson recommended, departmental hearing officials should conduct their own factual investigations. On December 31, 1947, Clifford referred Davidson's letter to White House aide Donald Dawson.

This matter had been raised at a Cabinet meeting, Dawson advised Clifford on January 7, 1948; it had been decided that only the FBI would conduct loyalty investigations. The Temporary Commission and the president's executive order, Dawson added, recognized that confrontation of witnesses and disclosure of sources would not be possible in all cases. Were the bureau required to disclose its sources, its investigative program and infiltration of "subversive organizations" could be compromised. Davidson should be informed that the loyalty program could not function if its investigative machinery were "destroyed"; those responsible for conducting the program were also committed to protecting individual liberties.[21]

The confidentiality issue resurfaced again, this time at the initiative of the powerful Secretary of the Treasury John Snyder (a close confidant of the president). Snyder criticized the unfairness and cumbersomeness of an April 8, 1948, Loyalty Review Board memorandum to all departments and agencies outlining how loyalty investigations and hearings were to be conducted. This memorandum should be reconsidered; the Treasury secretary requested a hearing at which Treasury representative Stephen Spingarn would outline why witnesses should be interrogated before accused employees were investigated. Twenty-five departments and agencies sent representatives to this requested hearing. Urging that the board not rely exclusively on FBI investigations, Spingarn obliquely criticized the bureau's investigative priorities. The FBI might be an excellent criminal investigative force, Spingarn conceded; its newly trained agents were amateurs in the loyalty field and tended to make political judgments. Not acceding to this suggestion, the board instead simply authorized the Treasury Department (which had its own investigative force) to conduct supplementary investigations and to interrogate accused employees in advance of an investigation.[22]

This limited change did not address broader, more serious problems—wherein the distinctly political nature of FBI investigations resulted in the dismissal of employees on rather questionable grounds and created the impression of a serious loyalty problem. Once again, Assistant Interior Secretary Davidson protested: the past year's operation of the loyalty program confirmed the need for changes to safeguard individual liberties, minimize embarrassment to the individual, and expedite loyalty hearings. Current loyalty investigation procedures should be altered because in effect they discouraged individuals holding liberal views from seeking federal employment. Citing a number of cases of improper FBI investigations and interrogations, the Interior Department official pointedly queried whether the departments and not the FBI should conduct loyalty investigations. The conservative chairman of the Loyalty Review Board summarily refuted Davidson's protest and characterized his suggestions as impugning the program's wisdom. Praising the FBI's investigative work, Richardson for one defended as wholly proper one of the instances cited by Davidson—wherein individuals were investigated on loyalty grounds simply because they opposed FBI investigations. The Loyalty Review Board chairman then dismissed Davidson's other examples of the FBI's politically-inspired investigations either as unavoidable or clearly exceptional.[23]

Almost concurrently, in two independent recommendations, Attorney General J. Howard McGrath and Loyalty Review Board official L. V. Moyer urged that the program's dismissal standard be drastically revised. The existing dismissal standard, Moyer protested in February 1949—namely, "on all evidence, reasonable grounds exist for the belief that the person involved is disloyal to the Government of the United States"—required a finding that the individual "is at present disloyal." This requirement was clearly undesirable as individuals were cleared "who are potentially disloyal or who are bad security risks." Loyalty clearances instead should be denied to applicants for federal employment "if there is a reasonable doubt as to their loyalty to the Government of the United States." By 1950, the board also recommended that this standard be applied to incumbent employees.[24]

The Loyalty Review Board renewed this request again in February 1951. Exploiting current doubts about the adequacy of the administration's internal security program which conservative Republicans had exploited effectively during the 1950 congressional elections Hiram Bingham, Richardson's successor as board chairman, urged that the dismissal standard be revised to "reasonable doubt as to the loyalty of the person involved."[25] Basing dismissal on mere suspicion as opposed to confirmed evidence of disloyalty, this recommendation would have fundamentally altered the character of the loyalty program. Under the proposed revision, loyalty hearings and investigations would inevitably focus on the individual's political beliefs and associations.

The president did not immediately implement this request—in part because in January 1951 he had appointed a special commission to investigate the loyalty program. Eventually on April 28, 1951, Truman issued Executive Order 10241 instituting this new standard.[26] Succumbing again to pressures from internal security bureaucrats, the president in 1952 extended loyalty check procedures to all presidential appointees (whether to advisory boards or as presidential consultants).[27]

The board's successes were not confined to revising the dismissal standards and extending coverage to presidential appointees. Whereas its functions had been limited to an advisory or supervisory role under Truman's March 1947 order, the board now exploited the (April 1951) amended dismissal standard and, on its own authority, assumed final denial of clearance responsibility.

Thus, on May 23, 1951, Loyalty Review Board Chairman Hiram Bingham ordered all federal departments and agencies to apply the new standards to the 565 cases still under consideration. Departments and agencies must review these cases whenever higher loyalty boards had on appeal reversed denial of clearance rulings of departmental loyalty boards. Any case (even if a clearance had been granted) should be reviewed if there was any reasonable doubt about the individual's loyalty; agency heads should report favorable rulings in these cases to the Loyalty Review Board so that they could be post-audited. Then, on December 21, 1951, agency and department heads were advised that henceforth the board would review periodically "as it deems necessary" any agency or department decision even when no appeal had been made.[28] In addition, the FBI exploited the program's requirement that all applicants for federal employment undergo a name check to justify its investigations of "subversive" or "potentially subversive" organizations.[29]

The president remained dissatisfied with this revised program. Truman's dissatisfaction, however, was confined to the program's lack of uniform standards and decentralized review procedures. Accordingly, he directed the National Security Council in 1951 to study the need to institute uniform standards and procedures and to centralize review decisions within the departments. After a thorough study, the Interdepartmental Committee on Internal Security (the NSC subcommittee having internal security responsibility) in April 1952 attributed one of the program's principal problems to its operation under three differing standards: suitability, security, and loyalty. The committee recommended further study to ensure "a single general program to cover eligibility for employment in the Federal Service, whether on grounds of loyalty, security, or suitability." Acting on this report, Truman first ordered the Civil Service Commission to formulate uniform procedures and then that those departments/agencies having security programs "re-examine their procedures."[30] Before these changes could be implemented, however, Truman's presidential tenure ended.

The newly elected Republican president was receptive to these proposed administrative changes. Ideological and partisan considerations particularly influenced the conservative anti-Communist Dwight Eisenhower to alter the Truman loyalty program. During the 1952 campaign Eisenhower successfully exploited popular concerns about the adequacy of the Truman loyalty procedures. Eisenhower's frequent campaign promises and the Republicans' 1952 platform planks seemingly constituted a commitment to implement more "effective" internal security safeguards. In addition, Eisenhower doubted the loyalty of individuals who held "New Dealish" (let alone radical) political beliefs or who since 1948 might have challenged the Truman administration's anti-Soviet policies from a leftist perspective. Moreover, his views on security needs were rather arbitrary—he believed individuals guilty only of "bungling" or wrongdoing should be thoroughly investigated and that U.S. security interests were adversely affected if information was leaked to the press. Inheriting a federal bureaucracy staffed by Roosevelt and Truman appointees, the president also concluded that responsible conservative government required purging New Deal–Fair Deal bureaucrats.[31]

Convinced of the inadequacy of existing procedures to preclude the employment of "potentially" dangerous individuals, the Eisenhower administration almost immediately began considering how to revise Truman's loyalty program. Expressing a rhetorical concern for fairness and due process, the Republican president was committed to the goal of absolute security. The result was a new security program, established by Executive Order 10450 on April 27, 1953, which abolished the Truman program's hearing and review procedures and was based on the principle that federal employment was a privilege and not a right. Ostensibly relying on that provision of Public Law 733 (Security Act of August 26, 1950) that authorized heads of sensitive departments and agencies summarily to dismiss disloyal employees, Eisenhower's executive order in effect extended this summary dismissal standard to all other federal agencies and departments. Responsible for administering the program, department/agency heads must ensure all their employees' "fitness." Eisenhower's dismissal standard, more importantly, extended beyond "loyalty" and/or "security" to "suitability"; responsible officials must certify that the employment was "clearly consistent with the interests of national security" and that all employees were "reliable, trustworthy, of good conduct and character, and of complete and unswerving loyalty to the United States."[32]

Given these priorities, subsequent changes simply tightened security procedures (until Supreme Court decisions of 1956 and 1959 required revision of this "security" program's authority, scope, and procedures). By Executive Order 10491 of October 14, 1953, and Executive Order 10548 of August 2, 1954, the president authorized the suspension of those federal employees who relied on the Fifth Amendment during testimony before congressional committees investigating "alleged disloyalty or other misconduct" or whose illness or mental condition might "cause significant defect in the [employee's] judgment or reliability." The administration's commitment to "strengthen" security standards also led to continuous reviews of the program's operation, pressures on department/agency heads to ensure that the program was handled expeditiously, and continuous examinations of "deficiencies in the department and agency programs which are inconsistent with or weaken the national security."[33]

Because of these "security" requirements intelligence agencies were able to conduct intrusive, continuing investigations of dissident political activities. These investigations did not, however, focus on disloyalty considerations. National Security Agency employee "suitability files" contained extremely personal information, much of which was dated and irrelevant to determining loyalty. The FBI's files, if those revealed in court cases are representative, contained information that was extremely personal as well as wholly irrelevant to security needs. In one case, for example, the vice-president of an engineering firm having a defense contract was denied a security clearance in 1953 because of his former wife's (whom he had divorced in 1943) political associations. In another case, the political activities of a soldier's mother-in-law resulted in his undergoing a security investigation. Ludicrously, this soldier's mother-in-law had died when he was ten years old and her death occurred ten years before he met his future wife.[34]

Under the Eisenhower administration's "suitability" program, political activists were penalized. In this sense, the program advanced the administration's more general political objectives. The Republicans had won control of both the White House and the Congress in 1952 in part by charging that the internal security procedures of the Truman administration (and the Democrats) had been inadequate and by pledging to institute a needed housecleaning of the "disloyal." To sustain this advantage, the administration resorted to a carefully formulated "numbers game": statistics were periodically released on how many federal employees had been removed under the Eisenhower administration's "security" reforms (in 1955 skeptical press questioning and a publicized congressional investigation forced abandonment of this practice). As a further aspect of this strategy, in November 1953 the administration consciously exploited the Harry Dexter White case to convey the impression that the lax security procedures of the Truman administration had been rejected, the FBI unleashed, and internal security safeguards strengthened. These themes were pointedly developed by Republican congressional candidates, Vice President Nixon (more indirectly President Eisenhower), and the Republican National Committee during the 1954 congressional campaign.[35]

The administration also attempted to replace New Deal–Fair Deal federal appointees with loyal, conservative Republicans. Patriotic businessmen, Eisenhower believed, must be attracted to Washington to replace "socialistic" Democratic officeholders. Because of civil service tenure, however, incumbent employees could be replaced only if their positions were reclassified or if they were dismissed or resigned. Resignations were directly related to fear of dismissal under the Eisenhower "security" program's broader "suitability" standards.[36]

The Eisenhower program's vague and extremely broad security standards encouraged agency heads to "play it safe" and to resolve in the government's favor any doubts about particular employees' "suitability." Not surprisingly, the administration seriously considered requiring security checks for private citizens who might travel overseas on State Department-sponsored cultural and sports programs; AEC counsel Harold Green was ordered to provide information about his colleagues' attitudes toward security; individuals denied a security clearance by ultraconservative departmental officials were granted clearance for more sensitive security positions (in one case, Wolf Ladejinsky was denied a Department of Agriculture clearance and was almost immediately appointed to the Mutual Security Administration); and individuals (notably, J. Robert Oppenheimer, John Carter Vincent, John Paton Davies, and William Greene) who had continuously received security clearances since the loyalty program's inception in 1947 and against whom no new information had been developed were denied security clearances under the Eisenhower program. The program's varying and capricious standards, impact on employee morale, and unfair procedures and requirements, however, soon precipitated congressional and press demands for an independent investigation.[37]

The administration at first dismissed these criticisms and sought to prevent Congress from creating an independent study commission. Convinced that they confronted simply a public relations problem, administration personnel in private affirmed that existing procedures were fair and sound. In their public responses, they extolled the fairness and effectiveness of the so-called Eisenhower security procedures. Their strategy failed; press and congressional revelations about abuses and capricious decisions had raised legitimate concerns about the program. These revelations eventually forced the administration to support an investigation by a specially created twelve-member Commission on Government Security (the so-called Wright Commission), one half appointed by the White House and the other half by the Congress.[38]

Pressured into supporting an external examination of its security procedures, the administration, nonetheless, was committed to delimiting the scope and thrust of this review even though the commission's membership was convinced that stringent security procedures were required. This objective was easily attained, in part because the commission's administrative director, FBI Assistant Director D. Milton Ladd, had effective power to determine the investigation's direction and focus. In addition, the administration carefully limited the commission's access to FBI files.

Throughout the Wright Commission investigation, the Justice Department and the FBI strongly opposed any changes which would permit employees to confront their accusers during denial of security clearance appeal hearings. Responding to these pressures, the commission ultimately recommended tighter safeguards, creation of a Central Security Agency to ensure greater uniformity and direction, legalization of wiretapping, additional legislation penalizing leaks of classified information, and extending classification restrictions. Individual rights, the commission concluded, were "adequately" protected under existing procedures "in the light of the necessity for protection of the national security."

The commission's anti-Communist recommendations, nonetheless, occasioned considerable debate and division within the administration. Sharing this same indifference to civil liberties, the administration's sole concern was whether the changes should be instituted by executive order or legislation; central to this intra-administration review was how best to ensure secrecy and executive discretion. Thus, proponents of statutory authority argued that new legislation would strengthen the administration's ability to withhold "necessarily confidential information from one accused." Those urging executive order changes, in contrast, counseled that reliance on legislation "would likely result in a detailed piece of legislation which hogties the Administration and robs both criteria and procedures of the necessary flexibility." Not surprisingly, then, even commission member James McGranery's dissent that the proposed recommendations unduly restricted individual liberties was summarily ignored.[39]

As part of these internal efforts to control changes in the president's security program, Assistant Attorney General William Tompkins had been appointed to head a special committee to coordinate federal employee security policy, the Personnel Security Advisory Committee. Then, upon receiving the Wright Commission report on June 21, 1957, and discussing its recommendations with the Cabinet, on June 28, 1957, the president directed all heads of departments and agencies to review those recommendations calling for "administrative action" and submit written comments to Tompkins for "interdepartmental study and subsequent consideration in the Cabinet." The Bureau of the Budget would continue to process legislative recommendations.

The Cabinet considered these recommendations on August 8, 1958. The Cabinet's discussion, however, centered on whether to establish an independent central security office within the executive branch. The consensus was to oppose such an office.[40]

The administration was not permitted the luxury of deciding how to react to the Wright Commission's conservative recommendations. Two U.S. Supreme Court decisions of 1956 and 1959 undermined this administration strategy of containment and compelled a different review of the security program.

On June 11, 1956, in *Cole v. Young*, the U.S. Supreme Court ruled that President Eisenhower had exceeded his authority when directing all federal agencies and departments summarily to dismiss employees holding nonsensitive positions. Public Law 733, the Court held, authorized the summary dismissal of only those employees holding "sensitive" positions. Delivering the majority opinion, Justice Harlan emphasized:

> (1) that the term "national security" is used in the Act [Public Law 733] in a definite and limited sense and relates only to those activities which are directly concerned with the Nation's safety, as distinguished from the general welfare; and (2) that no determination has been made that petitioner's position was affected with the "national security" as that term is used in the Act. It follows that his dismissal [under Executive Order 10450] was not authorized by the 1950 Act and hence violated the Veterans' Preference Act. [Cole was a World War II veteran.][41]

The Supreme Court might have skirted the issue of whether presidents possessed the independent authority to establish a loyalty/security program; its decision in *Cole*, nonetheless, might have impelled a more liberal administration to consider individual rights when mandating new procedures. The Eisenhower administration, however, remained committed to salvaging its security program at the same time technically complying with the Court's oblique and rather narrow ruling.

Thus, on August 1, 1956, Attorney General Brownell advised department and agency heads of administration policy in view of the Court's decision. Federal appointments should be classified either as sensitive or nonsensitive. Executive order 10450's provisions for summary suspension should continue to apply to sensitive positions but nonsensitive dismissals had to comply with the procedural requirements of the Lloyd-LaFollette and Veterans Preferences acts. (These measures required that the employee be notified of specific charges and be permitted to defend him/herself.) Those employees holding nonsensitive positions who had been summarily dismissed under Executive Order 10450 were to be reinstated. These restored employees, the attorney general added, should then be informed that suspension proceedings might be instituted "under appropriate legislative authority other than the Act of August 26, 1950."[42]

At the same time, the administration seriously considered how to regain summary dismissal ("suitability") authority for nonsensitive positions. In 1956 and 1957, accordingly, it supported legislation specifically authorizing the summary dismissal of any employee holding a position which affected the security or the "welfare" of the nation. When these measures were not immediately enacted by the Congress (one such bill passed the House but was held up in the Senate), the administration in late 1957 ceased openly to urge their passage. This changed stance, however, did not derive from civil libertarian considerations. Having by then received the Wright Commission report, the administration preferred to examine the commission's general recommendations before adopting a specific legislative stance. At issue, here, were other provisions of these congressional bills, and specifically the proposed establishment of a central security office. The administration's strong opposition to such an office and conviction that executive flexibility would be unduly restricted by any legislative change eventually led to the decision neither to draft nor to lobby for passage of alternative legislation. Instead, the administration considered but again decided against instituting executive order changes. Practical considerations again determined this decision: the recent Supreme Court decisions had indirectly raised serious questions about presidential authority to institute these changes.[43]

President Eisenhower's conservative views sharply delimited intra-administration deliberations over how to respond to the Court's rulings. Eisenhower's conceptions of constitutional rights, and his response to recent Supreme Court decisions, were pointedly conveyed in a May 12, 1958, letter to Attorney General William Rogers requesting a "succinct study" of the Court's recent decisions and of two bills to countermand these decisions. (One of these bills, sponsored by the conservative anti-Communist Senator William Jenner, would essentially have barred the Court from hearing and deciding specified types of "national security" cases. The second bill, championed by Congressman Francis Walter, proposed to clarify Congress's intent by the Smith Act prohibition and to contravene the Court's ruling in the *Yates* case.) Eisenhower pointedly queried:

> (d) While I understand that you have reported adversely against these particular bills, is there any necessity for any kind of additional legislation respecting the functioning of our Courts, especially the Supreme Court?
>
> (e) I believe that the Constitution accords to the Congress the right to pass certain laws affecting the Courts. Does this right extend

to the passing of laws affecting the functioning of the Courts and the kinds of cases they may properly decide?

Replying on May 27, 1958, the attorney general gently and politely lectured the president on constitutional history and the Supreme Court's constitutional authority. By subtly reminding Eisenhower of Franklin Roosevelt's 1937 "Supreme Court packing plan," Rogers effectively dissuaded him from publicly intervening to support these efforts to undercut the Supreme Court's recent libertarian rulings.[44]

If already troubled by the Court's decisions of 1956–57 (and, specifically *Cole v. Young*), the administration soon confronted a more formidable challenge in another Supreme Court decision, *Greene v. McElroy* of June 29, 1959. In *Greene*, a deeply divided majority ruled that denying to individuals whose security clearance was revoked the right to confront their accusers under the federal industrial security program was unconstitutional. The Court again did not directly rule on the federal security program's constitutionality or whether federal employees (or those employed by defense contractors) had a right to personal privacy absent provable instances of illegal activities. The Court only considered (in the words of Justice Harlan's concurring opinion) "whether the particular procedures here employed to deny clearance on security grounds were constitutionally permissible." In their concurrence, Justices Harlan, Frankfurter, and Whittaker further qualified this right of confrontation "on the ground that it has not been shown that either Congress or the President authorized the procedures whereby petitioner's security clearance was revoked, intimating no views as to the validity of those procedures." The Court in effect only held that the secretary of defense (the executive official responsible for administering the Industrial Security Program) could not on his own authority promulgate regulations prohibiting confrontation.[45]

The Court's tortured opinion left unresolved what alternative procedures were constitutionally permissible. It might have ruled that petitioner William Greene was entitled to confront his accusers during security clearance hearings but this right was qualified by the concurring opinion's implication that the Court might have ruled differently had either the Congress or the President specifically denied to individuals the right of confrontation. This case, moreover, involved specifically an individual employed by a private firm having a U.S. government defense contract. Nonetheless, the Court's ruling had possibly broader implications as the Court conceivably might require the same procedural safeguards for federal employees.

Given the breadth and narrowness of this ruling, the administration had three options. Recognizing the constitutional principle involved, and the proven unfairness of extant procedures, the administration could mandate the right of confrontation. Conversely, the administration could deny the right of confrontation whether by issuing an appropriate executive order or seeking specific legislation authorization.

Not surprisingly, administration officials did not even consider the first option. Rather, in lengthy and intensive intra-administration deliberations lasting from June 29, 1959, through February 20, 1960 (when the president issued Executive Order 10865), these officials considered how best to avert confrontation and preserve the confidentiality of FBI sources and reports. Administration officials might have considered legislation in passing; ultimately they chose the executive order option— preferring its greater flexibility and maximum secrecy and holding expansive views on presidential powers. When assessing the Court's specific ruling, moreover, intra-administration deliberations of 1959–60 concentrated exclusively on the industrial security program. The procedures might have to be extended to other security programs (including federal employees) administration officials recognized: this need not be done simultaneously. White House counsel Phillip Areeda justified this cautious approach when conceding that "the internal obstacles to the adoption of such reforms are great." These deliberations were principally governed by the need to preserve the confidentiality of FBI sources, extending even to "casual informants." The problem, then, was how to reconcile this objective with the Court's ruling. Some modifications in existing procedures were required to comport with the Court's emphases that the procedures of the industrial security program denying confrontation departed from "traditionally" fair procedures.

White House counsel Phillip Areeda assumed leadership in this review effort. The resort to confidentiality, Areeda concluded, might have to be the exception; nor could the president merely delegate blanket exception authority. Areeda stressed the need for a detailed executive order as opposed to a permissive directive authorizing the secretary of defense to accord nonconfrontation.

Areeda's position conflicted with those of the Departments of Defense and Justice. Both Defense and Justice sought to preserve confidentiality, even to the extent of not considering the full implications of the Court's ruling. A lengthy intra-administration debate thereby ensured over the proposed executive order's specific language and whether to grant discretionary authority to the secretary of defense. Ultimately, Defense and Justice bowed to White House counsel Areeda's position. (The Atomic Energy Commission, in contrast, supported Areeda and in addition advocated specific legislation.) These concessions were nonetheless limited and were based upon expansive conceptions of "national security" needs and presidential powers. The proposed order permitted confrontation only after "complete and careful consultation with the FBI Director." Second, a July 23, 1959, Areeda memorandum starkly expressed the administration's preference for executive order as opposed to legislative changes. A presidential "national security" claim, Areeda contended, would effectively disarm the Court:

> An executive order would probably be legally sufficient to establish
> a hearing procedure that allowed the use of evidence without con-
> frontation and cross-examination. The Court would find it most diffi-

cult to challenge an explicit determination by the President that the nation's security would be compromised unless access to classified data could be denied without confrontation in certain cases. . . . I do not believe the Court would second-guess the President's estimates of national security requirements.

Only if the administration decided upon a "greater departure from traditional due process procedures," Areeda reasoned, would exceptions from confrontation have to be grounded in statutory authority. Legislation then would make it more likely for any exceptions to "survive judicial scrutiny."

Moreover, Eisenhower's Executive Order 10865 did not clearly delimit when confrontation would be denied. Titled "Safeguarding Classified Information within Industry," this order sidestepped the civil liberties issue by advancing a "national security" rationale. Ostensibly authorizing oral or written cross-examinations, Executive Order 10865 nonetheless permitted vaguely worded discretionary exceptions. These included:

(1) *The head of the department supplying the statement certifies* that the person who furnished the information is a confidential informant who has been engaged in obtaining intelligence information for the Government and that disclosure of his identity would be substantially harmful to the national interest.

(2) *The head of the department concerned or his special designee* . . . has particularly determined, after considering information and the accuracy of the statement concerned, that the statement concerned appears to be reliable and material and the head of the department or such special designee has determined that failure to receive and consider such statement would, in view of the level of access sought, be substantially harmful to the national security and that the person who furnished the information cannot appear to testify (A) due to death, severe illness, or similar cause, in which case the identity of the person and the information to be considered shall be made available to the applicant, or (B) due to some other cause *determined by the head of the department to be good and sufficient.* (b) Whenever procedures under paragraphs (1) or (2) of subsection (a) of this section are used (1) the applicant shall be given a summary of the information which shall be *as comprehensive and detailed as the national security permits,* (2) *appropriate* consideration shall be accorded to the fact that the applicant did not have an opportunity to cross-examine such person or persons, and (3) a final determination adverse to the applicant shall be made only by the head of the department based upon his personal review of the case.[46] (Emphasis added)

These limited changes were not extended to the federal employee security program. President Eisenhower further amended the industrial security program on January 17, 1961. (Significantly, the consideration and approval of these revisions had been expedited to "avoid the necessity either of presenting it to the new President after January 20 on the basis of the views of present appointees, or of soliciting the views of new agency heads after that date.") In essence, the amended order authorized the payment of the expenses of two witnesses during security hearings and, more importantly, the extension of the industrial security program through agreements between the secretary of defense and other departments or agencies (specifically the General Services Administration).[47]

Thus, despite both the Supreme Court's challenge and the adverse publicity surrounding its arbitrary procedures, the Eisenhower administration successfully forged and preserved a politically repressive security program. The administration's exploitation of the then prevalent deferential acceptance of presidential "national security" and secrecy claims paved the way for a program focusing on the personal (political and social) activities of federal employees and private citizens (the latter because they might at some future time seek federal employment).

John F. Kennedy inherited this legacy when he assumed office in January 1961. An ardent anti-Communist, President Kennedy shared the Cold War consensus that the seriousness of the internal security threat justified radical departures from traditional values. Kennedy's anticommunism led him to support innovative measures (such as counterinsurgency) to combat communism's perceived worldwide subversive threat and to decide not to revise the Eisenhower "suitability" program. Under White House aide Lee White's leadership, Eisenhower's security program was "informally" reviewed in 1961. "For the most part," Kennedy White House officials concluded, the program was "functioning properly and serving its intended purpose of protecting the national security and safeguarding the rights of employees and applicants." The White House accordingly decided to continue the program "without opening up the subject to public debate."[48] Because of this passive policy, the Kennedy administration ironically created a potentially serious political problem.

Although never breaking radically from the past, the president's affinity for innovative tactics and reliance on new advisers (notably liberal academics who were unremitting Cold Warriors) precipitated a muted conflict with the conservative personnel administering the security program. Anti-Communists, these civil service tenured officials did not necessarily distinguish between liberal dissent and disloyalty. Because of the program's vague standards, incumbent security officials commanded wide latitude when finding particular appointees not "suitable." One such official was Otto Otepka, appointed deputy director of the State Department's Office of Security in January 1956 and since 1958 responsible for granting security clearances to all new appointees. An anti-Communist extremist, differing even from fellow security officials, Otepka had the zealot's view that a belief in world government, associations (familial or friendship) with radicals, or intellectual attraction to socialism denoted security problems.

Ironically, the Kennedy administration's initial confrontation with Otepka involved the possible appointment of Walt Whitman Rostow, an ardent anti-Communist who for later critics of the Vietnam War symbolized the fallacies of an unthinking anticommunism. Under consideration for a high-level State Department appointment, Rostow had in 1955 and 1957 been denied security clearance for appointment as a consultant to two presidential advisory panels. Following a December 1960 interview with Otepka, Attorney General–designate Robert Kennedy and Secretary of State–designate Dean Rusk concluded that Rostow might be denied a State Department security clearance. Whether or not because of this concern, Rostow was appointed deputy special assistant to the president for national security affairs—Otepka could only review Rostow's investigative files if he were appointed to a State Department and not a White House post.[49]

Bypassing Otepka could not solve the broader security standards problem. Dissatisfied with the quality of State Department personnel, President Kennedy increasingly relied on National Security Council staff officials for foreign policy advice. This institutional preference left unresolved the administration's broader concerns over how nonmajor foreign policy decisions were formulated and executed. Politically biased security officers like Otepka could effectively contravene the administration's activist and innovative preferences by ensuring that only conventional, noncontroversial personalities would pass the "security" test. Unwilling to invest the political capital required to revise Eisenhower's "security" standards, the Kennedy administration soon settled on a more indirect strategy to undercut Otepka's influence. On November 8, 1961, the administration announced the reduction in force of twenty-five State Department security officials for budgetary reasons. Ostensibly because of this reduction in personnel, Otepka was transferred from the post of deputy director of the Office of Security to chief of the Division of Evaluations. (If given a more honorific title, Otepka's "promotion" denied him administrative control over FBI investigative files on prospective appointees.)

This decision caused considerable concern to conservatives in the media and to the staff of the Senate Internal Security Subcommittee. The Internal Security Subcommittee, accordingly, convened hearings to ascertain whether the national security would be adversely affected by this reduction of State Department security personnel. Invited to testify during executive session hearings on November 16, 1961, Otepka soon developed a covert relation with the staff of the subcommittee. Although a less powerful security official (who could still delay or raise questions about security clearances), Otepka was thereafter able to leak classified State Department documents to the staff. Otepka's unauthorized leaking in turn enabled the subcommittee in 1962 to challenge the priorities of the administration's security program and the loyalty of certain State Department officials. State Department officials' concerns about these leaks, and suspicions that Otepka was their source, resulted in their close surveillance of the security official, including wiretapping his office phone. Eventually, because he had violated President Truman's March 1948 executive order prohibiting the unauthorized release of loyalty reports to the Congress, Otepka was dismissed from his governmental position.[50]

The Kennedy administration's resolution of the Otepka problem had not ensured a more restrained security program. Instead, partly influenced by the Internal Security Subcommittee's investigation, in April 1962 the president solicited FBI Director Hoover's advice on the Department of State's "inspection system." Special Assistant to the President Ralph Dungan followed up on this presidential request.[51] As one result of this solicitation and inaction, "security" investigations continued to focus on dissident political activities.

The Kennedy administration's concern about right-wing extremism, however, impelled the FBI director to order in June 1963 more intensive investigation of " 'rightist or extremist' groups operating in the anti-Communist field." FBI field offices were specifically directed "also [to] be alert to the activities of such groups which come within the purview of Executive Order 10450" or violate federal statutes.[52]

The Kennedy administration might not have reassessed Eisenhower's security standards but the Johnson administration would. William Crockett (deputy under secretary of state for administration) in May 1964 and John Macy (chairman of the Civil Service Commission) in October 1964 independently recommended a review of the security program. Their concern, however, stemmed from a conviction that security procedures could be tightened. Thus, Crockett bemoaned the lack of uniform standards and the cost of duplicative security reviews while Macy recommended the need for a reinvestigative program whereby all persons holding "sensitive positions or are occupying positions of sufficient importance to affect the public image of the Federal service" would undergo a "national agency check" every five years. Whether or not it was because of these recommendations, on February 22, 1965, White House aides Bill Moyers and Lee White urged President Johnson to appoint a special presidential task force to review "without general publicity" existing security procedures. Emphasizing the need to ensure against publicity (reflecting their extreme caution even when proposing the consideration of limited changes), these White House aides advocated this study less out of a civil liberties concern than "in terms of costs and efficiency."

President Johnson concurred and on February 24, 1965, appointed Civil Service Commission Chairman Macy to head the review force. The secretary of defense, the attorney general, and the Budget Bureau director were to designate "a principal official" to participate in this study group which was to report its findings to the president by August 31, 1965. Johnson specifically directed this group to assess: (1) which federal positions should be considered sensitive and which nonsensitive, (2) the effectiveness "and appropriateness" of current security standards, (3) the status of the attorney general's list, (4) how to update incumbent employee investigations, (5) the procedures for denying clearance to federal employees, (6) the rights of employees and applicants, (7) "the availability of confrontation and cross-examination in individual cases," and (8) the costs, timeliness and "productivity" of personnel investigations.

The study was conducted although the August deadline was not met. Reporting back on November 1, 1965, the committee (composed of Macy, Assistant Secretary of Defense Norman Paul, Assistant Attorney General J. Walter Yeagley, and Executive Assistant Bureau of the Budget Director William Carey) observed that the incumbent phase of the employee security program "has been largely completed"—adding that "very few" security removals had been effected since the *Cole* decision of 1956. Since *Cole*, federal agencies effected separation not on the executive order's dismissal provisions but on civil service regulations. "There are no compelling reasons" to modify substantially the program, the committee concluded, "such as would require the issuance of a new Executive Order or an amendment to the existing Order." Committee members instead recommended "improvements" within the framework of the existing order to "provide greater uniformity, promote more effective and equitable operation of the program and facilitate the reciprocal use of security clearances among agencies." Although these improvements might ensure a more efficient program, they would neither extend individual rights nor eliminate the invasion of personal privacy or the political criteria attendant to the existing program. In its assessment of the notorious attorney general's list, moreover, the committee recommended against its abolition "because it serves an important function in preventing the relitigation of the character of the designated organization. . . . [and further that] despite the desirability of bringing the list up to date, it is not practical to do so."

Johnson approved the recommended changes on November 3, 1965. Federal positions were to be classified as to whether they were sensitive or non-sensitive. Full field investigations should be conducted only for appointees to sensitive positions although full field investigations could be instituted "when [the agency or department head] considers such action appropriate." Provisions were spelled out for reinvestigating incumbent employees holding "critical-sensitive" positions and for permitting employees to challenge and refute derogatory information. Employees were not to be permitted to cross-examine their accusers, and the rights of employees and applicants were not specifically defined. The Department of Justice instead, the study group had recommended, should be consulted "to assure that the rights of employees are fully considered," advise departmental security officials "whether the proposed charges are fully supported," and further "the extent to which confrontation and cross-examination of witnesses will be required."[53]

These revised standards continued to shape the Johnson administration's security policy until 1966–67. In the interim, moreover, the administration seriously considered limiting use of the polygraph during interrogations of federal employees as well as other measures to advance employee rights.

Concurrently, administration officials pressured federal employees to support civil rights and purchase U.S. government bonds, and political tests continued to be employed for high-level Civil Service appointments.

Because of these latter requirements, the Subcommittee on Constitutional Rights of the Senate Judiciary Committee chaired by North Carolina Senator Sam Ervin, Jr., initiated hearings in September–October 1966 to "protect the constitutional rights of Government employees and prohibit unwarranted invasions of their privacy." The impetus for these hearings on governmental personnel policies derived from protests the subcommittee had received from employees involving various federal agencies' "sensitivity" sessions to ensure greater tolerance toward black Americans; detailed Civil Service questionnaires soliciting information about the employee's race, political beliefs, general attitudes, and finances; and suggestions (amounting to commands) that employees attend political lectures or meetings, subscribe to federal bonds, and support particular administration policy objectives. The resultant subcommittee hearings confirmed that applicant and incumbent employees were queried about their sexual activities, attitudes toward their parents, political beliefs, and attitudes toward birth control and high defense expenditures. In addition, the hearings disclosed that during punitive hearings employees were denied due process and hesitated to resist their superiors' suggestions which in essence amounted to coercion.

The subcommittee's hearings and final report of August 21, 1967, dramatized the arbitrariness of federal employee rules, the intrusiveness of Civil Service restrictions on federal employee privacy rights, and the high-handed attitudes of officials directing the federal employee security program. To Civil Service Commission officials, federal employment was a privilege, and not a right. When queried about abuses, these officials either defended the criticized procedures as necessary to fulfill the commission's mandate or as correctable only through administrative action. Civil Service Commission Chairman John Macy pointedly characterized the legislation proposed by Senator Ervin as unreasonably interfering with proper and harmonious employee-employer relations. (Cleared with the president, Macy's public testimony represented considered administration policy. Keenly sensitive to the Ervin committee hearings, the Johnson White House devised an informal strategy to limit their impact.)

Thus, Macy defended the requirement that applicants list their memberships in organizations having legislative objectives as essential to ascertaining whether the individual had or still belonged to organizations on the attorney general's list. When pressed, Macy had no reply to the point that some of the organizations specifically identified on federal application forms were not on this list (such as the John Birch Society, U.S. Chamber of Commerce, American Civil Liberties Union, Friends Committee on National Legislation). Psychological tests and other requests for intimate personal information were justified, Macy claimed, to ascertain the individual's "suitability," character, and fitness.

The Ervin subcommittee hearings constituted the first libertarian challenge to the independently established security program. The subcommittee's focus, however, was confined to the program's more sensational and arbitrary abuses. Accordingly, still prevalent "national security" considerations stringently limited the inquiry's impact. Thus, the subcommittee (highlighted by its proposed legislative remedies) was willing to exempt the NSA and the CIA from proposed bans on psychological testing and polygraphs if their directors certified a "national security" need. In addition, the subcommittee's proposed restrictions on governmental intrusions into personal privacy and constitutional rights were confined to Civil Service questionnaires and investigations; and the FBI was specifically exempted from these restrictions. In 1969, moreover, the Ervin subcommittee initiated hearings into the Health, Education and Welfare Department requirements that all scientific advisers and consultants undergo full field investigations and obtain clearance. In response, HEW Secretary Robert Finch instituted new rules prohibiting investigations into the political activities of advisers and consultants.[54]

Not surprisingly, then, the FBI responded to Nixon administration pressures and in 1970 extended its investigations of New Left organizations on the premise that "leaders" or anyone who "joined in membership" should be identified for "future reference" should they ever obtain "a sensitive Government position."[55]

The FBI's 1970 decision involved no departure in principle from an established program of compiling extensive information on dissident political activities. By April 1970 the Civil Service Commission employed individuals whose sole responsibility was to peruse and list individuals mentioned in radical newspapers. The commission relied on this clipping service, on other agencies' investigative reports (notably the Army and the FBI), and on the cooperation of so-called local police "Red Squads" to compile a data bank containing information on 1.5 million citizens. Like the FBI, Civil Service personnel justified this decision to compile files on nonfederal employees "containing information relating to Communist and other subversive activities" on the premise: "The file is an essential tool to the commission's legal function of investigating the fitness of people for federal employment for security positions."

Not surprisingly, then, serious consideration was in time given to permitting use of these files for purposes other than determining security clearances. During the 1960s, for example, Army intelligence officials used these files to compile reports identifying individuals who might participate in espionage, sabotage, riots, or subvert military discipline. In addition, in 1969 and 1970, Defense Department officials advocated legislation to open these intelligence files to industry. Business executive Mark Shepherd, Jr., president of Texas Instruments, most pointedly articulated this policy's rationale. During an executive meeting of the Defense Department's Industry Advisory Council, Shepherd affirmed:

Industry's immediate problem is to protect itself through some means from the violence oriented militant. Much of the legislation dealing with the social ills of our society over the past 15 or 20 years has unwittingly limited or eliminated many of the former methods used by companies to screen out this type of individual.

If the government does not share "its intelligence with industry in some appropriate manner," Shepherd continued, "industry may in effect have to establish an undercover organization of its own in order to protect itself."[56]

Whether or not industrialists established such an "undercover organization" is not known. In the different political climate of the 1970s, Congress proved unresponsive to the Defense Department proposal to open these files to private industry and to the Nixon administration's efforts to resuscitate the moribund Subversive Actitivies Control Board (SACB). (Established under the McCarran Internal Security Act of 1950, the SACB had been authorized to register Communist and Communist-action organizations.) The board had in effect been rendered inoperative by recent U.S. Supreme Court rulings holding the act's registration requirements unconstitutional.

President Nixon, however, was committed to reviving the SACB. On July 2, 1971, he issued an executive order, 11605, defining listing standards for proscribing organizations under the security program. Prepared under the direction of Assistant Attorney General Robert Mardian, Nixon's order revised existing standards for evaluating whether applicants had engaged in "subversive" activities and authorized the SACB to designate "subversive" organizations. The current security program contained two principal deficiencies, Mardian averred: an obviously dated attorney general's list and the requirement that federal agencies "individually evaluate information regarding membership in allegedly subversive organizations based on raw data" furnished by the FBI.

To rectify the first "deficiency," Executive Order 11605 revised Executive Order 10450 in three important ways. First, whereas subversive organizations had been defined as those adopting "a policy of advocating or approving" acts of force and violence, Nixon's order deleted the "approving" phrase and qualified the advocacy clause by adding the word "unlawful." Second, whereas such organizations had been identified as "having adopted" such a policy, Nixon's order cited "has" adopted. Last, whereas organizations which denied constitutional rights to others or unconstitutionally sought to alter the government had been listed, Nixon's order extended this to include "laws" of the United States "or any State" or "subdivision thereof." As such, Executive Order 11605 substantively extended the criteria for finding organizations to be subversive and encouraged the informal reporting relationship which had been formalized in 1963 between the FBI and local police "Red Squads."

To rectify the second "deficiency," Nixon's order permitted the SACB to designate subversive organizations. Any organization could be so listed by the SACB if it "unlawfully" damaged or destroyed property, injured persons, engaged in riots or "civil disorders," obstructed "the recruiting and enlistment service of the United States, impeding officers of the United States, or related crimes or offenses." Mardian tacitly admitted during congressional testimony that this proposed revision's purpose was not to limit FBI investigations and preclude investigations into political activities. "We have a new brand of radical in this country and we are trying to address ourselves to this new situation," Mardian affirmed. "With the investigative effort of the FBI we hope to present petitions to the Board in accordance with requirements of the Executive Order."[57]

The Nixon administration also tightened measures to preclude the unauthorized disclosure of classified information. It directed the FBI in 1969 to investigate targeted National Security Council and White House staff members and required other suspect executive branch officials to submit to polygraph tests. President Nixon's reasoning for requiring polygraphs for all employees having "top secret" clearance was not a belief in the reliability of such tests but to "immediately scare the bastards."[58]

The administration's public effort to redefine the SACB's functions, however, precipitated a successful congressional effort of 1972 (led by Senator Ervin) to forbid the SACB's use of congressionally appropriated funds to implement the executive order. Congress did not address the Nixon order's broader definition of "subversive" activities and the FBI's broader mandate to investigate individuals under the federal employee security program.[59]

In the absence of any legislative constraints, investigations conducted under the security program focused on dissident political activities. By the 1960s these investigations had been extended to include right-wing anti-Communist organizations and the conservative black nationalist Nation of Islam (Black Muslims). Having concluded that the Black Muslims were violating no federal law and could not be investigated under the Security Index program, FBI and Justice Department officials relied upon the provisions of Eisenhower's Executive Order 10450.

An informal FBI memorandum of July 10, 1974, outlined the FBI's conception of its responsibility under the security program: "The names of all civil applicants and incumbents of the Executive Branch [would be checked] against our records. In order to meet this responsibility FBIHQ [Federal Bureau of Investigation headquarters] records must contain identities of all persons connected with subversive or extremist activities, together with necessary identifying information. All FBI field offices, moreover, were directed on August 16, 1974, to report:

> Identities of subversive and/or extremist groups or movements (including front groups) with which subject has been identified, period of membership, positions held, and a summary of the type and extent of subversive or extremist activities engaged in by subject (e.g., attendance at meetings or other functions, fund raising or recruiting activities on behalf of the organization, contributions, etc.).

Given these criteria, not surprisingly in fiscal year 1974 alone the FBI, the Civil Service Commission, and military intelligence agencies conducted 367,000 name checks on "prospective" federal employees. No longer centering even tangentially on espionage or sabotage, federal employee loyalty/ security programs focused primarily on citizen involvement in nonconventional, dissident politics.[60]

Any changes to reduce the arbitrariness of this repressive program proved inconsequential. Issuing Executive Order 11785, President Nixon abolished the attorney general's list of proscribed organizations and outlined new criteria for evaluating prospective federal employees. This standard read:

> Knowing membership with the specific intent of furthering the aims of, or adherence to and active participation in, any foreign or domestic organization, association, movement, group, or combination of persons . . . which unlawfully advocates or practices the commission of acts of violence to prevent others from exercising their rights under the Constitution or laws of the United States or of any state, or which seeks to overthrow the Government of the United States or subdivision thereof by unlawful means.

Nixon's order permitted the continued listing of individuals engaged in dissident activities, a purpose reaffirmed by the Department of Justice's November 11, 1974, instructions to the FBI. The FBI should continue to "detect organizations with a potential" for falling within the order's standards; individuals who were members or affiliated with such organizations should continue to be investigated. The department further emphasized:

> It is not necessary that a crime occur before the investigation is initiated, but only that a reasonable evaluation of the available information suggests that the activities of the organization may fall within the prescription of the Order. . . . It is not possible to set definite parameters covering the initiation of investigations of potential organizations falling within the Order but once the investigation reaches a stage that offers a basis for determining that the activities are legal in nature, then the investigation should cease, but if the investigation suggests a determination that the organization is engaged in illegal activities or potentially illegal activities it should continue.[61]

The investigative focus of the federal employee security program was not substantively altered by the formal abolition of the attorney general's list. On the one hand, on November 13, 1974, Assistant Attorney General Henry Petersen advised FBI Director Clarence Kelley that a group which had been on the attorney general's list "would still come within the criteria" if it "may have engaged in activities" proscribed under the revised executive order. In a November 19, 1974, memorandum to Kelley, Assistant Attorney General Glen Pommerening reaffirmed that the amended order was not intended to be restrictive; the FBI should investigate organizations having "a potential" for violating federal statutes. To ascertain this potential, Prommerening noted, the FBI must investigate organizations which "may be" of this nature; a crime need not have occurred but "only that a reasonable evaluation" of available information suggested that the activities of the organization "may fall" within these criteria. "Definite parameters" could not be set.

Intelligence officials did not comply even with these *pro forma* changes. The Army, for one, simply ignored the president's order; as late as November 1975 Army security investigations continued to be based on the attorney general's list. Responding to news stories detailing that a former Young Socialist Alliance leader had been discharged from the Reserves, the Army confirmed that its regulations still specified that membership in organizations on the now repealed attorney general's list was considered presumptive evidence that an individual was subversive.[62]

Federal employee investigations continued to be based on these vague standards until September 1976. Then, influenced by the vastly different pressures resulting from congressional disclosures of federal intelligence agencies' abuses of power and recent Court decisions, the Civil Service Commisson announced its decision to drop questions 27, 28, and 29 from the standard Federal Job Form 171. Ever since Eisenhower's requirement that all employees "be of complete and unswerving loyalty to the United States," individuals had been questioned on whether they were a member of the Communist party or subdivision thereof; a member of any organization which "you knew was advocating or teaching that the government of the United States" should be overthrown by force, violence, or any unlawful measures; or as a member of such organization did the individual intend to overthrow the United States government unlawfully. A federal district court in 1969 had ruled that this program's loyalty oath requirement was unconstitutional. Accordingly, the oath had been dropped, but the written questions were retained on the job form. In 1976, however, California, Ohio, Connecticut, and Massachusetts federal district courts ruled that these questions constituted an encroachment on First Amendment rights. On September 8, 1976, and only then, the U.S. Civil Service Commission announced that these questions would be deleted from all federal job application forms "when they are next revised." Until then, Civil Service examining officers would "inform all applicants in writing not to answer these questions." Civil Service officials conceded that the difficulty of rephrasing the queries so that they could meet the courts' requirements against overbroad language encroaching on First Amendment rights had alone resulted in this decision. A Civil Service spokesman, however, emphasized that this did "not mean that in making a background investigation an investigator cannot ask those questions if loyalty were a factor in selection."[63] Apparently, then, the commission was only formally complying with the courts' prohibition against written questions—much as it had in 1969 dropped oaths while retaining the written questions. Civil Service officials clearly intended that security clearance investigations would continue to focus on political activities.

Neither changes in presidential administrations nor the issuance of "more liberalized" orders after 1953 had altered what began as a far-reaching and politically conservative security program. This program authorized (1) the compilation and retention of extensive files on American citizens on the premise that those listed might seek federal employment in the future and (2) far-ranging, continuous FBI investigations of dissident individuals and organizations. Indirectly, then, these programs helped create a chilling political climate. The existence of extensive data bank collections by the 1970s, moreover, permitted and encouraged presidents and intelligence agency officials to leak derogatory information for the political purpose of discrediting individuals or organizations holding unconventional political beliefs. Control over this information had the further effect of undermining whatever respect federal officials might have for First Amendment rights and whatever hesitancy they might have had not to comply with constitutional and/or legal restrictions on their authority.

Conclusion

The Politics of Intelligence

As long as it remains national policy, another important requirement is an aggressive covert psychological, political and paramilitary
organization more effective, more unique, and if necessary, more ruth-
less than that employed by the enemy. No one should be permitted to
stand in the way of the prompt, efficient, and secure accomplishment
of this mission.

It is now clear that we are facing an implacable enemy whose avowed
objective is world domination by whatever means and at whatever
cost. There are no rules in such a game. Hitherto acceptable norms
of human conduct do not apply. If the United States is to survive,
long-standing American concepts of "fair play" must be reconsidered.
We must develop effective espionage and counter-espionage services.
We must learn to subvert, sabotage and destroy our enemies by more
clever, more sophisticated, and more effective methods than those
used against us. It may become necessary that the American people
be made acquainted with, understand and support this fundamentally
repugnant philosophy.[1]

Doolittle Committee Report, September 1954

Just as "the power to wage war is the power to wage war successfully,"
so the power of the President to conduct foreign relations should be
deemed to be the power to conduct foreign relations successfully, by
any means necessary to combat the measures taken by the Communist
bloc, including both open and covert measures.[2]

Department of Justice Memorandum, January 17, 1962

While I share your uneasiness and distaste for any program which
tends to intrude upon an individual's private and legal prerogatives, I
believe it is necessary that the [CIA] maintain a central role in this
activity [drug testing], keep current on enemy capabilities the manipu-
lation of human behavior, and maintain an offensive capability.[3]

Memorandum, CIA Deputy Director for Plans Richard Helms,
December 17, 1963

During the ten years that I was on the U.S. Intelligence Board, . . .
never once did I hear any body, including myself, raise the question:
"Is this course of action which we have agreed upon lawful, is it
legal, is it ethical or moral?" We never gave any thought to this realm
of questioning, because we were just naturally pragmatists. The one

229

thing we were concerned about was this: will this course of action work, will it get us what we want, will we reach the objective that we desire to reach.[4]

Deposition, Former FBI Assistant Director William Sullivan,
November 1, 1975

Although the Department [of Justice] is of the firm view that activities similar in scope and authorization to those [mail opening] conducted by the CIA between 1953 and 1973 would be unlawful if undertaken, the Department has concluded that a prosecution of the potential defendants would be unlikely to succeed because . . . . The view both inside and, to some extent, outside the government was that, in response to exigencies of national security, the President's constitutional power to authorize collection of intelligence was of extremely broad scope. . . . In a very real sense, this case involves a general failure of the government, including the Department of Justice itself, over the period of the mail opening program ever clearly to address and to resolve for its own internal resolution the constitutional and legal restrictions on the relevant aspects of Presidential power.[5]

Department of Justice Press Release, January 14, 1977

It is quite obvious that there are certain inherently governmental actions which if undertaken by the sovereign in protection of the nation's security are lawful but which if undertaken by private persons are not . . . . But it is naive to attempt to categorize activities a president might authorize as "legal" or "illegal" without reference to the circumstances under which he concludes that the activity is necessary.[6]

Notarized Response, Former President Richard Nixon, March 9, 1976

Why did the intelligence agencies become politicized and seek to discredit dissident political movements? Why were intelligence bureaucrats and executive branch officials willing to violate legal and constitutional prohibitions? Why did the constitutional system of checks-and-balances and of broadly defined powers based on law not function in the recent past? The above quotations offer a partial explanation.

To understand the breakdown of the American constitutional system and the emergence of a "1984" society, we must at first recognize the radical impact of the Cold War on American values and institutions. For one, the Cold War encouraged a strong elite-dominated government with authority to make decisions and the gradual acceptance of the need for secrecy and uncritical deference to so-called national security claims. Internal security bureaucrats became increasingly insulated from external accountability and focused only on achieving their desired policy results. The steady rise in influence of the FBI, NSC, the CIA, and the White House staff to dominant policy-making roles and the resultant displacement of the State and Justice departments and the Cabinet—served to reduce the congressional oversight role. By the 1970s, therefore, the intelligence bureaucrats—whether J. Edgar Hoover of the FBI, Henry Kissinger of the NSC, or Richard Helms of the CIA—had become independent powers, effectively establishing national policy, even at times independent of the occupant of the oval office.

A secondary factor—though not without its own ironic importance—was the McCarthy phenomenon. McCarthyism scarred American politics. In response, executive officials avoided controversial appointments, sought to purify the federal bureaucracy, and uncritically acceded to recommendations represented as helping confirm their vigilant anticommunism. The resultant anti-Communist consensus ensured a rather paranoid politics. Conversely, Senator McCarthy's repudiation and the reaction exclusively to his irresponsible tactics (but not his anti-Communist principles and priorities), strengthened "executive privilege" claims and discredited intensive congressional investigations of the executive branch. Indirectly, Senator McCarthy damaged a politics of exposure, increased skepticism about congressional challenges to presidential prerogatives (or, at least, claimed prerogatives), and thereby rendered executive policy less immune to congressional investigations. By extending classification restrictions and basing "executive privilege" on both "national security" and separation-of-powers grounds, presidents after Dwight D. Eisenhower were increasingly able to circumvent the potential constraints on executive policy and on the federal intelligence agencies that had bedeviled Harry Truman. As part of this McCarthyite assault on Truman, conservatives had not only challenged that president's unilateral conduct of foreign and internal security policy and assertion of "executive privilege" claims but also between 1945 and 1953 the potential abuses of power resulting from executive branch officials' independent conduct of policy. During these years, conservatives pointedly railed against Franklin Roosevelt's unilateral decisions at Yalta, feared that the proposed creation of a central intelligence agency might result in a "gestapo," insisted upon constitutional amendments to restrict presidential foreign policy authority, and demanded investigations of the policies and personnel of the Central Intelligence Agency.

Until 1953, at least, American conservatives had supported limited government, feared centralized power, extolled the importance of individual rights, and (if not antireformist) believed that change could not be engineered but must be allowed to unfold organically. The libertarianism of American conservatives, however, was qualified by a preference for order and stability and a profound fear of disruptive change. American conservatives had been consistently (if episodically) in the forefront of efforts to curb the liberties of radicals and dissidents—whether the Populists in the 1890s, the IWW in the 1900s, alien radicals and trade unionists during the 1910s and 1920s, and New Dealers during the 1930s and 1940s. The antilibertarian predilections of American conservatives, nonetheless, were somewhat counterbalanced by a qualified legalism and a profound distrust of centralized power. Traditional conservatives resisted first Franklin Roosevelt's transformation of the office of the presidency between 1933 and 1939 and then his unilateral conduct of foreign policy during the 1939–45 years.

Harry Truman inherited this ambivalent conservative legacy. At once, conservatives sharply denounced the new president's proposal to create a central intelligence group in 1945–46, his refusal in 1948 and again in 1950 to comply with congressional requests for executive agency documents, his secretive diplomacy, and his extension of executive classification restrictions as usurpations of power, as controvening constitutional restrictions, and ultimately as undermining political freedom.

This conservative critique, however, was aborted during Eisenhower's presidency, even though Eisenhower acted even more secretively and unilaterally than had either Truman or Roosevelt. The series of quotes introducing this concluding chapter, notably that from the Doolittle Committee Report of September, 1954, highlight how traditional conservative positions had been repudiated.

During the Cold War years, conservatives came to reject these traditional conservative principles, particularly in the "national security" area. Success in the fight against communism at home or abroad required centralizing power, repudiating legal/constitutional constraints, rejecting moral values, and deference to the executive branch. The representative conservative position no longer was that of Senator Robert Taft or Felix Morley but instead, the messianic Cold War posturing of Senator Barry Goldwater or William Buckley, Jr. By the 1950s conservative political leaders enthusiastically endorsed methods and institutions that conservatives of the 1930s would have condemned as dictatorial and abhorrent. Conservative bureaucrats like FBI Director J. Edgar Hoover willingly violated the law, devised procedures to preclude discovery of their illegalities, and consciously sought to influence and manipulate public opinion and presidential policy. For American conservatives "law and order" became no more than an empty, if effective, political slogan—their preference was to ensure order and to impose conformity. This blindness to principle is most dramatically reflected in the right-wing heroes of the Cold War years—whether J. Edgar Hoover or Otto Otepka—bureaucrats who enthusiastically trampled on the rights of dissident Americans in the name of "national security" and who, though appointive, nonelected officials, independently sought to establish national policy. Traditional conservative fear of centralized power and its consequent abuses and insistence on the authority of the law no longer shaped American conservatives' political positions.

Not that American liberals were without sin. Too often liberals succumbed to rather than challenged conservative political pressures. Whether for reasons of belief or political expediency, Cold War liberals joined in the anti-Communist consensus, in the process qualifying their traditional commitment to individual liberties and constitutionalism. The American liberals' failure was, nonetheless, one of nerve. Liberals sought safety and purity, not because they were more committed to order than to liberty but because they feared that without establishing their anti-communism and that of their programs they would be vulnerable to the tactics of the McCarthyites—whether conservative bureaucrats like Hoover or Otepka, conservative journalists like William Buckley, George Sokolsky, or Walter Trohan, or conservative politicians like James Eastland, Pat McCarran, Richard Nixon, or Barry Goldwater.

These developments, however, were not the inevitable byproduct of the Cold War. International crisis might have provided the context for these far-reaching value and institutional changes; it did not necessitate them. Equally important factors were the formative presidencies of Harry S. Truman and Dwight D. Eisenhower.

The expansion of the federal intelligence agencies' investigative activities and independent authority might have begun during Franklin Roosevelt's presidency. Nonetheless, Roosevelt's informal administrative style, glib (and strained) interpretations of the law and of Supreme Court decisions (whether in his August 1936 oral decision on FBI investigative authority or his May 1940 wiretapping memorandum), and highly personal relationship with FBI Director Hoover had created no permanent authority or intelligence structure. In addition, the programs specifically authorized by Roosevelt were both defined and related directly to the World War II crisis. Truman thus inherited no fixed legacy, and had considerable leeway either to continue or terminate these relatively limited programs. He did not terminate them, however.

The radical expansion of the intelligence community's independent authority and investigative activities, then, was in part the product of Harry Truman's administrative priorities and incompetence. Truman's preference for orderly and rational procedures contributed to new institutional relations in the "national security" area. The National Security Council in time evolved as *the* central, coordinating instrument, permitting a high degree of centralization. Its personnel—conservative anti-Communists—effectively ensured this expansion. In combination, the secrecy shrouding CIA operations and the desire to exploit that secrecy to attain politically risky policy objectives permitted the CIA's role to expand to include covert activities. A secretive and independent national security bureaucracy evolved—no longer directly accountable to external controls. Congress's action of 1949 when exempting the CIA from traditional budget reporting requirements combined with the fact that because NSC personnel were not confirmed by the Senate they need not testify before congressional committees also contributed to this result.

Truman's incompetence helped ensure this expansion. Deferential to his principal advisers, Truman allowed policy to be made by powerful and ambitious personalities. The president might have enjoyed a close relationship and commanded the loyalty of Dean Acheson which the secretary of state exploited to shape administration policy; less loyal cabinet officials and intelligence bureaucrats similarly exploited Truman's deference to advance their own policy goals. Thus, Truman often failed to exercise his authority whether in Attorney General Clark's editing of Roosevelt's wiretapping directive, FBI Director Hoover's editing of Roosevelt's investigative authorization directive, or FBI officials' efforts to ensure a preventive detection program. Either misinformed or bypassed, Truman was often a president in name only: bureaucrats instead independently or insubordinately made policy.

In 1952, Republican presidential candidate Dwight Eisenhower won election to the presidency by pledging greater legislative-executive cooperation, an end to secrecy and executive unilateralism, the balancing of individual rights and national security, and government based on the rule of law, not the personal preferences of bureaucrats. These pledges did not, however, become the guiding principles of the new Republican administration. Although the authorization for far-reaching programs (involving preventive detention, FBI political surveillance investigations, or wiretapping) had been obtained during Truman's tenure by questionable means, the new president did not critically review these decisions. Instead, again by misinformation or selective briefings, intelligence bureaucrats secured reaffirmation. Nor were these activities merely sustained. Instead, the Eisenhower years witnessed a quantum jump in the independent authority and activities of the intelligence agencies—whether in the areas of electronic surveillance policy, the institution of the FBI's COINTELPRO, the CIA's mail intercept program, the FBI's preventive detention program, or the CIA's involvement in coups or planned assassinations.

These programs expanded further during the 1960s. Intelligence bureaucrats no longer needed to fear effective executive oversight or direction. Minor administrative reforms might have then been instituted—specifically by President Johnson's two attorneys general, Nicholas Katzenbach and Ramsey Clark, involving FBI electronic surveillance activities—but the principal checks to the federal intelligence bureaucracy's activities came from outside the executive branch. First, investigative hearings conducted in 1965–66 by the Subcommittee on Administrative Practice and Procedure of the Senate Judiciary Committee and then *Rampart's* magazine's revelations in 1967 threatened to compromise programs and activities of the intelligence bureaucracy. Not because of a concern for the law or a sensitivity to the limits of their authority but because of a fear of adverse publicity, intelligence bureaucrats in 1965–67 restricted their agencies' activities. This same fear of adverse publicity recurred in 1973–75 when, responding to other congressional investigations and press revelations, intelligence officials terminated still other programs and activities.

If, then, the history of this expansion and the resultant abuses of power derived from inadequate executive oversight, from the politics of secrecy and national security (insulating the intelligence bureaucracy from external controls), and from intelligence bureaucrat's disdain for the law and the Constitution, the revelation of these abuses of power in 1975–76 did not automatically ensure reform. These abuses' origins were institutional in nature; they were the product as well of the acceptance of Cold War "national security" and "executive privilege" claims. Ironically, however, in the very aftermath of these revelations of abuses, reforming the intelligence community did not surface as a major political issue during the 1976 presidential and congressional campaigns. Nor were the public and the congressional leadership willing to repudiate the secrecy and national security rationalizations which had contributed to the evolution of this problem.

This hesitancy to challenge Cold War norms and existing institutional relationships was evident as early as 1976. Following the numbing series of revelations brought out by the House and Senate select committees investigating the intelligence agencies and publicized by the media, Congress hesitated even to consider instituting legislative reforms. Instead, responding to the

December 24, 1975, assassination of CIA official Richard Welsh in Athens, Greece, and a strategy carefully orchestrated by the conservative congressional leadership and the Ford administration, the House of Representatives on January 29, 1976, voted decisively, 246–124, not to release the report of the Pike committee (the special House committee investigating the intelligence agencies). Senator Frank Church aptly characterized this action as confirming a greater concern for secrecy than abuses of power.[7]

A rather limited reform proposal, S. Res. 400, creating a special congressional oversight committee (which until then was conceded to be assured of congressional passage), at first appeared doomed to the same fate. Amended by the Senate Rules Committee to deny any legislative jurisdiction to the proposed committee and to be staffed predominantly with senators serving on existing oversight committees (notably Judiciary and Armed Services), the proposed establishment of an effective Senate oversight committee seemed destined to the same considerations that determined suppression of the Pike committee report. The proposal was rescued only with the April 1976 release of the Senate Select Committee on Intelligence Activities reports dramatizing the scope of past abuses of power and the ineffectiveness of executive oversight. When the amended S. Res. 400 thus came to the floor of the Senate for a vote, important revisions were instituted under the leadership of Senators Mike Mansfield, Robert Byrd, and Abraham Ribicoff. These included ceding final legislative jurisdiction to the proposed intelligence oversight committee and providing that seven of the fifteen committee members be selected at large with two each to be drawn from existing oversight committees (Armed Services, Judiciary, Appropriations, and Foreign Relations). The Senate approved these revisions on May 19, 1976, by the vote of 72–22.[8]

In the attempt to contain future reforms by capitalizing on this changed political climate, on February 18, 1976, President Ford had issued Executive Order 11905 allegedly to "preserve and respect our established concepts of privacy and civil liberties," "clarify the authority and responsibilities" of the intelligence agencies, and ensure that intelligence "activities are conducted in a Constitutional and lawful manner and never aimed at our own citizens." Despite this civil libertarian rhetoric, the executive order's provisions underscored the real commitment was to ensure presidential control over the agencies and to promote their effective operation. Ford did not prohibit surveillance operations and activities of questionable legality; rather his order merely required that all intelligence activities be formally authorized by agency heads subject to approval and review of personnel directly responsible to the president. Reflecting the executive preference for secrecy, and committed to curbing potentially embarrassing leaks, Executive Order 11905 required that all executive branch officials and government contractors sign an agreement not to disclose information about "intelligence sources and methods" and minimized any external oversight role, principally by the Congress.[9]

This attempt to delimit prospective reforms of the intelligence agencies to the policy preferences of the executive branch also underlay the series of guidelines that Attorney General Levi formulated for FBI investigations. Instituted on March 10, 1976, these internally imposed restrictions would have prohibited the more glaring abuses of past FBI investigative activities. Levi's prohibitions, however, were not absolute; for investigations could still be conducted even when no federal statute was violated. The FBI could continue to "detect and prevent . . . subversion . . . on behalf of foreign powers" and "to ascertain information" concerning the use of "force or violence and the violation of federal law, for the purpose of . . . impairing, for the purpose of influencing U.S. government policies or decisions . . . the functioning of the government of the United States. . . ." The broad language of Levi's guidelines permitted continued political surveillance investigations, both because the word "subversion" was meaningless and because demonstrations often times were intended to influence U.S. policies or, as in the case of some antiwar demonstrations, impair the "functioning" of the government. Under these guidelines, the FBI's use of informers, wiretaps, and political investigations was somewhat reduced; investigations to obtain political intelligence were not terminated. In fact, "domestic security" investigations continued thereafter but under different terminology—to combat "terrorism" or as "foreign counterintelligence." FBI Associate Director James Adams's March 1978 testimony confirmed that 250 informers who formerly had been assigned to "domestic security" investigations after 1976 were reclassified "foreign intelligence."[10]

In 1977–78, the Carter administration extended these administrative reforms. In effect, though, the Carter reforms (formally instituted by Executive Order 12036 on January 24, 1978) tightened administrative controls over the intelligence agencies, reduced intelligence agency personnel and interagency policy conflicts, retained the flexibility which the vague language of the National Security Act of 1947 provided for NSC and CIA operations (including "special activities" and "services of common concern"), and granted to the CIA director greater supervisory power over intelligence collection. Designated as the "primary adviser to the President and the NSC on national foreign intelligence," the CIA director was assigned "full and exclusive" authority to approve the National Foreign Intelligence budget submitted to the president. Domestic surveillance activities, moreover, were not barred. Executive Order 12036 only required that they be properly authorized; they need not be predicated on violations or "probable cause" violations of federal statutes. In contrast to earlier "national security" rationalizations (whether the nebulous phrases "subversive activities" or "Communist/ Fascist" influence), Carter's order justified surveillances of any person whom the executive branch independently concluded was an "agent of a foreign power." Implicitly, the president claimed to have the inherent power to authorize "without a judicial warrant" investigations on his (or the attorney general's) conclusion that "there is probable cause to believe that the United States person is an agent of a foreign power." Carter's order also authorized the CIA to "conduct counterintelligence activities within the United States, but only in coordination with the FBI and subject to the approval of the Attorney General" and granted the same authority and review requirement to the Department of Defense. The NSA, moreover, was authorized to collect, process, and disseminate "signals intelligence information for counterintelligence purposes." Investigations for "intelligence" purposes involving "terrorism" or groups primarily made up of alien residents or "foreign agents" were also permitted. (Not surprisingly, then, in his first press conference newly appointed FBI Director William Webster articulated the FBI's "emerging concern" about the possibility that terrorism might spread to the United States.) Carter's order thus might have formally limited the authority of intelligence agencies; it did not preclude the recurrence of the recently disclosed abuses. Like the Ford reforms, Executive Order 12036 was based on the principle of executive self-restraint and the need for a rationalized intelligence capability.

To curb leaks of "classified" information, the Carter administration also supported legislation penalizing the unauthorized leaks of classified information to the press and reducing from seven to one the number of congressional committees having access to intelligence information. The number of White House aides having access to covert intelligence information was reduced from forty to five while "secrecy agreements" were more expansively used within the national security bureaucracy to require employees not to divulge classified material. The Carter Justice Department, in addition, filed a legal brief during a suit (involving illegal wiretapping activities) arguing that former President Nixon and all other presidents should be immune from prosecution in illegal wiretap cases if they acted in "good faith" having concluded that "matters vital to" the national security were involved and thus that "no judicial question can be tolerated."[11]

Administration efforts to confine restrictions on the intelligence agencies' activities were not limited to executive order reforms. An additional problem for the administration involved the decision whether or not to prosecute intelligence officials for their participation in illegal activities in the recent past. Prosecution of these officials could serve as a powerful example, could deter the recurrence of illegal activities, and would symbolize a commitment to the rule of law. Prosecution, however, could also entail major political risks. First, such prosecutions could further demoralize the intelligence community, already buffeted by an adverse public reaction though nonetheless remaining convinced that past activities had been necessary and justified. Second, during trial proceedings additional secrets could be compromised and other procedures and activities could be publicly disclosed—for defense attorneys through disclosure motions or interrogation would surely attempt to establish the authority and commonality of the activities for which their clients had been indicted. (Indeed, such were the cases in the aborted trial of former FBI agent John Kearney, who was indicted on April 7, 1977, for illegal mail opening and wiretap activities, and in the May 1978 pre-trial motions of attorneys for former FBI officials L. Patrick Gray, W. Mark Felt and Edward Miller.) Third these trials would inevitably be highly publicized and this in turn could sustain public awareness of the scope of past abuses and possibly increase demands for reforms more stringent than those presidents could support.

Accordingly, the Ford administration decided in January 1977 not to prosecute CIA officials who had illegally opened the mail of American citizens. Attorney General Edward Levi conceded that mail opening was recognizably "unlawful." He nonetheless justified the department's decision not to prosecute on the twin premises of the Department of Justice's past failures "to address and resolve . . . the constitutional and legal restrictions" on presidential powers and on Cold War presidents' expansive conceptions of their constitutional powers in the "national security" area. Then, on October 31, 1977, the Carter administration agreed to permit former CIA Director Richard Helms to plead *nolo contendre* to two misdemeanor counts of failing to testify truthfully before a congressional committee. As part of this bargain, the department recommended that Helms be fined only $200. (The judge, instead, fined Helms $2,000.) The administration rationalized this decision on the basis of Helms' distinguished governmental career and the possibility that a trial "might jeopardize national secrets."

The administration confronted a more difficult and torturous decision, however, involving the illegal activities of FBI officials and agents. Unlike Helms, high-level FBI officials and FBI agents could not automatically claim higher authority. FBI break-ins, wiretaps, and mail intercepts of the early 1970s either violated recent Court decisions (*U.S. v. U.S. District Court*) or FBI Director Hoover's written orders of 1965 and 1966 terminating or stringently limiting these practices.

Attorney General Griffin Bell's willingness to initiate a grand jury investigation in 1977 precipitated a major crisis within the FBI and, in turn, within the Department of Justice. FBI agents protested the double standard wherein CIA officials were not prosecuted for illegal mail opening. These same agents defended past illegal activities as necessary and proper. Although hesitating to drop this investigation, given its pledge to restore respect for the law, the Carter administration found it distasteful. A distinct ambivalence ensued. At first, only former FBI supervisor John Kearney was indicted but not John Morley, his superior in the New York field office. Ultimately, on April 10, 1978, the department dropped prosecution of Kearney and obtained the indictment of former Acting FBI Director L. Patrick Gray, former FBI Associate Director W. Mark Felt, and former FBI Assistant Director Edward Miller. In the interim between the Kearney and the Gray-Felt-Miller indictments, the attorney general's obvious reluctance to indict higher-level FBI officials, and thereby risk court disclosure of FBI break-ins and other illegal activities, led five Justice Department attorneys to resign in protest. (In April 1978, moreover, the head of the department's criminal division, William Gardner, accused Attorney General Bell of having thwarted the indictment of eight other FBI officials.) Confronted by a time deadline which would foreclose any further indictments (because of the statute of limitations), in early April 1978 Justice Department officials had nonetheless preferred to negotiate plea bargaining agreements with attorneys for Mssrs. Gray, Felt, and Miller. Confident that the Government would not dare indict their clients, defense attorneys refused to agree to any plea unless the government first disclosed its evidence against their clients. Attorney General Griffin Bell rejected this demand and at an April 10, 1978, press conference announced the grand jury's decision to indict Gray, Felt, and Miller. During this press conference, Bell claimed to have uncovered documentary evidence that these high-level FBI officials had authorized illegal activities and implied further that authorization did not go higher, whether to President Nixon, Attorney General John Mitchell, or high-level Justice Department officials. The indictments effectively shifted the issue to the courtroom without resolving the question of whether these FBI officials had acted on their own authority. Thus, during pre-trial motions, Miller and Felt admitted authorizing the activities (Gray, however, denied any knowledge) but claimed that higher-level officials in the FBI, Justice Department and the Nixon White House knew and approved the use of these illegal investigative activities. As part of this effort, defense attorneys submitted massive discovery motions, including requests for documents pertaining to Nixon's presidency.[12]

Because somewhat sensitive to the political impact of Congressional investigations of 1975–76 disclosing wiretapping uses, however, the Ford and Carter Administrations abandoned the "inherent" presidential powers claim which had been affirmed during the Cold War years as the authority for warrantless "national security" wiretaps. These presidential claims had first been challenged by the *Keith* decision of 1972. After 1972, however, presidents claimed the right to authorize "foreign intelligence" wiretaps, instead of relying on the earlier "national security" rationale. The congressional disclosures of 1975–76 of how wiretaps of dissident political movements had been authorized by president's since Truman's administration on "national security" grounds, and thus of the abuses practiced in the name of "national security," compelled further presidential retreats. The Ford administration abandoned its initial opposition to support legislation, S. 3197, providing a limited warrant requirement for "national security" wiretaps. The administration nonetheless insisted upon retention of a clause reaffirming what had become the position of Cold War presidents: "Nothing contained in this chapter shall limit the constitutional power of the Presidents to order electronic survelilance. . . ."

More sensitive to the protests over the inherent power's claim and committed, at least symbolically, to a more open and less arrogant presidency, the newly elected Carter administration abandoned this claim and, in conjunction with leaders of the Senate, participated in drafting a bill—S. 1566 introduced by Senators Kennedy, Bayh, Eastland, Inouye, McClellan, Mathias, Nelson, and Thurmond on May 18, 1977—outlining procedures "to authorize applications for a court order approving the use of electronic surveillance to obtain foreign intelligence information." If a decided improvement over the broad exemption granted by section 2511(3) of the Omnibus Crime Control Act of 1968 and over S. 3197, S. 1566 nonetheless contained important loopholes. Wiretapping would not be confined to investigating violations of federal statutes (in this case the espionage laws); instead, individual citizens could be wiretapped if they secretly "collect or transmit information" that might harm the national security. Alien residents or visitors could be tapped if engaging in noncriminal and undefined "clandestine intelligence activities;" American citizens or foreigners who "aid or abet" someone engaged in these undefined activities could also be tapped. The prohibition of S. 1566, moreover, did not apply to NSA electronic surveillance of Americans living abroad although such surveillance would be somewhat curbed within the United States. Senator Birch Bayh astutely criticized this legislative deficiency: "To the extent that N.S.A. activities fall within the definition of electronic surveillance in the proposed bill, the act would protect the rights of Americans from improper N.S.A. surveillance. But most of what N.S.A. does is not covered by the bill." Other liberal senators expressed similar reservations about S. 1566.

These reservations eventually resulted in the introduction of a series of amendments to the originally proposed bill. Following relatively unpublicized hearings conducted by the Senate Committee on the Judiciary and by the Senate Select Committee on Intelligence, an amended S. 1566 was cleared for floor debate in February 1978. After perfunctory debate, this amended bill was overwhelmingly approved, by the vote of 95–1, on April 20, 1978. These amendments in effect strengthened the bill's intended safeguards for individual liberties. The principal amendments required a criminal standard as a condition for governmental requests for court approval of "foreign intelligence" electronic surveillances of citizens and alien residents. To minimize potential abuses, the amended bill also required that semi-annually the attorney general must fully inform designated congressional committees how this "foreign intelligence" authority had been used. Still dissatisfied, some liberal critics hoped to convince House members to adopt a tighter bill.[13]

The congressional failure to enact tighter legislative standards by 1978 left the wiretapping issue squarely to the discretion of the courts. Although Carter administration officials had informed the Congress in 1978 that it had not authorized any warrantless "foreign intelligence" investigation of American citizens, the February 1978 arrests of U.S. information officer Ronald Humphrey and Vietnamese expatriate David Truong soon disclosed that the president had personally authorized television and electronic surveillances and warrantless mail opening. During the resultant trial, government attorneys defended these actions claiming that in the national security area presidents may ignore the Fourth Amendment's prohibitions against illegal searches and seizures. To observers it appeared that the administration was inviting a court test of presidential powers; an undisclosed State Department official indeed told *New York Times* reporter Nicholas Horrock that the case had been brought "as a test of Presidential power and nothing else."

In addition, the Carter administration sought a modification of a judge's order demanding twenty-five years of FBI records of warrantless wiretaps, mail openings, and break-ins; claimed that presidents should be immune from prosecution for illegal wiretaps based on a "good faith" standard; and considered not complying with a judge's disclosure ruling involving the files of eighteen FBI informers. More importantly, the administration vigorously contested a suit brought against the Ford administration in 1976 by a House subcommittee for AT&T's records on "national security request letters." This congressional committee, chaired by Democratic Congressman John Moss, had attempted to assess the validity of administration claims of having reduced the number of wiretaps. While the Ford administration had claimed that wiretaps had declined from 190 in 1974 to 122 in 1975, Moss maintained that Justice Department requests to AT&T numbered 76 in 1972, 95 in 1973, 141 in 1974, 141 in 1975, and 58 for the first six months of 1976. This discrepancy, the department explained, was the result of a changed administrative requirement: before 1974 one letter might cover a number of wiretap requests; after 1974 a letter was required for each request.

Although this issue has not been resolved judicially—Federal Judge Oliver Gasch ordered the subcommittee and the administration to attempt to work out a settlement—another potentially more far-reaching judicial ruling was issued involving whether telephone companies could be required to assist law enforcement officers in installing telephone surveillance devices. Sustaining a lower federal court ruling, the U.S. Supreme Court in a 5–4 ruling of December 7, 1977, upheld such a requirement. Without such assistance, the majority opinion held, law enforcement officials could not conceivably carry out lawful surveillance orders. In a sharp dissent, Justice John Stevens characterized the ruling as "a sweeping grant of authority without precedent in our nation's history"; other dissenters regretted this violation of two hundred years of precedent limiting the government's powers to force private cooperation. Earlier, on January 18, 1977, the Supreme Court also ruled that evidence gathered from a technically illegal secret wiretap could be used during criminal trials.[14]

Given the court's and executive branch officials' unwillingness to limit the intelligence agencies' investigative activities, and thereby preclude the recurrence of the recently disclosed abuses of power, what has been the congressional response? Rather than seizing the initiative and seeking to reassert its authority, the Congress has been decidedly hesitant about grappling with this complex, explosive issue. It is almost as if most members of Congress hope that by delaying action the problem will simply go away. For example, on June 22, 1977, the Senate authorized the intelligence community's fiscal year 1978 budget without a roll call vote or amendments. Moreover, when Senator Daniel Inouye (the chairman of the Select Committee on Intelligence) invited other senators to read the classified report of the Select Committee's Subcommittee on Budget Authorization, based on intensive hearings and testimony, only three senators other than the seventeen members of the Select Committee responded to that invitation. The House was even less willing to oversee the intelligence agencies. Approving by the vote of 323–43 budgets for the intelligence agencies on June 6, 1978, without most members of the House knowing how much money was involved or how it would be used, the House uncritically acceded to the recommendation of the House Intelligence Committee that the disclosure of even the total budgetary allocation would create pressure for more details.

In striking contrast to this ostrich-like attitude, on April 5, 1977, Congressman Herman Badillo (and twenty-four other representatives supported by a host of civil liberties and civil rights organizations) introduced H.R. 6051, the Federal Intelligence Agencies Control Act of 1977, to limit stringently the activities of the intelligence agencies. Hearings on this bill, however, were delayed until the Carter administration's position on this and other proposed legislative measures was made public.

In the interim, the Senate Select Committee began lengthy deliberations to develop legislative charters for the intelligence agencies. Composed of conservatives (Barry Goldwater, Jake Garn, James Pearson, Richard Lugar, Malcolm Wallop, and Daniel Moynihan) and liberals (Birch Bayh, Adlai Stevenson, William Hathaway, Joseph Biden, Jr., Gary Hart, Clifford Case, and Charles Mathias), the committee spent its first year seeking to reach a consensus on a legislative measure which would "balance the right of the public and the Senate to be informed of the government's activities with the countervailing necessity to protect valid national secrets." The additional views of Senator Moynihan to the May 17, 1977, report of the Select Committee on its activities covering the first year of its existence graphically capture the magnitude of this problem. Although agreeing with the contents of the May 17 report, the New York senator then complained:

> I am nonetheless concerned that the committee has unintentionally produced a profoundly biased political document. . . . I would characterize the central position of the committee's report in terms of Walt Kelly's now classical aphorism in his comic strip "Pogo": "We have met the enemy and he is us." . . . There is a pattern of avoidance of the reality of totalitarian threat throughout this document. This seeming obliviousness to the international context in which our intelligence activities take place seems less an aberration than a mutant of classical isolationism. In my opinion, this may be a comforting world view, but it is a profoundly unrealistic one.

If such Cold War views continued to shape the context within which intelligence policy was publicly discussed, nonetheless, the Select Committee soon moved well beyond these alarmist fears. Accordingly, on February 9, 1978, Senator Walter Huddleston (as chairman of the Select Committee's Subcommittee on Charters and Guidelines) formally introduced S. 2525, the National Intelligence Reorganization and Reform Act of 1978. Supported by twenty senators (only Stevenson, Hathaway, and Case of the full Select Committee were not listed as co-sponsors), this massive 263-page bill defined its purpose "to improve the intelligence system of the United States by the establishment of a statutory basis for the national intelligence activities of the United States, and for other purposes." Whether or not enacted by the Congress or amended, S. 2525 constituted a radical improvement over both Presidents Ford's and Carter's executive orders.

The framers of S. 2525 had sought to attain three objectives: (1) to ensure that responsible executive officials could more effectively control and authorize intelligence agency activities, (2) to ensure that a fully-informed Congress could meet its oversight role, and (3) to ensure the future intelligence activities would be governed by definite rules and procedures based on legislatively defined guidelines. S. 2525 effectively prohibited the intelligence agencies' more glaring abuses of power of the recent past. For one, Do Not File procedures were prohibited by requiring full and complete written records of decisions and authorizations and specifically that heads of agencies, the attorney general, and designated congressional committees must certify the lawfulness of all intelligence activities. Second, the National Security Council, the attorney general, the president, a to-be-established Intelligence Oversight Board, and designated congressional committees were assigned review and approval responsibility. The bill required not only written authorization and full reporting within the executive branch, but also that responsible executive officials fully brief, and thus were accountable to, House and Senate select intelligence committees. Third, S. 2525 forbade particular investigative activities (like the FBI's COINTELPROs and political reporting to the White House) and delineated the parameters of the various intelligence agencies investigative authority. These specific guidelines were carefully outlined in sections defining permissible intelligence activities and in sections providing formal legislative charters for the CIA, FBI, and NSA.

The principal motivations of the drafters of this bill were dual: to ensure greater efficiency and rationality in the intelligence community and to limit violations of individual liberties. Based on the premise that reform must also improve the efficiency of the intelligence agencies, S. 2525 formally authorized continuance of CIA covert activities and did not predicate domestic investigations on violations or "probable cause" violations of federal laws. While not authorizing investigations of "subversive activities," S. 2525's authorization of "foreign intelligence," "counterintelligence," and "counterterrorist" investigations posed a potential problem. Because of their vagueness and breadth, these terms could permit the recurrence of abuses (if less dramatic than those disclosed during the 1970s). For example, foreign intelligence activities were broadly defined as pertaining to "the defense, national security, foreign policy *or related policies* of the United States" (emphasis added). The term "terrorism" is another troubling word, and recalls the rationalization offered by FBI, CIA, and White House officials during the 1950s, the 1960s, and early 1970s to justify far-reaching investigations of then-perceived internal security threats—whether the omnipresent term "subversive activities" or "communism, fascism." Last, the bill's "statement of purpose" section affirms, for one, the need "to insure that the executive and legislative branches are provided, in the most efficient manner, with such accurate, relevant, and timely information and analysis as those branches need to make sound and informed decisions regarding the security and vital interests of the United States and to protect the United States against foreign intelligence activities, international terrorist activities, *and other forms of hostile action* directed against the United States" (emphasis added).[15]

Whether or not S. 2525 will be seriously considered and enacted remains problematic. The congressional response, however, will highlight the permanent or transitory impact of the Cold War on American values and institutions. For by the 1970s the nation faced a serious constitutional crisis: in the recent past not only had laws been violated with impunity, not only had responsible executive officials failed to fulfill their assigned oversight role, but the Congress had been virtually excluded from its proper legislative and oversight functions. Senator Frank Church's letter transmitting the final reports of the Senate Select Committee on Intelligence Activities succinctly summarizes the problem confronting the Congress and the nation in the late 1970s:

> The root cause of the excesses which our record amply demonstrates has been failure to apply the wisdom of the constitutional system of checks and balances to intelligence activities. Our experience as a nation has taught us that we must place our trust in laws, and not solely in men. The founding fathers foresaw excess as the inevitable consequence of granting any part of government unchecked power. This has been demonstrated in the intelligence field where, too often, constitutional principles were subordinated to a pragmatic course of permitting desired ends to dictate and justify improper means.[16]

Abbreviations

AAPIFL	U.S. Senate, Select Committee to Study Governmental Operations with Respect to Intelligence Activities, Interim Report, *Alleged Assassination Plots Involving Foreign Leaders,* 94th Cong., 1st sess., 1975.
FMI	U.S. Senate, Select Committee to Study Governmental Operations with Respect to Intelligence Activities, Final Report, *Foreign and Military Intelligence,* Book I, 94th Cong., 2d sess., 1976.
HDIOIS	U.S. House, Committee on Internal Security, *Hearings on Domestic Intelligence Operations for Internal Security Purposes,* pt. I, 93rd Cong., 2d sess., 1974.
HIA	U.S. Senate, Select Committee to Study Governmental Operations with Respect to Intelligence Activities, *Hearings on Intelligence Activities,* 94th Cong., 1st sess., 1975.
HIDFBI	U.S. House, Committee on Government Operations, Subcommittee on Government Information and Individual Rights, *Hearings on Inquiry into the Destruction of Former FBI Director Hoover's Files and FBI Recordkeeping,* 94th Cong., 1st sess., 1975.
HJDIIP	U.S. House, Committee on Government Operations, Subcommittee on Government Information and Individual Rights, *Hearings on Justice Department Internal Investigation Policies,* 95th Cong., 1st sess., 1977.
IARA	U.S. Senate, Select Committee to Study Governmental Operations with Respect to Intelligence Activities, Final Report, *Intelligence Activities and the Rights of Americans,* Book II, 94th Cong., 2d sess., 1976.
JHWWES	U.S. Senate, Committee on the Judiciary, Subcommittees on Administrative Practice and Procedure and on Constitutional Rights, and U.S. Senate, Committee on Foreign Relations, Subcommittee on Surveillance, *Joint Hearings on Warrantless Wiretapping and Electronic Surveillance—1974,* 93rd Cong., 2d sess., 1974.
SDSRFMI	U.S. Senate, Select Committee to Study Governmental Operations with Respect to Intelligence Activities, Final Report, *Supplementary Detailed Staff Reports on Foreign and Military Intelligence,* Book IV, 94th Cong., 2d sess., 1976.

SDSRIARA   U.S. Senate, Select Committee to Study Governmental Operations with Respect to Intelligence Activities, Final Report, *Supplementary Detailed Staff Reports on Intelligence Activities and the Rights of Americans*, Book III, 94th Cong., 2d sess., 1976.

DDE   Dwight D. Eisenhower Library, Abilene, Kansas

HST   Harry S Truman Library, Independence, Missouri

JFK   John F. Kennedy Library, Boston, Massachusetts

LBJ   Lyndon B. Johnson Library, Austin, Texas

Notes

Preface

1. These filing procedures are discussed in detail in the text of this study. See also Athan Theoharis, "Bureaucrats above the Law: Double-Entry Intelligence Files," *Nation* 225 (Oct. 22, 1977), pp. 393–397 and "Should the FBI Purge Its Files?" *USA Today* (forthcoming but likely Sept. 1978).

2. *SDSRIARA*, pp. 458 n336, 464. May 13, 1954, Entry, James Hagerty Papers–Diary Entries, May 1954, DDE.

3. *SDSRFMI*, pp. 138–141, 139 n106a, 141 n108. *AAPIFL*, pp. 55–60, 56 n2.

4. *Report of the Department of Justice Concerning Its Investigation and Prosecutorial Decisions with Respect to Central Intelligence Agency Mail Opening Activities in the United States* (Jan. 14, 1977), pp. 11–12, 471, *FMI*, pp. 45–46, 51–52, 54–56, 59, 60, 86, 107, 112, 283, 294, 309–310, 360, 385 n2, 386–391, 394, 398–399, 401, 403–408, 404 n77, 406 n83, 409–411, 410 n95, 418–419, 421, 423, 427, 428, 440, 447, 459–460, 471–474, 475 nl, 480–481, 483 n34, 499 n100. *AAPIFL*, pp. 3, 6–7, 10–12, 25–26, 33, 44–45, 53, 55–64, 67–70, 93, 95–96, 99–108, 114–135, 148–180, 182–188, 246–254, 261–279. *SDSRFMI*, pp. 28, 30, 35, 46, 50–51, 70–71, 128–131, 128 n34, 129 n44, 132–133. *SDSRIARA*, pp. 596, 599, 623, 689, 743 n27, 745 n33, 746, 761, 762, 768–770, 783, 808–809, 808 n148, 811, 813. U.S. House, Committee on Government Operations, Special Subcommittee on Government Information, *Hearings on Availability of Information for Federal Departments and Agencies*, pt. 8, 85th Cong., 1st sess., 1957, pp. 2011–2012. *Milwaukee Journal*, May 9, 1978, p. 2. *New York Times*, May 14, 1978, p. 3E. In addition, although his assertions were self-serving and based on a concern to avoid any admission of illegal conduct, Richard Nixon's responses to a series of interrogatories posed by staff members of the Senate Select Committee on Intelligence Activities also highlights this practice. The former president never directly denied knowing of any of the activities cited by the staff; instead he consistently affirmed that he could not recall or did not remember being briefed. We are left, then, with the irresolvable dilemma: either Nixon had not been briefed or he was being unresponsive in March 1976. See *SDSRFMI*, pp. 144–149, 152, 154, 155–156, 158–159, 161–167. William Corson, moreover, has enumerated a series of incidents wherein presidents were incompletely briefed or where intelligence agency officials effectively established policy. Corson, *The Armies of Ignorance*, pp. 19–20, 22, 26–27, 28, 31–32, 70–71, 85–86, 88–91, 140, 211–214, 344–345, 347–352, 354–358, 360–366, 385–386, 392–393, 448. Seymour Hersh, "The Angleton Story," *New York Times Magazine* (June 25, 1978), p. 15.

Introduction

1. Athan Theoharis, "Misleading the Presidents: Thirty Years of Wire Tapping." *Nation*, 212 (June 14, 1971), p. 747.

2. Ibid.
3. Ibid., pp. 748–749.
4. Clinton Rossiter, *The American Presidency* (New York: Harcourt, Brace, 1956), pp. 10, 25–27, 29, 62–81, 94, 159–160, 163. Walter Johnson, *1600 Pennsylvania Avenue: Presidents and the People Since 1929* (Boston: Little, Brown, 1963), pp. vii–viii, 25, 26, 41, 49–50, 56, 83–84, 107–108, 113, 127, 188, 192, 195, 200, 223–224, 240, 246, 286, 293, 295, 303, 312, 318, 323, 324, 332. George Kennan, *The Cloud of Danger: Current Realities of American Foreign Policy* (Boston: Atlantic–Little, Brown, 1977), pp. 3–9, 25–26, 40, 48–49. The literature on the presidency is impressively surveyed in an unpublished paper of Thomas Cronin, "The Textbook Presidency and Political Science," introduced into the *Congressional Record* by Senator Gordon Allott, U.S. *Congressional Record*, 91st Cong., 2d sess., 1970, vol. 116, pt. 26, pp. 34915–34928. The references to the excessive role of public opinion and the need for more independent political elites were offered by Peter Viereck and Talcott Parsons, and echoed by Seymour Lipset and Richard Hofstadter in essays they contributed to a collection edited by Daniel Bell, *The Radical Right* (Garden City: Doubleday, 1963), pp. 95, 165, 228–229, 326. See also George Kennan, *American Diplomacy, 1900–1950* (Chicago: The University of Chicago Press, 1951); Walter Lippmann, *Essays in the Public Philosophy* (Boston: Little, Brown, 1955); Hans Morgenthau, "The Decline and Fall of American Foreign Policy," *New Republic* 135 (Dec. 10, 1956), p. 11; Norman Graebner, *The New Isolationism: A Study in Politics and Foreign Policy since 1950* (New York: Ronald Press, 1956); and Thomas Bailey, *The Man in the Street: The Impact of American Public Opinion on Foreign Policy* (New York: F. S. Crofts, 1948). For other studies of the presidency, see Richard Neustadt, *Presidential Power* (New York: Wiley, 1960); Grant McConnell, *The Modern Presidency* (New York: St. Martin's Press, 1967); John Murphy, *The Pinnacle: The Contemporary American Presidency* (Philadelphia: Lippincott, 1974); James MacGregor Burns, *Presidential Government* (Boston: Houghton Mifflin, 1966); Aaron Wildavsky, ed., *The Presidency* (Boston: Little, Brown, 1969); Richard Pious, "Is Presidential Power Poison," *Political Science Quarterly* 89 (Fall 1974), pp. 627–643; and Michael Grossman and Francis Rourke, "The Media and the Presidency: An Exchange Analysis," *Political Science Quarterly* 91 (Fall 1976), pp. 455–470. See also the essays by Abraham Safaer, Barton Bernstein, and William Van Alystyne in *Law and Contemporary Problems* 40 (Spring 1976).
5. These instances are discussed variously in Richard Polenberg, *Reorganizing Roosevelt's Government: The Controversy over Executive Reorganization, 1936–1939* (Cambridge: Harvard, 1966); Athan Theoharis, *The Yalta Myths: An Issue in U.S. Politics, 1945–1955* (Columbia: University of Missouri Press, 1970); Athan Theoharis, *Seeds of Repression: Harry S. Truman and the Origins of McCarthyism* (Chicago: Quadrangle, 1971); Athan Theoharis, "The Politics of Scholarship: Liberals, Anti-Communism, and McCarthyism," in Robert Griffith and Athan Theoharis, eds., *The Specter: Original Essays on the Cold War and the Origins of McCarthyism* (New York: New Viewpoints, 1974), pp. 271–275; Thomas Ross, "Spying in the United States," *Society* 12 (March/April 1975), pp. 64–65; Corey Ford, *Donovan of OSS* (Boston: Little, Brown, 1970), pp. 109, 300–305; R. Harris

Smith, *OSS: The Secret History of America's First Central Intelligence Agency* (Berkeley: University of California Press, 1972), pp. 363–365; and Stephan Garrett, "Foreign Policy and the American Constitution: The Bricker Amendment in Contemporary Perspective," *International Studies Quarterly* 16 (June 1972), pp. 187–200. Memorandum, William Donovan to President, Feb. 23, 1945, Conway File, OSS—Donovan Intelligence Service WHCF Misc, HST. Contrast William Buckley's recent columns in the *National Review* on "executive privilege" with the book on McCarthy he co-authored with L. Brent Bozell, *McCarthy and His Enemies: The Record and Its Meaning* (Chicago: Regnery, 1954).

6. These five involved Truman's refusal to provide: (1) in 1948 the loyalty report on Edward Condon to the House Committee on Un-American Activities; (2) in 1950 the files of the so-called 81 cases identified by Senator McCarthy to the Tydings Committee; (3) in 1951 the Senate Judiciary Committee's request for the loyalty files of federal employees and in return the Committee offered to report special legislation exempting members of the Nimitz commission from "conflict of interest" regulations; (4) in 1952 the loyalty file of John Carter Vincent to the Senate Subcommittee on Internal Security; and (5) in 1952 a Department of Justice résumé of the action taken on all civil and criminal cases from 1945 to 1951 to a subcommittee of the House Judiciary Committee chaired by Congressman Frank Chelf.

7. Arthur Schlesinger, Jr., *The Imperial Presidency* (Boston: Houghton Mifflin, 1973), pp. 155–159, 247–250. Raoul Berger, *Executive Privilege: A Constitutional Myth* (New York: Bantam, 1975), pp. vii, 1–2, 5, 7, 53, 240, 263–269. When first claiming executive privilege on May 17, 1954, President Eisenhower stated: "It is essential to efficient and effective administration that employees of the Executive Branch be in a position to be completely candid in advising with each other on official matters." The president continued that "it is not in the public interest that any of their conversations or communications, or any documents or reproductions, concerning such advice be disclosed" and further that the president had the constitutional responsibility to "preclude the exercise of arbitrary power by any branch of the Government." The historical context for this letter is surveyed in Robert Griffith, *The Politics of Fear: Joseph R. McCarthy and the Senate* (Lexington: The University Press of Kentucky, 1970), pp. 243–269.

8. *Washington Post*, May 20, 1954; *New York Times*, May 18, 1954.

9. Johnson, *1600 Pennsylvania Avenue*, pp. 290, 293. William Fulbright, "Reflections: In Thrall to Fear," *The New Yorker* (Jan. 8, 1972), pp. 41–62. Daniel Ellsberg, "Laos: What Nixon Is Up To," *New York Review of Books* 16 (Mar. 11, 1971), pp. 13–17. The impact of McCarthyism on how intellectuals viewed the presidency is sketched in Athan Theoharis, "The Politics of Scholarship," in Griffith and Theoharis, *The Specter*, pp. 264–280. This theme is also sketchingly made by Griffith and Theoharis in their introductory comments, pp. ix–xiv. See also Michael Rogin, *McCarthy and the Intellectuals: The Radical Specter* (Cambridge: MIT Press, 1976) and Leslie Gelb, "Vietnam: The System Worked," *Foreign Policy* (Summer 1971), pp. 104–167.

10. *New York Times*, May 23, 1973, pp. 1, 28, 29; June 6, 1973, pp. 1, 33, 34, 35; June 7, 1973, p. 44; June 8, 1973, pp. 1, 18; June 10, 1973, p. 1E; June 17, 1973, pp. 1, 44, 45; June 27, 1973, pp. 1, 48, 52; June 29, 1973,

pp. 1, 22, 26, 27; July 17, 1973, pp. 1, 26; July 18, 1973, pp. 1, 20; Nov. 6, 1973, p. 25; Dec. 9, 1973, pp. 1, 76; Dec. 26, 1973, p. 44. *Milwaukee Journal*, Apr. 16, 1973, p. 8; May 3, 1973, p. 9; May 10, 1973, pp. 1, 15; May 16, 1973, pp. 1, 2, 4; May 23, 1973, pp. 1, 2, 18, 19; May 24, 1973, pp. 1, 3, 4; May 25, 1973, pp. 1, 6; June 3, 1973, pp. 1, 7; June 4, 1973, pp. 1, 2; June 21, 1973, p. 4; July 18, 1973, p. 3; Aug. 24, 1973, pp. 1, 8; Nov. 16, 1973, p. 14; Dec. 5, 1973, p. 3.

11. *The White House Transcripts* (New York: Bantam, 1974), p. 163.

12. Ibid., pp. 99, 105–106, 113, 129–131, 201–221, 262, 276–277. *New York Times*, Apr. 11, 1973, p. 1; Mar. 3, 1973, p. 1. *Boston Globe*, May 5, 1973, p. 1. *U.S. v. Nixon*, 418 U.S. 683 (1974).

13. Schlesinger, *The Imperial Presidency*, pp. 301–307. U.S., *Congressional Record*, 93rd Cong., 1st sess., vol. 119, no. 113 (July 1973), H6231–H6284; vol. 119, no. 153 (Oct. 12, 1973), H8948–H8963; vol. 119, no. 170 (Nov. 7, 1973), S20093–S20116, H9641–H9661. Athan Theoharis, "Classification Restrictions and the Public's Right to Know: A New Look at the Alger Hiss Case," *Intellect* 104 (Sept./Oct. 1975), p. 89. *Milwaukee Journal*, Nov. 21, 1974; Nov. 22, 1974. *New York Times*, Feb. 16, 1975, p. 16E. See also plaintiff's memorandum of law, May 15, 1975 in *Weinstein v. Levi*.

14. Schlesinger. *The Imperial Presidency*. See also, John W. Dean, *Blind Ambition: The White House Years* (New York: Simon and Schuster, 1976); Leon Jaworski, *The Right and the Power: The Prosecution of Watergate* (New York: Reader's Digest, 1976); J. Anthony Lukas, *Nightmare: The Underside of the Nixon Years* (New York: Viking, 1976); Jeb S. Magruder, *An American Life: One Man's Road to Watergate* (New York: Atheneum, 1974); Mary McCarthy, *The Mask of State: Watergate Portraits* (New York: Harcourt, Brace, Jovanovich, 1973); Clark Mollenhoff, *Game Plan for Disaster: An Ombudsman's Report on the Nixon Years* (New York: Norton, 1976); Ronald Pynn, ed., *Watergate and the American Political Process* (New York: Praeger, 1975); Dan Rather and Gary Gates, *The Palace Guard* (New York: Harper & Row, 1974); Jonathan Schell, *The Time of Illusion* (New York: Knopf, 1976); William Shannon, *They Could Not Trust the King: Nixon, Watergate and the American People* (New York: Macmillan, 1974); Theodore White, *Breach of Faith: The Fall of Richard Nixon* (New York: Atheneum, 1975); Bob Woodward and Carl Bernstein, *All the President's Men* (New York: Simon and Schuster, 1974) and *The Final Days* (New York: Simon and Schuster, 1976). In contrast to these critical accounts of Richard Nixon's presidency, conservative authors Victor Lasky and William Safire attempt to defend this conservative president. Their defense minimizes the Nixon abuses of power, contends that the media was "out to get" Nixon and thus distorted by exaggerating the particular actions, or concludes that earlier presidents (notably Kennedy) had similarly abused power but that the liberal press consciously chose to ignore these abuses. Victor Lasky, *It Didn't Start with Watergate* (New York: Dial, 1977) and William Safire, *Before the Fall: An Inside View of the Pre-Watergate White House* (Garden City: Doubleday, 1975). See also Richard Nixon, *RN: The Memoirs of Richard Nixon* (New York: Grosset & Dunlap, 1978), pp. 625–653, 773–912, 926–1090.

15. *New York Times*, Dec. 22, 1974, pp. 1, 26; Dec. 30, 1974, pp. 1, 13; Jan. 12, 1975, pp. 1, 13; Jan. 19, 1975, p. 3E. *Milwaukee Journal*, Jan. 9, 1975, pp. 1, 6; Jan. 10, 1975, pp. 1, 10; Jan. 16, 1975, pp. 1, 2. William

Corson, *The Armies of Ignorance: The Rise of the American Intelligence Empire* (New York: Dial, 1977), pp. 435–437.

16. *New York Times*, Nov. 24, 1974, p. 3E; Jan. 5, 1975, pp. 1, 42; Feb. 2, 1975, pp. 1, 40; Feb. 16, 1975, pp. 1, 48; Feb. 28, 1975, pp. 1, 11; *Milwaukee Journal*, Nov. 16, 1974, pp. 1, 24; Jan. 26, 1975, pp. 1, 8; Feb. 10, 1975, pp. 1, 9; Mar. 9, 1975, pp. 1, 20; Mar. 21, 1975, pp. 1, 10. U.S. House, Committee on the Judiciary, Subcommittee on Civil and Constitutional Rights, *Hearings on FBI Counterintelligence Programs*, 93rd Cong., 2d sess., 1974, pp. 9–15, 21–23, 44–47 and *Hearings on FBI Oversight*, ser. no. 2, pt. 1, 94th Cong., 1st sess., 1975, pp. 4–11, 15–19, 34.

17. *IARA*, pp. 343–354.

18. Corson, *The Armies of Ignorance*, pp. 439–442, 444, 447. *FMI*, pp. 7–8. *IARA*, p. ix n7.

19. David Wise, *The American Police State* (New York: Random, 1976) and Morton Halperin, Jerry Berman, Robert Borosage, and Christine Marwick, *The Lawless State: The Crimes of the U.S. Intelligence Agencies* (New York: Penguin, 1976). For a more radical interpretation see Noam Chomsky's introduction to Nelson Blackstock, *COINTELPRO: The FBI's Secret War on Political Freedom* (New York: Vintage, 1976), pp. 3–26. See also Jerry Berman and Morton Halperin, eds., *The Abuses of the Intelligence Agencies* (Washington: Center for National Security Studies, 1975); Pat Watters and Stephen Gillers, eds., *Investigating the FBI* (Garden City: Doubleday, 1973); *Privacy in a Free Society* (Cambridge: Roscoe Pound–American Trial Lawyers Foundation, 1974); Richard Cotter, "Notes toward a Definition of National Security," *Washington Monthly* 7 (Dec. 1975), pp. 4–16; Sanford Unga, *FBI* (Boston: Atlantic Monthly/Little, Brown, 1975); Norman Dorsen and Stephen Gillers, eds., *None of Your Business: Government Secrecy in America* (New York: Penguin, 1975); Richard Harris, "Reflections: Crime in the F.B.I.," *The New Yorker*, (Aug. 8, 1977), pp. 30–42; Corson, *The Armies of Ignorance*; and Victor Navasky, "The FBI's Wildest Dream," *Nation* 226 (June 17, 1978), pp. 716–718.

Chapter One

1. The Sanders cartoon ran in the June 27, 1973, issue of the *Milwaukee Journal*. It is reprinted in Bill Sanders, *Run for the Oval Office* (Milwaukee: Alpha Press, 1974), p. 191. See also ibid., pp. 1, 401. Representative of how the liberal press covered the administration's justification and the release of the Huston Plan are *Milwaukee Journal*, May 23, 1973, pp. 1, 2, 18; May 24, 1973, pp. 1, 4; June 1, 1973, pp. 1, 2; June 4, 1973, p. 2; June 7, 1973, pp. 1, 2; Aug. 24, 1973, pp. 1, 8; *New York Times*, May 23, 1973, p. 28; June 7, 1973, pp. 1, 36, 37, 44; June 8, 1973, p. 18; June 10, 1973, p. 1E; June 11, 1973, pp. 1, 27; June 17, 1973, p. 44. See also U.S. Senate, Select Committee on Presidential Campaign Activities, Hearings and Final Reports, 93rd Cong., 2d sess., 1974; Schlesinger, *The Imperial Presidency*, pp. 216–218, 259–260, 274, 380, 446 n106; Halperin et al., *The Lawless State*, pp. 10, 120, 130, 149, 229. A representative reaction by the conservative media is that of the *National Review*, May 25, 1973, pp. 565–566, 573, 598–599; June 8, 1973, pp. 615–618, 624, 650–651; June 22, 1973, pp. 666–667, 674, 685, 702–704; July 6, 1973, pp. 720–722, 726, 755; July 13, 1973, p. B94; July 20, 1973, pp. 770, 778; Aug. 3, 1973, pp. 820–823, 829, 858–859;

Aug. 10, 1973, pp. B113–114; Aug. 17, 1973, pp. 876, 879–880, 910–911; Aug. 24, 1973, p. B124; Aug. 31, 1973, pp. 922, 926–927, 934, 945, 961, 962; Sept. 7, 1973, pp. B129, B134; Sept. 14, 1973, pp. 981, 982–983, 986–988, 990–997, 1014; Sept. 21, 1973, pp. B140–142; Sept. 28, 1973, pp. 1034, 1038; Oct. 12, 1973, pp. 1096–1098, 1138–1139; Oct. 26, 1973, pp. 1167–1170; Nov. 9, 1973, pp. 1220–1222; Nov. 23, 1973, pp. 1281–1284; Nov. 30, 1973, p. B177. See also Lasky, *It Didn't Start with Watergate*, pp. 330–332.

2. Unlike his predecessors, Richard Nixon did not rely on the investigative services of the FBI, CIA, NSA, or IRS. Instead, in 1971 he created the White House Plumbers group and in 1969 appointed former New York City police officer John Caulfield to the White House staff. Responsible for political intelligence investigations for the White House, Caulfield, for example, installed a tap on the phone of syndicated national columnist Joseph Kraft. Responding to Caulfield's suggestion that the White House request FBI assistance, White House aide John Ehrlichman complained that the bureau was a "sieve" and could not be trusted to keep the matter secret (Wise, *The American Police State*, pp. 15–18).

3. Nixon's conviction that electronic surveillance was a legitimate intelligence method is ironically captured in his 1968 presidential campaign decision to hire a former FBI electronics expert, John Ragan, to sweep his law offices, his campaign headquarters trailer at the Republican National Convention, and his hotel rooms and those of key staff aides to ensure that he and his staff had not been tapped or bugged. That such surveillance might have been illegal did not lead the Republican presidential candidate to conclude that electronic surveillance was not normal. This incident is discussed at length in Wise, *The American Police State*, pp. 4, 9–12, 13.

4. *Milwaukee Journal*, Nov. 5, 1976, p. 2; Nov. 7, 1976, p. 8; Nov. 8, 1976, p. 2; Nov. 9, 1976, pp. 1, 2; Nov. 10, 1976, pp. 1, 2; Nov. 15, 1976, p. 4; Feb. 3, 1977, p. 2; March 21, 1977, p. 5; June 7, 1977, pp. 1, 2; June 8, 1977, pp. 1, 11; Sept. 6, 1977, p. 15; March 22, 1978, p. 2; April 20, 1978, p. 10. *New York Times*, Nov. 5, 1976, p. 4; Nov. 7, 1976, p. 2; Nov. 8, 1976, p. 2; Nov. 9, 1976, pp. 1, 22; Nov. 10, 1976, pp. 1, 14, 15; Nov. 14, 1976, pp. 1, 24, 25; Nov. 15, 1976, pp. 14, 15; Nov. 16, 1976, p. 34; Nov. 17, 1976, p. 18; Nov. 21, 1976, pp. 1, 41; June 2, 1977, p. 1E; March 12, 1978, p. 16; March 26, 1978, p. 5E.

5. The Helms memorandum is reprinted in *HIA*, vol. 2, Huston Plan, p. 401. See also ibid., pp. 400, 402–403. The NSA "Watch List" program is discussed in *SDSRIARA*, pp. 736–764, 781–782; *HIA*, vol. 5, The National Security Agency and Fourth Amendments Rights, pp. 7–24, 31–33, 145–163. The administration's desire to formalize FBI political reporting to the White House is detailed in *HIA*, vol. 6, Federal Bureau of Investigation, pp. 368–369, 642. FBI reports on foreign embassy contacts by members of Congress and congressional staff are discussed in ibid., pp. 162, 479. Operation CHAOS is discussion in Commission on CIA Activities within the United States, *Report to the President* (Washington: U.S. Government Printing Office, June 1975), pp. 130–150. These activities are discussed in greater detail in the subsequent chapters of this study. See also *IARA*, pp. 12, 13, 96–102, 104–105, 108–109, 174. The U.S. military's domestic surveillance activities were investigated by the U.S. Senate, Subcommittee on Constitutional Rights, Committee on the Judiciary, *Hearings on Federal Data Banks, Computers and the*

Bill of Rights, Pts. I and II, 92d Cong., 1st sess., 1971, and Report, *Military Surveillance of Civilian Politics*, 93rd Cong., 1st sess., 1973.

6. *IARA*, pp. 112, 172. *SDSRIARA*, pp. 501–502, 508–509, 518–525, 699–700, 924, 928–929. *HIA*, vol. 2, Huston Plan, pp. 10–12, 28–30, 85–86, 103–105, 108, 125–126, 128–129, 134–135, 203–206, 287–312, 401–403. Commission on CIA Activities within the United States, *Report to the President* (Washington: U.S. Government Printing Office, June 1975), p. 121.

7. For a perceptive analysis of the Cold War conservatives, see Ronald Lora, "A View from the Right: Conservative Intellectuals, the Cold War, and McCarthy," in Griffith and Theoharis, *The Specter*, pp. 42–70.

8. *IARA*, pp. 12, 105–106, 111–113, 143. *SDSRIARA*, pp. 256–259, 300–302, 355, 365, 485–487, 508–509, 522–525, 601, 634–635, 668–671, 924–925, 928–934, 948–949, 972; *HIA*, vol. 2, Huston Plan, pp. 3, 23, 60, 67–69, 83–84, 96–99, 101, 114–115, 120, 124, 127–128, 205–206, 273–276, 309–312. Brennan and Sullivan were not the only FBI officials frustrated by Hoover's restrictions. *SDSRIARA*, p. 671.

9. The incident involved the March 1969 disappearance of Colorado University history professor Thomas Riha. The subsequent role of CIA officials in the resultant police investigation precipitated this rift and FBI Director Hoover's decision to terminate liaison with the CIA. Wise, *The American Police State*, pp. 258–273. *SDSRIARA*, p. 933.

10. *IARA*, pp. 112–113; *HIA*, vol. 2, Huston Plan, pp. 283–286, 342–356.

11. *IARA*, p. 112 n537; *SDSRIARA*, pp. 932–933, 946–947; *HIA*, vol. 2, Huston Plan, pp. 67–69. Memo, unsigned (but probably Marvin Watson) to President, Sept. 23, 1966, WHCF Name Files, Hoover, J. Edgar. LBJ.

12. *SDSRIARA*, p. 965.

13. Ibid., pp. 357–358.

14. Ibid., p. 934.

15. Ibid., pp. 929–930.

16. *IARA*, p. 113; *SDSRIARA*, pp. 936–938; *HIA*, vol. 2, Huston Plan, pp. 3–4, 9, 16–17, 60, 396–399.

17. *HIA*, vol. 2, Huston Plan, pp. 207–212.

18. *SDSRIARA*, pp. 938–939; *HIA*, vol. 2, Huston Plan, pp. 4–5, 9, 57.

19. *HIA*, vol. 2, Huston Plan, pp. 213–215.

20. *SDSRIARA*, p. 966.

21. *HIA*, vol. 2, Huston Plan, pp. 219–226, 229–234; *SDSRIARA*, pp. 939–942; *IARA*, p. 147 n43.

22. *HIA*, vol. 2, Huston Plan, pp. 168–181, 187–188, 193–197. These discussions also considered having the FBI assume responsibility for the NSA's SHAMROCK program (under which the agency received from RCA, ITT, and Western Union copies of most international telegrams leaving the United States). This idea was dropped, however, because Sullivan could not commit the FBI to accept responsibility for the program and because the NSA feared that its working relationship with these companies would be jeopardized. *SDSRIARA*, p. 776.

23. *HIA*, vol. 2, Huston Plan, p. 5.

24. Ibid., p. 218.

25. Ibid., pp. 227–228.

26. Ibid., pp. 235–236; *SDSRIARA*, p. 943.

27. *HIA*, vol. 2, Huston Plan, pp. 237–239.

28. *SDSRIARA*, pp. 942–943. Wise, *The American Police State*, p. 272.

29. *HIA*, vol. 2, Huston Plan, pp. 173, 176, 178, 181, 186.

30. *SDSRIARA*, pp. 943 n75, 943–945; *HIA*, vol. 2, Huston Plan, pp. 6, 7, 189–192.

31. *HIA*, vol. 2, Huston Plan, pp. 189–197.

32. *SDSRFMI*, p. 154. During his May 19, 1977, television interview with David Frost, Richard Nixon claimed that presidents had the right to violate the law to safeguard the national security and that such actions were not illegal. Irrespective of the questionable basis for such an asserted claim, Nixon had not recognized such a right as president—otherwise he would have directly authorized in writing the Huston Plan. The former president would also not have recalled Huston's authorization memorandum when advised by Attorney General Mitchell of Hoover's intention to request in writing the attorney general's express authorization each time a break-in or another illegal technique was employed. *Milwaukee Journal*, May 20, 1977, p. 1. *New York Times*, May 20, 1977, p. 1.

33. *SDSRIARA*, pp. 951, 955; *HIA*, vol. 2, Huston Plan, p. 198.

34. *HIA*, vol. 2, Huston Plan, pp. 199–202.

35. Ibid., pp. 313–316; *SDSRIARA*, pp. 956–957.

36. Hoover's proposed method would have seriously compromised the attorney general. In the event an individual who had been the subject of one of these illegal activities would be indicted, the attorney general would then have to decide whether: (1) not to prosecute because of the risk of disclosing this program, (2) to comply fully with court-ordered disclosure motions and disclose the program, or (3) to affirm falsely that the individual had not been the subject of illegal governmental activities and thereby avert public knowledge of the plan. Hoover's proposed method had not provided for separate file-keeping procedures, as had earlier been done whenever the bureau conducted illegal or embarrassing programs.

37. *SDSRIARA*, pp. 957–958; *SDSRFMI*, pp. 153–154.

38. *HIA*, vol. 2, Huston Plan, pp. 8–9, 14–15, 24–25, 42, 247–248; *SDSRIARA*, pp. 958–959.

39. *HIA*, vol. 2, Huston Plan, pp. 42, 249–253; *SDSRIARA*, pp. 959–960.

40. *HIA*, vol. 2, Huston Plan, pp. 13, 15–16, 17, 21–22, 25–27, 33–34, 36, 51–54, 57–59, 85, 92–93, 105, 131–132, 174, 176, 177–178, 193–195. *HIA*, vol. 5, The National Security Agency and Fourth Amendment Rights, pp. 28–29, 32, 44–45, *IARA*, pp. 12, 114, 143, 150; *SDSRIARA*, pp. 594 n131, 596–598, 668, 763–764, 926, 946, 947–948, 962–965, 972; *SDSRFMI*, pp. 144–148, 155–156.

41. *SDSRIARA*, pp. 946, 948, 972–973, 973 n246. There is a possibility, however, that former President Nixon directed the FBI to resume the use of break-ins in May 1971. In pre-trial motions, defense attorneys for former Acting FBI Director L. Patrick Gray and former FBI Assistant Director Edward Miller claimed that Nixon had directed Hoover in May 1971 "to use all means possible" or "pull no punches" when investigating terrorist activities. Defense attorneys specifically sought a "missing memorandum" which pertained to a May 26, 1971, telephone conversation between the president and the FBI director. *New York Times*, May 28, 1978, p. 5E; June 23, 1978, p. B2. *Detroit News*, June 22, 1978, p. A10.

42. *HIA*, vol. 2, Huston Plan, pp. 100, 102–103, 116–117, 126, 137–138, 317–341; *IARA*, pp. 111 n528, 116; *SDSRIARA*, pp. 259, 525–531, 927, 978–979. After his death in May 1972, Hoover's restrictions on the number of electronic surveillances were lifted. Accordingly, the number of taps increased from around 100 (102 in 1970, 101 in 1971, 108 in 1972) to 123 in 1973 and 190 in 1974. Ibid., pp. 301, 303.

43. *HIA*, vol. 2, Huston Plan, pp. 42, 108, 255–257; *IARA*, pp. 115, 123, 143 n26; *SDSRIARA*, pp. 500–505, 974.

44. *HIA*, vol. 2, Huston Plan, pp. 258–260.

45. Ibid., p. 261.

46. Ibid., pp. 42, 108, 262–266; *IARA*, pp. 115–116, 123; *SDSRIARA*, pp. 505, 536–537, 824–825, 974–977.

47. *HIA*, vol. 2, Huston Plan, p. 267; *SDSRIARA*, p. 976.

48. *HIA*, vol. 2, Huston Plan, pp. 42, 70–71, 268–272; *SDSRIARA*, pp. 977–978.

Chapter Two

1. For a good legislative history of the Internal Security Act of 1950, see William Tanner and Robert Griffith, "Legislative Politics and 'McCarthyism': The Internal Security Act of 1950," in Griffith and Theoharis, eds., *The Specter*, pp. 174–189 and William Tanner, "The Passage of the Internal Security Act of 1950" Ph.D. diss., University of Kansas, 1971).

2. *SDSRIARA*, pp. 408–409.

3. Ibid., pp. 413–414; *HIA*, vol. 6, Federal Bureau of Investigation, pp. 409–411.

4. *SDSRIARA*, p. 414.

5. Ibid., pp. 414, 417–418; *IARA*, pp. 34–35.

6. *IARA*, pp. 34–35; *SDSRIARA*, pp. 418–419. *Federal Records of World War II: Civilian Agencies* (Washington: U.S. Government Printing Office, 1950). p. 789. The FBI objected to the department's plan involving American citizens. Rather than rely on prosecution under appropriate statutes, the department should consider "the possibility of utilizing denaturalization proceedings" and undertake a study to "control suspected citizens." See also Theoharis, "Should the FBI Purge Its Files?"

7. *HIA*, vol. 6, Federal Bureau of Investigation, pp. 412–413.

8. Ibid., pp. 414–415. Hoover's decision to ignore Attorney General Biddle's 1943 order was not unprecedented. This insubordination dated from May 1924 when he had been appointed acting director of the bureau. (Attorney General Harlan Fiske Stone appointed Hoover permanent director in December of that year.) In May, Stone had also announced a series of restrictions on bureau investigations to preclude the recurrence of recently disclosed abuses of power. Stone's restrictions included dissolving the bureau's General Intelligence Division (which had been developing files on the political activities of radicals and dissidents), prohibiting wiretaps, and limiting FBI investigations to violations of federal statutes. Nonetheless, recently released FBI documents confirm that in August, October, and November 1927 the FBI investigated ACLU meetings (including who attended and what was said at those meetings) and kept track of ACLU bank accounts and deposits. Begun in 1920, this investigation of the ACLU was not discontinued in May

1924 despite Stone's ban but continued throughout the 1920s and succeeding decades. *Civil Liberties*, 318 (July 1977), pp. 1, 8. *Milwaukee Journal*, June 19, 1977, p. 3. *Washington Post*, June 19, 1977, pp. 1A, 4A. Ungar, *FBI*, pp. 48–49, 54.

9. *SDSRIARA*, pp. 429–430. To ensure a political climate favorable to this program, Ladd also recommended "that an effort should be made now to prepare educational material which can be released through available channels." A two day training conference should also be convened to brief fully all FBI field office "Communist supervisors." *Ibid.*

10. Ibid., pp. 430, 436. Hoover's failure to apprise the attorney general of the bureau's 1943 action partially explains why the bureau declined to respond to a January 17, 1946, request from members of the President's Temporary Commission of Employee Loyalty for "the approximate number of names in [FBI] subversive files . . . and whether the Bureau had a file of names of persons who could be picked up in the event of a war with Russia." Minutes of the President's Temporary Commission on Employee Loyalty, Jan. 17, 1946, Stephen Spingarn Papers, HST.

11. *SDSRIARA*, pp. 436–438. When preparing the memorandum to brief department officials on FBI standards for classifying potentially dangerous persons, FBI Assistant Director Ladd did not specify "Espionage Suspects and Government Employees in Communist Underground" because "the Bureau does not have evidence, whether admissable or otherwise, reflecting actual membership in the Communist Party. It is believed that for security reasons, examples of these logical suspects should not be set forth at this time." Hoover concurred with this decision, noting: "There are too many leaks." Ibid., pp. 436–437.

12. Ibid., p. 438.

13. Ibid. See also Michal Belknap, *Cold War Political Justice: The Smith Act, the Communist Party, and American Civil Liberties* (Westport: Greenwood, 1977) and Richard Freeland, *The Truman Doctrine and the Origins of McCarthyism* (New York: Knopf, 1971), pp. 210–219, 293–298, 337–338.

14. *SDSRIARA*, p. 439; *HIA*, vol. 6, Federal Bureau of Investigation, pp. 416–420, 424–425. Daniel Yergin, *Shattered Peace: The Origins of the Cold War and the National Security State* (Boston: Houghton, Mifflin, 1977), p. 357.

15. A number of factors support the conclusion that Truman had not been briefed. In July 1946, for example, Attorney General Clark secured Truman's assent to expand FBI wiretapping authority by selectively quoting from a May 21, 1940, Roosevelt directive and implying that this 1946 request merely reaffirmed that directive. In fact, when quoting from the authorization paragraph of Roosevelt's directive, Clark deleted a key sentence and thereby secured Truman's authorization for FBI wiretapping of "subversive activities." Clark employed the same technique on August 17, 1948. Citing Roosevelt's directives of September 6, 1939, and January 8, 1943, the attorney general urged the president to issue a "third statement"—implying that the recommended statement merely reaffirmed these earlier Roosevelt directives. Clark's proposed statement did not conform with those of Roosevelt and, if issued, would have provided the first formal presidential authorization for FBI investigations of "subversive activities." In addition, in 1947 and 1948 the Justice Department unsuccessfully sought White House approval for certain

internal security legislative proposals. These included making the unauthorized disclosure of "national defense" information a crime, authorizing the attorney general to order wiretapping in national security cases, and extending the foreign-agent registration provisions to the Communist party and its alleged front organizations. All agency and departmental legislative requests after 1947, however, required Bureau of the Budget clearance and this bill was denied such clearance. Nonetheless, department officials continued to lobby Congress and conveyed the impression to key Democratic congressional leaders that these measures commanded White House support. Moreover, while there is no written record of presidential concurrence, in 1947 and 1949 Secretaries of Defense James Forrestal and Louis Johnson, claiming to speak for Truman, directed the international telecommunications companies RCA, Western Union, and ITT to intercept illegally certain international messages. Stressing national defense needs, the secretaries assured these executives that compliance with this request would not subject their companies to prosecution in the federal courts (for violating the prohibitions incorporated in Section 605 of the Federal Communications Act of 1934). Theoharis, "Misleading the Presidents," pp. 744–745. Theoharis, *Seeds of Repression*, pp. 132, 134–135. Theoharis, "The FBI's Stretching of Presidential Directives, 1936–1953," *Political Science Quarterly* 91 (Winter 1976/1977), pp. 661–663. *SDSRIARA*, pp. 765–776. *HIA*, vol. 5, The National Security Agency and Fourth Amendment Rights, pp. 47–55, 57–64.

There is the possibility, however, that President Truman might have been briefed after the fact on the department portfolio. In a letter of August 7, 1950, to Presidential National Security Consultant Sidney Souers (with the only other copy to Attorney General McGrath), FBI Director Hoover forwarded a memorandum "setting forth the main programs of this Bureau designed to meet the present threats to the internal security of this country." Hoover then enumerated and described nineteen different programs. Among these was: "IV. *Detention of Dangerous Persons in the Event of a War Emergency.* A. Detailed plans have been drawn up and all field offices fully instructed, with the exception of certain details which the Department has under consideration." The description might have been sketchy and vague; this briefing nonetheless predated congressional passage of the McCarran Act. Letter, Hoover to Souers, Aug. 7, 1950, and accompanying memo, PSF, FBI I, HST.

16. *SDSRIARA*, pp. 439–440.

17. *Foreign Relations of the United States, 1949. Vol. I. National Security Affairs, Foreign Economic Policy* (Washington: U.S. Government Printing Office, 1976), pp. 271–277. The quote is from p. 274.

18. Ibid., pp. 282–284, 291–292, 296–298, 313–314, 345–347, 381–384. The Kennan quotes are from pp. 382, 383.

19. NSC 68 is reprinted in *Naval War College Review* (May–June 1975). The quote is from p. 101. The only other specific internal security reference is on p. 106. See also *Foreign Relations of the United States 1950. Vol. I. National Security Affairs, Foreign Economic Policy* (Washington: U.S. Government Printing Office, 1977), pp. 213–226, 234–324.

20. *SDSRIARA*, p. 440.

21. Ibid., pp. 440–441; *IARA*, pp. 55, 55 n193. The FBI did not provide this information when Attorney General McGrath in July 1950 requested an

analysis of the Security Index. At the time, the Congress was considering Title II (the emergency detention provision) of the Internal Security Act of 1950.

22. *HIA*, vol. 6, Federal Bureau of Investigation, pp. 416–420, 424–425.

23. Ibid., p. 421.

24. Ibid.; *SDSRIARA*, p. 442; *IARA*, pp. 54–55.

25. *HIA*, vol. 6, Federal Bureau of Investigation, p. 421; *SDSRIARA*, p. 442. While continuing to provide the department with the names of individuals listed on its Security Index, the bureau did not forward the names of certain espionage subjects "for security reasons." Apprehension of such persons in an emergency "would destroy chances of penetration and control of an operating Soviet espionage parallel or would destroy known chances of penetration and control of a 'sleeper' parallel." Ibid., pp. 442–443.

26. Ibid., p. 443; *HIA*, vol. 6, Federal Bureau of Investigation, pp. 419–420, 422, 424–425.

27. *SDSRIARA*, pp. 443–444.

28. Ibid., p. 444; *HIA*, vol. 6, Federal Bureau of Investigation, pp. 422–423.

29. *HIA*, vol. 6, Federal Bureau of Investigation, p. 423, *SDSRIARA*, p. 444.

30. *HIA*, vol. 6, Federal Bureau of Investigation, p. 423.

31. Ibid., pp. 416–417, 423–424.

32. Ibid., pp. 416–417, 420, 424–426.

33. Ibid., p. 426; *SDSRIARA*, p. 455.

34. *SDSRIARA*, p. 455; *HIA*, vol. 6, Federal Bureau of Investigation, p. 427.

35. *SDSRIARA*, p. 445.

36. Friday, June 11, 1954, Hagerty Papers–Diary Entries, Hagerty Diary, June 1954, DDE.

37. Ibid.

38. *SDSRIARA*, p. 446; *HIA*, vol. 6, Federal Bureau of Investigation, p. 424.

39. *SDSRIARA*, p. 446.

40. Ibid., p. 447; *HIA*, vol. 6, Federal Bureau of Investigation, pp. 659–661. In this letter, Hoover outlined the revised standards for listing individuals on the now named Reserve Index. These included membership in or leadership of "revolutionary" organizations, "subversive" organizations, or "subversive front" organizations. These criteria were rather nebulous, even capricious. Individuals were listed who had been identified as members but "investigation has failed to substantiate allegations of membership in a revolutionary organization within the past five years, coupled with some evidence or information indicating activity, association, or sympathy for the subversive cause within the same period, and no reliable evidence of defection." Ibid., p. 661.

41. *HIA*, vol. 6, Federal Bureau of Investigation, pp. 824, 826; *SDSRIARA*, pp. 465–466. Acting independently in November 1960 FBI Director Hoover directed special agents in charge to recommend for inclusion on the Security Index individuals who were active in "pro-Castro" groups or activities. After the 1961 Bay of Pigs invasion and the 1962 Cuban missile crisis, Hoover expanded these criteria to include individuals active in anti-administration "demonstrations" or efforts to "influence public opinion." Ibid., pp. 467–468.

42. *SDSRIARA*, p. 468. At this time, the White House might have authorized the FBI to employ break-ins in the investigation of the radical Weathermen organization. *New York Times*, May 28, 1978, p. 5E.

43. *SDSRIARA*, p. 468.

44. Ibid., p. 469; *HIA*, vol. 6, Federal Bureau of Investigation, p. 666.

45. *HIA*, vol. 6, Federal Bureau of Investigation, p. 667.

46. *SDSRIARA*, pp. 513–516.

47. Ibid., pp. 516–518. This expansion is discussed in detail in *IARA*, pp. 89–90.

48. *HIA*, vol. 6, Federal Bureau of Investigation, pp. 676–677.

49. Those in attendance were Messrs. John Mohr, William Sullivan, Charles Brennan, Thomas Bishop, Nicholas Callahan, Joseph Casper, W. Mark Felt, James Gale, Alex Rosen, Leonard Walters, Tavel, and Beaver.

50. Ibid., pp. 700–702.

51. *SDSRIARA*, pp. 542, 544. In language reminiscent of the strategy of the department's Portfolio, a September 21, 1971, Cotter memorandum emphasized that "should this country come under attack from hostile forces, foreign or domestic, there is nothing to preclude the President from going before a joint session of Congress and requesting necessary authority to apprehend and detain those who would constitute a menace to national defense. At this point it would be absolutely essential to have an immediate list, such as the SI, for use in making such apprehensions. The SI, backed by our investigative files, would provide documentation of subversive backgrounds during any hearings which might be required following apprehensions." Ibid., pp. 542–543.

52. Ibid., pp. 543–544.

53. *HIA*, vol. 6, Federal Bureau of Investigation, pp. 655–657.

54. Ibid., p. 658.

55. Ibid.; *SDSRIARA*, p. 545.

56. *SDSRIARA*, pp. 545–547; *IARA*, p. 126.

57. *IARA*, p. 127.

58. *HIA*, vol. 6, Federal Bureau of Investigation, pp. 645–646.

59. Ibid., pp. 645–652; *IARA*, p. 128 n639.

60. *SDSRIARA*, pp. 551, 551 n639.

61. Ibid., p. 552.

62. Ibid., pp. 557–558; *IARA*, pp. 133–135. *Milwaukee Journal*, May 7, 1978, pp. 1, 8.

Chapter Three

1. *Milwaukee Journal*, Jan. 11, 1976, p. 1.

2. U.S. Senate, Committee on the Judiciary, Subcommittee on Constitutional Rights, *Hearings on Federal Data Banks, Computers and the Bill of Rights*, pt. I, 92d Cong., 1st sess., 1971, pp. 597–598, 602–603, 861.

3. Hoover's letter is reprinted in Watters and Gillers, eds., *Investigating the FBI*, p. 467.

4. 407 U.S. 297 (1972); 418 U.S. 683 (1974).

5. Brennan's testimony is cited in John Elliff, "The FBI and Domestic Intelligence," in Richard Blum, ed., *Surveillance and Espionage in a Free Society* (New York: Praeger, 1973), p. 25. In an October 28, 1975, memorandum analyzing FBI authority for "domestic security intelligence investi-

gations" and in testimony the bureau offered the same rationale to the Senate Select Committee on Intelligence Activities. *HIA*, vol. 6, Federal Bureau of Investigation, pp. 547–575 and particularly pp. 560–575. Other students of the FBI concur that the directives constitute the sole basis for FBI political surveillance authority. See Frank Donner "Hoover's Legacy: A Nationwide System of Political Surveillance Based on the Spurious Authority of a Press Release," *Nation* 218 (June 1, 1974), pp. 678–699 and "How J. Edgar Hoover Created His Intelligence Powers," *Civil Liberties Review* 3 (Feb./March 1977), pp. 34–51; Jerry Berman and Morton Halperin, eds., *The Abuses of the Intelligence Agencies* (Washington: Center for National Security Studies, 1975). Cf. Elliff, "The FBI and Domestic Intelligence," pp. 21–22; Cotter, "Notes toward a Definition of National Security," pp. 4–16. Don Whitehead, *The FBI Story* (New York: Pocket Books, 1959); Victor Navasky, *Kennedy Justice* (New York: Atheneum, 1970), p. 36; and the essays by Vern Countryman, William Turner, John Elliff, and Thomas Emerson in Walters and Gillers, *Investigating the FBI*, pp. 49, 51, 114, 256, 261, 419. Significantly when ruling that the federal government had prempted state sedition laws in *Pennsylvania v. Nelson*, the U.S. Supreme Court cited Roosevelt's September 1939 directive. 350 U.S. 497 (1956), pp. 504–505. Following its extensive inquiry into this question and after reviewing the FBI's files, the staff of the Senate Select Committee on Intelligence Activities reached the same conclusion. See *IARA*, pp. 267–270.

6. *HDIOIS*, pp. 3568–3569, 3572, 3606–3607. Contrast Wannall's testimony with that of Deputy Assistant Attorney General Kevin Maroney: see pp. 3333, 3335, 3363, 3364, 3365, 3366, 3369–3370, 3385, 3388–3390, 3392, 3393, 3396, 3438–3439. During testimony before the Senate Select Committee on Intelligence Activities, former FBI Assistant Directors Cartha De Loach and Charles Brennan reiterated this rationale; see *HIA*, vol. 6, Federal Bureau of Investigation, p. 192 and *HIA*, vol. 2, Huston Plan, pp. 118, 123. Attorney General Edward Levi, however, only generally cited executive orders and directives as one basis for FBI investigative authority but specifically not the 1936, 1939, 1943, 1950, or 1953 directives. *HIA*, vol. 6, Federal Bureau of Investigation, pp. 313–314. In any event, the FBI had investigated political activities before 1936. Hoover's comments on Communist influence in trade unions and in the federal government during his August 24, 1936, meeting with President Roosevelt confirm that the FBI already had been conducting such political surveillance. Recently released FBI files also confirm that the bureau's surveillance of the ACLU dated from 1920 and continued after Attorney General Harlan Fiske Stone's May 1924 ban on such political surveillance. The FBI not only conducted its own investigations (in 1932, for example, investigating the Bonus March) but filed information from military intelligence officials. In 1936 and 1939, then, Hoover was seeking authority to conduct investigations already conducted by the FBI. *HIA*, vol. 6, Federal Bureau of Investigation, p. 560; *IARA*, pp. 25, 25 n9; *SDSRIARA*, pp. 393–394. *Civil Liberties*, 318 (July 1977), pp. 1, 8; *Milwaukee Journal*, June 19, 1977, p. 3; *Washington Post*, June 19, 1977, pp. 1A, 4A; Ungar, *FBI*, pp. 48–49, 54. Corson, *The Armies of Ignorance*, pp. 69–70.

7. *HIA*, vol. 6, Federal Bureau of Investigation, p. 560; *IARA*, pp. 25, 25 n9; *SDSRIARA*, pp. 393–394.

8. Hoover was referring to a 1916 amendment to an appropriations statute of 1871. The 1871 statute had authorized the attorney general to expend

funds for the "detection and prosecution of crimes against the United States." The 1916 amendment revised this to permit the attorney general to appoint officials "to conduct such other investigations regarding official matters under the control of the Department of Justice or the Department of State, as may be directed by the Attorney General." *SDSRIARA*, p. 379. Open-ended investigations of political activities were not authorized by this amendment, but only the dynamiting of a consulate or the suspicious movements of a diplomatic attaché. Donner, "How J. Edgar Hoover Created His Intelligence Powers," p. 36.

9. *SDSRIARA*, pp. 393–395; *HIA*, vol. 6, Federal Bureau of Investigation, pp. 560–561; Whitehead, *The FBI Story*, pp. 188–191. Until the Select Committee investigation, Whitehead's account (based on privileged access to FBI documents and interviews with FBI Director Hoover) constituted the principal source for this 1936 directive. As the committee staff's more detailed account confirms, Whitehead's account is not always reliable.

10. *SDSRIARA*, pp. 392, 394–396; *HIA*, vol. 6, Federal Bureau of Investigation, pp. 561–562.

11. *SDSRIARA*, p. 395 n71.

12. *HIA*, vol. 6, Federal Bureau of Investigation, pp. 562–563. Donner, "How J. Edgar Hoover Created His Intelligence Powers," p. 38. *SDSRIARA*, p. 255.

13. *HIA*, vol. 6, Federal Bureau of Investigation, p. 562.

14. *SDSRIARA*, p. 396. The numerous errors in Hoover's September 10 memorandum—the reference to one conference on September 1 whereas there were two conferences on August 24 and 25—combined with the thrust of Hoover's briefing of Cummings further suggest that Hoover's role was not simply a trusted subordinate carrying out his superiors' orders. Apparently, the FBI director relied on the general desire for confidentiality, that there be no written record, and higher-level executive officials' trust in his good faith when assuming the role of coordinator and source of information on decisions and authority. To suggest duplicity and an attempt to maneuver responsible superiors rests not only on contrasting the language of Hoover's August 24 and 25 with his September 5 and 10 memorandums but also Cummings's response to Secretary of War George Dern's January 1936 proposal. A February 19, 1938 Cummings memorandum describes the attorney general's impression of this conversation that "there was no particular urgency." Ibid., p. 393 n67.

15. Ibid., pp. 397–399; *IARA*, pp. 25–27; *HIA*, vol. 6, Federal Bureau of Investigation, pp. 563–567. Corson, *The Armies of Ignorance*, pp. 79–86, 88–91. *New York Times*, June 25, 1938.

16. In a separate memorandum, however, the president directed the State Department to continue its "intelligence work." HIA Vol. 6 pp. 567–570; *SDSRIARA*, pp. 400–403.

17. *SDSRIARA*, pp. 403–404; *HIA*, vol. 6, Federal Bureau of Investigation, pp. 570–572. Donner, "How J. Edgar Hoover Created His Intelligence Power," p. 40.

18. The statement is reprinted in *HDIOIS*, pp. 3336–3337 and *SDSRIARA*, p. 404.

19. *SDSRIARA*, pp. 404–405. Moreover, when issuing an executive order and proclaiming a national emergency on September 8, 1939, and in a subsequent press conference, President Roosevelt defined the FBI's additional

duties as "strengthening of our national defense within the limits of peacetime authorizations," and protecting the nation from "some of the things that happened" prior to U.S. involvement in World War I. Roosevelt specifically listed "sabotage," "a great deal of propaganda by both belligerents, and a good many definite plans laid in this country by foreign governments to try to sway American public opinion." Ibid., p. 405; *IARA*, p. 27 n19.

20. *SDSRIARA*, p. 406.

21. The statement is reprinted in *HDIOIS*, p. 3337.

22. Biddle's action is discussed in greater detail in chapter two. The pertinent section of Biddle's letter quoted above is reprinted in *HIA*, vol. 6, Federal Bureau of Investigation, p. 412. During Robert Jackson's tenure as attorney general, however, when the FBI's Custodial Detention program had been authorized, a Special War Policies Unit had been created and had also been assigned supervisory responsibility over this program. This unit contained a section, named the Subversives Administrative Section, which worked with the FBI and had the assigned responsibility to direct investigations of and organize evidence relating to subversive activities carried on by Nazi, Communist, and Fascist elements in the United States and to recommend prosecutive and other actions. The nature of this section's activities and the particular meaning applied to the term "subversive activties" cannot presently be ascertained. Further research into this question is needed, as also whether Attorney General Biddle's 1943 order terminating the Custodial Detention program and dissolving the Subversives Administrative Section, also terminated investigations involving "subversive activities." *Federal Records of World War II*, p. 789.

23. *SDSRIARA*, pp. 407–412.

24. Ibid., pp. 423–424; *HIA*, vol. 6, Federal Bureau of Investigation, pp. 572–573.

25. Memo, for Clark Clifford, Aug. 9, 1948; Memo, George Elsey, Aug. 16, 1948; Draft Speech, Aug. 18, 1948; Elsey Notes, Aug. 26, 1948; all in George Elsey Papers, Internal Security—Congressional Loyalty Investigations (2), HST. Democratic National Committee, "Files of the Facts, V., Loyalty and Subversive Activities," Elsey Papers, 1948 Campaign Reference Material—Loyalty, HST. Truman's "red herring" press conference remark and other critical comments on congressional investigations are in *Public Papers of the Presidents of the United States: Harry S. Truman, 1948*, pp. 186–190, 431–435, 457–461, 844–845, 882–888, 925–930, 959–962, 963–966. Presidential Platform Material, prepared by Stephen Spingarn, Oct. 13, 1948. Memo, Spingarn to Attorney General Clark, Sept. 9, 1948; Memo, Spingarn, Sept. 10, 1948; Department of Justice Press Release, Sept. 29, 1948; all in Stephen Spingarn Papers, White House Assignments, HST.

26. Memo, Attorney General Clark to President Truman, Aug. 17, 1948. Draft Statement by the President, undated; Memo, Spingarn to Clifford, Sept. 21, 1948; all in Truman Papers, OF 10–B, FBI, HST.

27. Memo, Pat Coyne, April 8, 1949, Spingarn Papers, National Defense–Internal Security (2), HST. Souers Draft Statement by the President, undated, Truman Papers, OF 10–B, FBI, HST. Letter, Elsey to Souers, Aug. 19, 1948; Memo, Elsey to Murphy, Aug. 26, 1948; Memo, Elsey to Clifford, Aug. 27, 1948; all in Elsey Papers, Internal Security—Congressional Loyalty Investigations (2), HST.

28. Memo, Pat Coyne, April 8, 1949; Memo, Spingarn to Clifford, April 11, 1949; Memo, Spingarn, April 11, 1949; Memo, Spingarn to Clifford, April 22, 1949; all in Spingarn Papers, National Defense–Internal Security (2), HST; Memo, Pat Coyne, April 14, 1949, Clifford Papers, National Military Estimate Security Council, HST. In contrast to Truman's March 23, 1949, directive, the delimitation agreement of February 23, 1949, worked out between the FBI and the various military intelligence agencies specifically concluded that on the basis of presidential directives of September 6, 1939, October 30, 1947 (the first time this directive had ever been cited), the delimitation agreement of February 9, 1942, and Roosevelt's June 26, 1939, memorandum, "responsibility for the investigation of all activities coming under the categories of espionage, counterespionage, subversion and sabotage," would be "delimited as indicated hereinafter." The FBI would inform the military agencies about groups "classed as subversive and whose activities are a potential danger to the security of the United States." *HDIOIS*, pp. 3369–3374.

29. *HIA*, vol. 6, Federal Bureau of Investigations, pp. 572–572; *SDSRIARA*, p. 462.

30. Memo, Murphy to Lay, July 12, 1950; Memo, Elsey to Murphy, July 12, 1950; Letter, Attorney General McGrath to Murphy, July 11, 1950; all in Murphy Files, National Security Council, HST. Concerned about Senator McCarthy's impact, the Truman administration considered (1) dratfing internal security legislation, (2) establishing a special presidential commission on loyalty, and (3) assessing how best to establish its solid anti-Communist credentials and respond to Senator McCarthy. See Memo, Spingarn, July 21, 1950, and Memo, Spingarn, July 22, 1950, in Spingarn Papers, National Defense, Internal Security–Individual Rights (1), HST. Memo, Spingarn, Aug. 11, 1950, Murphy Files, Internal Security, HST. Memo, Spingarn to Hopkins, May 11, 1950, Spingarn Papers, Loyalty Commission, Civil Rights (1), HST. See also Athan Theoharis, "The Rhetoric of Politics: Foreign Policy, Internal Security, and Domestic Poltitics in the Truman Era," in Barton Bernstein, ed., *Politics and Policies of the Truman Administration* (Chicago: Quadrangle, 1970), pp. 229–231.

31. Statement by the President, July 24, 1950, Truman Papers, PPF 1–F Jan.–July 1950, HST. Memo, Bell to Spingarn, Elsey, Murphy, July 24, 1950, Elsey Papers, Central Intelligence, HST. *SDSRIARA*, p. 458 n336.

32. Statement, FBI Director Hoover, July 26, 1950, Eleanor Bontecou Papers, Internal Security File FBI (1), HST. Department of Justice Release, July 28, 1950, Spingarn Papers, National Defense . . . , vol. 2, Folder 3, HST.

33. *IARA*, p. 46.

34. The statement is reprinted in *HDIOIS*, pp. 3337–3338. At a May 13, 1954, NSC meeting Attorney General Brownell urged the president to issue a suggested statement (as recorded by presidential press secretary James Hagerty) "re-emphasizing the need for the citizens of this country to report to the FBI any spying in this country." Rather than issue a formal statement, the president expressed his intent to raise the matter during a press conference. May 13, 1954, Entry, James Hagerty Papers–Diary Entries, May 1954, DDE.

35. *SDSRIARA*, pp. 458 n336, 464. Lewis Strauss Appointment Logs, Dec. 1, 1953, Dec. 2, 1953, Dec. 3, 1953, Dec. 10, 1953, Dec. 11, 1953,

Dec. 14, 1953, and Dec. 15, 1953. Records of the U.S. Atomic Energy Commission, U.S. Energy Research and Development Administration Files (henceforth cited as AEC). Lewis Strauss Telephone Logs, Dec. 2, 1953, Dec. 3, 1953, Dec. 9, 1953, Dec. 10, 1953, Dec. 14, 1953, and Dec. 15, 1953, AEC. Memo, Strauss to Charles Bates, Nov. 23, 1953; Memo, Strauss to K. D. Nichols, Dec. 15, 1953 and reply, Dec. 24, 1953; all in AEC.

36. The text of the 1946 act is reprinted in U.S. Congress, Joint Committee on Atomic Energy, *Atomic Energy Legislation through 91st Cong., 2d sess.*, 91st Cong., 2d sess., 1971. Section 10 (5c) specifically requires: "All violations of this Act shall be investigated by the Federal Bureau of Investigation of the Department of Justice." p. 265.

37. Telephone Calls, Dec. 2, 1953, Eisenhower Papers–Diary, Box 3, Phone Calls July–Dec. 1953, DDE. Note for Diary, Dec. 2, 1953, Eisenhower Papers–Diary, Box 2, DDE Diary, Nov. 1953, DDE. Jack Holl, "In the Matter of J. Robert Oppenheimer: Origins of the Government's Security Case" (paper delivered at the American Historical Association meetings, December 28, 1975; the author expresses his appreciation to Dr. Holl for providing him with a copy of this paper), p. 12. Griffith, *The Politics of Fear*, p. 216. *New York Times*, July 10, 1953, p. 1; Aug. 11, 1953, p. 12. Richard Fried, *Men Against McCarthy* (New York: Columbia University Press, 1976), pp. 272–274. Harold Green, "The Oppenheimer Case: A Study in the Abuse of Law," *Bulletin of the Atomic Scientists* (Sept. 1977), pp. 12–16, 56–61.

38. Herbert Parmet, *Eisenhower and the American Crusades* (New York: Macmillan, 1972), pp. 333–335. Holl, "In the Matter of J. Robert Oppenheimer," p. 12. Speech, Attorney General Herbert Brownell, Chicago, Ill., Nov. 6, 1953, Murphy Files, Truman-Brownell, HST. Brownell's charges were known to the president and, following the furor they precipitated, the administration carefully considered how to retain the initiative. See, Telephone Calls, Nov. 5, 11, and 16, 1953, all in Eisenhower Papers–Diary, Box 3, Phone Calls July–Dec. 1953, DDE. Minutes of Cabinet Meeting, Nov. 12, 1953, Eisehower Papers, Cabinet Minutes, DDE. Press Conference Notes, Nov. 18, 1953, Eisenhower Papers, Press Conference, Box 1, Press Conf. 11/18/53, DDE. Letter, President Eisenhower to General Alfred Gruenther, Nov. 23, 1953, Eisenhower Papers–Diary, Box 2, DDE Diary, Nov. 1953, DDE. C. D. Jackson Logs, Nov. 27, 1953, Jackson Papers, DDE. Sherman Adams, *Firsthand Report: The Story of the Eisenhower Administration* (New York: Popular Library, 1962), p. 135. Holl, "In the Matter of J. Robert Oppenheimer," pp. 13–14. Earl Latham, *The Communist Controversy in Washington: From the New Deal to McCarthy* (Cambridge: Harvard University Press, 1966), pp. 369–372. Telephone Calls, Dec. 2, 1953, Eisenhower Papers–Diary, Box 2, DDE Diary, Nov. 1953, DDE. U.S. Senate, Committee on the Judiciary, Subcommittee on Internal Security, *Hearings on Interlocking Subversives in Government*, pt. 16, 83rd Cong., 1st sess., 1953. See also, Bentley, Elizabeth—Testimony, Nov. 20, 1953. Official and Confidential FBI Files, J. Edgar Hoover Building.

39. Telephone Calls, Dec. 2, 1953, Eisenhower Papers–Diary, Box 3, Phone Calls July–Dec. 1953, DDE. Note for Diary Dec. 2, 3, 1953, Eisenhower Papers–Diary, Box 2, DDE Diary Nov. 1953, DDE. C. D. Jackson Logs, Nov. 27, 1953, DDE. Adams, *Firsthand Report*, p. 135. Holl, "In the Matter of J. Robert Oppenheimer." pp. 13–14; Griffith, *Politics of Fear*, pp.

217–220, 244–249, 260. Latham, *Communist Controversy*, pp. 326, 403. Fried, *Men Against McCarthy*, pp. 272–274. Indeed, the Eisenhower administration adopted this strategy in May 1954 during the later Army-McCarthy hearings when refusing to provide McCarthy's committee with transcripts or documents pertaining to the administration's strategy in dealing with McCarthy. Griffith, *The Politics of Fear*, pp. 243–269. Green, "The Oppenheimer Case," p. 16. David Caute, *The Great Fear: The Anti-Communist Purge under Truman and Eisenhower* (New York: Simon and Schuster, 1978), pp. 473–479. Fred Cook, *The Nightmare Decade: The Life and Times of Joe McCarthy* (New York: Random, 1971), pp. 438–450, 461–465.

40. *HIA*, vol. 6, Federal Bureau of Investigation, pp. 821–826. For quote, see p. 824.

41. *SDSRIARA*, p. 465. See also note 30 above.

42. *HDIOIS*, pp. 3401–3403.

43. *SDSRIARA*, p. 464; *HIA*, vol. 6, Federal Bureau of Investigation. p. 574.

44. *Federal Register*, vol. 27, p. 5169.

45. *HIA*, vol. 6, Federal Bureau of Investigation, p. 574; *SDSRIARA*, p. 464. It is unknown whether FBI Director Hoover briefed Lyndon Johnson about the bureau's claimed investigative authority under the 1939 presidential directive. Responding to criticisms of FBI and Secret Service coordination following John Kennedy's assassination and the Warren Commission's Report on February 3, 1965, the bureau and the Secret Service executed an agreement outlining their respective investigative and reporting responsibilities. While in no case an authorization document, this agreement confirmed the then common assumption that the FBI had authority to investigate "subversive activities." The agreement recognized the FBI's "general jurisdiction" over, "supervision" of, and responsibility to report to the Secret Service information about "subversives, ultrarightists, racists and fascists" who expressed "strong or violent anti-U.S. sentiment" or made "statements indicating a propensity for violence and antipathy toward good order and government." *IARA*, pp. 85, 85 n374. Agreement between the FBI and the Secret Service Concerning Presidential Protection, Feb. 3, 1965. Official and Confidential FBI Files, J. Edgar Hoover Building.

46. FBI Annual Report of 1964, p. 23. Documentary Supplement, Department of Justice, vol. XIII, FBI, pt. XIXb, LBJ. Hoover's annual reports for 1965, 1966, 1967, and 1968 repeated this claim. Ibid.

47. The Huston Plan's history is discussed in detail in chapter one.

48. *SDSRIARA*, pp. 507–508. Yeagley's successor as head of the Internal Security Division, Robert Mardian, sought to expand the scope of internal security investigations by revising the federal employee security program. Drafted by Mardian and issued by President Nixon on July 2, 1971, the new executive order 11605 substantially expanded FBI investigative authority by revising the attorney general's standards for listing groups to include those advocating the use of force to deny individuals rights under the "laws of any State" and the overthrow of the government of "any State or subdivision thereof." *IARA*, p. 123. This order is discussed in greater detail in chapter seven.

49. See chapter two for a more detailed discussion of this question.

50. *HIA*, vol. 6, Federal Bureau of Investigation, pp. 655–657.

51. Ibid., p. 658.

52. The conference's proceedings were published in 1973, See Watters and Gillers, *Investigating the FBI*. A later FBI document discloses that the paper which Brandeis political scientist John Elliff had presented at this conference had caused bureau personnel to reappraise whether FBI surveillance authority could be based on presidential directives.

53. See U.S. Senate, Committee on the Judiciary, Subcommittee on Constitutional Rights, *Hearings on Federal Data Banks, Computers and the Bill of Rights*, pts. I and II, 92nd Cong., 1st sess., 1971. The 1965 hearings of the Senate Subcommittee of Administrative Practice and Procedure had focused on questionable investigative techniques of the IRS. While branching out to include other federal agencies, at no time did these meetings explore federal investigative authority and surveillance of dissident political activities.

54. *SDSRIARA*, p. 549.

55. Ibid., pp. 549–550.

56. Ibid., pp. 550–551.

57. *HIA*, vol. 6, Federal Bureau of Investigation, pp. 540–546.

58. Ibid., p. 541.

59. Ibid., pp. 542–543.

60. Ibid., pp. 543–544.

61. Ibid., pp. 544–545.

62. Ibid., p. 546.

63. *JHWWES*, pp. 31–32.

64. *SDSRIARA*, p. 553. This program is discussed in greater detail in chapter five.

65. *IARA*, p. 318.

66. *HJDIIP*, pp. 157, 171–172. *Milwaukee Journal*, May 7, 1978, pp. 1, 8.

Chapter Four

1. *SDSRIARA*, p. 968.

2. *Milwaukee Journal*, March 22, 1976, pp. 5, 10. See also Frank Donner, "Intelligence on the Attack: The Terrorist as Scapegoat." *Nation*, 226 (May 20, 1978), pp. 590–594.

3. 47 U.S.C. 605 (1934).

4. Augelli's ruling is reprinted in U.S. Senate, Subcommittees on Criminal Laws and Procedures and on Constitutional Rights, *Hearings on Electronic Surveillance for National Security Purposes*, 93rd Cong., 2d sess., 1974, pp. 571–577. For the quote, see p. 576.

5. The government's memorandum is reprinted in ibid., pp. 417–437. The quote is from pp. 431–432. In that memorandum, the government quoted the Court of Appeals ruling: "In enacting #605, the Congress did not address the statute's possible bearing on the President's constitutional duties as Commander-in-Chief and as administrator of the nation's foreign affairs. The Senate and House reports suggest that the purpose of the Communications Act was to create a commission with regulatory power over all forms of electrical communications. . . . There appears to have been little or no discussion at all in Congress regarding #605. . . . In the absence of any indication that the legislators considered the possible effect of #605 in the foreign affairs field, we should not lightly ascribe to Congress an intent that #605 should reach electronic surveillance conducted by the President in furtherance of his foreign affairs responsibilities." Ibid., p. 433.

6. For a review of the changing justifications for electronic surveillance, see Athan Theoharis and Elizabeth Meyer, "The 'National Security' Justification for Electronic Eavesdropping: An Elusive Exception," *Wayne Law Review* 14 (Summer 1968), pp. 749–771.

7. Good histories of foreign policy attitudes during the 1930s, the Nye committee, and neutrality legislation include John Wilz, *In Search of Peace: The Senate Munitions Inquiry, 1934–1936* (Baton Rouge: Louisiana State University Press, 1963), Wayne Cole, *Senator Gerald Nye and American Foreign Relations* (Minneapolis: University of Minnesota Press, 1962), and Robert Devine, *The Illusion of Neutrality* (Chicago: The University of Chicago Press, 1962). In 1938, moreover, Congress seriously considered a proposed constitutional amendment requiring a national referendum before war could be declared—the so-called Ludlow Amendment. Then, during the early 1950s, Congress seriously considered (the Senate narrowly rejecting by one vote) the so-called Bricker Amendment requiring congressional approval of all treaties and executive agreements affecting the domestic society.

8. Victor Navasky and Nathan Lewin, "Electronic Surveillance," in Watters and Gillers, eds., *Investigating the FBI*, pp. 313–314. *Nardone v. United States* 302 U.S. 379 (1937) [the Roberts quote is from pp. 382–384]; 308 U.S. 338 (1939). See also Theoharis and Meyer, "The 'National Security' Justification for Electronic Eavesdropping," pp. 756–759.

9. Memorandum, President Roosevelt to Attorney General Jackson, May 21, 1940, Stephen Spingarn Papers, National Defense—Internal Security Folder 2, HST. Apparently, the president hurriedly prepared this memorandum after talking with Attorney General Jackson. According to Francis Biddle, Jackson was shocked by the vagueness of the president's phrase "persons suspected of subversive activities." Despite these reservations, the attorney general allowed the FBI director to institute taps without his approval in each case. During his tenure as attorney general, Biddle claimed, he reviewed FBI applications carefully; at times he requested additional information and at other times rejected these requests completely. Francis Biddle, *In Brief Authority* (Garden City: Doubleday, 1967), p. 167. In a February 21, 1941, letter to Congressman Thomas Eliot, Roosevelt reiterated this narrow view of legitimate wiretapping: "I have no compunction in saying that wiretapping should be used against persons not citizens of the United States, and those few citizens of the United States, who are traitors to their country, who today are engaged in *espionage or sabotage* against the United States" (emphasis added). Elliff, "Electronic Surveillance for 'National Security.'" When subsequently justifying this authorization, the department did not claim inherent presidential powers; it simply offered an interpretation as to what the Supreme Court had and had not prohibited. A March 17, 1941, letter from Attorney General Jackson to Congressman Hatton Summers articulated this view: "The only offense under the present law is to *intercept* any communication and *divulge or publish* the same. . . . Any person, with no risk or penalty, may tap telephone wires . . . and act upon what he hears or make any use of it that does not involve divulging or publication" (emphasis added). Elliff, "Electronic Surveillance for 'National Security,'" and Navasky and Lewin, "Electronic Surveillance," pp. 318–319. This tortuous reasoning, representing the FBI and the Justice Department as a single person and claiming that the FBI could wiretap for preventive reasons but that such informa-

tion could not be used for prosecutive purposes, provided the sole legal underpinning for the administration's claimed authority to order FBI wiretapping.

10. Attorney General Biddle privately affirmed this view in an October 9, 1941, memorandum to FBI Director Hoover. Biddle began by describing his recent press conference comments concerning revelations that the FBI had wiretapped labor leader Harry Bridges. He had defended the department's decision to authorize wiretapping in espionage, sabotage, and kidnapping cases by pointing out that the 1934 act had not prohibited interceptions—there must "be both interception and divulgence or publication." "The Courts," Biddle continued, "had held only that evidence could not be used which resulted from wiretapping; that the Courts had never defined what divulgence and publication was; that I would continue to construe the Act, until the Courts decided otherwise" as permitting interception. *SDSRIARA*, p. 281.

11. Attorney General Biddle interpreted this directive broadly—at least in one instance. On November 19, 1941 (approximately two weeks before Pearl Harbor), Biddle authorized a tap on the Los Angeles Chamber of Commerce. When approving this tap, Biddle conceded that the Chamber had "no record of espionage at this time." He then added the *caveat* that "unless within a month from today there is some evidence connecting the Chamber of Commerce with espionage, I think the surveillance should be discontinued." Ibid., p. 315; *IARA*, p. 37.

12. Letter, Attorney General Clark to President Truman, July 17, 1946, Stephen Spingarn Papers, National Defense—Internal Security Folder 2, HST. In November 1945, Attorney General Clark authorized an FBI wiretap of Thomas Corcoran, a former aide to President Roosevelt, in part because Truman (according to Clark) was "particularly concerned" about Corcoran's activities and "his associates." The purpose was "if possible to see that such activities did not interfere with the proper administration of government." *SDSRIARA*, p. 315 n156. Barton Bernstein, "The Road to Watergate and Beyond: The Growth and Abuse of Executive Authority Since 1940," *Law and Contemporary Problems* 40 (Spring 1976), p. 63. Robert Donovan, *Conflict and Crisis: The Presidency of Harry S. Truman, 1945–1948* (New York: Norton, 1977), pp. 29–30.

13. *New York Times*, June 2, 1949, p. 3; June 3, 1949, p. 2; June 4, 1949, p. 2; June 8, 1949, p. 1; June 9, 1949, p. 1; June 10, 1949, p. 10; June 11, 1949, p. 6; June 12, 1949, p. 1; June 16, 1949, p. 15; Dec. 1, 1949, p. 28; Dec. 16, 1949, p. 20; Jan. 12, 1950, p. 9; Feb. 2, 1950, p. 14; Nov. 3, 1950, p. 24. See also *Coplon v. U.S.* 191 F. 2d 749 (D.C. Cir. 1951), 342 U.S. 926 (1952); *U.S. v. Coplon* 185 F. 2d 629 (2d Cir. 1950), 342 U.S. 920 (1952); Navasky and Lewin, "Electronic Surveillance," p. 322; Thomas Emerson, "The FBI as a Political Police," in Watters and Gillers, eds., *Investigating the FBI*, pp. 241, 243, 245. Frank Donner, "Electronic Surveillance: The National Security Game," *Civil Liberties Review* 2 (Summer 1975), pp. 21–23.

14. Letters, Clifford Durr to President Truman, June 20, 1949 and Jan. 19, 1950; Letter, President Truman to Clifford Durr, June 23, 1949; all in Harry S. Truman Papers, OF 10–B, FBI, HST. Press Release, Feb. 24, 1950, and Speech, Joseph Rauh, Feb. 24, 1950, Stephen Spingarn Papers, National Defense—Internal Security, Folder 2, HST.

15. Memo, FBI Director to SAC, Boston, Oct. 13, 1949, FBI Files, Alger Hiss, Harvard University Library.

16. Press Releases, Department of Justice, March 31, 1949, and Jan. 8, 1950, Department of Justice Library. *New York Times*, Jan. 9, 1950.

17. Memo, Attorney General to FBI Director, Dec. 1, 1949; Letter, Attorney General to President Truman, Dec. 1, 1949; Memo, Director Hoover to Attorney General, Dec. 22, 1949; Letter, President Truman to Attorney General McGrath, Dec. 6, 1949; Letter, Attorney General McGrath to President Truman, Dec. 7, 1949; Letter, President Truman to Attorney General McGrath, Dec. 17, 1949; all in J. Howard McGrath Papers, The President, HST. Letter, J. Edgar Hoover to Harry Vaughan, Jan. 14, 1950, Harry S. Truman Papers, PSF, FBI N, HST. *Detroit News*, Aug. 25, 1977, p. 106. *Milwaukee Journal*, Aug. 28, 1977, Accent, p. 6. *New York Times*, Aug. 28, 1977, p. 3E. Letters, FBI Director to Attorney General, June 20, 1949, #1670, and Hoover to Lyle Wilson, June 28, 1949, #1668; Memo, Nichols to Tolson, June 28, 1949, #1669; all in FBI files, National Lawyers Guild. See also Cedric Belfrage, *The American Inquisition* (Indianapolis: Bobbs-Merrill, 1973), pp. 93–100.

18. *Washington Post*, Jan. 17, 1950, and Feb. 22, 1950, in Stephen Spingarn Papers, National Defense—Internal Security Folder 1, HST.

19. Memo, George Elsey to President Truman, Feb. 2, 1950; Memo, Elsey to Spingarn, Feb. 2, 1950; Draft Memorandum for the Attorney General, Feb. 7, 1950; all in Spingarn Papers, National Defense—Internal Security Folder 2, HST. See also *HDIOIS*, pp. 3390–3391, 3468–3469.

20. One of the purposes of Bureau Bulletin No. 34 was to preclude departmental knowledge of FBI wiretapping. Given this ignorance of key Department of Justice officials of FBI activities, can we reasonably expect effective presidential oversight of the bureau? Numerous cases of departmental ignorance can be cited. During 1972 pretrial hearings involving the Berrigan case, former Attorney General Ramsey Clark characterized as "equivocal" the government's response to a defense disclosure motion for all evidence obtained through electronic surveillance. Clark described his own experiences as attorney general, conceding that FBI electronic surveillance activities had caused the Justice Department "deep embarrassment" many times. "Often we would go into court and say there had been no electronic surveillance and then we would find out we had been wrong." The attorney general continued, "Often you could not find out what was going on . . . frequently agents lost the facts." Justice Department ignorance of FBI activities recurred during a damages suit brought by the Socialist Workers party against the U.S. government for the FBI's harassment and intimidation initiated in its 1961 CO-INTELPRO-SWP. On April 3, 1976, it was publicly disclosed that FBI agents had broken into SWP offices ninety-two times between 1962 and 1966 and that the FBI had not informed Justice Department attorneys defending the government of this fact. Two years earlier, in 1974, departmental attorneys had specifically assured SWP lawyers that the party had not been the subject of any FBI break-ins. Furthermore, those Justice Department officials who had been assigned responsibility to conduct a general investigation of past FBI break-ins became aware of the bureau's SWP break-ins only the day before the documents confirming them were released to SWP lawyers. *New York Times*, Apr. 4, 1976, p. 29. Then, after June 1976, it was

further learned that the FBI continued until July 1976 to receive reports and other materials stolen from SWP offices. Not only had these SWP reports been illegally secured; in addition bureau officials consistently claimed (including 1975 testimony before the Senate Select Committee on Intelligence Activities) that FBI break-ins had terminated in 1966 (excepting for foreign intelligence purposes) following former FBI Director Hoover's July 1966 order. *New York Times*, July 20, 1975, p. 2E; June 27, 1976, p. 16. *Time* (July 5, 1976), pp. 33–34. *Milwaukee Journal*, Sept. 20, 1974, p. 4; July 14, 1975, p. 1; July 2, 1976, p. 2; July 9, 1976, p. 5. These revelations led to a Justice Department inquiry into alleged FBI criminal misconduct, including illegal (in these cases, presumably unauthorized) wiretapping and bugging, physical assaults on radicals, and burning of automobiles. *New York Times*, July 11, 1976, pp. 20, 2E. Last, on September 28, 1964, in another case, *U.S. v. Baltch*, U.S. Attorney Hoey denied in open court that there had been any illegal electronic surveillance. Hoey made this statement after having first checked with the FBI. On September 29, Hoey informed the court again after checking with the Department of Justice that no leads had been secured through eavesdropping or other illegal activity. Only on October 2, 1964, did the U.S. attorney learn that the FBI had in fact bugged and unlawfully entered the Baltch's apartment. *HIA*, vol. 6, Federal Bureau of Investigation, pp. 203, 828–829. In this case, which was eventually dropped, the FBI had also opened the Baltch's mail; significantly, FBI officials had not reported this fact to the attorney general or to the prosecuting attorney.

21. *U.S. v. Coplon*, 185 F. 2d 629 (2d Cir. 1950); *Coplon v. U.S.*, 191 F. 2d 749 (D.C. Cir. 1951); *U.S. v. Coplon*, 342 U.S. 920 (1952).

22. The author discusses this White House attempt in greater detail in *Seeds of Repression*, pp. 138–140 and "The Threat to Civil Liberties" in Thomas Paterson, ed., *Cold War Critics* (Chicago: Quadrangle, 1971), pp. 286–288.

23. The Department since 1947 periodically sought White House authorization and then congressional enactment of wiretapping legislation. *New York Times*, Jan. 15, 1949, and April 7, 1949; Memo, Stephen Spingarn for the Files, Feb. 3, 1949; Memo, Spingarn to Lynch, Jan. 26, 1949; Letter, Attorney General Clark to Speaker of House, Jan. 14, 1949; Letter, Frank Pace to Attorney General, April 16, 1948; Memo, Spingarn to the President, July 14, 1950; all in Spingarn Papers, National Defense—Internal Security, HST. Memo, Murphy to Attorney General, Feb. 14, 1949, and Memo, Murphy to Souers, Jan. 7, 1949, Murphy Files, Internal Security, HST. Letter, Peyton Ford to James Webb, April 9, 1948, Clifford Files, HST. Letter, Attorney General McGrath to President Truman, Nov. 19, 1951, Philleo Nash Files, HST. See also Theoharis and Meyer, "The National Security' Justification for Electronic Eavesdropping," pp. 757, 761, 763–766.

24. *JHWWES*, p. 29. When reprinting this memorandum the subcommittee erroneously added an additional paragraph (beginning with the sentence "Previous interpretations . . ."); this paragraph came from Attorney General Brownell's May 20, 1954, memorandum. McGrath's cryptic reference to "other Federal Agencies (when known)" does suggest that already by 1952 the CIA and the predecessor of NSA were involved in electronic interception and that the attorney general at least suspected that domestic organizations and citizens had been targeted.

25. 316 U.S. 129 (1942).
26. *SDSRIARA*, p. 294 n74. *HIA*, vol. 2, Huston Plan, pp. 97–99, 111–113, 129–131, 273–280.
27. The Department of Justice also concluded that Roosevelt's 1940 requirement was "limited to wiretapping" and thus the attorney general's prior authorization did not apply to microphone surveillances. *JHWWES*, p. 23.
28. *SDSRIARA*, p. 295. Wise, *The American Police State*, p. 151.
29. *SDSRIARA*, pp. 295, 301. The committee did obtain statistics from the FBI detailing the number of illegal entries to install microphones for the years since 1960. See ibid., p. 371. See also Attorney General Levi's testimony in *HIA*, vol. 5, The National Security Agency and Fourth Amendment Rights, p. 86; see also pp. 67–71. Wise, *The American Police State*, p. 152.
30. Wise, *The American Police State*, p. 152.
31. 347 U.S. 128 (1958).
32. *SDSRIARA*, pp. 296–297. Wise, *The American Police State*, p. 153.
33. *SDSRIARA*, pp. 284–285. Memo, De Loach to Tolson, July 6, 1966, Official and Confidential FBI Files, J. Edgar Hoover Building.
34. *JHWWES*, p. 27.
35. *IARA*, p. 141. In 1960, moreover, Hoover approved a microphone surveillance of a "black separatist group," at least forty-nine microphone installations in "internal security, intelligence, and counterintelligence" investigations, and at least eleven in "criminal" investigations. Ibid., p. 61 n234, 61 n236.
36. *SDSRIARA*, p. 285. See also, Memos, De Loach to Tolson, July 6, 1966, Official and Confidential FBI Files, J. Edgar Hoover Building. Under Kennedy, this authority was widely used. The number of wiretaps increased dramatically from 115 in 1960 to 260 in 1964. The attorney general's expansive "national security" view, moreover, led him in 1963 to approve wiretaps on the Rev. Martin Luther King, Jr., and in 1961 and 1962 on three executive branch employees, a congressional staff member, and two lobbyists. When approving the King tap in October 1963, Kennedy required an FBI evaluation after sixty days. The bureau failed to do so; rather, in December 1963, it evaluated this wiretap informally and independently decided to extend it for another three months. The attorney general would not protest this failure. The assassination of the attorney general's brother, President John Kennedy, in the interim probably explains his failure to follow up on his October conditional authorization. The same extenuating circumstance, however, did not apply to the 1961–62 sugar lobby taps. That investigation had been initiated, as one bureau document records, because of the president's interest to obtain "a picture of what was behind pressures exerted on behalf of [a foreign country] regarding sugar quota deliberations in Congress . . . in connection with conduct of the Administration's foreign policy toward that country"; only in the loosest sense does this qualify as a "national security" matter. Indeed, an April 15, 1961, FBI memorandum recounts a meeting wherein the attorney general concluded that "now [that] the law has passed he did not feel there was justification for continuing this extensive investigation." The bureau similarly concluded that "undoubtedly, data from our coverage contributed heavily to the administration's success in [passage of the bill it desired]." Ibid., pp. 88, 88 n34, 115–118, 301, 318, 328–330, 345–346.

37. Theoharis and Meyer, "The 'National Security' Justification for Electronic Eavesdropping," pp. 752, 765–766. See also Victor Navasky, *Kennedy Justice* (New York: Atheneum, 1970), pp. 39–40, 72–79, 94.

38. Navasky, *Kennedy Justice*, pp. 448–449.

39. Ibid., pp. 78–95. *IARA*, pp. 60–61, 61 n234, 141. Memos, De Loach to Tolson, July 6, 1966, Official and Confidential FBI Files, J. Edgar Hoover Building.

40. *IARA*, pp. 61, 61 n234, 61 n235, 61 n236, 117–118, 117 n575. *SDSRIARA*, pp. 120–126, 301. Although welcoming this freedom, Hoover did not welcome the risks and responsibilities basic to this unreviewed authorization policy. Accordingly, when the department prepared a supplemental memorandum informing the Supreme Court of departmental policy involving bugs in *U.S. v. Black*, Hoover wanted it stated that every attorney general since Herbert Brownell had authorized warrantless microphone surveillance. Not believing this to be the case, Attorney General Nicholas Katzenbach approved a memorandum which simply stated that the particular microphone installations had been authorized by long-standing "practice." Ibid., p. 670. See also Memos, De Loach to Tolson, July 6, 1966, Official and Confidential FBI Files, J. Edgar Hoover Building.

41. *HIA*, vol. 6, Federal Bureau of Investigation, pp. 203–204, 828–829. *HIA*, vol. 4, Mail Opening, pp. 233–234. Memo, De Loach to Tolson, July 6, 1966 and Memo, De Loach to Tolson, July 6, 1966, both in Official and Confidential FBI Files, J. Edgar Hoover Building.

42. *SDSRIARA*, pp. 286–287, 302, 307–310; *HIA*, vol. 6, Federal Bureau of Investigation, pp. 357–359, 830–835; *IARA*, pp. 286, 286 n80. Memorandum, Mike Manatos to the Files, Feb. 25, 1965, WHCF Confidential File, FG 400–FG 600, FG 431, Senate Committees, LBJ. Letter, Edward Long to Donald Hornig, Aug. 11, 1966, WHCF FG 431/L-P, FG 431/A-C, LBJ. Letter, Edward Long to J. Patrick Coyne, Aug. 11, 1966, and accompanying instructions for Subcommittee Questionnaire; Letter, Patrick Coyne to Edward Long, Aug. 24, 1966; all in WHCF, FG 431, FG 431/A, LBJ. Memorandum, Lee White to President, July 8, 1965, WHCF, FG 431/F, FG 431/H-K, LBJ. Memorandum, Sheldon Cohen to Marvin Watson, Nov. 30, 1965, WHCF Confidential Files, JL-LA 6, JL Judicial Legal Matters, LBJ. Memorandum, Marvin [Watson] to President, Nov. 30, 1965, WHCF Confidential File, FG 110 (1967)-FG 115 (1965), FG 110–9 Internal Revenue Service, LBJ.

43. *SDSRIARA*, pp. 285–286, 298, 305–306. Theoharis and Meyer, "The 'National Security' Justification for Electronic Eavesdropping," pp. 755–756. Donner, "Electronic Surveillance," p. 30. On April 8, 1966, Attorney General Katzenbach urged President Johnson to issue an executive order limiting wiretapping to "national security" uses and prohibiting wiretapping by all federal agencies without the attorney general's prior approval. The president issued this order on June 30, 1965. Ibid., p. 286. Memo no. 493, Acting Attorney General to All U.S. Attorneys, Nov. 3, 1966, WHCF, Department of Justice, vol. III, Wiretaps and Electronic Surveillance, LBJ.

44. *SDSRIARA*, p. 301.

45. *SDSRIARA*, pp. 286–287, 299.

46. *SDSRIARA*, pp. 287, 299. Consistent with this view, and reflecting expansive "national security" conceptions, Attorney General Katzenbach approved FBI wiretap requests for the Student Non-Violent Coordinating

Committee, Students for a Democratic Society, and the editor of an anti-Communist newsletter. *IARA*, p. 105.

47. Theoharis, "Misleading the Presidents," pp. 747–749. The text of the 1968 act is reprinted in U.S. Senate, Subcommittees on Criminal Laws and Procedures and on Constitutional Rights, *Hearings on Electronic Surveillance for National Security Purposes*, 93rd Cong., 2d sess., 1974, pp. 5–15.

48. Theoharis, "Misleading the Presidents," pp. 746–747. See also Athan Theoharis, "Illegal Surveillance: Will Congress Stop the Snooping?" *Nation* 218 (Feb. 2, 1974), pp. 138–142.

49. Wise, *The American Police State*, pp. 41, 42–43. Donner, "Electronic Surveillance," pp. 36–40, 41. *SDSRIARA*, pp. 303, 307 n123, 323–326, 327, 337–338, 342–344, 349–351. See also "The Second Deposing of Richard Nixon," *Civil Liberties Review* 3 (June/July 1976), pp. 13–23, 84–95. The deposition of Nixon was taken by the American Civil Liberties Union in the suit it brought on behalf of Morton Halperin. The Senate Select Committee also deposed the former President. Relevant testimony is reprinted in *SDSRFMI*, pp. 146–147, 148, 149–152. *JHWWES*, pp. 311–332, 335–349, 352–378.

50. Wise, *The American Police State*, pp. 77–79. *SDSRIARA*, pp. 344, 540–541, 541 n606. *IARA*, pp. 124–125. When *Time* magazine reported in May 1973 that the records of these taps had been removed from the FBI files, Justice Department officials doubted that this could have been done. *Milwaukee Journal*, May 7, 1973, p. 3. See also Ibid., Feb. 26, 1973, p. 8. In *The American Police State*, David Wise quotes an October 1971 FBI memorandum stressing: "Knowledge of this coverage represents a potential source of tremendous embarrassment to the Bureau and political disaster for the Nixon administration. Copies of the material itself could be used for political blackmail and the ruination of Nixon, Mitchell, and others of this administration," p. 76. U.S. Senate, Subcommittee on Administrative Practice and Procedure et al., *Joint Hearings on Warrantless Wiretapping and Electronic Surveillance—1947*, 93rd Cong., 2d sess., 1974, pp. 365–369. The Nixon administration's quest for secrecy was not confined to this one instance. Indeed, in 1969, the administration sought to pressure the Supreme Court to reverse its ruling in *Alderman v. U.S.* entitling defendants to examine wiretap transcripts to support a taint contention. The administration even threatened to conceal from the courts records of sensitive surveillances if the court did not permit a "foreign intelligence" exception. Donner, "Electronic Surveillance," pp. 30–32.

51. 407 U.S. 297 (1972).

52. To effect this strategy, the White House cultivated former FBI Assistant Director William Sullivan to secure his assistance in providing details of similar political abuses by the Johnson and Kennedy administrations. Wise, *The American Police State*, pp. 76, 284–286. See also ibid., p. 154. *White House Transcripts* (New York: Bantam, 1974), pp. 72–78, 82–85, 95–96, 100–105, 108, 122–123. *JHWWES*, pp. 55–57, 485–486. *Time* (June 18, 1973), p. 22. *Chicago Sun-Times*, May 8, 1973, p. 3. *New York Times*, May 23, 1973, pp. 1, 28, 29; June 6, 1973, pp. 1, 33, 34, 35; June 7, 1973, p. 44; June 8, 1973, pp. 1, 18; June 10, 1973, p. 1E; June 17, 1973, pp. 1, 44, 45; June 27, 1973, pp. 1, 48, 52; June 29, 1973, pp. 1, 22, 26, 27; July 17, 1973, pp. 1, 26; July 18, 1973, pp. 1, 20; Nov. 6, 1973, p. 23; Dec. 9, 1973, pp. 1, 76; Dec. 26, 1973, p. 44; Feb. 9, 1975, p. 5E. *Milwaukee Journal*, April 16,

1973, p. 8; May 3, 1973, p. 9; May 10, 1973, pp. 1, 15; May 16, 1973, pp. 1, 2, 4; May 23, 1973, pp. 1, 2, 18, 19; May 24, 1973, pp. 1, 3, 4; May 25, 1973, pp. 1, 6; June 3, 1973, pp. 1, 7; June 4, 1973, pp. 1, 2; June 21, 1973, p. 4; July 18, 1973, p. 3; Aug. 24, 1973, pp. 1, 8; Nov. 16, 1973, p. 14; Dec. 5, 1973, p. 3; March 13, 1974, p. 1; May 14, 1974, p. 3. *HIA*, vol. 6, Federal Bureau of Investigation, pp. 539, 720, 732. This attempt to justify the administration's 1972 efforts to limit the FBI investigation into the Watergate break-in was not atypical, even though it proved counterproductive. In 1971, the Nixon administration adopted a similar "national security" rationale when responding to Congressman Hale Boggs's allegations about FBI wiretapping of members of Congress, and to the revelations about FBI surveillance brought out in the raid on the Media (Pa.) FBI office and public release of these files. *Milwaukee Journal*, March 24, 1971, pp. 1, 6; March 25, 1971, p. 6; April 15, 1971, pp. 1, 2; April 16, 1971, pp. 1, 2, 7. See also *HIA*, vol. 2, Huston Plan, pp. 141–197.

53. *Milwaukee Journal*, Jan. 6, 1974, pt. 5, p. 3; Jan. 9, 1974, p. 21; Feb. 4, 1974, p. 9; March 29, 1974, p. 9; April 24, 1974, p. 2; April 26, 1974, p. 16; May 2, 1974, p. 10; May 9, 1974, p. 10; July 27, 1974, p. 9; Aug. 23, 1974, p. 14. *New York Times*, Feb. 17, 1974, p. 13E. Letters, Lewis Paper (legislative counsel to Senator Gaylord Nelson) to Athan Theoharis, March 4, 1974, May 8, 1974, June 12, 1974, July 25, 1974. Press Releases, Senator Gaylord Nelson, May 9, 1974, May 31, 1974, Aug. 15, 1974. U.S. *Congressional Record*, 93rd Cong., 2d sess. (Feb. 4, 1974), S1138–1142; (June 18, 1974), S11301–11310. Letter, Howard Feldman (chief counsel, U.S. Senate Permanent Subcommittee on Investigations) to Athan Theoharis, May 30, 1974. Press Release, Senator Henry Jackson, May 31, 1974. Association of the Bar of the City of New York, Committees on Federal Legislation and on Civil Rights, "Judicial Procedures for National Security Electronic Surveillance" (Association of the Bar of the City of New York, 1974). U.S. *Congressional Record*, 93rd Cong., 2d sess. (Aug. 22, 1974), S15710–15728. *JHWWES*, pp. 254–278, 287–297.

54. U.S. Senate, Subcommittees on Criminal Laws and Procedures and on Constitutional Rights, *Hearings on Electronic Surveillance for National Security Purposes*, 93rd Cong., 2d sess., 1974, pp. 252–253. For the testimony of Attorney General Saxbe, see pp. 233–236, 241.

55. U.S. Senate, Committee on the Judiciary, Report No. 94–1035, July 15, 1976, *Foreign Intelligence Surveillance Act of 1976*, 94th Cong., 2d sess., 1976, p. 12. Moreover, in a letter filed by the Department of Justice on May 9, 1975, during John Ehrlichman's trial for having illegally authorized the break-in to the office of Dr. Lewis Fielding (Daniel Ellsberg's psychiatrist), Assistant Attorney General John Keeney outlined the department's current position that the executive branch had the independent right to authorize what would normally be considered illegal activities. The Fielding break-in was illegal because it had not been properly authorized, Keeney wrote. Break-ins must be carefully controlled, involve "foreign espionage or intelligence," be conducted with "minimum" intrusion, and be authorized in advance by the president or the attorney general; "activities so controlled are lawful under the Fourth Amendment." The department further maintained that "warrantless searches involving physical entries into private premises are justified under the proper circumstances when related to foreign espionage or

intelligence." *HIA*, vol. 2, Huston Plan, pp. 281–282. Wise, *The American Police State*, p. 160.

56. These new guidelines required: (1) the attorney general's written "personal approval" for all non-court authorized electronic surveillances; (2) submission of wiretapping requests in writing detailing the "relevant factual circumstances" justifying the proposed surveillances; and (3) the identity of the individuals requesting and approving this request. Authorizations were limited to ninety days or less; the attorney general's "specific approval" was required for continuance beyond this period. Electronic surveillance would be authorized only if he were "satisfied that the subject of the surveillance is either assisting a foreign power or foreign-based political group, or plans unlawful activity directed against a foreign power or foreign-based political group." *SDSRIARA*, pp. 291–292.

57. *New York Times*, Sept. 22, 1974, p. 49; June 29, 1975, p. 2E; July 6, 1975, p. 4E; July 13, 1975, p. 34; July 20, 1975, p. 3E; Dec. 21, 1975, p. 27; March 7, 1976, pp. 1, 27; March 21, 1976, p. 4E. *Milwaukee Journal*, June 2, 1974, p. 24; Feb. 20, 1976, Accent, p. 6; May 19, 1975, Accent, p. 3; June 25, 1975, p. 4; June 26, 1975, p. 2; July 2, 1975, p. 4; July 6, 1975, p. 9; Oct. 16, 1976, Accent, p. 6; Feb. 18, 1976, pp. 1, 2; March 7, 1976, p. 1; March 22, 1976, p. 5; March 24, 1976, p. 6; April 14, 1976, Accent p. 8; Apr. 20, 1976, p. 8; May 2, 1976, p. 10; June 3, 1976, p. 4. Letters, Lewis Paper (legislative counsel to Senator Gaylord Nelson) to Athan Theoharis, March 17, 1975, March 31, 1975. Letters, Ira Shapiro (legislative counsel to Senator Gaylord Nelson) to Athan Theoharis, May 4, 1976, June 16, 1976, and Aug. 3, 1976. Interview, Lewis Paper, April 29, 1975 (Washington, D.C.). Interviews, Ira Shapiro, Oct. 24, 1975 (Washington, D.C.) and Feb. 19, 1976 (Milwaukee, Wis.). See also U.S. Senate, Committee on the Judiciary, Report 94–1035, *Foreign Intelligence Surveillance Act of 1976*, 94th Cong., 2d sess., 1976. Letter, Senator Gaylord Nelson to Senator Birch Bayh (chairman, Subcommittee on the Rights of Americans, Senate Intelligence Committee), undated but July 1976, Xerox in author's possession. See also Donner, "Terrorism on the Attack," pp. 590–594.

58. *Milwaukee Journal*, Aug. 7, 1976, p. 2; Sept. 3, 1976, p. 13; Accent, p. 12; Sept. 21, 1976, p. 4. April 27, 1978, pp. 1, 26; May 20, 1978, p. 2. *New York Times*, May 8, 1977, p. 2E; June 15, 1976; July 2, 1976. April 16, 1978, pp. 1, 36; May 24, 1978, p. A20. Jay Miller, "Washington Report: We Must Stop New Surveillance Act." *Civil Liberties* (Sept. 1976), pp. 1, 3. U.S. Senate, Select Committee on Intelligence, Report No. 94–1161, *Foreign Intelligence Surveillance Act of 1976*, Aug. 24, 1976, 94th Cong., 2d sess., 1976. *Boston Globe*, June 30, 1976. Christopher Pyle, "A Bill to Bug Aliens," *Nation* 222 (May 29, 1976). U.S. Senate, Select Committee on Intelligence, Report No. 95–217, Annual *Report to the Senate*, May 18, 1977, 95th Cong., 1st sess., 1977, pp. 5–6.

59. *Milwaukee Journal*, July 23, 1976, p. 6; July 29, 1976, pt. 2, p. 8; Nov. 3, 1976, p. 2; April 21, 1977, p. 8, *New York Times*, July 25, 1976, p. 32; Aug. 8, 1976, p. 15E.

60. *IARA*, p. 58; *SDSRIARA*, p. 423.

61. *SDSRIARA*, pp. 740–741, 765–770. *HIA*, vol. 5, The National Security Agency and Fourth Amendment Rights, pp. 58–60. As in the case of other sensitive programs, the NSA devised separate filing procedures for

Operation SHAMROCK. Whereas NSA officials in September 1975 assured the Senate Select Committee on Intelligence Activities that all NSA documents pertaining to SHAMROCK had been provided, on March 25, 1976, NSA officials informed the committee of the "discovery" of a file containing additional documents and memorandums about SHAMROCK. These files allegedly had been held by a lower-level NSA employee who brought them to his superiors' attention on March 1, 1976. *SDSRIARA*, p. 767.

62. *SDSRIARA*, pp. 806–814. Similarly, this program was formally terminated when the Senate Subcommittee on Constitutional Rights initiated an investigation into Army surveillance activities following revelations about the scope and political nature of this program in a January 1970 *Washington Monthly* article. Ibid., pp. 787–834. See also Christopher Pyle, "CONUS Intelligence: The Army Watches Civilian Politics," *Washington Monthly* (Jan. 1970), pp. 4–16. U.S. Senate, Subcommittee on Constitutional Rights, *Hearings on Federal Data Banks, Computers and the Bill of Rights*, 92d Cong., 1st sess., 1971; ibid., *Hearings on Military Surveillance*, 93rd Cong., 2d sess., 1974; ibid., Staff Report, *Army Surveillance of Civilians: A Documentary Analysis*, 92d Cong., 2d sess., 1972; Report, *Military Surveillance of Civilian Politics*, 93rd Cong., 1st sess., 1973. Athan Theoharis, "Second-Term Surveillance: The Froehlke Affair," *Nation* 215 (Dec. 18, 1972), pp. 623–626.

63. *SDSRIARA*, pp. 423, 735–738, 740, 743, 744–748, 750, 765–766, 767–776; *IARA*, p. 108, 145; *HIA*, vol. 5, The National Security Agency and Fourth Amendment Rights, pp. 1, 3, 6, 7, 10–11, 12, 14, 145–146.

64. *HIA*, vol. 5, The National Security Agency and Fourth Amendment Rights, pp. 11, 13, 149–155; *SDSRIARA*, pp. 521, 739, 741, 743–744, 746, 748–749, 751, 752–756, 762; *IARA*, pp. 108–109, 147, 189.

65. *SDSRIARA*, pp. 739, 739 n18, 756–761. *HIA*, vol. 5, The National Security Agency and Fourth Amendment Rights, pp. 15, 158, 162–163. Athan Theoharis, "Illegal Surveillance," pp. 140–141. *New York Times*, June 6, 1976, p. 35; June 7, 1973, pp. 1, 36, 37; June 8, 1973, p. 19; June 11, 1973, pp. 1, 27; June 26, 1973, p. 37; July 10, 1973, p. 29; Oct. 15, 1973, pp. 1, 25; Oct. 16, 1973 pp. 1, 7; Oct. 21, 1973, p. 2E; Nov. 6, 1973, p. 22; Dec. 9, 1973, pp. 1, 76; Jan. 17, 1974, p. 30. *Milwaukee Journal*, May 24, 1973, pp. 1, 4; May 27, 1973, pp. 1, 3; June 1, 1973, pp. 1, 2; July 10, 1973, p. 3; Aug. 1, 1973, p. 3. *Des Moines Register*, Oct. 4, 1973, p. 6. *Village Voice*, Oct. 25, 1973, pp. 8, 9, 14. *Detroit Free Press*, Oct. 16, 1973, p. 1. *Detroit News*, June 5, 1973, p. 16A. *Chicago Sun-Times*, Sept. 9, 1973, p. 3. Order of Judge Keith, June 5, 1973. Order of Judge Keith, July 9, 1973. Proceedings on Motion for Extension of Time, Sept. 12, 1973. See also, Schlesinger, *The Imperial Presidency*, pp. 252–277, 378–381. *JHWWES*, pp. 312–334, 496.

66. Wise, *The American Police State*, pp. 142–182. Athan Theoharis, "Bell Limits FBI Prosecutions," *Nation* 225 (Sept. 10, 1977), pp. 198–199. *HIDFBI*, pp. 35, 44, 46–47, 173. *HIA*, vol. 2, Huston Plan, pp. 97–99, 111–113, 129–131, 273–280. *HIA*, vol. 6, Federal Bureau of Investigation, pp. 12–14, 352–359. *SDSRIARA*, pp. 355–371. *New York Times*, April 4, 1976, p. 29; April 25, 1976, p. 28; June 27, 1976, pp. 16, 3E; July 11, 1976, pp. 20, 2E; Aug. 1, 1976, pp. 1, 33, 3E; Aug. 15, 1976, pp. 28, 4E; Aug. 22, 1976, pp. 26, 3E; Dec. 12, 1976, p. 30; May 1, 1977, p. 1E; May 10, 1977, pp. 1,

34; May 22, 1977, p. 26; Aug. 14, 1977, p. 3E; Aug. 21, 1977, p. 16. May 22, 1978, p. A21; May 23, 1978, pp. A1, 15; May 28, 1978, p. 5E. *Milwaukee Journal*, Aug. 24, 1973, p. 1; Sept. 20, 1974, July 14, 1975, p. 1; July 16, 1975, p. 6; July 22, 1975, p. 6; March 29, 1976, p. 2; April 4, 1976, p. 3; May 10, 1976, Accent, p. 9; May 13, 1976, p. 18; July 2, 1976, p. 2; July 9, 1976, p. 5; July 15, 1976, p. 12; July 29, 1976, pp. 1, 6; Aug. 9, 1976, p. 7; Aug. 12, 1976, p. 27; Aug. 14, 1976, p. 6; Aug. 27, 1976, p. 6; Aug. 30, 1976, p. 2; Oct. 7, 1976, p. 3; Oct. 11, 1976, p. 9; Oct. 21, 1976, p. 7; Oct. 28, 1976, p. 11; Feb. 28, 1977, p. 6; March 31, 1977, p. 21; April 1, 1977, p. 5; April 2, 1977, p. 9; April 8, 1977, p. 5; April 15, 1977, p. 2; April 27, 1977, p. 5; April 28, 1977, p. 10; May 9, 1977, p. 11; May 12, 1977, p. 5; May 13, 1977, p. 3; May 18, 1977, p. 11; May 19, 1977, p. 5; May 21, 1977, p. 8; June 9, 1977, pp. 1, 16; July 6, 1977, p. 11; Aug. 31, 1977, p. 10; Dec. 7, 1977, p. 9; Dec. 11, 1977, Accent, p. 17; Dec. 14, 1977, p. 12. March 28, 1978, p. 8; April 22, 1978, p. 6; April 27, 1978, pp. 1, 2; April 29, 1978, p. 2; May 23, 1978, p. 3. *Detroit News*, June 23, 1976, p. 4A; Aug. 19, 1976, p. 4D; Aug. 21, 1977, p. 23C. *Time* (July 5, 1976), pp. 33–34. FBI documents of actual break-ins to the New York City offices of the Socialist Workers party are reproduced in Blackstock, *COINTELPRO*, pp. 204–211. These documents detail the procedures employed to ensure against disclosure— memorandums were forwarded to the personal folder of the special agent in charge and not the general field office files—and raise two additional questions. First, the extensive deletions made by the FBI at the bottom of the page, and the positioning of these deletions, suggest that these memorandums were widely circulated in the field office and in Washington and undoubtedly resulted in formal recommendations for action. Second, the deletion of the second line in the bureau's caption program description, that deletions were made on pre-1960 documents (preceding formal initiation of the FBI's COINTELPRO-SWP), and that these documents were released in the spring of 1976 after the FBI's "Do Not File" procedure had become known—all suggest that break-ins were conducted as part of a broader FBI surveillance program which entailed cross-referencing and filing of documents seperately. Otherwise, why would the bureau have deleted this line in 1976? Conceivably, extensive files still exist that provide insights into FBI break-ins and other illegal activities. *HJDIIP*, pp. 3, 42–46, 48–57, 62–66, 86–87, 90–91, 149– 150, 152–154, 156–159, 163–166, 172–173, 175–177. *U.S. v. Kearney*, CR 77–245, Defendant's Reply to Government's Response Opposing Supplemental Discovery Motion, June 28, 1977, p. 8, and Government's Response to Defendant's Supplementary Motion for Discovery and Inspection, Oct. 31, 1977, p. 14. Memo, De Loach to Tolson, July 6, 1966, and Memo, De Loach to Tolson, July 6, 1966; both in Official and Confidential FBI Files, J. Edgar Hoover Building. Letter, Anthony Marro (Washington bureau, *New York Times*) to Athan Theoharis, June 5, 1978.

67. *HIDFBI*, pp. 96–99, 103–104, 116–118, 123–146, 154–170, 173. Memos, Hoover to Tolson, Tamm, Ladd, and Clegg, March 19, 1946; Hoover to Tolson, Tamm, and Ladd, March 20, 1946; and Hoover to Tolson, Tamm, and Ladd, March 21, 1946; all in Hoover's "Official and Confidential" File on Alger Hiss, Harvard University Library. See also Theoharis, "Should the FBI Purge Its Files," and "Unanswered Questions," *Inquiry* 1 (June 12, 1978), pp. 21–24.

68. *HIA*, vol. 4, Mail Opening, pp. 148–161, 167–168, 238–240, 245–248. *HIA*, vol. 6, Federal Bureau of Investigation, pp. 828–835. *SDSRIARA*, pp. 636–677.

69. *SDSRIARA*, pp. 561–636. *HIA*, vol. 4, Mail Opening, pp. 407, 16–17, 24, 31, 34–38, 45–49, 60–61, 71–75, 80–95, 113–114, 119–128, 148–150, 154–156, 167–168, 175–183, 189, 192, 195–196, 199–205, 219–223, 238–240, 245–248. [Presidential] Commission on CIA Activities within the United States, *Report to the President* (June 1975), pp. 20–21, 102–106, 110–114.

70. Presidential Commission on CIA Activities, pp. 22–24, 26–27, 117–138, 144–148, 152–154. *IARA*, pp. 96–105. *SDSRIARA*, pp. 681–732.

71. *New York Times*, Mar. 14, 1976, pp. 4E, 14E.

72. *HJDIIP*, pp. 137–138, 162–163.

Chapter Five

1. *IARA*, pp. 66, 211 n1. *SDSRIARA*, p. 16. Allen Weinstein, *Perjury: The Hiss-Chambers Case* (New York: Knopf, 1978), pp. 9n, 275–276, 280, 358–359, 365–366. John Chabot Smith, "The Debate of the Century (Con't.)." *Harper's* (June 1978), pp. 81–85. Gary Wills, *Nixon Agonistes* (New York: New American Library, 1971), pp. 36–37. Peter Irons, "American Business and the Origins of McCarthyism: The Cold War Crusade of the United States Chamber of Commerce," in Griffith and Theoharis, eds., *The Specter*, pp. 79–82. For other examples of similar pre-COINTELPRO activities, see Caute, *The Great Fear*, pp. 169–181, 474, 481–482.

2. *HIA*, vol. 6, Federal Bureau of Investigation, pp. 88–89, 170–172, 186–188, 486–494, 535–538, 761, 766–784, 817. Memo, Marvin Watson to President Lyndon Johnson, July 10, 1967, WHCF FG135, A12, FG135–6, 1/14/67 —6/30/68, LBJ. *New York Times*, June 4, 1978, p. 6E. Ungar, *FBI*, pp. 277–278, 283–288, 355–358, 373–386. *IARA*, pp. 242–243, 242 n105, 242 n106, 242 n109. Robert Friedman, "FBI: Manipulating the Media," *Rights*, 23 (May/June 1977), pp. 13–14. *Milwaukee Journal*, Nov. 22, 1977, p. 2; Nov. 23, 1977, pp. 1, 8; Nov. 24, 1977, pp. 1, 9; Dec. 9, 1977, Accent, p. 4; Dec. 11, 1977, pp. 1, 15. Weinstein, *Perjury*, pp. 5, 366. Whitehead, *The FBI Story*, pp. 252–253. Walter Goodman, "J. Edgar Hoover and Me," *Nation*, 226 (Mar. 25, 1978), p. 325. Robert Wall, "Special Agent for the FBI," *New York Review of Books*, 13 (Jan. 27, 1972), pp. 140–167.

3. The more important Supreme Court rulings were *Communist Party v. Subversive Activities Control Board* (1956), 351 U.S. 115; *Pennsylvania v. Nelson* (1956), 350 U.S. 497; *Peters v. Hobby* (1955), 349 U.S. 331; *Service v. Dulles* (1957), 354 U.S. 363; *Slochower v. Board of Education* (1956), 350 U.S. 551; *Cole v. Young* (1956), 351 U.S. 536; *Watkins v. United States* (1957), 354 U.S. 178; *Yates, et al. v. United States* (1957), 354 U.S. 298; and *Jencks v. United States* (1957), 353 U.S. 657. *SDSRIARA*, pp. 16–17. Belknap, *Cold War Political Justice*, pp. 156, 175, 190–192, 216–220, 228–230, 236–248, 261, 263, 265.

4. John Elliff, "Aspects of Federal Civil Rights Enforcement: The Justice Department and the FBI, 1939–1964," *Perspectives in American History*, V (1971), pp. 643–647. *HIA*, vol. 6, Federal Bureau of Investigation, p. 473. *IARA*, p. 180. *SDSRIARA*, pp. 450–451.

5. Not principally concerned over legal restrictions and holding alarmist "national security" views, FBI officials were committed simply to obtaining practical results. *IARA*, pp. 14, 14 n82, 66, 211 n1. *SDSRIARA*, pp. 3, 10–11, 15, 16–17, 108, 469–470. *HIA*, vol. 6, Federal Bureau of Investigation, p. 70.

6. *HIA*, vol. 6, Federal Bureau of Investigation, pp. 372–376. *IARA*, pp. 66–67, 211, 211 n2. *SDSRIARA*, pp. 5, 17, 110–111. Similar considerations underlay Bureau efforts to develop a "responsible" leader for the civil rights movement. Navasky, "The FBI's Wildest Dream," pp. 716–718.

7. *IARA*, pp. 146–147, 151, 156, 281. *SDSRIARA*, pp. 9 n39, 27, 62, 63–64.

8. *IARA*, p. 281. *SDSRIARA*, p. 65. *HIA*, vol. 6, Federal Bureau of Investigation, pp. 819–820.

9. Minutes of Cabinet Meeting, Nov. 6, 1958, Cabinet Minutes, DDE. *IARA*, pp. 281–282. *SDSRIARA*, pp. 69–70.

10. *HIA*, vol. 6, Federal Bureau of Investigation, pp. 821–826. *SDSRIARA*, p. 66.

11. *IARA*, p. 282. *SDSRIARA*, pp. 465–466.

12. *HIA*, vol. 6, Federal Bureau of Investigation, p. 377. *SDSRIARA*, pp. 17–18.

13. Navasky, *Kennedy Justice*, pp. 105–106.

14. *New York Times*, June 27, 1964; *Washington Post*, June 17, 1964.

15. Don Whitehead, *Attack Against Terror: The FBI Against the Ku Klux Klan in Mississippi* (New York: Funk and Wagnalls, 1970), pp. 90–91.

16. *SDSRIARA*, pp. 18, 471–472.

17. Ibid., pp. 19–20; *HIA*, vol. 6, Federal Bureau of Investigation, pp. 378–382, 602–604.

18. *HIA*, vol. 6, Federal Bureau of Investigation, pp. 513–514.

19. Ibid., p. 515.

20. Ibid., pp. 202, 206–207, 213–217, 218, 231–232, 243–247.

21. *IARA*, pp. 151–152. *SDSRIARA*, p. 64 n261. Annual FBI Reports of 1964, 1965, 1966, 1967, and 1968. Documentary Supplement, Department of Justice, vol. XIII, FBI, pt. XIXb, LBJ. The FBI's 1966 report inaccurately identified this counterintelligence program as "designed to identify foreign intelligence personnel working against the United States and to determine their objectives so that protective measures and counter moves can be devised. These investigations are largely preventive in nature and their effectiveness cannot be measured on the basis of convictions or other statistics. Also, by the very nature of the investigations and the information obtained from them, a detailed outline of accomplishments cannot be publicly recorded." Ibid., 1966 Report, p. 23. While other annual reports were neither so specific nor so dishonest, these same themes were generally reiterated. See also the bland descriptions of the FBI's "internal security" responsibilities in Narrative History, Department of Justice, vol. XIX, Federal Bureau of Investigation, pp. 22–39, LBJ.

22. *HIA*, vol. 6, Federal Bureau of Investigation, pp. 516–527.

23. Ibid., pp. 221, 224, 232–235, 240–241.

24. *SDSRIARA*, p. 69.

25. Ibid., pp. 474–475; *HIA*, vol. 6, Federal Bureau of Investigation, pp. 679–680.

26. *SDSRIARA*, pp. 108, 179, 475–483; *HIA*, vol. 6, Federal Bureau of Investigation, p. 681. See also Navasky, "The FBI's Wildest Dream," pp. 716–718 for an account of FBI cointelpro-type activities directed at civil rights leader Martin Luther King, Jr.

27. *HIA*, vol. 6, Federal Bureau of Investigation, pp. 383–385. *SDSRIARA*, pp. 20–21. *Milwaukee Journal*, Mar. 11, 1978, p. 3.

28. *HIA*, vol. 6, Federal Bureau of Investigation, pp. 386–392.

29. *SDSRIARA*, pp. 22, 187–188, 528–531.

30. *HIA*, vol. 6, Federal Bureau of Investigation, pp. 528–534. *IARA*, pp. 83–84. *SDSRIARA*, pp. 487–501.

31. *SDSRIARA*, pp. 23–27, 483–489. *HIA*, vol. 6, Federal Bureau of Investigation, pp. 393–397. Wise, *The American Police State*, p. 311.

32. *Milwaukee Journal*, Mar. 24, 1971, pp. 1, 6. Wise. *The American Police State*, pp. 281, 314n. Ungar, *FBI*, pp. 136–140, 484–492. *IARA*, p. 127 n635.

33. *Milwaukee Journal*, March 24, 1971, pp. 1, 6; March 25, 1971, p. 6; Apr. 15, 1971, pp. 1, 2; April 16, 1971, pp. 1, 2.

34. *HIA*, vol. 6, Federal Bureau of Investigation, pp. 30, 605. *IARA*, p. 285. Wise, *The American Police State*, p. 314n. Ungar, *FBI*, p. 488. *HDIOIS*, p. 3832.

35. *HIA*, vol. 6, Federal Bureau of Investigation, pp. 30, 49, 90, 165, 330–332, 486–488. *SDSRIARA*, pp. 13–14. *IARA*, p. 246. *Milwaukee Journal*, Mar. 23, 1975, p. 14.

36. *SDSRIARA*, p. 73. *Milwaukee Journal*, Dec. 7, 1973, p. 5; Dec. 9, 1973, p. 18; March 8, 1974, pp. 1, 7. *HDIOIS*, pp. 3540–3544, 3831–3913.

37. *HIA*, vol. 6, Federal Bureau of Investigation, pp. 540–575. *SDSRIARA*, p. 553. The background to FBI Director Kelley's August 7, 1973, proposal and the response are more fully discussed in chapter three.

38. *SDSRIARA*, p. 553. U.S. House Committee on the Judiciary, Subcommittee on Civil and Constitutional Rights, *Hearings on FBI Counterintelligence Programs*, 93rd Cong., 2d sess., 1974, pp. 9–16, 20–23, 44–47.

39. *HIA*, vol. 6, Federal Bureau of Investigation, pp. 270–272, 430–433; *IARA*, pp. 130–131, 271 n20; *SDSRIARA*, pp. 12, 42, 73–76, 195–198, 553–554. U.S. House, Committee on the Judiciary, Subcommittee on Civil and Constitutional Rights, *Hearings on FBI Counterintelligence Programs*, 93rd Cong., 2d sess., 1974, pp. 9–16, 20–23, 44–47. Justice Department officials' indifference and willingness to minimize FBI COINTELPRO activities are also graphically demonstrated in Deputy Assistant Attorney General Kevin Maroney's April 8, 1974, testimony before the House Committee on Internal Security. Even though COINTELPRO documents had been released to NBC reporter Carl Stern in December 1973 and March 1974 and disclosed programs dating from 1961, Maroney nonetheless testified: "As has been indicated in the press by virtue of some documents made available by the Department, it [Cointel] was a program operated for about 3 years and discontinued in 1971." *HDIOIS*, p. 3533.

40. *HIA*, vol. 6, Federal Bureau of Investigation, pp. 316–320; *IARA*, pp. 135, 316–320; *SDSRIARA*, p. 76 n314. *Kansas City Star*, Aug. 13, 1975, p. 1. *Milwaukee Journal*, April 4, 1975, p. 7; Dec. 11, 1975, p. 18; Feb. 17, 1976, p. 2; Feb. 18, 1976, pp. 1, 2; Feb. 28, 1976, p. 1; March 12, 1976, Accent, p. 9; April 9, 1976, Accent, p. 14. *New York Times*, Dec. 10, 1976, p. 76; March 14, 1976, p. 4E.

41. *HIA*, vol. 6, Federal Bureau of Investigation, pp. 24–29, 31–34, 42–48, 50–59, 65–80, 83, 88–90, 92–95, 99–101, 103–104, 118, 151, 171, 271–272, 370–371, 398–407, 430–442, 486–494, 535–538, 606–622, 684–685, 689–702, 762–818. *IARA*, pp. 10–12, 17–18, 93–94, 180, 215–219, 242–248. *SDSRIARA*, pp. 7–11, 27–61, 95–96, 96 n68, 188–223, 242 n63, 251–252, 850–855. Blackstock, *COINTELPRO*, pp. 28–192. *HJDIIP*, pp. 113, 114, 235–236. *Milwaukee Journal*, Nov. 22, 1977, p. 2; Nov. 23, 1977, pp. 1, 8; Nov. 24, 1977, pp. 1, 9; Nov. 26. 1977, p. 11.

Chapter Six

1. In addition, whenever the FBI acquired information on members of Congress or their families, an agent would be dispatched to inform this congressman that this information had been acquired by chance but that no one would ever learn about it. Wise, *The American Police State*, p. 276. During February 1975 testimony before a House subcommittee, Attorney General Edward Levi further admitted that Hoover's files included forty-eight folders dealing with "public figures or prominent personalities" including presidents, Cabinet officers, and seventeen members of Congress. Ibid., p. 282. U.S. House, Committee on the Judiciary, Subcommittee on Civil and Constitutional Rights, *Hearings on FBI Oversight*, ser. no. 2, pt. 1, 94th Cong., 1st sess., 1975, pp. 4–11, 15–19, 34.

2. *IARA*, p. 31.

3. *HIDFBI*, pp. 154–155. These "official confidential files" included derogatory or potentially embarrassing information on prominent individuals. Ibid., pp. 87–88, 97, 139–140. U.S. House, Committee on the Judiciary, Subcommittee on Civil and Constitutional Rights, *Hearings on FBI Oversight*, ser. no. 2, pt. 1, 94th Cong., 1st sess., 1975, pp. 4–11, 15–19, 34.

4. These procedures are described in chapter four. See also ibid., pp. 96–99, 103–104, 116–118, 123–146, 154–170, 173. Memos, FBI Director to SAC, Boston, Oct. 13, 1949; Hoover to Tolson, Tamm, Ladd, and Clegg, March 19, 1946; Hoover to Tolson, Tamm, and Ladd, March 20 and 21, 1946; all in FBI Files, Alger Hiss, Harvard University Library. *SDSRIARA*, pp. 441, 562, 628, 632, 658–659, 675–676.

5. *IARA*, p. 32. *SDSRIARA*, p. 415.

6. These anti-FDR criticisms are fully discussed in Ronald Radosh, *Prophets on the Right: Profiles of Conservative Critics of American Globalism* (New York: Simon and Schuster, 1975), Michele Flynn Stenehjem, *An American First: John T. Flynn and the America First Committee* (New Rochelle: Arlington House, 1976), Wayne Cole, *American First: The Battle against Intervention 1940–41* (Madison: University of Wisconsin Press, 1953), and Warren Cohen, *The American Revisionists: The Lessons of Intervention in World War I* (Chicago: The University of Chicago Press, 1967). For an excellent bibliography, see Justus Doenecke, *The Literature of Isolationism: A Guide to Non-Interventionist Scholarship, 1930–1972* (Colorado Springs: Ralph Myles, 1972), pp. 13–45. See also Theoharis, "Should the FBI Purge Its Files?"

7. *HIA*, vol 6, Federal Bureau of Investigation, pp. 452–454. Wise, *The American Police State*, pp. 286–287. Bernstein, "The Road to Watergate and Beyond," p. 63.

8. *IARA*, pp. 32, 33, 37, 49. *SDSRIARA*, pp. 315 n154, 415–417.

9. *SDSRIARA*, pp. 415–417, 421–422. *IARA*, pp. 37, 227. Diary Entry, May 11, 1945, Harold Smith Papers, Box 1, HST. Peter Irons, " 'The Test Is Poland': Polish Americans and the Origins of the Cold War," *Polish American Studies* 30 (Autumn 1973), pp. 17–19, 21–22, 24, 26, 27–28, 44. Bernstein, "The Road to Watergate and Beyond," pp. 63, 65. Biddle, *In Brief Authority*, pp. 182–183, 237, 258–259. William Sullivan, "Personal Observations and Recommendations on Privacy," in *Privacy in a Free Society* (Cambridge: Roscoe Pound–American Trial Lawyers Foundation, 1974), pp. 94–95. During the prewar and wartime years, military intelligence agencies sought information on dissident political activists who opposed the war and military preparedness. These officials considered such activists subversive. *SDSRIARA*, pp. 423–424. Blackstock, *COINTELPRO*, p. 19. Wise, *The American Police State*, p. 286.

10. Letter, Harry Vaughan to J. Edgar Hoover, April 23, 1945, Truman Papers, OF 10–B, FBI, HST.

11. *IARA*, p. 37. Donovan, *Conflict and Crisis*, pp. 29–30.

12. Letter, Hoover to Vaughan, March 31, 1948, Truman Papers, PSF, FBI T, HST.

13. Letter, Hoover to Vaughan, Jan. 27, 1948; Letter, Hoover to Vaughan, Jan. 19, 1948; Letter, Hoover to George Allen, Sept. 20, 1946; all in Truman Papers, PSF, FBI Communist–Data, HST. Letter, Hoover to Vaughan, Mar. 3, 1948, Truman Papers, PSF, FBI S, HST. Letter, Hoover to Vaughan, Jan. 27, 1948; Letter, Hoover to Vaughan, Dec. 19, 1947, and photostatic copy of report "Democratic Party Committee to Elect Henry Wallace President of the United States"; and Letter, Hoover to Vaughan, June 25, 1947; all in Truman Papers, PSF, FBI W, HST.

14. Letter, Hoover to Vaughan, June 25, 1947, Truman Papers, PSF, FBI S, HST. Letter, Hoover to Matthew Connelly, Jan. 27, 1950, Truman Papers, PSF, FBI N, HST.

15. Letter, Hoover to Vaughan, June 18, 1947, Truman Papers, PSF, FBI Argentina, HST. Letter, Hoover to Sidney Souers, Feb. 20, 1951, Truman Papers, PSF, FBI I, HST.

16. Letter, Hoover to Vaughan, Oct. 23, 1946, Truman Papers, PSF, FBI W, HST. Letter, Hoover to Allen, Feb. 10, 1947, Truman Papers, PSF, FBI S, HST. Letter, Hoover to Vaughan, Jan. 8, 1948, Truman Papers, PSF, FBI Atomic Bomb–data, HST. Letter, Hoover to Vaughan, Sept. 15, 1948, and Letter, Hoover to Vaughan, Feb. 25, 1947, both in Truman Papers, PSF, FBI C, HST. Letter, Hoover to Vaughan, Mar. 29, 1947, Truman Papers, PSF, FBI L, HST. Bernstein, "The Road to Watergate," p. 66. Green, "The Oppenheimer Case," pp. 57, 58. Letter, Hoover to Vaughan, Jan. 5, 1949, Truman Papers, PSF, FBI Communist–Data, HST.

17. Letter, Hoover to Vaughan, Dec. 4, 1947, and Letter, Hoover to Vaughan, Jan. 11, 1946, both in Truman Papers, PSF, FBI Personal–FBI; Letter, Hoover to Vaughan, Feb. 6, 1946, Truman Papers, PSF, FBI A. Letter, Hoover to Vaughan, March 8, 1946, PSF, FBI F. Letter, Hoover to Vaughan, Dec. 23, 1948, Truman Papers, PSF, FBI N. Letter, Hoover to Vaughan, March 31, 1948, Truman Papers, PSF, FBI P. Letter, Hoover to Vaughan, Dec. 7, 1945, Truman Papers, PSF, FBI L. Letters, Hoover to Vaughan, Jan. 5, 1946; Hoover to Vaughan, Feb. 28, 1948; Hoover to Vaughan, Jan. 17, 1946; Hoover to Vaughan, Feb. 11, 1946; Hoover to Vaughan, Jan. 29, 1946; Hoover to Vaughan, June 21, 1946; Hoover to

Vaughan, Oct. 1, 1947; Hoover to Vaughan, Jan. 13, 1948; Hoover to Vaughan, March 16, 1948; Hoover to Vaughan, March 16, 1948; Hoover to Vaughan, Jan. 12, 1950; Hoover to Vaughan, April 13, 1948; Hoover to Vaughan, April 7, 1948; all in Truman Papers, PSF, FBI Communist–Data. Letters, Hoover to Vaughan, March 7, 1946; Hoover to Vaughan, Nov. 28, 1945; Hoover to Vaughan, June 21, 1948; Hoover to Vaughan, Nov. 15, 1945; Hoover to Vaughan, Dec. 12, 1947; Hoover to Allen, Sept. 25, 1946; Hoover to Vaughan, Feb. 20, 1946; Hoover to Vaughan, March 12, 1946; Hoover to Vaughan, Dec. 6, 1945; Attorney General Tom Clark to Matthew Connelly, July 23, 1946; all in Truman Papers, PSF, FBI C. Letter, Hoover to Vaughan, Nov. 13, 1947, Truman Papers, PSF, FBI R. Letter, Hoover to Allen, May 29, 1946, Truman Papers, PSF, FBI P. All in HST. Bernstein, "The Road to Watergate," p. 66.

18. Letters, Hoover to Vaughan, Oct. 31, 1945, Truman Papers, PSF, FBI C; Hoover to Vaughan, Jan. 29, 1946, Truman Papers, PSF, FBI M; Hoover to Vaughan, Jan. 25, 1946, Truman Papers, PSF, FBI M; Hoover to Vaughan, May 15, 1946, Truman Papers, PSF, FBI Maritime; Hoover to Vaughan, Nov. 29, 1945, Truman Papers, PSF, FBI Maritime; Hoover to Allen, June 10, 1946, Truman Papers, PSF, FBI Maritime; Hoover to Vaughan, Aug. 6, 1947, Truman Papers, PSF, FBI Personal–FBI; Hoover to Vaughan, June 5, 1946, Truman Papers, PSF, FBI Railroad–Data; Hoover to Allen, Dec. 13, 1946, Truman Papers, PSF, FBI T. All in HST.

19. Letter, Hoover to Vaughan, Dec. 6, 1946, Truman Papers, PSF, FBI I, HST. Harry S. Truman, *Memoirs*, vol. 1, *Year of Decisions* (Garden City: Doubleday, 1955), pp. 553–555.

20. Memo, George Elsey to Clark Clifford, Aug. 25, 1948, Elsey Papers, General File 1948, HST. *New York Times*, July 14, 1948, p. 2.

21. *SDSRIARA*, p. 430. *IARA*, p. 66. Wills, *Nixon Agonistes*, pp. 36–47. Nixon, *RN*, p. 58. Peter Irons, "American Business and the Origins of McCarthyism: The Cold War Crusade of the United States Chamber of Commerce" in Griffiith and Theoharis, eds., *The Specter*, pp. 79–82. William Gill, *The Ordeal of Otto Otepka* (New Rochelle: Arlington House, 1969), p. 32. John Chabot Smith, *Alger Hiss: The True Story* (New York: Penguin, 1977), pp. 143–148, 200–201, 229–230, 232, 285, Allen Weinstein, "The Hiss Case: An Exchange," *New York Review of Books* 23 (May 27, 1976), p. 39. Caute, *The Great Fear*, p. 463. Weinstein, *Perjury*, pp. 186, 190, 275–276, 280, 358–359, 365–366, 410. Memos, Hoover to Tolson, Tamm, Ladd and Clegg, March 19, 1946; Hoover to Tolson, Tamm, and Ladd, March 20 and 21, 1946; all in Official and Confidential Files, Alger Hiss, Hiss Papers, Harvard University Library.

22. *HIA*, vol. 6, Federal Bureau of Investigation, p. 486. *IARA*, pp. 239, 239 n91. *SDSRIARA*, pp. 35, 175–177, 209, 219–220. See the extensive Hoover-Trohan correspondence in the Walter Trohan Papers, J. Edgar Hoover File, Herbert Hoover Library. Memo, Marvin Watson to President Lyndon Johnson, July 10, 1967, WHCF, FG 135 A12, FG 135–6 1/14/67–6/30/68, LBJ. Robert Friedman, "FBI: Manipulating the Media," *Rights* 23 (May/June 1977), pp. 13–14. Caute, *The Great Fear*, pp. 113–114. Weinstein, *Perjury*, p. 366. *Milwaukee Journal*, Nov. 23, 1977, pp. 1, 8; Nov. 24, 1977, pp. 1, 9; Dec. 11, 1977, Accent, pp. 1, 15. Memo, Nichols to Tolson, June 28, 1949, #1669 and Letter, Hoover to Lyle Wilson, June 28, 1949, #1668, FBI files, National Lawyers Guild. FBI Cointelpro-type activities

might not have been confined to leaking information to "friendly" reporters or editors. FBI Director Hoover's 1947 testimony before the House Appropriations Committee strongly suggests that bureau officials also sought to influence public opinion by leaking information to "friendly" committees. Hoover's testimony is only suggestive; but this matter can be resolved when still closed files of congressional committees (notably HUAC and the Senate Internal Security Subcommittee) or of the FBI are open to research. In his 1947 testimony, the FBI director affirmed: "Committees of Congress have served a very useful purpose in exposing some of these activities which no Federal agency is in a position to do, because the information we obtain is either for intelligence purposes or for use in prosecution, and committees of Congress have a wider latitude." The Hoover quote is cited in U.S. *Congressional Record*, 93rd Cong., 2d sess., 1974, vol. 120, p. 8936.

  23. *IARA*, p. 240. *HIA*, vol. 6, Federal Bureau of Investigation, pp. 187–188. Ungar, *FBI*, pp. 355–356. Athan Theoharis, "Second-Term Surveillance: The Froehlke Affair," *Nation* 215 (Dec. 18, 1972), pp. 623–624. Berman and Halperin, eds., *The Abuses of the Intelligence Agencies*, pp. 20–21. *Milwaukee Journal*, Oct. 28, 1972, p. 1. *New York Times*, June 4, 1978, p. 6E. Wise, *The American Police State*, p. 276.

  24. *IARA*, pp. 9, 50, 51–52, 180, 232, 237, 238. On March 6, 1956, National Security Council staff member J. Patrick Coyne summarized that month's FBI reports to the White House as providing information "regarding attempts being made by the National Association for the Advancement of Colored People to send instructed delegations to high-ranking Government officials to tactfully draw out their positions concerning civil rights." Ibid., p. 233 n39. Bernstein, "The Road to Watergate," p. 71.

  25. *IARA*, pp. 7–8, 50, 52, 227.

  26. Ibid., pp. 48–50, 81, 175, 232–233, 233 n40. *SDSRIARA*, p. 449–451. COMINFIL's conservative political purposes were consistent with those leading to COINTELPRO. *IARA*, pp. 66, 250 n151.

  27. *IARA*, p. 239. *HIA*, vol. 6, Federal Bureau of Investigation, p. 160.

  28. Memo, Frederick Dutton to All White House Staff, Feb. 13, 1961, WHCF, FG 11–8–1 Dutton, F, Box 117, JFK. Memo, Attorney General Kennedy to Heads of Departments and Agencies, Aug. 17, 1962, WHCF, FG 11–5 NSC, Box 114, JFK. See also, Letter, McGeorge Bundy to David Bell, Feb. 3, 1961, Kennedy Papers, POF Bureau of Budget to 7/61, Box 70, JFK. Memo, McGeorge Bundy to Frederick Dutton, Feb. 1, 1961, and Letter, McGeorge Bundy to Senator Henry Jackson, Sept. 4, 1961, WHCF, FG 11–5, NSC, Box 114, JFK.

  29. *HIA*, vol. 6, Federal Bureau of Investigation, pp. 821–826.

  30. For one example, see Memo, Frederick Dutton (special assistant to the president) to Angela Novello (personal secretary of Attorney General Kennedy), Feb. 8, 1961, WHCF, FG 135 1–1–61—4–30–62, Box 146, JFK. In this memo, Dutton acknowledged receipt of a Hoover memo ("the second of these that has been forwarded to me") on the Bronx Civil Liberties Committee. Dutton added: "If there is any special action I should be taking, please let me know. I have absolutely no knowledge of the contents of this memorandum."

  31. *IARA*, pp. 52–53, 228.

  32. Ibid., p. 53. *SDSRIARA*, pp. 457, 483, 891–896. Bernstein, "The Road to Watergate," p. 71. In November 1963, moreover, administration officials

urged extending FBI coverage of segregationist groups to the Mississippi
White Citizens Council. See Memo, Burke Marshall to the Attorney General,
Nov. 13, 1963, Marshall Papers, Attorney General Nov. 63–Jan. 64, JFK.
For the administration's concern over the "radical right," see Memo, Leo
White to Ted Sorensen, Dec. 16, 1961; Confidential Report #6, Feb. 19,
1962; Confidential Report #9, June 12, 1962; all in White Papers, The Radi-
cal Right, JFK.

33. Memo, Angie Novello to Evelyn Lincoln, April 12, 1962 (and enclosed Memo, gp to Ed); Cover memo, Attorney General to the President,
April 12, 1962; Memo, FBI Director to Attorney General, April 12, 1962;
all in Kennedy Papers, POF, Justice 4162–6162, Box 80, JFK.

34. *IARA*, p. 63, 63 n248. *SDSRIARA*, Book III, p. 321.

35. *SDSRIARA*, pp. 321–322. FBI officials also requested authorization
to tap a former FBI agent who had disclosed "confidential" bureau information during a public forum. Instituted in 1962 without the attorney general's
prior authorization, the tap was discontinued for a time to be briefly reinstituted during 1963. *IARA*, pp. 63–64.

36. *IARA*, pp. 9, 64, 64 n259, 64 n262, 65, 65 n263, 201, 227, 233–234.
SDSRIARA, pp. 313, 328–330, 346.

37. *SDSRIARA*, pp. 449–450.

38. Ibid., pp. 466–467.

39. *IARA*, pp. 49, 176.

40. *SDSRIARA*, p. 87.

41. Ibid., pp. 86–88, 87 n26.

42. Ibid., pp. 88–90, 92–93, 93 n57, 95–96, 98–99, 105–107, 109–116,
121–123, 131–146, 151–154, 158–163, 174–177, 480–481. *IARA*, pp. 16,
52, 159, 199, 219–223, 249, 250, 275–277. *HIA*, vol. 6, Federal Bureau of
Investigation, pp. 30–34, 42–43, 55–58, 68–69, 77–80, 102, 167–170, 183–
185, 208–210, 609–611, 695–697. This quest for evidence to confirm Communist influence, even when earlier investigations established the contrary,
determined bureau policy. In an April 24, 1964, letter to the New York field
office, FBI officials in Washington argued: "The Bureau does not agree with
the expressed belief of the field office that [name of individual deleted] is not
sympathetic to the Party cause. While there may not be evidence that [name
deleted] is a Communist neither is there any substantial evidence that he is
anti-Communist." *IARA*, p. 7. Navasky, "The FBI's Wildest Dream," pp.
716–718.

43. This was no personal vendetta but bureau policy and is indirectly
confirmed by the FBI's continued surveillance of the NAACP. Even though
FBI investigations since 1940 had established the Communists' failure to
direct this civil rights organization, FBI surveillance continued on the premise
that Communists continued to exploit civil rights and might be more successful in the future. In April 1964, the FBI also sought and secured Attorney
General Kennedy's authorization to wiretap a black nationalist leader. This
leader was "forming a new group" which would be "more aggressive" and
would "participate in racial demonstrations and civil rights activities," and
had urged blacks to secure firearms for their self-protection. Bureau concern
expanded during the racial unrest of the 1960s. Because Soviet control could
not be confirmed, FBI officials sought to ascertain Chinese Communist,
Cuban, and "foreign influences on racial strife and the upsurge of black
nationalism." *IARA*, pp. 81, 105, 180, 206. *SDSRIARA*, p. 520. See also

Memo, Bill Moyers to President, May 15, 1964, WHCF, FG 135 A/2, Box 188, FG 135–6 11/23/63–11/30/64, LBJ. Memo, Brooks [Hays] to Bill [Moyers], Dec. 14, 1964, WHCF Confidential File, FG 135–6 FBI, LBJ. Letter, Hoover to Moyers, April 9, 1965, WHCF, Gen HU2, LBJ. Memo, Attorney General Katzenbach to President, Aug. 17, 1965, WHCF, FG 135 A/2, Box 188, FG 135–6 12/1/64–4/13/67, LBJ. Memo, De Loach to Tolson, July 6, 1966, Official and Confidential FBI Files, J. Edgar Hoover Building.

44. The FBI's COINTELPROs are described in detail in chapter five.

45. *IARA*, pp. 76, 257. *SDSRIARA*, pp. 448, 485, 487–488. Memo, Marvin [Watson] to President, May 16, 1967, WHCF Confidential File, FG 135–6 FBI Folder, LBJ. FBI coverage of campus dissent intensified in 1965. When *Ramparts* magazine publicly exposed CIA uses of the National Students Association in 1967, however, FBI Director Hoover examined the FBI's campus program principally because of fears about possible political embarrassment. On February 21, 1967, Hoover warned: "It is possible that this current controversy [over CIA links with the National Students Association] could focus attention on the Bureau's investigations of student groups on college campuses." Groups such as the Students for a Democratic Society (SDS), the FBI Director warned, might attempt to exploit this controversy "as a vehicle to create some incident to embarrass the Bureau." Special agents should continue "investigations to keep abreast of subversive influence on campus groups . . . conducted in a most discreet and circumspect manner. Good judgment and common sense must prevail so that the Bureau is not compromised or placed in an embarrassing position." Then, in response to the report to President Johnson of the special presidential commission investigating this matter recommending certain changes, Hoover tightened FBI procedures for contacting students and faculty. *SDSRIARA*, p. 486.

46. *IARA*, pp. 9, 16, 73, 241, 248. *HIA*, vol. 6, Federal Bureau of Investigation, pp. 393–397, 612–615. Memo, Marvin Watson to President, July 10, 1967, WHCF FG 135 A 12, Box 188, FG 135–6 1/14/67–6/30/68, LBJ. FBI efforts to shape national politics were not confined to the Vietnam War debate. In November 1964, exploiting their good relationship with the chairman of the board of a national news magazine, FBI officials "squelched" an "unfavorable article against the Bureau," "postponed publication" of another article involving an FBI case, "forestalled" publication of an article written by Reverend King, and received information about proposed editing of articles concerning King. In September 1965, moreover, the FBI sent anonymous letters to several community leaders decrying the "communist background" of George Crockett, a Detroit lawyer running for election to the City Council. That same month the bureau under a fictitious name sent another letter to a television station on which Crockett was to appear, enclosing a series of questions to be asked about his law clients and activities. When Crockett sought election to the Detroit Recorders Court in 1967, FBI agents used a local anti-Communist group to distribute fliers and write letters opposing his candidacy. In 1968, moreover, FBI officials pressured the Internal Revenue Service to tax audit a Midwestern college professor to prevent his attendance at the Democratic National Convention and planted a series of derogatory articles in the news media about Reverend King and the Poor People's Campaign. Friendly reporters received this information from FBI officials on the condition that "the Bureau must not be revealed as the source." *IARA*, pp. 16, 94, 248.

47. *IARA*, pp. 105, 251. *SDSRIARA*, pp. 483–485. *HIA*, vol. 6, Federal Bureau of Investigation, p. 683.
48. *SDSRIARA*, p. 489. *IARA*, pp. 8, 117, 229, 229 n13, 230, 238. *HIA*, vol. 6, Federal Bureau of Investigation, pp. 638–639. Memo, Marvin [Watson] to President, May 16, 1967, WHCF Confidential File, FG 135–6 FBI, LBJ. Memo, Director to Attorney General, April 7, 1967, and Memo, Ramsey [Clark] to Marvin Watson, April 8, 1967, with accompanying FBI report on SANE, WHCF, FG 135–6, HU 6, LBJ. Letter, McGeorge Bundy to Director Hoover, Dec. 9, 1965, WHCF Name File, Hoover, J. Edgar. Letter, Edgar [Hoover] to President, June 2, 1965, WHCF, FG 135 A12, Box 188, FG 135–6 12/1/64–4/13/67, LBJ. Memo, Joe Califano to President, Nov. 15, 1967, WHCF, Ex JL 3, LBJ.
49. *IARA*, pp. 8, 120, 171, 229. *SDSRIARA*, pp. 313–314. *HIA*, vol. 6, Federal Bureau of Investigation, pp. 162, 478–479, 720. In his inside account of the Johnson administration, historian and former Johnson aide Eric Goldman reports how the president privately praised the FBI and the CIA for fully briefing him about the antiwar movement. "Liberal critics!" Goldman quoted the president as declaiming. "It's the Russians who are behind the whole thing." Antiwar senators were in close contact with the Russians "who think up things for the Senators to say. I often know before they do what their speeches are going to say." Eric Goldman, *The Tragedy of Lyndon Johnson* (New York: Knopf, 1969), p. 500.
50. *IARA*, p. 100. *SDSRIARA*, pp. 681–682, 688–699. Commission on CIA Activities, *Report to the President*, pp. 22–27, 130–138, 152–154. When submitting a CIA report to the president on September 4, 1968, entitled "Restless Youth," CIA Director Helms stressed: "Some time ago you requested that I make occasional round-up reports on youth and student movements world wide. Responding to this request and guided by comments and suggestions from Walt Rostow, we have prepared the attached study. *You will, of course, be aware of the particular sensitivity which attached to the fact that CIA has prepared a report on student activities both here and abroad*" (emphasis added). *SDSRIARA*, p. 697.
51. Ibid., pp. 788–791, 794–806. *IARA*, p. 77. U.S. Senate, Committee on the Judiciary, Subcommittee on Constitutional Rights, Report, *Military Surveillance of Civilian Politics*, 93rd Cong., 1st sess., 1973, pp. 4–9, 11–14, 16–21, 28–31, 34–47, 52–83. Ibid., *Hearings on Federal Data Banks, Computers and the Bill of Rights*, pt. I, 92d Cong., 1st sess., 1971, pp. 85–467. Ibid., pt. II, 92d Cong., 1st sess., 1971, pp. 1047–1311.
52. *IARA*, pp. 117, 227 n3, 228–229, 229 n12, 229 n13, 230. *HIA*, vol. 6, Federal Bureau of Investigation, pp. 721–724. Letter, Mildred [Stegall] to Watson, June 30, 1965, WHCF, FG 135 A12, Box 188, FG 135–6 12/1/64–4/13/67, LBJ. Letter, Hoover to Watson, Nov. 16, 1966, WHCF, General FBI Reports, 1966, LBJ. Letter, Hoover to Watson, Nov. 23, 1966, WHCF, General FBI Reports 1966, LBJ. Letter, Hoover to Stegall, July 18, 1967, WHCF, General FBI Reports June-Present 1967, LBJ. Memo, Stegall to De Loach, May 24, 1965, WHCF, General Misc. 1965–1967, LBJ. Because their requests for name check were so extensive, White House aides were ordered as early as 1964 to forward future requests through the president's secretary, Mrs. Mildred Stegall. Memo, Walter Jenkins to White House Staff, Oct. 7, 1964, WHCF, FG 135 A12, Box 188, FG 135–6 11/23/63–11/30/64, LBJ. Memo, Bill Moyers to White House Personnel, Dec. 3, 1964, WHCF, FG 135 A12, Box 188, FG 135–6 12/1/64–4/13/67, LBJ. Memo, Mildred

[Stegall] to Marvin Watson, Nov. 23, 1965, WHCF General Misc., 1965–1967, LBJ. Letter, "Deke" [Cartha De Loach] to Mildred Stegall, Aug. 19, 1966, WHCF General Misc. 1966, LBJ.

53. *IARA*, pp. 65 n266, 105; *SDSRIARA*, pp. 323, 339, 340. The apparent catalyst to this FBI request was a William Gill article, "The Strange Case of Otepka's Associates," on a "top secret" State Department project which was published in the September 28, 1964, issue of the American Security Council *Washington Reports*. Assigned to investigate this "leak," State Department security official Jack Norpel interviewed Gill. Gill, *The Ordeal of Otto Otepka*, p. 377. In 1964, however, when Gill volunteered information to the FBI about alleged State Department security improprieties, Hoover promptly forwarded this information to then Attorney General Robert Kennedy. The attorney general apparently did not share Hoover's concern. Why the FBI director sought authority later to wiretap this editor for "internal security" reasons remains unclear. Hoover had expressed concern to the president in 1962 about the State Department's inspection system. (The Otepka case is discussed in greater detail in chapter seven.) Memo, Ralph Dungan (special assistant to the president) to FBI Director Hoover, April 4, 1962, WHCF, FG 135–6 FBI, Box 146, JFK.

54. *SDSRIARA*, p. 479. See also Navasky, "The FBI's Wildest Dream," pp. 716–718.

55. Attorney General Kennedy had not authorized the bugging of Reverend King's hotel room or of SNCC headquarters. In his August 29, 1964, report on the FBI's special squad's role at the convention, De Loach specifically claimed: "Through our counterintelligence efforts, Jenkins, et al., were able to advise the President in advance regarding major plans of the MFDP delegates. The White House considered this of prime importance." A January 29, 1975, internal FBI report on the Atlantic City operation, submitted in response to questions from the Senate Select Committee, conceded that political information had been forwarded to the White House and that part of the purpose had been to ensure that "there was nothing which would 'embarrass the President.' " Ibid., pp. 123, 335, 346–348. *IARA*, pp. 117–118, 239. *HIA*, vol. 6, Federal Bureau of Investigation, pp. 174–180, 189–190, 495–510, 623–638, 713–717. The White House particularly welcomed these reports and later that year formally thanked De Loach for his assistance. Note (unsigned), Aug. 19, 1964; Letter, De Loach to Moyers, Sept. 10, 1964; Letter, Lyndon Johnson to "Deke" [De Loach], Nov. 14, 1964; all in WHCF Name File, De Loach, Cartha, LBJ. Wise, *The American Police State*, pp. 288–292.

56. Wise, *The American Police State*, p. 293. *HIA*, vol. 6, Federal Bureau of Investigation, pp. 192, 194–195, 539.

57. *HIA*, vol. 6, Federal Bureau of Investigations, pp. 732–739, 756–759. As early as July 1967, moreover, Connell had contacted Marvin Watson (with a copy of his memorandum to Cartha De Loach) urging that "something should be undertaken, either in or out of government" concerning the planned September 1967 Chicago convention of the left-liberal, antiwar National Conference for New Politics. Memo, Bill [unsigned stationery from the Office of the Vice President] to Marvin [Watson], July 24, 1967, WHCF Confidential File, FG 120 1966, FG 135 Department of Justice (1967), LBJ.

58. *HIA*, vol. 6, Federal Bureau of Investigation, pp. 737–755.

59. Ibid., pp. 254, 535–537.

60. Ibid., pp. 164–165, 193, 195–196, 251–253, 483–484. *IARA*, pp. 120, 228, 228 n10, 228 n11. *SDSRIARA*, pp. 314–315.
61. *HIA*, vol. 6, Federal Bureau of Investigation, pp. 368–369, 642–644. The bureau's correspondence with Vice President Agnew on Ralph Abernathy is reprinted in ibid., pp. 490–494, 640–641. See also, *IARA*, pp. 117, 231. The FBI's "Summary of Extremist Activities" is described in *SDSRIARA*, p. 533.
62. *SDSRIARA*, pp. 245, 246, 314, 314 n149, 532, 551. *IARA*, pp. 7, 74, 76, 117, 120, 175–176, 230–231, 230 n16, 238, 257. *Milwaukee Journal*, Mar. 8, 1976, Accent, p. 3.
63. The Huston Plan has been discussed in detail in chapter one.
64. Since 1969, moreover, the Nixon administration had been pressuring the FBI to expand ongoing FBI investigative programs. On March 3, 1969, for example, Assistant Attorney General J. Walter Yeagley ordered FBI Director Hoover to utilize "existing sources" to collect information about "campus disorders." The department was then seriously considering "conducting a grand jury investigation under antiriot and other statutes." *HIA*, vol. 2, Huston Plan, p. 272. *HIA*, vol. 6, Federal Bureau of Investigation, pp. 693–694, 690–702. *IARA*, pp. 8–9, 76, 76 n324. *SDSRIARA*, p. 541.
65. *SDSRIARA*, pp. 842, 876–878, 880–886. *IARA*, pp. 95–96, 168. *HIA*, vol. 2, Huston Plan, p. 395. FBI and CIA officials specifically requested the tax returns of particular dissident individuals and organizations. The CIA obtained Victor Marchetti's returns (a former CIA employee and author of a book the agency was seeking to suppress) and FBI officials obtained the files of individuals targeted under COINTELPRO. *SDSRIARA*, pp. 848, 850, 854–855, 857, 858. The FBI also requested the tax returns of individuals and foundations when attempting to ascertain funding sources of the New Left movement. In a March 12, 1970, memorandum to William Sullivan (disseminated widely throughout the bureau), FBI official Charles Brennan outlined White House political objectives and the FBI's concern for secrecy: "By letter dated 2/27/70, in response to a specific request, we furnished the White House with material concerning income sources of revolutionary groups. Such an inquiry is indicative of the high-level interest in the financial aspects of revolutionary activity. Because of the sensitive nature of any direct intensive financial investigation of large foundations or funds, prominent wealthy individuals who limit their activities to financial support, or politically oriented groups such as the Vietnam Moratorium Committee, embarrassment to the Bureau would likely result." *HIA*, vol. 2, Huston Plan, pp. 309–312.
66. *HIA*, vol. 2, Huston Plan, p. 401. *IARA*, pp. 100, 102.
67. *HIDFBI*, pp. 20–33.
68. *SDSRIARA*, pp. 323, 541. *New York Times*, July 19, 1974, pp. 1, 12–19. Wise, *The American Police State*, pp. 13–18, 109–114, 117–139.
69. *IARA*, pp. 121, 121 n598, 122, 231. *SDSRIARA*, pp. 323, 336–337, 343, 344.
70. *New York Times*, May 9, 1969, p. 1; July 17, 1973, pp. 1, 4; July 18, 1973, pp. 1, 4.
71. *White House Transcripts* (New York: Bantam, 1974), pp. 77–78, 82–85, 95–96, 100–105, 108, 122–123.
72. Not one of the supporting documents accompanying FBI wiretap authorization requests of 1969 and 1970 cited "national security." Two of those

tapped, moreover, were White House domestic advisers who had no access to classified foreign policy documents; the initiative to tap one White House speech writer stemmed from his having been overheard (from a tap on another White House aide) agreeing to provide a reporter with background information on a presidential speech on revenue sharing and welfare reform. *SDSRIARA*, p. 337.

73. Ibid., pp. 324–326, 337, 343, 345, 350–351. *IARA*, pp. 10, 122, 200, 201, 207–208, 231, 232, 235–236. *New York Times*, Aug. 23, 1973, p. 1; June 9, 1974, p. 1; July 14, 1974, p. 1; July 19, 1974, pp. 1, 12–18; Sept. 29, 1974, p. 1. *Milwaukee Journal*, July 18, 1974, pp. 1, 16; Jan. 18, 1976, pp. 1, 22. Wise, *The American Police State*, pp. 31–73, 102–103.

74. *Milwaukee Journal*, Jan. 11, 1974, p. 1; Jan. 12, 1974, p. 1. *New York Times*, Jan. 13, 1974, p. 1. *SDSRIARA*, pp. 326–327, 343.

75. *SDSRIARA*, pp. 292, 331–332, 338–341, 339 n310, 339 n311. *IARA*, pp. 106–107, 107 n503, 206–207. *HIA*, vol. 2, Huston Plan, pp. 268–271, 334–341.

76. An FBI report on former FCC member and political activist Clifford Durr, which the bureau disseminated to the CIA and the State Department in 1964, highlights this political objective: "Clifford Durr is a well-known proponent of civil rights for all and has been outspoken in his opposition to Government loyalty investigations and investigating committees in the past. . . . Mrs. Durr . . . is extremely active on behalf of integration activities at present." John Rosenberg, "The FBI Shreds Its Files: Catch in the Information Act," *Nation* 226 (Feb. 4, 1978), pp. 108–111.

Chapter Seven

1. All New York State Medical Society members had to take loyal oaths; the American Bar Association urged all states to enact laws requiring loyalty oaths of all lawyers; Newark (New Jersey) Housing Authority tenants had to affirm their loyalty; and as one condition for being licensed by the state of Indiana all boxers and wrestlers had to take loyalty oaths. Harold Chase, *Security and Liberty: The Problem of Native Communists 1947–1955* (Garden City): Doubleday, 1955), p. 2. Caute, *The Great Fear*, pp. 267–348, 403–538. In December 1947, Attorney General Tom Clark released the department's list of subversive organizations. This list is reprinted in Eleanor Bontecou, *The Federal Loyalty-Security Program* (Ithaca: Cornell University Press, 1953), pp. 352–358. During 1948 testimony before the House Committee on Un-American Activities, FBI Director Hoover enumerated the bureau's criteria for determining whether to list an organization—criteria which were clearly political and conservative. Ibid., pp. 363–364. In *The Truman Doctrine and the Origins of McCarthyism*, Richard Freeland discusses the Truman administration's strategy when releasing the attorney general's list in December 1947 and cites examples of the political uses of this list. See pp. 208–213. Moreover, a private detective agency, the Wackenhut Corp., compiled files on 2.5 million individuals (including information on their political beliefs and activities) which it used during pre-employment and insurance claim investigations for private corporations. *Washington Post*, Jan. 27, 1977.

2. Bontecou, *The Federal Loyalty-Security Program*, pp. 8–21, 272–273, 284–287, 289–290, 310–312. Athan Theoharis, "The Escalation of the

Loyalty Program," in Barton Bernstein, ed., *Politics and Policies of the Truman Administration*, (Chicago: Quadrangle, 1970), pp. 244–245. *SDSRIARA*, p. 255. Schlesinger, *The Imperial Presidency*, p. 117. Richard Polenberg, *War and Society: The United States, 1941–1945* (Philadelphia: Lippincott, 1972), pp. 49–50. Freeland, *The Truman Doctrine and the Origins of McCarthyism*, pp. 118–120. Chase, *Security and Liberty*, p. 37.

3. Latham, *The Communist Controversy in Washington*, pp. 203–216. *The Report of the Royal Commission, Appointed under Order in Council, P.C. 411 of February 5, 1946, To Investigate the Facts Relating to and the Circumstances Surrounding the Communication by Public Officials and Other Persons in Positions of Trust of Secret and Confidential Information to Agents of a Foreign Power, June 27, 1946* (Ottawa: E. Cloutier, 1946), pp. 82–83, 686–689. Weinstein, *Perjury*, pp. 357–366. Smith, "The Case of the Century," pp. 81–85. Memos, Hoover to Tolson, Tamm, Ladd, and Clegg, March 19, 1946; Hoover to Tolson, Tamm, and Ladd, March 20 and 21, 1946; Memo, Bentley, Elizabeth, Testimony, Nov. 20, 1953; all in Official and Confidential FBI Files, J. Edgar Hoover Building.

4. U.S. House, Committee on the Civil Service, *Report of Investigation with Respect to Employee Loyalty and Employment Policies and Practices in the Government of the United States*, in A. Devitt Venech Papers, Advisory Loyalty Commission, HST.

5. Letter, Jennings Randolph to Truman, July 25, 1946; Letter, Arthur Flemming to Clark, July 22, 1946; Memo, George Elsey to Clark Clifford, Aug. 16,1946; Memo, John Steelman to Latta, Aug. 21, 1946; Memo, John Collet to Steelman, Sept. 18, 1946; all in OF252–I, HST. Letter, Harry Mitchell to Truman, Sept. 8, 1946, OF2 (1945–1946), HST. Memo, J. Edgar Hoover to Attorney General, July 25, 1946, and Memo, Attorney General to J. Edgar Hoover, July 31, 1946, both in A. Devitt Vanech Papers, Advisory Loyalty Commission, HST. Memo, for Matthew Connelly, Oct. 1, 1946, PSF General File, General–I, HST. Freeland, *The Truman Doctrine and the Origins of McCarthyism*, pp. 122–123.

6. These included A. Devitt Vanech (Justice), John Peurifoy (State), Edward Foley (Treasury), Kenneth Royall (War), John Sullivan (Navy), and Harry Mitchell (Civil Service). The working subcommittee was composed of L. V. Meloy (Civil Service), Marvin Ottilie (Navy), Stanley Goodrich (State), Harold Baynton (Justice), Stephen Spingarn (Treasury), and Kenneth Johnson (War). Innes Randolph (War) served as military adviser and P. B. Nibecker as naval adviser. Report of the President's Temporary Commission on Employee Loyalty, Feb. 20, 1947, p. 2, A. Devitt Vanech Papers, Advisory Loyalty Commission, HST. Letter, James Webb to Tom Clark, Nov. 20, 1946, and Executive Order 9806, Nov. 25, 1946, both in OF252–I, HST. Memo, J. Edgar Hoover to Attorney General, July 25, 1946, and Memo, Attorney General to J. Edgar Hoover, July 31, 1946, both in A. Devitt Vanech Papers, Advisory Loyalty Commission, HST.

7. Letters, A. Devitt Vanech to all agency and department heads, the FBI, the Military Intelligence Division, and the Office of Naval Intelligence, Dec. 26, 1946, OF252–I, HST.

8. In part, Hoover's interest in a federal employee loyalty program stemmed from a conservative objective to purge the federal bureaucracy. Hamstrung by existing Civil Service rules, possessing information which because merely derogatory or illegally obtained could not be used prosecutively, the

FBI director sought additional avenues to effect this objective. Even prior to the creation of the Temporary Commission, in late 1945 and early 1946, for one, Hoover forwarded a number of reports to the Truman White House and to Cabinet officials to prevent Harry Dexter White's appointment as a director of the International Monetary Fund and to force the dismissal of twenty-six other federal employees. Hoover's reports were based not on hard evidence but on the unsubstantiated testimony of Elizabeth Bentley and information obtained through illegal wiretaps. See Weinstein, *Perjury*, pp. 357–359, 364–366. U.S. Senate, Committee on the Judiciary, Subcommittee on Internal Security, *Hearings on Interlocking Subversives in Government*, pt. 16, 83rd Cong., 1st sess., 1953. Memo, Bentley, Elizabeth, Testimony, Nov. 20, 1953, Official and Confidential FBI Files, J. Edgar Hoover Building. Minutes, Commission meetings, Jan. 8, 1947, Jan. 13, 1947, Jan. 15, 1947, Jan. 17, 1947, Jan. 23, 1947, Feb. 17, 1947, Feb. 18, 1947, all in Stephen Spingarn Papers, Pres. Temp. Comm., vol. II, HST. Memorandums for the Files, Stephen Spingarn, Jan. 14, 1947, Jan. 17, 1947, Jan. 20, 1947, Feb. 20, 1947, all in Spingarn Papers, Pres. Temp. Comm., vol. II, HST. Notes on meeting of subcommittee, Stephen Spingarn, Jan. 24, 1947, Spingarn Papers, Pres. Temp. Comm., vol. II, HST. Memo, Spingarn to Foley, Jan. 19, 1947; Memo, Spingarn to Vanech, Jan. 20, 1947; Memo, Johnson to Meloy, Jan. 20, 1947; Memo, Spingarn to Foley, Jan. 28, 1947; Memo, Spingarn to Foley, Feb. 7, 1947; Memo, Goodrich and Spingarn to Vanech, Feb. 12, 1947; Memo, Spingarn to Foley, Feb. 20, 1947; all in Spingarn Papers, Pres. Temp. Comm., vol. II, HST. Memo, FBI Director to Attorney General, Jan. 29, 1947, Vanech Papers, FBI Loyalty, HST. Report of the President's Temporary Commission, Feb. 20, 1947, Vanech Papers, Adv. Loyalty Commission, HST. Letter, Acting Attorney General Douglas MacGregor to President, March 21, 1947, George Elsey Papers, Int Sec—FELP—E09835, HST. Memo, Clark to Vanech, Feb. 14, 1947; Letter, Hoover to Vanech, Jan. 3, 1947; Letter, Thomas Inglis to Vanech, Jan. 8, 1947; Letter, S. J. Chamberlin to Vanech, Feb. 11, 1947, all in OF252–I, HST. Letter, James Webb to Attorney General Clark, March 21, 1947, and Executive Order 9835, March 22, 1947, both in OF252–K, HST.

9. Thus, on the one hand the commission report and the executive order stipulated: "Each department or agency shall be responsible for the loyalty investigation of any of its employees whenever it is deemed necessary. Those departments and agencies not having investigative organizations will use the investigative facilities of the Civil Service Commission." The report and executive order continued: "There shall be a loyalty investigation of all persons entering the employ of any department or agency. All investigations of persons entering the competitive service shall be conducted by the Civil Service Commission, except in such cases as are covered by a special agreement between the Commission and any given department or agency." Investigating noncompetitive service employees "shall be the responsibility of the employing department or agency." On the other hand, during the preliminary check, loyalty investigators must consult all pertinent sources of information, including the FBI. The FBI, moreover, was ceded "the continuing responsibility to inquire into cases involving alleged subversive activities on the part of incumbent Federal employees." In addition, both the report and the executive order required: "At the request of the head of any department or agency an investigative agency shall make available [personally to each agency or de-

partment head or designated officer or officers] all investigative material and information collected by the investigative agency on any employee or prospective employee. . . . Notwithstanding the foregoing requirement, however, the investigative agency may refuse to disclose the names of confidential informants, provided it furnished sufficient information about such informants on the basis of which the requesting department or agency can make an adequate evaluation of the information furnished by them, and provided it advises the requesting department or agency in writing that it is essential to the protection of the informants or to the investigation of other cases that the identity of the informants not be revealed. It is not intended that investigative agencies should use this discretion to decline to reveal sources of information where such action is not essential." Report of the President's Temporary Commission, pp. 31–34 and Executive Order 9835, Vanech Papers, Advisory Loyalty Commission, HST. Memo, Clark to Vanech, Feb. 14, 1947, Vanech Papers, Pres. Temp. Comm., HST. Memo, FBI Director to Attorney General, Jan. 29, 1947, Vanech Papers, FBI Loyalty, HST. Memo, Spingarn to Foley, Feb. 20, 1947 and Memo for the File, Spingarn, Feb. 20, 1947, both in Spingarn Papers, Pres. Temp. Comm., vol. II, HST.

10. Memo, FBI Director to Attorney General, March 19, 1947, Vanech Papers, FBI Loyalty, HST. Attorney General, March 28, 1947, Vanech Papers, Loyalty, HST.

11. Letter, Harry Mitchell (president, Civil Service Commission) to Attorney General, March 28, 1947, and Letter, Mitchell to Edward Foley (assistant secretary of treasury), April 2, 1947, Spingarn Papers, Pres. Temp. Comm., vol. II, HST. Memo, FBI Director to Attorney General, March 31, 1947, Vanech Papers, Loyalty, HST. Memo, on FBI investigative jurisdiction in loyalty cases, undated and initialed D.H., Spingarn Papers, General Loyalty Files Folder 1, HST.

12. The bureau's claim of 4,000 Communist employees is cited in Memo, Spingarn to Foley, April 4, 1947, Spingarn Papers, Pres. Temp. Comm., vol. II, HST. Memo, FBI Director Hoover to Attorney General, April 3, 1947; Memo, Derrenger to Vanech (undated but probably April 17, 1947); and Memo, FBI Director to Attorney General, April 5, 1947; all in Vanech Papers, FBI Loyalty, HST.

13. Memo, Spingarn to Foley, April 4, 1947, Spingarn Papers, Pres. Temp. Comm., vol. II, HST. Memo, Spingarn to Foley, April 9, 1947, and Memo for File, Spingarn, April 9, 1947, both in Spingarn Papers, General Loyalty Files Folder 1, HST.

14. Letter, Mitchell and Perkins to President, April 25, 1947, and Memo, President to Webb, April 28, 1947, both in PSF General File, Civil Service Commission, HST. Note, CMC [Clark Clifford], May 2, 1947; Note, for CMC, May 2, 1947; Notes, May 1, 1947; all in George Elsey Papers, Internal Security FELP E09835, HST.

15. Note, CMC [Clark Clifford], May 2, 1947; Note, for CMC, May 2, 1947; Notes, May 1, 1947; Handwritten Rough Draft Memo for Clifford (never used), May 2, 1947; Typed Draft Memo for Clifford, May 2, 1947; CMC Summary, May 5, 1947; Notes, Montague of Budget, May 5, 1947; Note, Mitchell and Perkins, May 5, 1947; Recommendations, GME [George Elsey] to CMC, May 5, 1947; Draft Memo for President (prepared by Elsey), Clark Clifford, May 6, 1947; Memo, Clifford to President, May 7, 1947; all in George Elsey Papers, Internal Security FELP EO 9835, HST.

FBI comments on Executive Order 9835 and Loyalty Program, undated, A. Devitt Vanech Papers, EO 9835—Loyalty, HST.

16. Memo, Clifford to President, May 9, 1947, and Letter, Truman to Mitchell, May 9, 1947, Elsey Papers, Internal Security FELP EO 9835, HST. Press Release, May 9, 1947, and Statement by the President, Nov. 14, 1947, OF 10–B, FBI, HST. Memo, FBI Director to Attorney General, May 12, 1947; Letter, President to Speaker of House, May 9, 1947; Letter, James Webb (director, Bureau of Budget) to President, May 7, 1947; all in Vanech Papers, FBI Loyalty, HST. Memo, Dawson to President, Oct. 24, 1947, PSF General File, Loyalty Review Board, HST. Memo, Clifford to President, May 23, 1947, PSF Cabinet, J. Howard McGrath, HST. Memo, Webb to Truman, April 30, 1947; Memo, Attorney General to President, May 1, 1947; Memo, Clifford to President, May 9, 1947; Letter, President to Harry Mitchell, May 9, 1947; all in OF 252–K (1945–1947), HST.

17. Memo, FBI Director to Attorney General, May 21, 1947, Vanech Papers, FBI Loyalty, HST. Reiterating this position in January 1948, Hoover protested Secretary of the Army Kenneth Royall's effort to have the military intelligence services handle an investigation of "the St. Louis situation." Memo, FBI Director to Attorney General, Jan. 8, 1948, Vanech Papers, FBI Loyalty, HST.

18. Memo, Special Assistants to the Attorney General David Edelstein and Joseph Duggan to Assistant Attorney General Douglas McGregor, July 24, 1947, Vanech Papers, Loyalty Criteria, HST.

19. Memo, FBI Director to Attorney General, April 25, 1947, Vanech Papers, FBI Loyalty, HST.

20. Order N. 3464, Supplement No. 4, Office of the Attorney General, July 8, 1947, OF 285–M (Nov. 1951–June 10, 1952), HST. On September 3, 1947, the attorney general amended this order to permit the release of FBI investigative reports to federal district judges, U.S. commissioners, and probate officers whenever these reports pertained to "criminal cases" in which those officers had legitimate interests and could facilitate their work. Order N. 3464, Supplement No. 5, Office of the Attorney General, Sept. 3, 1947, OF 285–M (Nov. 1951–June 10, 1952), HST. *New York Times*, Dec. 28, 1947, p. 28. This concern to preserve the confidentialty of FBI informers remained until the 1970s. Unwilling to comply with a lower court order to turn over the files on eighteen FBI informers Attorney General Griffin Bell in June 1978 was instead considering being cited for contempt of court. *Milwaukee Journal*, June 12, 1978, p. 12. *New York Times*, June 18, 1978, p. 3E.

21. Letter, Davidson to Clifford, Dec. 29, 1947, Charles Murphy Files, Loyalty, HST. *Washington Post*, Jan. 8, 1948, p. 2. Memo, Dawson to Clifford, Jan. 7, 1948, OF252–K (1948), HST.

22. A number of such instances of politically motivated dismissals are cited in Caute, *The Great Fear*, pp. 267–345, 364–368, 473–484. Letter, Synder to Richardson, Apr. 15, 1948, John Snyder Papers, "Personnel 1946–1952," HST. Transcript, Loyalty Review Board Hearing, undated 1948, Spingarn Papers, CIC Prog. and Res., Folder 1, HST.

23. Davidson's letter is not available but is extensively quoted in Richardson's reply. Letter, Richardson to Davidson, Jan. 3, 1949, OF252–K (1949), HST. Significantly, in those few instances where confidential sources were independently examined, the damning nature of the derogatory information

quickly evaporated. Because these were the exception, the result was a highly political loyalty program which (1) sanitized the federal service since only those holding conventional political views and untainted by an unorthodox past would be seriously considered for federal employment and (2) raised the specter of a serious loyalty problem justifying extending the authority and responsibility of internal security agencies and refining loyalty/security procedures. For examples of political dismissals, see Letter, Norman Stoll (chairman, Auxiliary Loyalty Board No. 5 of the Department of Interior) to Martin G. White (solicitor, Department of Interior), Feb. 28, 1950, Spingarn Papers, Federal Loyalty Program, Folder 2, HST. Memo, Edward Condon (director, Bureau of Standards, Department of Commerce) to President, Aug. 6, 1951, PSF General File, C General #2, HST.

24. Letter, Moyer to Civil Service Commission, Feb. 2, 1949, OF252–K, HST. Attorney General McGrath echoed this recommendation in a December 23, 1949, letter to White House aide Donald Dawson. Administrative reforms were needed to close loopholes and prevent employment of individuals of "doubtful" loyalty "potentially" dangerous to the national security. Letter, McGrath to Dawson, Dec. 23, 1949, OF252–I, HST.

25. Letter, Bingham to Mitchell, Feb. 15, 1951, OF252–K, HST.

26. Theoharis, "The Escalation of the Loyalty Program," pp. 257–259.

27. Athan Theoharis, "The Threat to Civil Liberties," Thomas Paterson, ed., in *Cold War Critics*, (Chicago: Quadrangle, 1971), pp. 290–291.

28. Letter, Bingham to all heads of departments and agencies, May 23, 1951, and Letter, Bingham to all heads of departments and agencies, Dec. 21, 1951, both in OF252–K, HST.

29. *IARA*, p. 261.

30. Chase, *Security and Liberty*, pp. 44–45.

31. Memo, Eisenhower to Attorney General, Nov. 4, 1953, Eisenhower Papers–Diary, DDE Diary, Nov. 1953, DDE. Letters, Eisenhower to Postmaster General Arthur Summerfield, May 25, 1953, and reply, June 3, 1953, both in Eisenhower Papers, Summerfield, A 1952–54 (2), DDE. First Draft, Campaign Speech on Communism, Sept. 12, 1952, Benedict Papers, 2–12–52, DDE. Speech, Dwight Eisenhower, Oct. 4, 1952, Benedict Papers, 10–3–52, DDE. Letter, Leonard Hall to Kermit Mason, Hall Papers, Comments 1953–11, DDE. Letter, Senator William Jenner to President, Sept. 16, 1953; Memo, Gerald Morgan to Secretary of State, Oct. 9, 1953; Memo, Jeffrey Kitchen to Gerald Morgan, Oct. 12, 1953; Letter, Gerald Morgan to Senator Jenner, Nov. 6, 1953; Memo, John Foster Dulles to President, Nov. 23, 1953; Letter, President to Senator Jenner, Nov. 30, 1953; all in OF133 E–1, Communism 1953–1955, DDE. *Public Papers of the Presidents of the United States: Dwight D. Eisenhower, 1953*, pp. 24–25, 213–215. Peter Lyon, *Eisenhower: Portrait of the Hero* (Boston: Little, Brown, 1974), pp. 421n, 491, 492, 506. Dwight Eisenhower, *The White House Years: Mandate for Change 1953–1956* (Garden City: Doubleday, 1963), pp. 38, 46, 57, 83, 90, 111, 125, 308, 309. Barton Bernstein, "Election of 1952," in Arthur Schlesinger, Jr., *History of American Presidential Elections 1789–1968* (New York: Chelsea House, 1971), vol. IV, pp. 3233, 3241, 3242, 3245, 3246, 3257–3258, 3260, 3262–3263, 3281–3283, 3286, 3299, 3301. Hagerty Papers–Diary Entries, Hagerty Diary, March 1955, DDE. Memo, Eisenhower to Attorney General, April 27, 1953 and reply May 1, 1953, Eisenhower Papers, Brownell, Herbert, 1952–1954 (2), DDE. The administration's anticom-

munism was so alarmist that when the Cleveland bar association provided legal council to local Communists indicted under the Smith Act Assistant Attorney General William Tompkins criticized the bar association and characterized those lawyers who provided such legal assistance as dupes of the Communists. Belknap, *Cold War Political Justice*, pp. 227–230.

32. Letter, Hiram Bingham to President, Feb. 12, 1953; Memo, Sherman Adams to Bernard Shanley, Feb. 13, 1953; Letter, Shanley to Assistant Attorney General J. Lee Rankin, Feb. 16, 1953; Memo, Rankin to Shanley, Feb. 19, 1953; Letter, Adams to Bingham, Feb. 20, 1953; all in OF 104–J, Security and Loyalty Program 1952–53, DDE. Memo, Special Committee on Government Organization to Eisenhower, Dec. 31, 1952, GF 1–B–9, Loyalty and Security . . . 1952–53, DDE. Letter, Sherman Adams to Attorney General, Jan. 21, 1953, OF 103–K, E.O. on Classified Information (1), DDE. Letter, Edward Rees to Gerald Morgan, Jan. 22, 1953, Morgan Files, Security Order 10450 #1, DDE. Memo, Max Rabb to Adams, Jan. 26, 1953, OF 133, National Defense 1953, DDE. Memo, Joseph Dodge (director, Bureau of Budget) to Heads of all Departments and Agencies, Feb. 27, 1953; Memo, Charlie Willis to Adams, June 13, 1953; Memo, Dodge to Attorney General, April 2, 1953; Letter, Attorney General to President, April 17, 1953; Memo, George Moore to Philip Young, April 20, 1953; Executive Order 10450, April 27, 1953; Letter, President to Young, April 27, 1953; Memo, President to Heads of Departments and Agencies, April 27, 1953; all in OF 104–J 1954 (4), DDE. Hagerty Press and Radio Conference, April 27, 1953, OF 104–J, 1955, DDE. Order No. 12–53, Department of Justice, April 29, 1953, and Order No. 25–53, Department of Justice, Aug. 31, 1953, both in Rogers Papers, Orders A–G–II, DDE. Departmental Circular No. 708, U.S. Civil Service Commission, May 1, 1953, OF 104–J, Security and Loyalty Program . . . 1952–53, DDE. Chase, *Security and Liberty*, pp. 45–46. Green, "The Oppenheimer Case," pp. 15–16, 56–57.

33. Letter, Attorney General to President, May 20, 1954; Letter, W. R. Reid to William Hopkins, May 20, 1954; Executive Order 10491, May 27, 1954; all in OF 104–J, 1954 (1), DDE. Executive Order 10491, Oct. 13, 1953; Executive Order 10531, May 27, 1954; Executive Order 10548, Aug. 2, 1954; Letter, Attorney General to President, July 30, 1954; Memo, Rowland Hughes (director, Bureau of Budget) to Bernard Shanley, Aug. 4, 1954; Departmental Circular No. 782, U.S. Civil Service Commission, Dec. 29, 1954; all in F 104–J, 1954 (4), DDE. Letter, Philip Young to Sherman Adams, Oct. 16, 1953; Memo, Roger Steffan to Adams, Oct. 20, 1953; Letter, Steffan to Young, Oct. 20, 1953; all in OF 104–J, Security and Loyalty Program 1952–53, DDE. Memo, Eisenhower to Vice President et al., March 5, 1954, Hagerty Papers, State Department, DDE. Executive Order 10550, Aug. 5, 1954, and Order No. 70–55, Department of Justice, Jan. 20, 1955, both in Rogers Papers, Orders –A–G–II, DDE.

34. *SDSRIARA*, pp. 452–454, 779. *IARA*, p. 43. Caute, *The Great Fear*, p. 299.

35. Fried, *Men Against McCarthy*, pp. 273–274, 277–279. Lyons, *Eisenhower*, pp. 565, 567, 586, 599n. *Public Papers of the Presidents of the United States: Dwight D. Eisenhower, 1953*, pp. 802, 806, 841–844. Ibid., *1954*, pp. 12–13, 54–57, 202–204, 208–209, 526, 534, 611–612, 754, 781, 871–874, 881, 893, 896, 906, 937, 965, 971, 975–976, 982, 986, 987, 1008. Richard

M. Nixon, "Television Address on 'McCarthyism,' March 13, 1954," in Arthur Schlesinger, Jr., ed., *History of U.S. Political Parties* (New York: Chelsea House, 1973), vol. IV, pp. 3064–3066. Fact Papers Nos. 33, 53, 60, 63, 66, Young and Rubicam Files, Campaign publications . . . (1), DDE. Report on Anti-Communist Bills 8–11–54; The Eisenhower Program: Legislative Accomplishments—Anti-Communist Legislation; Justice Department; all in Young and Rubicam Files, Administrative Achievements of Eisenhower Administration, DDE. Memo, Charles Masterson to Jim Austin, May 28, 1954, Masterson Papers, Straight from the Shoulder, DDE. Memo, Masterson to Murray Snyder, Jan. 14, 1955, Masterson Papers, Chrono 1955, DDE. Communism and Internal Security, Masterson Papers, 1954 Election, DDE. Press Release, Oct. 23, 1953; Press Release, Dec. 2, 1953; Departmental Circular No. 737, U.S. Civil Service Commission, Dec. 28, 1953; Memo, Morgan to Robert Cutler, Feb. 15, 1954; all in Morgan Staff Files, Security Program, DDE. Speech, Attorney General Herbert Brownell, April 9, 1954, Morgan Staff Files, Communism (Leg.), DDE. Letter, Robert Sanford to President, April 2, 1954, and reply Murray Snyder to Sanford, April 20, 1954, GF 1–B–9, Loyalty and Security 1954, DDE. Press Conference Notes, March 3, 1954, Hagerty Papers, Pres. Press. Conf. 3–3–54, DDE. Letter, Edward Rees to President, Feb. 10, 1954, and replies, Morgan to Rees Feb. 17 and 23, 1954; Letter, Rees to President, March 5, 1954, and reply President to Rees, March 16, 1954; all in OF 104–J, 1954 (1) DDE. Memo, Young to Adams, June 2, 1954, OF 104–J, 1954 (3), DDE. Press Release, June 2, 1954, OF 133–E, Internal Security Subversive Activity (1), DDE. Letter, William Rogers to Adams, July 23, 1954, OF 133–E–10, Blacklist organizations (2), DDE. Testimony, Philip Young (chairman, Civil Service Commission), Senate Post Office and Civil Service Committee, March 2, 1954. Memo, Bentley, Elizabeth, Testimony, Nov. 20, 1953, Official and Confidential FBI Files, J. Edgar Hoover Building.

36. Lyons, *Eisenhower*, p. 506. Letter, Charles Willis to Homer Gruenther, June 25, 1954, and accompanying descriptive brochure describing "Operation Peoples' Mandate," Gruenther Papers, Office-General, DDE. Memo, Willis to President, Oct. 15, 1954, Willis Papers, Corr. White House Staff, DDE. Herbert Parmet, *Eisenhower and the American Crusades* (New York: Macmillan, 1972), pp. 215–217, 237–246.

37. Letter, Philip Young to John Moss, Jan. 19, 1954, Morgan Staff Files, Security Program, DDE. Memo, Edward McCabe to Jim Hagerty, March 29, 1956, OF 133, 1956, DDE. Letter, Hubert Humphrey to Philip Young, Feb. 16, 1955, Morgan Files, Investigations-Cong., DDE. S.J. Res. 21, Jan. 18, 1955, and H.R. 2590, Jan. 20, 1955, both in Morgan Files, Bills-Resolutions, DDE. Bernard Shanley to Millicent Fenwick, April 1, 1955, and Memo, Shanley to Goodpaster, March 9, 1955, both in OF 104–J, 1955, DDE. Department of State Press Release, Nov. 5, 1954, OF 104–J, 1954 (4), DDE. Eisenhower Papers–Diary, Phone Calls July-Dec. 1953 and DDE Diary Nov. 1953, DDE. Address, Attorney General Brownell, Nov. 6, 1953, Murphy Files, Truman-Brownell, HST. Eisenhower Papers–Diary, Phone Calls July–Dec. 1953 and DDE Diary Nov. 1953, DDE. Minutes of Cabinet Meeting, Nov. 12, 1953, Cabinet Minutes, DDE. Press Conference Notes, Nov. 18, 1953, Press Conference, Press Conf. 11/8/53, DDE. Green, "The Oppenheimer Case," p. 16. Caute, *The Great Fear*, pp. 292–293, 307–309, 315, 366–368, 473–484.

38. Letter, Thomas Curtis to Wilton Persons, July 14, 1954; Memo, Rodney Southwick to Paul Carroll, Aug. 6, 1954; Memo for Information, undated and unsigned but stamped received by Central Files, Aug. 9, 1954; all in OF 104–J, 1954 (3), DDE. Memo, George Moore to Philip Young, Dec. 8, 1954; Memo, Young to Sherman Adams, Jan. 13, 1955; Memo, Charles Masterson to Adams, Jan. 13, 1955; all in OF 104–J, 1955, DDE. Memo, M. B. Folson to Sherman Adams, Jan. 25, 1955, and recommendations of the Department of Health, Education and Welfare, Jan. 18, 1955, both in OF 104–J, 1956, DDE. Letter, Attorney General to President, March 4, 1955, Morgan Files, Security Order 10450 #2, DDE. Memo, Young to Donegan, June 21, 1955; Memo, Donegan to Morgan, Oct. 18, 1955; Summary of Activities, undated; all in Morgan Files, Security Order 10450 #1, DDE. Letter, Deputy Attorney General William Rogers to Sherman Adams, March 4, 1955, and accompanying draft statement; Memo, Gerald Morgan, March 7, 1955; both in Morgan files, Investigations-Cong., DDE. Memo, Morgan to Adams, undated but stamped received by Central Files, March 21, 1955, Rogers Papers, White House Correspondence, vol. I, 53–56–II, DDE.

39. Letter, Morgan to Wright, March 5, 1956; Directive, President to Heads of Departments and Agencies, March 6, 1956; Memo, Rabb to Strauss, March 30, 1956; Letter, Young to Tompkins, April 27, 1956; Memo, Donegan to Personnel Security Advisory Committee, May 23, 1956; Memo, Rabb to Adams, Jan. 29, 1958; all in Morgan Files, Security Order 10450 #1, DDE. Letter, Wright to Morgan, Dec. 7, 1956, Morgan Files, Security Order 10501 #1, DDE. Letter, Rogers to President, March 26, 1959, OF 104–J, 104–J 1958–60 (1), DDE. Letter, McGranery to President, June 18, 1957 and dissent, OF 104–J–1, (2), DDE. Recommendation #A–1, Nov. 29, 1956, and Recommendation #A–2, April 16, 1957, both in Rothschild Papers, Legislation, DDE. Tentative Recommendations of Supervisory Staff, Dec. 4, 1956, Rothschild Papers, Privilege . . . Self-Incrimination, DDE. Recommendations #A–3 and #A–4, April 16, 1957, Rothschild Papers, Document Classification, DDE. Recommendations #IV–2 and #V–2–a, Rothschild Papers, Civilian Employees (3), DDE. Recommendations #VII–D–2–g and #VIII–J–2–a, Rothschild Papers, Civilian Employees (4), DDE. Recommendations #IX–2 and # XV–2, Rothschild Papers, Civilian Employees (5), DDE. Recommendation #SVI–1, Rothschild Papers, Civilian Employees (6), DDE. Letter, Attorney General Brownell to Wright, Sept. 5, 1956, and Statement by Attorney General, Rothschild Papers, Corr. Sept. 1956, DDE. Letter, Wright to Rothschild, Feb. 20, 1957; Memo, Ladd to Wright, Jan. 8, 1957; Letter, Tompkins to Wright, Jan. 18, 1957; all in Rothschild Papers, Corr. Feb. 1957 (4), DDE. Letter, Wright to Rothschild, March 16, 1957, Rothschild Papers, Corr. March 1957 (2), DDE. Memo, Contor to Edwards Dec. 11, 1956, and Dec. 20, 1956, Rothschild Papers, Correspondence April 57 (2), DDE. Memo, Rothschild, June 8, 1957; Letter, Wright to Rothschild, June 5, 1957; Letter, Wright to Rothschild, June 28, 1957; Statement Lloyd Wright, July 1, 1957; Press Release, June 23, 1957; Rothschild Papers, Corr. June 57—May 57, DDE. Letter, Moss to Rothschild, Oct. 1, 1957; Letter, Rothschild to Moss, Oct. 2, 1957; Letter, Rothschild to Wright, Oct. 2, 1957; all in Rothschild Papers, Corr. April 58–Oct. 57, DDE.

40. Memo, Tompkins to Heads of All Departments and Agencies, April 9, 1957, OF 104–J–2, PSAC, DDE. Letter, President to Wright, June 21, 1957,

OF 104–J–1 (2), DDE. Memo, Rabb to President, July 22, 1957 and Directive, All Heads of Departments and Agencies, July 22, 1957, both in OF 104–J–2 (2), DDE. Press Conference Notes July 3, 1957, Morgan Files, Press Conferences, DDE. Memo, Rabb to Adams, Jan. 29, 1958, Morgan Files, Security Order 10450 #1, DDE. Cabinet Paper 58–84, Aug. 6, 1958, Cabinet Minutes, Cabinet Paper 58–84, DDE. Criminal Statutes, undated but 1958, Cabinet Secretariat, Security, DDE. Letter, Attorney General to President, Mar. 26, 1959, OF 104–J, 104–J 1958–60 (1), DDE. Cabinet Minutes, June 28, 1957, Cabinet Minutes, DDE. Memo, Rabb to Summerfield, April 2, 1958, OF 104–J, 1958–60 (1), DDE. Letter, Wright to President, June 19, 1959, and reply June 24, 1959, both in OF 104–J, 1958–60 (2), DDE.

41. *Cole v. Young* 351 U.S. 536 (1956). In other rulings involving the Truman loyalty program the Supreme Court narrowed the effect of federal loyalty/security policies on individual liberties. See *Peters v. Hobby* 349 U.S. 331 (1957) and *Service v. Dulles* 354 U.S. 363 (1957).

42. Departmental Circular No. 859, June 14, 1956 OF 104–J, 1956, DDE. Memo, Attorney General Brownell to Heads of All Departments and Agencies, Aug. 1, 1956, Morgan Files, Security Order 10450 #1, DDE. Memo, William Tompkins to All Heads of Departments and Agencies, May 1, 1957, OF 104–J, 1957, DDE. Memo, Roger Jones (chairman, U.S. Civil Service Commission) to Gerald Morgan, April 6, 1959 and memorandum, OF 104–J, 1958–60 (1), DDE.

43. Letter, Young to Murray, July 5, 1956, Morgan Files, Security Order 10450 #1, DDE. *Report of the Attorney General, 1957*, pp. 23–24, 64–65, Rogers Papers, Reports–Department of Justice, DDE. Letter, Ellsworth to Murray, July 2, 1958; Letter, Summerfield to Rogers, July 17, 1958; Letter, Rogers to Summerfield, July 28, 1958; Letter, Walsh to Johnston, July 24, 1958; Letter, Dechert to Johnston, July 17, 1958; Memo, Brown to Siciliano, July 16, 1958; all in Morgan Files, Legislation Pending, DDE. Letter, Summerfield to Stans, Aug. 29, 1958, and Letter, Summerfield to Morgan, Aug. 29, 1958, both in Morgan Files, Security Order 10450 #1, DDE. Memo, Robert Gray to Rogers, March 24, 1959, Rogers Papers, White House Correspondence III, DDE. Letter, Rogers to President, March 26, 1959, Areeda Papers, Industrial Security Program, DDE. Letter, Summerfield to Rogers, July 17, 1958; Letter, Summerfield to Anderson, July 17, 1958; Memo, Siciliano to Anderson, July 25, 1958; Letter, Morgan to Murray, Sept. 27, 1958; Memo, Siciliano for the Files, April 1, 1959; Memo, Jones to Morgan, April 7, 1959, and accompanying memo, OF 104–J, 1958–60 (1), DDE. Letter, Francis Walter to President, April 12, 1960; Letter, McPhee to Walter, April 19, 1960; Letter, Walter to President, Sept. 7, 1960; Letter, Kendall to Walter, Sept. 16, 1960; all in OF 104–J, 1958–60 (2), DDE.

44. Letter, President Eisenhower to Attorney General Rogers, May 12, 1958, Eisenhower Papers, Rogers, William 1958 (5), DDE. Letter, Rogers to Eisenhower, May 27, 1958, and reply, May 28, 1958, both in Eisenhower Papers, Rogers, William, 1958 (4), DDE. Belknap, *Cold War Political Justice*, pp. 254–258.

45. *Greene v. McElroy*, 360 U.S. 508 (1959).

46. Industrial Security Program, An Informal Chronology, undated; Memo, Areeda to Kendall, July 2, 1959; Memo, Meloy to Jones, July 2,

1959; Memo, Meloy to Jones, July 6, 1959; Memo, Hughes to Areeda, July 6, 1959; Memo, Robert Dechert, July 7, 1959; Letter, Dechert to Areeda, July 17, 1959; Memo, Port to Dechert, July 20, 1959; Memo, Niederlehner to Areeda, July 22, 1959; Defense Draft Executive Order, July 23, 1959; Memo, Areeda to Kendall, July 23, 1959; Memo, Draft Executive Order, July 30, 1959; Draft 3 Executive Order, Aug. 4, 1959; Areeda Draft Executive Order, Aug. 4, 1959; Draft Executive Order, Aug. 7, 1959; Memo, Areeda, Aug. 11, 1959; Draft Executive Order, Aug. 11, 1959; Memo, Meloy to Jones, Aug. 13, 1959; Memo, Areeda to Morgan, Sept. 15, 1959; Letter, Macomber to Stans, Aug. 19, 1959; Letter, Focke to Stans, July 28, 1959; Letter, Johnson to Focke, July 13, 1959; Letter, Dechert to Stans, July 7, 1959, and Draft Executive Order, July 7, 1959; Letter, Houston to Focke, July 14, 1959; Letter, Jones to Focke, July 16, 1959; Letter, Hoegh to Stans, July 23, 1959; Memo, Niederlehner to Focke, July 21, 1959; Letter, Floberg to Focke, July 31, 1959; Letter O'Connell to Stans, Aug. 10, 1959; Letter, unsigned and undated but from Atomic Energy Commission to Focke; Memo, Kendall to Rogers, Sept. 19, 1959; Memo, Kendall to Walsh, Sept. 19, 1959; Memo, Kendall to Rankin, Sept. 19, 1959; Draft Executive Order, Sept. 19, 1959; Draft Executive Order, Sept. 18, 1959; Memo, Areeda to Kendall, Sept. 30, 1959; Memo, Sherlock to Secretary of Army, et al., Nov. 24, 1959; Draft Executive Order, Nov. 24, 1959; Letter, Olson to Areeda, Dec. 22, 1959; Letter, Olson to Yeagley, Dec. 22, 1959; Defense Draft Executive Order, Dec. 11, 1959; Justice Draft Executive Order, Dec. 14, 1959; Letter, Burke to Stans, Jan. 7, 1960 and enclosed Draft Executive Order; Memo, Kendall to Attorney General, Jan. 16, 1960; Letter, Focke to Department of Commerce et al., Jan. 11, 1960; Memo, Bantz to Secretary of Defense, Jan. 13, 1960, and Department of Navy Comments on Draft Executive Order; Memo, Doherty to Kendall, Feb. 4, 1960; Draft Executive Order, Feb. 4, 1960; Memo, Areeda to Yeagley, Feb. 10, 1960; Memo, Areeda to Bartimo, Feb. 10, 1960; Draft Press Release, undated; Letter, Rogers to Stans, Feb. 17, 1960; Memo, Focke to Kendall, Feb. 18, 1960; Memo, Focke to Areeda, Feb. 11, 1960; Draft Executive Order, undated; Letter, McCone to Focke, Feb. 18, 1960; White House Press Release, Feb. 20, 1960; Executive Order 10865, Feb. 20, 1960; all in Areeda Papers, Industrial Security Program, DDE. Memo, Areeda to Kendall, Aug. 12, 1959 and Memo, Areeda to Morgan, Sept. 15, 1959, both in Morgan Files, Industrial Security Program, DDE.

47. Letter, Focke to Rogers, Jan. 9, 1961; Letter, Focke to Stans, Jan. 4, 1961; Letter, Quesada to Stans, Jan. 2, 1961; Letter, Jones to Focke, Dec. 28, 1960; Letter, O'Connell to Stans, Dec. 23, 1960; Letter, Hoegh to Stans, Dec. 20, 1960; Letter, Ray to Stans, Dec. 16, 1960; Letter, McCone to Focke, Dec. 15, 1960; Letter, Rogers to Stans, Dec. 13, 1960; Letter, Macomber to Stans, Dec. 13, 1960; Letter, Focke to Stans, Dec. 2, 1960; Letter, Johnson to Stans, Nov. 30, 1960; Letter, Weitzel to Stans, Nov. 29, 1960; Letter, Burke to Stans, Nov. 3, 1960; White House Press Release, Jan. 18, 1961; Executive Order 10865, as amended, Jan. 17, 1961; all in OF 103–K (6), DDE.

48. Memo, Bill Moyers to President [Johnson], Feb. 24, 1965, WHCF Confidential Files, PE 2 (1966)–PL/ST, PE 6 Investigations, LBJ.

49. Gill, *The Ordeal of Otto Otepka*, pp. 12, 14–21, 22–25, 29–33, 47–56, 71–76, 87–99, 150–153.

50. Ibid., pp. 3, 113, 117–125, 128–142, 146–149, 160–177, 180–186, 221–228, 230–280, 286–305, 314–323, 384–392, 460–470. Otepka's dismissal made him a political symbol for right-wing anti-Communists. His cause was championed by, among others, William Gill, Senators James Eastland and Thomas Dodd, and other conservative activists who actively lobbied the Johnson administration to reverse Otepka's dismissal. See, for example, Memo, Bill Moyers to President, May 13, 1964, WHCF, PE4 Health-Safety, PE 6 Investigations, LBJ. Letter, Mrs. Elvina Moore to President Johnson, Aug. 5, 1965; Route Slip, Hobart Taylor to Secretary of State, Aug. 11, 1965; Memo, Benjamin Read to McGeorge Bundy, Aug. 30, 1965; Letter, James Greenfield to Mrs. Elvina Moore, Aug. 27, 1965; all in WHCF Gen, PE 6 Investigations, PE 6 Investigations 11/23/63–8/27/65, LBJ.

51. Memo, Ralph Dungan to FBI Director Hoover, April 4, 1962, WHCF, FG 135–6FBI, JFK.

52. *SDSRIARA*, p. 457.

53. Memo, William Crockett to Walter Jenkins, May 8, 1964; Memo, Phillip Hughes to Myer Feldman, July 1, 1964; Memo, Myer Feldman to Walter Jenkins, July 22, 1964; Memo, Walter Jenkins to All Heads of Executive Departments and Agencies, Sept. 10, 1964; Letter, W. Willard Wirtz to President, Feb. 19, 1965; Memo, Matthew Coffey, April 2, 1965; all in WHCF, PE4 Health-Safety, PE 6 Investigations, LBJ. Letter, President Johnson to John Macy, Nov. 3, 1965, WHCF Confidential File, PE 2 (1966)–PLIST, PE 6 Investigations, LBJ. Letter, President Johnson to Attorney General Katzenbach, Feb. 24, 1965, WHCF Confidential File, FG 120 1966, FG 135 Department of Justice, LBJ. Letter, Lee White to Jerry Sonosky, Dec. 2, 1964, WHCF Gen, PE 6 Investigations, PE 6 Investigations 11/23/63–8/27/65, LBJ. Letter, John Macy to Lee White, Oct. 31, 1964; Draft Memo, Lyndon Johnson to Secretary of Defense, et al., undated; Draft Memo, Bill Moyers to President, undated; Memo, John Macy to Bill Moyers, Feb. 22, 1965; Memo, Lee White to Bill Moyers, Feb. 26, 1965; Memo, Bill Moyers to President, Feb. 24, 1965; Attachment B Proposed Text of Memorandum from Chairman Macy, undated; Attachment C Draft Letter, President Johnson to John Macy, undated; Letter, Macy et al. to President, Nov. 1, 1965, and Attachment A; all in WHCF Confidential File, PE 6 (1966)–PLIST, PE6 Investigations, LBJ.

54. U.S. Senate, Subcommittee on Constitutional Rights, Committee on the Judiciary, *Hearings on Privacy and the Rights of Federal Employees*, 89th Cong., 2d sess., 1966, pp. 1, 3, 5–6, 10–12, 23–25, 88, 89, 116, 117, 123–126, 137–140, 143–158, 172–173, 175–176, 198–199, 201, 218–219, 393–421, 455–456, 463, 495–497, 507–520, 530–534, 555–560, 566–570, 581–596, 619–687, 712–721, 726–785. *Senate Report No. 534*, Aug. 21, 1967, pp. 3, 4, 5, 7, 8–9, 10, 31, 33, 34, 35, 37, 38, 40, 41, 44. Memo, unsigned to President, May 27, 1966, WHCF Confidential File, LE/F 18—LEIPO, LE/LG—LEIPO, LBJ. Memo, Harry McPherson to President, Nov. 28, 1966, and Memo, Ruth [McCawley] to [DeVier] Pierson, June 5, 1967, both in WHCF McPherson Files, Security Investigations, *LBJ*. Memo, Lee White to Heads of Departments and Agencies, June 12, 1964; Memo, Lee White to Norbert Schlei, July 17, 1964, and reply; Memo, Norbert Schlei to Lee White, undated; all in WHCF Gen, PE/FG 140, PE 1 11/22/63–9/30/64, LBJ. Memo, Robert Kintner to President, Aug. 25, 1966, WHCF Confidential Files, PE 2 (1966)—PLIST, PE 6 Investigations, LBJ. Letter, Sam Ervin

to Donald Hornig, Oct. 13, 1966, WHCF, FG 4311L–P, FG 4311A–C, LBJ. Memo, John Warner to Mike Manatos, Aug. 31, 1967, and accompanying CIA analysis of S. 1035, WHCF, LE/PE 1, LE/PE 1, LBJ. Memo, Lawrence O'Brien to John Macy, Feb. 25, 1967, and Draft Memorandum, Joe Califano to President, Mar. 31, 1967, WHCF, EX PE 1 10/1/64, PE 1 7/26/66–9/18/67, LBJ. Memo, Bill Moyers to President, July 7, 1966, WHCF Name File, Ervin, Sam J., Ervin, Sam J. 1/5/66–12/31/66, LBJ. Memo, Ruth McCrawley to Juanita Roberts, Sept. 6, 1966, Memo, unsigned to Harry [McPherson], undated; Memo, Harry [McPherson] to DeVier [Pierson], May 10, 1967; Memo, John Macy to Harry McPherson, Feb. 24, 1967; Memo, John Macy to President, Feb. 24, 1967; Memo, Harry McPherson to Joe Califano, Feb. 2, 1967; Draft Memorandum, Lyndon Johnson to Heads of Departments and Agencies, undated [but 1967]; Note, DeVier [Pierson] to Harry McPherson, May 11, 1967; Memo, Wilt Rommel to Harry McPherson, Sept. 27, 1966; Letter, John Macy to James Eastland, undated [but 1966]; Memo, Helen Hill to Harry McPherson, Sept. 30, 1966; Memo, Ruth Mc-Cawley to Juanita Roberts, Sept. 7, 1966; Memo, Harry McPherson to President, Aug. 25, 1966; Memo, Attorney General to Harry McPherson, Aug. 24, 1966; Memo, Harry McPherson to Attorney General, Aug. 15, 1966; Memo, Harry McPherson to John Macy, Aug. 22, 1966; Memo, Harry Mc-Pherson to John Macy, Aug. 18, 1966; Memo, John Macy to Harry Mc-Pherson, Aug. 17, 1966; Memo, Harry McPherson to John Macy, Aug. 10, 1966; Memo, Mike Manatos to Harry McPherson, Aug. 4, 1966; all in WHCF DeVier-Pierson Files, Pierson Invasion of Privacy (2), LBJ. Memo, Ramsey Clark to Marvin Watson, Feb. 18, 1965; Memo, William Simkin to Joseph Califano, June 2, 1966; Memo, John Macy to George Christian, Jan. 14, 1967; Memo, Joe Califano to President with attached memorandum of Feb. 13, 1968, from William Gaud, Feb. 13, 1968; Draft Memorandum Lyndon Johnson to Heads of Departments and Agencies, undated [but Dec. 1966]; Letter, William Carey et al. to President, Dec. 27, 1966; Memo, John Macy to President, April 15, 1968; Memo, Larry Temple to President, April 25, 1968; Memorandum, John Macy to President, April 15, 1968; Memo, John Macy to President, June 10, 1968; Memo, Larry Temple to President, June 10, 1968; all in WHCF, PE 4 Health and Safety, PE 6 Investigations, LBJ. Letter, Phillip Burton et al. to John Macy, March 21, 1968; Draft Letter, John Macy to Phillip Burton, March 27, 1968; Memo, John Macy to George Christian, March 28, 1968; Memo, John Macy to Marvin Watson, March 14, 1968; Memo, John Macy to Marvin Watson, March 14, 1968; Memo, Larry Temple to Marvin Watson, March 15, 1968; all in WHCF, EX PE1 10/1/64, PE 1 9/9/67–4/30/68, LBJ. As a result of the Ervin com-mittee hearings the Civil Service Commission promulgated rules stringently restricting use of polygraphs. Exceptions were permitted, during "national security" employee investigations. These more liberalized rules were, none-theless, criticized by the ACLU and federal employee union officials during 1974 hearings. U.S. House, Subcommittee of the Committee on Govern-ment Operations, *Hearings on the Use of Polygraphs and Similar Devices by Federal Agencies.* 23rd Cong., 2d sess., 1974, pp. 1–144, 384–394, 408–663. U.S. Senate, Committee on the Judiciary, Subcommittee on Constitutional Rights, *Hearings on Military Surveillance of Civilian Politics*, 93rd Cong., 1st sess., 1973, p. 1.

55. *IARA*, p. 73 n296.

56. *Milwaukee Journal*, April 19, 1970, Accent, p. 6; May 30, 1971, p. 6; Sept. 9, 1976, Accent, p. 13; Sept. 14, 1976, p. 6. U.S. Senate, Committee on the Judiciary, Subcommittee on Constitutional Rights, *Report on Military Surveillance of Civilian Politics*, 93rd Cong., 1st sess, 1973, p. 61.

57. *SDSRIARA*, pp. 123–124. The extent of FBI-"Red Squad" cooperation is suggested in recently released Birmingham (Alabama) city records. *New York Times*, June 18, 1978, p. 19.

58. Wise, *The American Police State*, pp. 31–73, 352–366.

59. *SDSRIARA*, p. 539. *New York Times*, Aug. 8, 1971, p. 3E. Schlesinger, *The Imperial Presidency*, pp. 245–246.

60. *SDSRIARA*, pp. 554–555, *IARA*, pp. 131–132, 254.

61. *IARA*, pp. 132, 132 n658. *SDSRIARA*, pp. 478–479, 555, 555 n653.

62. *SDSRIARA*, p. 555. *HIA*, vol. 6, Federal Bureau of Investigation, pp. 706–708. *Milwaukee Journal*, Nov. 13, 1975, p. 5.

63. *Milwaukee Journal*, Sept. 9, 1976, p. 9; Sept. 14, 1976, Accent, p. 2. *New York Times*, Sept. 12, 1976, p. 9E. *Civil Liberties*, Nov. 1976, pp. 1–2.

Conclusion

1. *FMI*, p. 9. *SDSRFMI*, p. 52 n9. Corson, *The Armies of Ignorance*, p. 347.

2. *FMI*, pp. 36, 497.

3. *FMI*, p. 394.

4. *SDSRIARA*, p. 968.

5. *HJDIIP*, p. 163.

6. *SDSRFMI*, p. 157. *Washington Star*, July 27, 1976, p. 3. Halperin et al., *The Lawless State*, pp. 243–244.

7. Ira Shapiro, "Civil Liberties and National Security: The Outlook in Congress," *Intellect* 105 (Feb. 1977), p. 231. *New York Times*, Jan. 30, 1976, pp. 1, 24; Feb. 8, 1976, pp. 1, 35; Feb. 29, 1976, p. 4E. *Wichita Eagle*, Dec. 29, 1976, p. 15A. *Milwaukee Journal*, Dec. 12, 1975, p. 1; Jan. 7, 1976, pp. 1, 13; Jan. 24, 1976, p. 2; Feb. 12, 1976, pp. 1, 2; Feb. 29, 1976, pp. 1, 4. I. F. Stone, "The Schorr Case: The Real Dangers," *New York Review of Books* 23 (April 1, 1976), pp. 6–11. Corson, *The Armies of Ignorance*, pp. 444–445, 450. J. Leiper Freeman, "Investigating the Executive Intelligence: The Fate of The Pike Committee," *Capitol Studies* 5 (Fall 1977), pp. 103–118.

8. Corson, *The Armies of Ignorance*, pp. 449–450. Shapiro, "Civil Liberties and National Security," pp. 231–232. *New York Times*, Dec. 21, 1975, p. 2E; Feb. 29, 1976, p. 4E. *Milwaukee Journal*, Jan. 24, 1976, p. 2; April 1, 1976, p. 10; April 27, 1976, pp. 1, 2; April 28, 1976, p. 10; April 29, 1976, pp. 1, 10; May 18, 1976, p. 2; May 20, 1976, p. 8. Reflecting the greater conservatism of the House, a comparable oversight committee was not created until June 1977. *Milwaukee Journal*, March 31, 1977, p. 7; May 29, 1977, p. 3. Freeman, "Investigating the Executive Intelligence," p. 116.

9. Corson, *The Armies of Ignorance*, pp. 445–446, 449. Halperin et al., *The Lawless State*, pp. 246–251. *IARA*, pp. 209–302, 305, 310 n38, 332, 333–334.

10. *Milwaukee Journal*, Sept. 15, 1976, p. 10; Oct. 12, 1976, Accent, p. 6; Nov. 10, 1977, p. 11; Dec. 9, 1976, p. 4; Jan. 6, 1977, p. 2. May 7, 1978, pp. 1, 8. *New York Times*, Aug. 15, 1976, p. 4E. Halperin et al., *The Law-*

less State, pp. 251–253. *IARA*, pp. 318–319, 324, 326. Donner, "Intelligence on the Attack," pp. 590–594.

11. John Shattuck, "You Can't Depend on It: The Carter Administration and Civil Liberties," *Civil Liberties Review* 4 (Jan./Feb. 1978), pp. 13–14. John Shattuck, "Congress Faces Major Civil Liberties Battles," *Civil Liberties*, 321 (Jan. 1978), p. 3. *Detroit News*, Dec. 24, 1977, p. 2A. *Chicago Sun Times*, May 19, 1977, p. 48. *New York Times*, June 12, 1977, pp. 1, 40; Aug. 14, 1977, p. 28; April 30, 1978, p. 24, May 14, 1978, pp. 1, 24, May 24, 1978, p. A 20. *Milwaukee Journal*, June 14, 1977, Accent, p. 7; July 10, 1977, p. 18; Aug. 4, 1977, p. 2; Aug. 9, 1977, pp. 1, 6; Aug. 10, 1977, p. 10; Nov. 10, 1977, p. 11; Nov. 12, 1977, p. 5; Nov. 16, 1977, Accent, p. 3; Nov. 22, 1977, p. 10; Dec. 3, 1977, p. 8; Dec. 5, 1977, Accent, p. 9; Jan. 8, 1978, p. 3; Jan. 23, 1978, p. 2; Jan. 24, 1978, p. 3; March 30, 1978, pt. 2, p. 5. Executive Order 12036, United States Intelligence Activities, Jan. 24, 1978. Press Release, American Civil Liberties Union and Center for National Security Studies, undated, on Carter Administration Executive Order.

12. Shattuck, "You Can't Depend on It," p. 14. *HJDIIP*, pp. 42–46, 48–57, 63–74, 152–153, 157–159, 162–165, 185, 233. Halperin et al., *The Lawless State*, pp. 243–244. *Washington Star*, July 27, 1976, p. 3. Theoharis, "Bell Limits FBI Prosecutions," pp. 198–199. *Detroit News*, Aug. 19, 1976, p. 40; Aug. 21, 1977, p. 23C. *New York Times*, July 18, 1976, p. 22; Aug. 1, 1976, pp. 1, 33; Aug. 15, 1976, p. 28; Aug. 22, 1976, pp. 26, 3E; Sept. 5, 1976, pp. 21, 27; Dec. 12, 1976, p. 30; May 1, 1977, pp. 56, 1E; May 10, 1977, pp. 1, 34; Aug. 14, 1977, p. 3E; Aug. 21, 1977, p. 16; Oct. 9, 1977, pp. 1, 24, 3E; Nov. 6, 1977, p. 1E; April 16, 1978, p. 2E; May 23, 1978, pp. A1, 15; May 28, 1978, p. 5E; June 18, 1978, p. 36. *Milwaukee Journal*, July 15, 1976, p. 12; July 29, 1976, pp. 1, 6; Aug. 9, 1976, p. 7; Aug. 12, 1976, p. 27; Aug. 14, 1976, p. 6; Aug. 15, 1976, pt. 2, p. 13; Aug. 27, 1976, p. 6; Aug. 30, 1976, p. 2; Sept. 11, 1976, p. 8; Sept. 21, 1976, Accent, p. 3; Sept. 29, 1976, p. 6; Oct. 11, 1976, p. 9; Oct. 28, 1976, p. 11; Oct. 21, 1976, p. 7; Feb. 28, 1977, p. 6; March 31, 1977, p. 21; April 1, 1977, p. 5; April 2, 1977, p. 9; April 8, 1977, p. 5; April 15, 1977, p. 2; April 21, 1977, p. 8; April 27, 1977, p. 5; April 28, 1977, p. 10; May 9, 1977, p. 11; May 12, 1977, p. 5; May 13, 1977, p. 3; May 18, 1977, p. 11; May 19, 1977, p. 5; May 21, 1977, p. 8; June 9, 1977, pp. 1, 16; July 6, 1977, p. 11; Aug. 24, 1977, p. 2; Aug. 31, 1977, p. 10; Sept. 29, 1977, p. 3; Oct. 5, 1977, p. 2; Oct. 7, 1977, pp. 2, 3; Oct. 9, 1977, pp. 4, 11; Oct. 12, 1977, p. 5; Oct. 19, 1977, Accent, p. 5; Nov. 1, 1977, p. 2; Nov. 9, 1977, Accent, p. 8; Dec. 7, 1977, p. 9; Dec. 11, 1977, Accent, p. 17; Dec. 14, 1977, p. 12; Jan. 4, 1978, p. 3; Feb. 10, 1978, p. 3; Feb. 26, 1978, p. 3; April 2, 1978, p. 3; April 11, 1978, pp. 1, 4; April 12, 1978, p. 3; April 13, 1978, p. 2; April 22, 1978, p. 6; April 27, 1978, pp. 1, 2; April 29, 1978, p. 2; May 23, 1978, p. 3. *U.S. versus Kearney*, 77 Cr. 245, Opinion and Order, Feb. 9, 1978; Court transcript, Jan. 3, 1978; Opinion and Order, July 28, 1977. Letter, David Kendall to Athan Theoharis, April 7, 1978. *Milwaukee Sentinel*, April 14, 1978, pp. 1, 17. Letter, Anthony Marro to Athan Theoharis, June 5, 1978.

13. John Shattuck and Sally Berman, "Washington Report," *Civil Liberties*, 318 (July 1977), p. 3. Shattuck, "You Can't Depend on It," pp. 14–16. John Shattuck, "Washington Report," *Civil Liberties*, 323 (May 1978), p. 3. *S. 3197*, March 23, 1976. *S. 1566*, May 18, 1977. U.S. Senate, Committee on the Judiciary, Report No. 94–1035, *Foreign Intelligence Surveil-*

lance Act of 1976, 94th Cong., 2d sess., 1976. U.S. Senate, Select Committee on Intelligence, Report No. 94–1161, *Foreign Intelligence Surveillance Act of 1976*, 94th Cong., 2d sess., 1976. *Chicago Sun-Times*, May 19, 1977, p. 8. *New York Times*, May 1, 1977, p. 17E; May 8, 1977, p. 2E; Aug. 14, 1977, p. 3E; April 19, 1978, p. 40; April 23, 1978, p. 4E. *Milwaukee Journal*, Sept. 21, 1976, p. 4; March 29, 1977, p. 12; April 7, 1977, p. 3; April 30, 1977, p. 6; May 19, 1977, p. 5; July 20, 1977, p. 3; Aug. 9, 1977, pp. 1, 6; Nov. 20, 1977, p. 17; Feb. 28, 1978, p. 3; March 16, 1978, p. 9; April 19, 1978, p. 4; April 21, 1978, pt. 2, p. 10. U.S. Senate, Select Committee on Intelligence, Report No. 95–701, *Foreign Intelligence Surveillance Act of 1978*, 95th Cong., 2d sess., 1978.

14. *New York Times*, July 25, 1976, p. 32; Aug. 8, 1976, p. 15E; April 16, 1978, pp. 1, 36; June 18, 1978, p. 3E. *Milwaukee Journal*, Feb. 25, 1976, p. 8; July 23, 1976, p. 6; July 29, 1976, pt. 2 p. 8; Nov. 3, 1976, p. 2; Jan. 19, 1977, p. 10; April 21, 1977, p. 8; May 25, 1977, p. 5; June 15, 1977, p. 3; Sept. 3, 1977, p. 3; Oct. 9, 1977, p. 11; Dec. 8, 1977, p. 8; Jan. 11, 1978, p. 2; Feb. 10, 1978, p. 9; March 7, 1978, p. 3; April 27, 1978, pp. 1, 26; May 20, 1978, p. 2; June 12, 1978, p. 12.

15. *S. 2525*, Feb. 9, 1977, pp. 9–11, 13, 21, 22, 30, 43–50, 64, 66, 72–92, 95, 99–101, 104, 106, 108, 120–121, 126, 130, 160, 163, 179, 184, 197–198, 207, 211–214, 218–219, 221, 248, 254, 261. U.S. Senate, Select Committee on Intelligence, Report No. 95–217, *Annual Report to the Senate*, 95th Cong., 1st sess., 1977, pp. 1, 23–25, 27–35, 43. *H. R. 6051*, April 5, 1977. Shattuck, "You Can't Depend on It," p. 16. John Shattuck, "Washington Report," *Civil Liberties*, 321 (Jan. 1978), p. 3. Corson, *Armies of Ignorance*, p. 454. *Washington Post*, June 24, 1977. *New York Times*, May 22, 1977, p. 2E. *Milwaukee Journal*, Feb. 1, 1977, Accent, p. 8; Apr. 6, 1977, p. 4; Apr. 26, 1977, p. 2; May 19, 1977, p. 4; Aug. 9, 1977, pp. 1, 6; Sept. 20, 1977, p. 7; Feb. 10, 1978, p. 12, June 7, 1978, p. 10. See also Donner, "Intelligence on the Attack," pp. 590–594.

16. *IARA*, p. iii.

Bibliography

Primary Sources

Boston Globe.
Chicago Sun-Times.
Civil Liberties.
Civil Liberties Review.
Cole v. Young 351 U.S. 536 (1956).
Commission on CIA Activities within the United States. *Report to the President.* Washington: U.S. Government Printing Office, June 1975.
Communist Party v. Subversive Activities Control Board 351 U.S. 115 (1956).
Coplon v. U.S. 191 F. 2d 749 (D.C. cir. 1951); 342 U.S. 926 (1952).
Des Moines Register.
Detroit Free Press.
Detroit News.
Dwight D. Eisenhower Library: Phillip Areeda Papers; Benedict Papers; Eisenhower Papers–Brownell, Herbert; Eisenhower Papers Cabinet Minutes; Eisenhower Papers Cabinet Secretariat; Eisenhower Papers–Diary; Eisenhower Papers Press Conferences; Eisenhower Papers–Rogers, William; Eisenhower Papers–Summerfield, A; GF 1–B–9; Homer Gruenther Papers; Leonard Hall Papers; James Hagerty Papers; James Hagerty Papers–Diary Entries; C. D. Jackson Papers; Charles Masterson Papers; Gerald Morgan Files; OF 103–K; OF 104–J; OF 133; William Rogers Papers; Louis Rothschild Papers; Charles Willis Papers; Young and Rubicam Files.
Executive Order 12036, January 24, 1978.
Federal Records of World War II; Civilian Agencies. Washington: U.S. Government Printing Office, 1950.
Foreign Relations of the United States, 1949. Vol. I. National Security Affairs, Foreign Economic Policy. Washington: U.S. Government Printing Office, 1976.
Foreign Relations of the United States, 1950. Vol. I. National Security Affairs, Foreign Economic Policy. Washington: U.S. Government Printing Office, 1977.
Goldman v. U.S. 316 U.S. 129 (1942).
Greene v. McElroy 360 U.S. 508 (1959).
Hiss, Alger, Papers, FBI Files, Harvard University Library.
Hoover, Herbert, Library: Walter Trohan Papers.
H.R. 6051, April 5, 1977.
Irvine v. California 347 U.S. 128 (1954).
Jencks v. U.S. 353 U.S. 657 (1957).
Lyndon Baines Johnson Library: Documentary Supplement Department of Justice; Narrative History Department of Justice; WHCF Confidential Files FG 110; WHCF Confidential Files FG 135; WHCF Confidential Files FG 431; WHCF Confidential Files LE/LG; WHCF Confidential Files PE 6; WHCF Department of Justice; WHCF DeVier Pierson Files;

WHCF Ex JL 3; WHCF Gen HU 2; WHCF Gen PE; WHCF General FBI Reports; WHCF General Misc; WHCF LE/PE; WHCF Harry McPherson Files; WHCF Name Files.

Kansas City Star.

John F. Kennedy Library: Kennedy Papers POF Bureau of Budget; Kennedy Papers POF Justice; Bourke Marshall Papers; Lee White Papers; WHCF FG 11–5 NSC; WHCF FG 11–8–1 Dutton F; WHCF FG 135.

Milwaukee Journal.

Milwaukee Sentinel.

Nardone v. U.S. 302 U.S. 379 (1937); 308 U.S. 338 (1939).

National Review.

Naval War College Review (May–June 1975).

New York Times.

Official and Confidential FBI Files, J. Edgar Hoover Building.

Pennsylvania v. Nelson 350 U.S. 497 (1956).

Peters v. Hobby 349 U.S. 331 (1955).

Press Releases, Department of Justice, Department of Justice Library.

Public Papers of the Presidents of the United States: Dwight D. Eisenhower. Washington: U.S. Government Printing Office.

Public Papers of the Presidents of the United States: Harry S. Truman. Washington: U.S. Government Printing Office.

Records of the U.S. Atomic Energy Commission, U.S. Energy Research and Development Files: Lewis Strauss Appointment Logs; Lewis Strauss Telephone Logs.

Report of the Department of Justice Concerning Its Investigation and Prosecutorial Decisions with Respect to Central Intelligence Agency Mail Opening Activities in the United States (January 14, 1977).

The Report of the Royal Commission, Appointed under Order in Council, P.C. 411 of February 5, 1946, to Investigate the Facts Relating to and the Circumstances Surrounding the Communication by Public Officials and Other Persons in Positions of Trust of Secret and Confidential Information to Agents of a Foreign Power, June 27, 1946. Ottawa: E. Cloutier, 1946.

S. 1566, May 18, 1977.

S. 2525, February 9, 1978.

S. 3197, March 23, 1976.

Service v. Dulles 354 U.S. 363 (1957).

Slochower v. Board of Education 350 U.S. 551 (1956).

Time.

Truman, Harry S., Library: Eleanor Bontecou Papers; Clark Clifford Papers; Rose Conway Files; George Elsey Papers; J. Howard McGrath Papers; Charles Murphy Files; Philleo Nash Files; OF 10–B; OF 252–I; OF 252–K; OF 252–M; John Snyder Papers; Stephen Spingarn Papers; Truman Papers PPF; Truman Papers PSF; Truman Papers PSF FBI; Truman Papers PSF General File; Truman Papers PSF Cabinet J. Howard McGrath; A. Devitt Vanech Papers.

U.S. v. Coplon 185 F. 2d 629 (2d Cir. 1950); 342 U.S. 920 (1952).

U.S. v. Kearney CR 77–245.

U.S. v. Nixon 418 U.S. 683 (1974).

U.S. v. U.S. District Court 407 U.S. 297 (1972).

U.S. Congress, Joint Committee on Atomic Energy. *Atomic Energy Legislation Through 91st Cong., 2d sess.* 91st Cong., 2d sess., 1971.

U.S. *Congressional Record.*
U.S. House, Committee on Government Operations, Special Subcommittee on Government Information. *Hearings on Availability of Information for Federal Departments and Agencies.* Pt. 8. 85th Cong., 1st sess., 1957.
U.S. House, Committee on Government Operations, Subcommittee on Government Information and Individual Rights. *Hearings on Inquiry into the Destruction of Former FBI Director Hoover's Files and FBI Recordkeeping.* 94th Cong., 1st sess., 1975.
————. *Hearings on Justice Department Internal Investigation Practices.* 95th Cong., 1st sess., 1977.
U.S. House, Committee on Internal Security. *Hearings on Domestic Intelligence Operations for Internal Security Purposes.* Pt. I. 93rd Cong., 2d sess., 1974.
U.S. House, Committee on the Judiciary, Subcommittee on Civil and Constitutional Rights. *Hearings on FBI Counterintelligence Programs.* 93rd Cong., 2d sess., 1974.
————. *Hearings on FBI Oversight.* Ser. no. 2, pt. I. 94th Cong., 1st sess., 1975.
U.S. House, Subcommittee of the Committee on Government Operations. *Hearings on the Use of Polygraphs and Similar Devices by Federal Agencies.* 93rd Cong., 2d sess., 1974.
U.S. Senate, Committee on the Judiciary. Report No. 94–1035, July 15, 1976. *Foreign Intelligence Surveillance Act of 1976.* 94th Cong., 2d sess., 1976.
————, Subcommittee on Constitutional Rights. *Hearings on Federal Data Banks, Computers and the Bill of Rights.* Pts. I and II. 92d Cong., 1st sess., 1971.
————. *Hearings on Military Surveillance.* 93rd Cong., 2d sess., 1974.
————. *Hearings on Privacy and the Rights of Federal Employees.* 89th Cong., 2d sess., 1966.
————. Report, *Military Surveillance of Civilian Politics.* 93rd Cong., 1st sess., 1973.
————. *Senate Report No. 534.* August 21, 1967. 90th Cong., 1st sess., 1967.
————. Staff Report, *Army Surveillance of Civilians: A Documentary Analysis,* 92nd Cong., 2d sess., 1972.
————. Subcommittee on Internal Security. *Hearings on Interlocking Subversives in Government.* Part 16. 83rd Cong., 1st sess., 1953.
————. Subcommittee on Administrative Practice and Procedure and on Constitutional Rights, and U.S. Senate, Committee on Foreign Relations, Subcommittee on Surveillance. *Joint Hearings on Warrantless Wiretapping and Electronic Surveillance—1974.* 93rd Cong., 2d sess., 1974.
————. Subcommittees on Criminal Laws and Procedures and on Constitutional Rights. *Hearings on Electronic Surveillance for National Security Purposes.* 93rd Cong., 2d sess., 1974.
U.S. Senate, Select Committee on Intelligence. Report No. 94–1161, August 24, 1976. *Foreign Intelligence Surveillance Act of 1976.* 94th Cong., 2d sess., 1976.
————. Report No. 95–217, May 18, 1977. *Annual Report to the Senate.* 95th Cong., 1st sess., 1977.
————. Report No. 95–701, March 14, 1978. *Foreign Intelligence Surveillance Act of 1978.* 95th Cong., 2d sess., 1978.

U.S. Senate, Select Committee on Presidential Campaign Activities. *Hearings* and *Final Reports.* 93rd Cong., 2d sess., 1974.
U.S. Senate, Select Committee to Study Governmental Operations with respect to Intelligence Activities. Final Report, *Foreign and Military Intelligence.* Book I, 94th Cong., 2d sess., 1976.
————. Final Report, *Intelligence Activities and the Rights of Americans.* Book II. 94th Cong., 2d sess., 1976.
————. Final Report, *Supplementary Detailed Staff Reports on Foreign and Military Intelligence.* Book IV. 94th Cong., 2d sess., 1976.
————. Final Report, *Supplementary Detailed Staff Reports on Intelligence Activities and the Rights of Americans.* Book III. 94th Cong., 2d sess., 1976.
————. *Hearings on Intelligence Activities.* Vol. 2. The Huston Plan. 94th Cong., 1st sess., 1975.
————. *Hearings on Intelligence Activities.* Vol. 4. Mail Opening. 94th Cong., 1st sess., 1975.
————. *Hearings on Intelligence Activities.* Vol. 5. The National Security Agency and Fourth Amendment Rights. 94th Cong., 1st sess., 1975.
————. *Hearings on Intelligence Activities.* Vol. 6. Federal Bureau of Investigation. 94th Cong., 1st sess., 1975.
————. Interim Report. *Alleged Assassinations involving Foreign Leaders.* 94th Cong., 1st sess., 1975.
Washington Post.
Washington Star.
Watkins v. U.S. 354 U.S. 178 (1957).
The White House Transcripts. New York: Bantam, 1974.
Wichita Eagle.
Yates v. U.S. 354 U.S. 298 (1957).

Secondary Sources

Adams, Sherman. *Firsthand Report: The Story of the Eisenhower Administration.* New York: Popular Library, 1962.
Association of the Bar of the City of New York, Committees on Federal Legislation and on Civil Rights. *Judicial Procedures for National Security Electronic Surveillance.* New York: Association of the Bar of the City of New York, 1974.
Bailey, Thomas. *The Man in the Street: The Impact of American Public Opinion on Foreign Policy.* New York: F. S. Crofts, 1948.
Belknap, Michal. *Cold War Political Justice: The Smith Act, the Communist Party, and American Civil Liberties.* Westport: Greenwood, 1977.
Bell, Daniel, ed. *The Radical Right.* Garden City: Doubleday, 1963.
Berger, Raoul. *Executive Privilege: A Constitutional Myth.* New York: Bantam, 1975.
Berman, Jerry, and Morton Halperin, eds. *The Abuses of the Intelligence Agencies.* Washington: Center for National Security Studies, 1975.
Bernstein, Barton. "Election of 1952." In Arthur Schlesinger, Jr., *History of American Presidential Elections, 1789–1968.* New York: Chelsea House, 1971.
————. "The Road to Watergate and Beyond: The Growth and Abuse of Executive Authority Since 1940." *Law and Contemporary Problems* 40 (Spring 1976), pp. 58–86.

Biddle, Francis. *In Brief Authority*. Garden City: Doubleday, 1967.
Blackstock, Nelson. *COINTELPRO: The FBI's Secret War on Political Freedom*. New York: Vintage, 1976.
Bontecou, Eleanor. *The Federal Loyalty-Security Program*. Ithaca: Cornell University Press, 1953.
Buckley, William, and L. Brent Bozell. *McCarthy and His Enemies: The Record and Its Meaning*. Chicago: Regnery, 1954.
Burns, James MacGregor. *Presidential Government*. Boston: Houghton Mifflin, 1966.
Caute, David. *The Great Fear: The Anti-Communist Purge under Truman and Eisenhower*. New York: Simon and Schuster, 1978.
Chase, Harold. *Security and Liberty: The Problem of Native Communists*. Garden City: Doubleday, 1955.
Cole, Wayne. *American First: The Battle against Intervention, 1940–1941*. Madison: University of Wisconsin Press, 1953.
———. *Senator Gerald P. Nye and American Foreign Relations*. Minneapolis: University of Minnesota Press, 1962.
Cook, Fred. *The Nightmare Decade: The Life and Times of Joe McCarthy*. New York: Random, 1971.
Corson, William. *The Armies of Ignorance: The Rise of the American Intelligence Empire*. New York: Dial, 1977.
Cotter, Richard. "Notes toward a Definition of National Security." *Washington Monthly* 7 (December 1975), pp. 4–16.
Cronin, Thomas. "The Textbook Presidency and Political Science." Paper delivered at American Political Science Association meetings (Sept. 1970, Los Angeles).
Dean, John W. *Blind Ambition: The White House Years*. New York: Simon and Schuster, 1976.
Divine, Robert. *The Illusion of Neutrality*. Chicago: The University of Chicago Press, 1962.
Doenecke, Justus. *The Literature of Isolationism: A Guide to Non-Interventionist Scholarship, 1930–1972*. Colorado Springs: Ralph Myles, 1972.
Donner, Frank. "Electronic Surveillance: The National Security Game." *Civil Liberties Review* 2 (Summer 1975), pp. 15–47.
———. "Hoover's Legacy: A Nationwide System of Political Surveillance Based on the Spurious Authority of a Press Release. *Nation* 218 (June 1, 1974), pp. 678–699.
———. "How J. Edgar Hoover Created His Intelligence Powers." *Civil Liberties Review* 3 (February/March 1977), pp. 34–51.
———. "Intelligence on the Attack: The Terrorist as Scapegoat." *Nation* 226 (May 20, 1978), pp. 590–594.
Donovan, Robert. *Conflict and Crisis: The Presidency of Harry S. Truman, 1945–1948*. New York: Norton, 1977.
Dorsen, Norman, and Stephen Gillers, eds. *None of Your Business: Government Secrecy in America*. New York: Penguin, 1975.
Eisenhower, Dwight D. *The White House Years: Mandate for Change, 1953–1956*. Garden City: Doubleday, 1963.
Elliff, John. "Aspects of Federal Civil Rights Enforcement: The Justice Department and the FBI, 1939–1964." *Perspectives in American History* 5 (1971), pp. 605–673.
———. "The FBI and Domestic Intelligence." In Richard Blum, ed., *Surveillance and Espionage in a Free Society*. New York: Praeger, 1973.

Ford, Corey. *Donovan of OSS*. Boston: Little, Brown, 1970.

Ellsberg, Daniel. "Laos: What Nixon Is Up To." *New York Review of Books* 16 (March 11, 1971), pp. 13–17.

Freeland, Richard. *The Truman Presidency and the Origins of McCarthyism*. New York: Knopf, 1971.

Freeman, J. Leiper. "Investigating the Executive Intelligence: The Fate of the Pike Committee." *Capitol Studies* 5 (Fall 1977), pp. 103–118.

Fried, Richard. *Men Against McCarthy*. New York: Columbia University Press, 1976.

Friedman, Robert. "FBI: Manipulating the Media." *Rights* 23 (May/June 1977), pp. 13–14.

Fulbright, William. "Reflections: In Thrall to Fear." *The New Yorker* (January 8, 1972), pp. 41–62.

Garrett, Stephan. "Foreign Policy and the American Constitution: The Bricker Amendment in Contemporary Perspective." *International Studies Quarterly* 16 (June 1972), pp. 187–200.

Gelb, Leslie. "Vietnam: The System Worked." *Foreign Policy* (Summer 1971), pp. 104–167.

Gill, William. *The Ordeal of Otto Otepka*. New Rochelle: Arlington House, 1969.

———. "The Strange Case of Otepka's Associates." *Washington Reports* (September 28, 1964).

Goldman, Eric. *The Tragedy of Lyndon Johnson*. New York: Knopf, 1969.

Graebner, Norman. *The New Isolationism: A Study in Politics and Foreign Policy Since 1950*. New York: Ronald, 1956.

Green, Harold. "The Oppenheimer Case: A Study in the Abuse of Law." *Bulletin of the Atomic Scientists* (September 1977), pp. 12–16, 56–61.

Griffith, Robert. *The Politics of Fear: Joseph R. McCarthy and the Senate*. Lexington: The University Press of Kentucky, 1970.

Grossman, Michael, and Francis Rourke. "The Media and the Presidency: An Exchange Analysis." *Political Science Quarterly* 91 (Fall 1976), pp. 455–470.

Halperin, Morton, Jerry Berman, Robert Borosage, and Christine Marwick. *The Lawless State: The Crimes of the U.S. Intelligence Agencies*. New York: Penguin, 1976.

Harris, Richard. "Reflections: Crime in the FBI." *The New Yorker* (August 8, 1977), pp. 30–42.

Holl, Jack. "In the Matter of J. Robert Oppenheimer: Origins of the Government's Security Case." Paper delivered at the American Historical Association meetings, December 28, 1975, Atlanta.

Irons, Peter. "American Business and the Origins of McCarthyism: The Cold War Crusade of the United States Chamber of Commerce." In Robert Griffith and Athan Theoharis, eds., *The Specter: Original Essays on the Cold War and the Origins of McCarthyism*. New York: New Viewpoints, 1974.

———. "The Test Is Poland: Polish Americans and the Origins of the Cold War." *Polish American Studies* 30 (Autumn 1973), pp. 5–63.

Jaworski, Leon. *The Right and the Power: The Prosecution of Watergate*. New York: Reader's Digest Press, 1976.

Johnson, Walter, *1600 Pennsylvania Avenue: Presidents and the People Since 1929*. Boston: Little, Brown, 1963.

Kennan, George. *American Diplomacy, 1900–1950*. Chicago: The University of Chicago Press, 1951.
————. *The Cloud of Danger: Current Realities of American Foreign Policy*. Boston: Atlantic–Little, Brown, 1977.
Lasky, Victor. *It Didn't Start with Watergate*. New York: Dial, 1977.
Latham, Earl. *The Communist Controversy in Washington: From the New Deal to McCarthy*. Cambridge: Harvard University Press, 1966.
Lippmann, Walter. *Essays in Public Philosophy*. Boston: Little, Brown, 1955.
Lora, Ronald. "A View from the Right: Conservative Intellectuals, the Cold War, and McCarthy." In Robert Griffith and Athan Theoharis, eds., *The Specter: Original Essays on the Cold War and the Origins of McCarthyism*. New York: New Viewpoints, 1974.
Lukas, J. Anthony. *Nightmare: The Underside of the Nixon Years*. New York: Viking, 1976.
Lyon, Peter. *Eisenhower: Portrait of the Hero*. Boston: Little, Brown, 1974.
McCarthy, Mary. *The Mask of State: Watergate Portraits*. New York: Harcourt, Brace, Jovanovich, 1973.
McConnell, Grant. *The Modern Presidency*. New York: St. Martin's Press, 1967.
Magruder, Jeb S. *An American Life: One Man's Road to Watergate*. New York: Atheneum, 1974.
Mollenhoff, Clark. *Game Plan for Disaster: An Ombudsman's Report on the Nixon Years*. New York: Norton, 1976.
Morgenthau, Hans. "The Decline and Fall of American Foreign Policy." *New Republic* 135 (December 10, 1956), p. 11.
Murphy, John. *The Pinnacle: The Contemporary American Presidency*. Philadelphia: Lippincott, 1974.
Navasky, Victor. *Kennedy Justice*. New York: Atheneum, 1970.
————. "The FBI's Wildest Dream." *Nation* 226 (June 17, 1978), pp. 716–718.
Neustadt, Richard. *Presidential Power*. New York: Wiley, 1960.
Nixon, Richard. *RN: The Memoirs of Richard Nixon*. New York: Grosset & Dunlap, 1978.
Parmet, Herbert. *Eisenhower and the American Crusades*. New York: Macmillan, 1972.
Pious, Richard. "Is Presidential Power Poison." *Political Science Quarterly* 89 (Fall 1974), pp. 627–643.
Polenberg, Richard. *Reorganizing Roosevelt's Government: The Controversy over Executive Reorganization, 1936–1939*. Cambridge: Harvard University Press, 1966.
————. *War and Society: The United States, 1941–1945*. Philadelphia: Lippincott, 1972.
Privacy in a Free Society. Cambridge: Roscoe Pound–American Trial Lawyers Foundation, 1974.
Pyle, Christopher. "A Bill to Bug Aliens." *Nation* 222 (May 29, 1976), pp. 645–648.
————. "CONUS Intelligence: The Army Watches Civilian Politics." *Washington Monthly* (January 1970), pp. 4–16.
Pynn, Ronald, ed. *Watergate and the American Political Process*. New York: Praeger, 1975.

Radosh, Ronald. *Prophets on the Right: Profiles of Conservative Critics of American Globalism.* New York: Simon and Schuster, 1975.

Rather, Dan, and Gary Gates. *The Palace Guard.* New York: Harper & Row, 1974.

Rogin, Michael. *McCarthy and the Intellectuals: The Radical Specter.* Cambridge: MIT Press, 1967.

Rosenberg, John. "The FBI Sheds Its Files: Catch in the Information Act." *Nation* 226 (February 4, 1978), pp. 108–111.

Ross, Thomas. "Spying in the United States," *Society* 12 (March/April 1975), pp. 64–70.

Rossiter, Clinton. *The American Presidency.* New York: Harcourt, Brace, 1956.

Safire, William. *Before the Fall: An Inside View of the Pre-Watergate White House.* Garden City: Doubleday, 1975.

Sanders, Bill. *Run for the Oval Office.* Milwaukee: Alpha Press, 1974.

Schell, Jonathan. *The Time of Illusion.* New York: Knopf, 1976.

Schlesinger, Arthur, Jr. *The Imperial Presidency.* Boston: Houghton Mifflin, 1973.

"The Second Deposing of Richard Nixon," *Civil Liberties Review* 3 (June/July 1976), pp. 13–23, 84–95.

Shannon, William. *They Could Not Trust the King: Nixon, Watergate and the American People.* New York: Macmillan, 1974.

Shapiro, Ira. "Civil Liberties and National Security: The Outlook in Congress." *Intellect* 105 (February 1977), pp. 230–233.

Shattuck, John. "You Can't Depend on It: The Carter Administration and Civil Liberties. *Civil Liberties Review* 4 (January/February 1978), pp. 10–27.

Smith, John Chabot. *Alger Hiss: The True Story.* New York: Penguin, 1977.

———. "The Case of the Century (Con't.)." *Harper's* (June 1978), pp. 81–85.

Smith, R. Harris. *OSS: The Secret History of America's First Central Intelligence Agency.* Berkeley: University of California, 1972.

Stenehjem, Michele Flynn. *An American First: John T. Flynn and the American First Committee.* New Rochelle: Arlington House, 1976.

Stone, I. F. "The Schorr Case: The Real Dangers." *New York Review of Books* 23 (April 1, 1976), pp. 6–11.

Tanner, William. "The Passage of the Internal Security Act of 1950." Ph.D. dissertation, University of Kansas, 1971.

——— and Robert Griffith. "Legislative Politics and 'McCarthyism': The Internal Security Act of 1950." In Robert Griffith and Athan Theoharis, eds., *The Specter: Original Essays on the Cold War and the Origins of McCarthyism.* New York: New Viewpoints, 1974.

Theoharis, Athan. "Bell Limits FBI Prosecutions." *Nation* 225 (September 10, 1977), pp. 198–199.

———. "Bureaucrats above the Law: Double-Entry Intelligence Files." *Nation* 225 (October 22, 1977), pp. 393–397.

———. "Classification Restrictions and the Public's Right to Know: A New Look at the Alger Hiss Case." *Intellect* 104 (September/October 1975), pp. 86–89.

———. "The Escalation of the Loyalty Program." In Barton Bernstein, ed., *Politics and Policies of the Truman Administration.* Chicago: Quadrangle, 1970.

―――. "The FBI's Stretching of Presidential Directives, 1936–1953." *Political Science Quarterly* 91 (Winter 1976/1977), pp. 649–672.

―――. "Illegal Surveillance: Will Congress Stop the Snooping?" *Nation* 218 (February 2, 1974), pp. 138–142.

―――. "Misleading the Presidents: Thirty Years of Wiretapping." *Nation* 212 (June 14, 1971), pp. 244–250.

―――. "The Politics of Scholarship: Liberals, Anti-Communism, and McCarthyism." In Robert Griffith and Athan Theoharis, eds., *The Specter: Original Essays on the Cold War and the Origins of McCarthyism*. New York: New Viewpoints, 1974.

―――. "The Rhetoric of Politics: Foreign Policy, Internal Security and Domestic Politics in the Truman Era, 1945–1950." In Barton Bernstein, ed., *Politics and Policies of the Truman Administration*. Chicago: Quadrangle, 1970.

―――. "Second-Term Surveillance: The Froehlke Affair." *Nation* 215 (December 18, 1972), pp. 623–626.

―――. *Seeds of Repression: Harry S. Truman and the Origins of McCarthyism*. Chicago: Quadrangle, 1970.

―――. "Should the FBI Purge Its Files?" *USA Today* (forthcoming but likely September 1978).

―――. "The Threat to Civil Liberties." In Thomas Paterson, ed., *Cold War Critics*. Chicago: Quadrangle, 1971.

―――. "Unanswered Questions." *Inquiry* 1 (June 12, 1978), pp. 21–24.

―――. *The Yalta Myths: An Issue in U.S. Politics, 1945–1955*. Columbia: University of Missouri Press, 1970.

――― and Elizabeth Meyer. "The 'National Security' Justification for Electronic Surveillance: An Elusive Exception." *Wayne Law Review* 14 (Summer 1968), pp. 749–771.

Truman, Harry S. *Memoirs, Vol. I: Year of Decisions*. Garden City: Doubleday, 1955.

Ungar, Sanford. *FBI*. Boston: Atlantic Monthly–Little, Brown, 1975.

Watters, Pat, and Stephen Gillers, eds. *Investigating the FBI*. Garden City: Doubleday, 1973.

Weinstein, Allen. "The Hiss Case: An Exchange." *New York Review of Books* 23 (May 27, 1976), pp. 34–39, 42–44, 46–48.

―――. *Perjury: The Hiss-Chambers Case*. New York: Knopf, 1978.

White, Theodore. *Breach of Faith: The Fall of Richard Nixon*. New York: Atheneum, 1975.

Whitehead, Don. *Attack Against Terror: The FBI Against the Ku Klux Klan in Mississippi*. New York: Funk and Wagnalls, 1970.

―――. *The FBI Story*. New York: Pocket Books, 1959.

Wildavsky, Aaron, ed. *The Presidency*. Boston: Little, Brown, 1969.

Wills, Garry. *Nixon Agonistes*. New York: New American Library, 1971.

Wilz, John. *In Search of Peace: The Senate Munitions Inquiry, 1934–1936*. Baton Rouge: Louisiana State University Press, 1963.

Wise, David. *The American Police State*. New York: Random, 1976.

Woodward, Bob, and Carl Bernstein. *All the President's Men*. New York: Simon and Schuster, 1974.

―――. *The Final Days*. New York: Simon and Schuster, 1976.

Yergin, Daniel. *Shattered Peace: The Origins of the Cold War and the National Security State*. Boston: Houghton, Mifflin, 1977.

Index

Abernathy, Ralph, 187, 289n61
Adams, James, 93, 236
Adams, Sherman, 81, 165
Administrative Index (ADEX), 60–63, 87, 259n51
Agnew, Spiro, 186, 289n61
Alderman v. U.S., 17
Allen, George, 160
Allen, Lew, 121, 124–125
Alsop, Joseph, 189
Amerasia, 199
America First Committee, 158, 159
American Christian Action Council, 188
American Civil Liberties Union (ACLU), 63, 93, 198, 222, 242, 301n54; and FBI surveillance of, 255n8
American Destiny Party, 159
American League for Peace and Democracy, 197
American Legion, 70, 134
American Nationalist Party, 159
American Polish Labor Council, 160
American Slav Congress, 160
American Telephone and Telegraph Company (AT&T), 119, 241
American Youth Congress, 158
Americans for Democratic Action (ADA), 102, 161, 187
Anderson, Dillon, 165
Anderson, Jack, 194
Angleton, James, 19–20, 35
Areeda, Phillip, 216–217
Army: and domestic surveillance, 88, 120–121, 178–179, 223, 276n62; and insubordination, 227
Army Security Agency (ASA), 120
Arnett, Peter, 179
Atomic Energy Act, 81, 82, 84, 85
Atomic Energy Commission (AEC), 164
attorney general's list, 196, 220, 221, 226, 227, 290n1

Badillo, Herman, 242
Bailey, Thomas, 4
Baker, Bobby, 179–180
Baldwin, Hanson, 120
Banoff, Barbara, 151
Barnett, Ross, 173
Barth, Roger, 189
Baruch, Bernard, 156, 165
Baumgardner, F. J., 50, 180
Bayh, Birch, 239, 240, 242
Beard, Charles, 158
Beecher, William, 191, 192
Bell, Griffin: and FBI break-ins, 128–129, 238–239; and FBI informers, 294n20
Belmont, Alan H., 49, 50, 51, 108, 136
Bennett, Donald, 24, 26, 29, 30
Benson, Ezra Taft, 54
Bentley, Elizabeth, 199, 291n8
Berger v. New York, 17
Berrigan, Philip, 188
Biddle, Francis, 76; and Custodial Detention program, 43–44, 262 n22; and loyalty program, 198; and political reports from FBI, 159–160; and Roosevelt's 1943 directive, 75–76; and wiretapping, 159, 267n9, 268n10, 268n11
Bingham, Hiram, 208–209
Birch, John, Society, 156, 166, 189, 222
Black, Fred B., 17, 112
black nationalist groups, 145–147, 188, 194; and COINTELPRO, 143; and Security Index program, 58–59
Black Panther Party (BPP), 147, 153, 165
Black v. U.S., 112, 272n40
Blackstone Rangers, 153
Boardman, C. V., 136
Boggs, Hale, 273n52
Boggs, Marion, xii

Bork, Robert, 152
Bowles, Chester, 161
Braden, Spruille, 161
Brandon, Henry, 192
break-ins, 11, 125–129, 133, 238–239, 269n20, 276n66; and FBI Director Hoover's 1966 ban, 15, 18, 35, 113; and Huston Plan, 13, 29, 33; and microphone surveillance (bugging), 105, 107–109; and Nixon administration, 254n41, 259n42; and separate filing procedures, 106, 112
Brennan, Charles, 18, 23, 39, 66, 148, 150, 259n49, 289n65; and FBI break-ins, 126; and FBI political surveillance authority, 260 n6; and wiretapping, 183–184
Breslin, Jimmy, 189
Brinkley, David, 179
Brown, Clarence, 5
Brownell, Herbert, xii, 112, 127; and electronic surveillance, 108–111, 174; and FBI political surveillance authority, 81–82, 263n34; and Harry Dexter White, 82–83; and loyalty/security program, 213–214; and Security Index program, 54–55
Brubeck, William, 171
Buchanan, Pat, 17
Buckley, William, Jr., 6, 232
Buffham, Benson, 35
bugging (microphone surveillance), 94; and attorney general controls, 17–18, 110–111, 114; and authority, 106, 112–113; and ban, 105; and break-ins, 125; and FBI policy, 106, 112; and Huston Plan, 13, 25, 29, 33
Bundy, McGeorge, 84, 171, 172, 176; and Security Index program, 56
Bureau Bulletin No. 34, 269n20
Butler, Smedley, 68
Butterfield, Alexander, 20
Byrd, Robert, 235
Byrnes, James F., 129, 164

Cambodia, 20, 21, 115, 191
Canadian Royal Commission, 199
Cardenas, Lazaro, 163

Carter, Jimmy: and Executive Order 12036, 236–237; and efforts to curb leaks, 237
Carter, Marshall, 19
Carter administration: and foreign intelligence, 119; and oversight of intelligence agencies, 237–239; and wiretapping, 237, 239–241; and wiretapping legislation, 119, 239–240
Caulfield, John, 190, 190n, 252n2
Central Intelligence Agency (CIA), 5, 22, 94, 123, 163, 170–171, 231, 233, 236; and domestic surveillance, 11, 16; and Eisenhower administration, 6; and electronic surveillance, 270n24; and Huston Plan, 37, 38; and illegal activities, 131–132; and IRS, 189, 289n65; and legislative charter, 242–243; and loyalty program, 223; and mail opening, xiii, 35, 130–132, 230, 234; and National Student Association, 286n45; and Operation CHAOS, 10, 15–16, 35, 92, 131–132, 178, 189–190, 287n50; and Operation MINARET, 121; and relations with FBI, 18–19
Chamber of Commerce, 222; and Los Angeles branch, 159, 268n11
Chambers, Whittaker, 164
Chappaquidick, 190
Chennault, Anna, 156, 185–186
Chicago Tribune, 5, 164
Christian Front and Mobilizers, 159
Christopher, Warren, 144
Church, Frank, 235, 244
Citizens' Commission to Investigate the FBI, 148
Civil Rights Act of 1964, 180
Civil Service Commission: and Circular No. 222, 197–198; and loyalty programs, 196, 203–206, 209, 220–223, 227, 292n9, 301n54
Clark, Ramsey, 67, 112, 145; and IDIU, 147; and oversight of FBI, 142–145, 269n20; and wiretapping, 17, 113, 114, 183–184, 185, 275n56
Clark, Tom C., 161, 164; and Alger Hiss, 129; and August 1948 directive, 76–78, 256n15; and confiden-

tiality of FBI sources, 206–208, 294n20; and FBI political investigations, 160; and insubordination, 233; and loyalty program, 199–204, 206–207; and Operation SHAMROCK, 120; and Security Index program, 44–48; and wiretapping, 99–100, 102, 104, 105, 110, 256n15, 268n12

Clifford, Clark, 163, 193; and loyalty program, 205–208

Code of Federal Regulations, 67, 85, 86

COINTELPRO, xiii, 93, 133–155, 175, 234, 243, 279n21, 280n39, 289n65; and black nationalist groups, 145–147, 152, 153; and Communist party, 135–139, 152; and Department of Justice, 10, 92; and Huston Plan, 35; and New Left, 147–149, 151–152; and Socialist Workers party, 127, 139–140, 152; and termination, 35, 148–151; and white hate groups, 140–146, 152

Colby, William, 10

Cold War: and abuses of power, 234; and American conservatives, 17, 196–197; and impact of, 12, 13, 39, 97, 132, 156, 230–231, 244; and institutional/value changes, 94; and presidential power, 14; and secrecy, 40

Cole v. Young, 135, 210, 213, 215, 221

Columbia University, 148

COMINFIL, 166, 172

COMINT, 13, 25, 32

Commager, Henry Steele, 165

Commission on Government Security (Wright Commission), 212–213, 214

Committee for a SANE Nuclear Policy, 177

Common Cause, 189

Communist, 157, 159, 167

Communist Control Act of 1954, 134

Communist Index, 48, 55, 56, 62

Communist party, 135–139, 158, 161–162, 167–168, 173, 177, 183, 184, 197–198, 256n11

Comsab, 48

Condon, Edward, 101, 161

Congress: and FBI, 57, 154, 176, 177–178; and intelligence agencies, 48, 88, 130–132, 156, 234–235, 239–240, 241–244, 266n53, 276n62; and legislation, 170–171; and loyalty programs, 212, 214, 215, 219, 221–223, 225; and oversight of intelligence agencies, 116–117; and presidential powers, 94, 97; and reform of intelligence agencies, 242–243; and repeal of emergency detention, 259n51

Congress on Industrial Organization (CIO), and Political Action Committee (PAC), 161, 162

Connell, Bill, 181–182, 288n57

Connelly, Matthew, 160

conservatives: and abuses of power, 250n14; and anti–New Deal politics, 197–200; and FBI, 133–134; and Huston Plan, 13, 251n1; and Kennedy administration, 168–169; and lawlessness, 132; and politics of anti-communism, 14, 17, 34, 76, 80–81, 86, 132, 133, 175, 180, 189–190, 196, 209, 211, 218–220, 223–224, 231–232, 242, 301n50; and presidency, 4–7, 231–232

Cooley, Harold, 171

Coolidge Committee, xiii

Coplon, Judith, 100–101, 104, 105

Corcoran, Thomas, 159, 160, 163, 268n12

Corson, William, 247n4

Cotter, Richard, 60; and ADEX, 259n51

Coughlin, Charles, 68

Cox, Archibald, 92

Cox, Edward, 200

Cox, Hugh, 43

Coyne, J. Patrick, 166, 284n24

Crockett, George, 286n46

Crockett, William, 220

Cronin, John, 129, 133, 164

Crum, Bartley, 162

Cuba, 173; and dissent over U.S. policy, 163, 168, 172, 258n41

Cummings, Homer, 67, 72, 261n14; and FBI political reports, 158; and FDR's 1936 order, 68–72

Custodial Detention, 157, 255n6; and Department of Justice, 262 n22
Cutler, Robert, 137, 165, 166

Dalbey, D. J., 60
D'Antonio, Emil, 187
Davidson, C. Girard, 206, 208
Davidson, Daniel, 192
Davies, John Paton, 211
Dawson, Donald, 207
Dean, John W., III, 8, 116, 192; and Huston Plan, 36, 37
Defense Intelligence Agency (DIA), 22, 123
Delimitation Agreement of 1940, 76
Delimitation Agreement of 1949, 78, 84, 263n28
De Loach, Cartha, 20, 22, 23, 24, 26, 126, 127, 144, 288n57; and FBI break-ins, 128; and FBI political surveillance authority, 260 n6; and Johnson administration, 178–182; and 1964 FBI squad, 288n55
Democratic National Convention, and FBI investigations, 10, 180–185
Dennis v. U.S., 135
Department of Defense, and loyalty program, 216–217, 223–224
Department of Justice, 94, 188; and Alien Control Unit, 43; and Civil Disturbance Group, 16; and CO-INTELPRO, 10, 92, 149–154; and Coplon case, 105; and electronic surveillance, 96–97, 107, 237, 267 n9, 271n27; and emergency detention programs, 40, 45, 63; and FBI break-ins, 125–129, 269n20; and FBI investigative authority, 68, 69, 72–73; and inherent powers of the presidency, 229, 266n5, 274n55; and internal security legislation, 256n15; and investigation of South Korea scandal, 14–15; and investigations of internal security bureaucracy, xiii, 132, 226–227; and investigations of racial groups, 147; and IRS, 169, 189; and loyalty programs, 199, 200–

206, 208, 211–214, 216–217, 224, 226–227; and mail opening, 36, 230; and Neutrality Laws Unit, 42; and Nixon administration, 86; and Operation MINARET, 124–125; and oversight of FBI, 61, 88–89, 101, 106, 109–113, 138–155, 225, 269n20, 280n39; and reforms of FBI, 154; and Security Index program, 46, 48–55, 58; and Special War Policies Unit, 42–43, 262 n22; and Truman's 1950 directive, 79–80; and wiretapping legislation, 105, 270n23
Department of State, and NSC 20/4, 47

Dern, George, 67, 261n14
destroyer-bases deal, 158
Detcom, 48
Dies, Martin, 197
Dondero, George, 200
Do Not File, 125–126, 137, 191, 243
Doolittle Committee Report, 229, 232
Douglas, William, 156, 165
Dudley, Tilford, 161
Duffy, Joseph, 187
Duggan, Joseph, 201
Dulles, Allen, 140–141
Dungan, Ralph, 220
Durr, Clifford, 102, 290n76
Dutton, Frederick, 284n30

Early, Stephen, 72, 158–159
Earth Day, 187
Eastland, James, 200, 232, 301n50
Edelstein, David, 201
Ehrlichman, John, 16, 20, 21, 37, 190, 193, 252n2
Eightieth Congress, 76
Eisenhower, Dwight D., xii, 6, 67, 109, 231–234; and COINTEL-PRO, 137–138; and Executive Order 10450, 210; and Executive Order 10865, 216–217; and executive privilege, 6–7, 249n7, 264 n39; and FBI political surveillance authority, 80, 83, 87, 263n34; and FBI reports, 165–168, 284n24; and Security Index program, 54–55; and Senator McCarthy, 82–83

Eisenhower administration: and abuses of power, 211; and civil liberties, 54–55; and COINTEL-PRO, 137–138; and electronic surveillance, 107–112; and Harry Dexter White, 211; and McCarthyism, 81–83; and oversight of intelligence agencies, 138–139; and political reports, xiv; and politics of anti-communism, 135, 214–215; and rationalizing political intelligence, 166; and security program, 135, 209–218

Elliff, John, 90, 266n52

Ellsberg, Daniel, 7, 123, 151, 190–191, 274n55

Elsey, George, 79, 103–104, 205; and political use of FBI, 103

ELSUR Index, 113, 193

Emergency Relief Act of 1939, 197

Ervin, Sam, 88–91, 117, 222–223, 301n54

Evans, Courtney, 171

Executive Order 9835, 202, 292n9

Executive Order 10241, 208

Executive Order 10450, 210, 213, 214, 218, 220, 224, 225, 227

Executive Order 10865, 216–217

Executive Order 11605, 224–225, 265n48

Executive Order 11785, 226–227

Executive Order 11828, 10

Executive Order 11905, 93, 235, 242

Executive Order 12036, 236–237, 242

executive privilege, xiii, 12; and abuses of power, 39, 195; and Eisenhower administration, 6, 249 n7; and McCarthyism, 231; and Nixon administration, 116; and Truman administration, 249n6; and wiretap records, 119

Fair Play for Cuba Committee, 169, 172

fascist, 157

Federal Bureau of Investigation (FBI), 94, 123; and abuse of power, 155, 164; and ADEX, 259 n51; and break-ins, 125–129, 238–239, 254n41, 259n42, 269n20, 276

n66; and bugging, 106, 269n20; and CIA, 253n9; and CIA mail program, 35; and civil rights, 135; and COINTELPRO, xiii, 10; and COMINFIL, 166, 172; and Congress, 48–53, 127, 134; and conservative politics, 133–156, 172–179, 194–195, 285n43; and Crime Records Division, 133–134, 165; and Custodial Detention, 255n6; and Democratic National Conventions, 180–182, 288n55; and Domestic Intelligence Division, 89, 173–174, 180, 183, 188; and efforts to influence public opinion, 166–167, 286n46; and Harry Dexter White, 82–83; and Hoover's restrictions of 1965–1966, 17, 18, 35, 38, 113, 130, 234; and informers, 18, 26, 29, 33, 36, 42, 63; and Inlet, 186–187; and insubordination, 40, 44, 45, 143, 155, 279n21; and insubordination of Sullivan, 17; and investigation of conservatives, 195, 220; and investigation of Joseph Kraft, 191; and investigation of press, 191–194; and investigation of prominent personalities, 177–179; and IRS, 189, 286n46, 289n65; and Johnson administration, 113; and lawlessness, 93, 101, 130, 136–155; and leaks to media and Congress, 129–130, 133–134, 142, 144, 154–155, 161, 164–165, 172–177, 184–185, 256 n9, 286n46; and legislative charter, 242–243; and Levi guidelines, 235–236; and loyalty programs, 196, 198, 200–208, 223, 292n9; and mail opening, 36, 130–131, 269n20; and Media (Pa.) raid, 148; and New Left, 280n65; and Nixon administration, 188, 289 n61, 289n64, 289n72; and NSA, 19, 27; and Operation MINARET, 121, 124–125; and Operation SHAMROCK, 253n22; and political surveillance, 11, 149, 156–195, 223, 288n45, 290n76; and political surveillance authority, xii, xiii, 12, 65–93, 133, 196, 225–226,

FBI (*cont.*)
228, 237, 259n5, 266n52; and politics of anti-communism, 135, 138–139, 155, 173–174, 183–184, 285n42; and politics of intelligence, xiii, xiv, 10, 15, 71–72, 93, 95, 101–103, 111, 133, 152–154; and presidential authority, 60, 63; and preventive detention programs, 36, 40–64; and Red Squads, 303n57; and reliability of informers, 294n23; and reports to White House, 133, 157–160, 171; and response to court ruling, 135; and Roosevelt's 1936 directive, 66; and Roosevelt's 1939 directive, 66–67, 90; and secrecy, 130–131, 137, 150, 155, 177, 215–218, 256 n11, 294n20; and Security Index, 256n11, 257n21, 258n25; and sensitivity toward conservatives, 141–142; and separate filing procedures, xi–xii, 102, 106, 112, 115–116, 125–131, 157–158, 185, 191–194, 269n20, 276n66; and smear tactics, 167, 173; and statutory authority, 41–44, 45, 49, 51–52, 58–61, 66–69, 71–73, 89, 92; and surveillance of congressmen, 19, 165, 187–188, 273n52, 281n1; and terrorism, 95; and VIDEM, 175; and wiretapping, 17, 98–99, 101–102, 114, 170, 182–184, 185, 271n36; and wiretapping legislation, 117
Federal Communications Act of 1934, 95, 96, 97, 99, 106, 110, 114, 120, 256n15, 266n5, 268n10
Federal Communications Commission (FCC), 121
Feldman, Myer, 171
Felt, W. Mark, 237, 238–239, 259 n49; and FBI break-ins, 128; and political intelligence, 187
Fielding, Lewis, 8, 191, 274n55
Finch, Robert, 223
Flemming, Arthur, 199
Flynn, John, 158
Ford, Gerald, 9, 10; and Executive Order 11905, 93, 235

Ford, Peyton, 51, 53, 163; and Security Index program, 47, 49, 50; and wiretapping, 103
Ford administration: and Church Committee, 92–93; and executive privilege, 241; and non-prosecution of abuses of power, 132; and reform of intelligence agencies, 92, 235–236; and wiretapping, 117–119, 241; and wiretapping legislation, 239
Ford Foundation, 189
foreign intelligence: and electronic surveillance, 96–97; and politics of, 117–119, 236, 240–241, 243
Forrestal, James, 45, 46, 47, 78, 120, 256n15
Fort Monmouth, 83
Frankfurter, Felix, 160, 215
Freedom of Information Act of 1966 (FOIA), xiv, 9, 151
Fulbright, J. William, 7, 156, 177, 193

Gandy, Helen, 157
Gardner, William, 238
Gasch, Oliver, 119, 241
Gayler, Noel, 15, 24, 26, 27, 29, 30; and Huston Plan, 38
Gilbert, Ben, 179
Gill, William, 288n53
Godwin, Mills, 144
Goldman, Eric, 278n49
Goldman v. U.S., 106
Goldwater, Barry, 156, 181, 232
Goodell, Charles, 189
Goodman, William, 123–124
Gray, Gordon, 165, 166
Gray, L. Patrick, 89, 237, 238–239, 254n41; and ADEX, 63; and FBI break-ins, 128–129; and FBI investigative authority, 89
Green, Harold, 211
Greene, William, 210, 211, 215
Greene v. McElroy, 210, 215
Gruening, Ernest, 189
Gubitchev, Valentin, 100
Guy, Ralph, 123

Hagerty, James, xii
Haig, Alexander, 193

Haldeman, H. R., 8, 20, 21, 34, 37, 115, 193; and Huston Plan, 31
Halperin, Morton, 95, 115, 156, 192–194
Halperin v. Nixon et al., 119
Harlan, John, 215
Hart, Philip, 4
Harvey, Paul, 165
Hatch Act, 197, 198, 201–203, 204, 206
Helms, Richard, 15, 16, 21, 22, 24, 26, 178, 231; and CIA drug testing, 229; and FBI Director Hoover, 18, 20; and Huston Plan, 38; and lawlessness, 189; and Operation CHAOS, 15–16; and perjury, 10, 238
Hennrich, C. E., 51
Hersh, Seymour, 10
Hess, Karl, 165
Hickenlooper, Bourke, 164
Higby, Larry, 187
Hiss, Alger, 129–130
Hobson, Timothy, 164
Holland, Spessard, 4
Holtzoff, Alexander, 106, 107
Hoover, Herbert, 6
Hoover, J. Edgar, xi, xii, 20, 36, 89, 149, 231; and Alger Hiss, 164; and break-ins, 125–128; and bugging, 105–109, 111–112, 271n35, 272n40, 288n55; and CIA, 16, 18–19; and COINTELPRO, 136–151, 153–154, 279n21; and concern about political risks, 150–151, 286 n45; and concern for secrecy, 142, 146, 176; and confidentiality of FBI files, 206–208; and conservative politics, 161–165, 172–179, 258n41, 290n1; and Delimitation Agreement of 1949, 78; and efforts to influence public opinion, 133, 283n22; and Eisenhower's 1953 directive, 80–82; and emergency detention programs, 40–64; and FBI investigative authority, 65, 71, 72, 88–89, 93; and FBI political surveillance authority, 201–206, 260n6, 260n8, 265n45; and FDR's 1936 directive, 39, 67–72; and FDR's September 1939

directive, 60, 67, 72–76, 80–81, 83–89, 157, 203; and FDR's 1943 directive, 60; and Harry Dexter White, 180; and Huston Plan, 14, 21, 23–24, 29, 31–34, 37–38, 40, 254n32, 254n36; and insubordination, 43–44, 70, 110–111, 137–139, 142–145, 148, 155, 255n8, 261n14; and intelligence agencies, 29; and investigations of conservatives, 288n53; and investigations of press, 191–194; and Joseph McCarthy, 82; and labor unions, 162; and lawlessness, 232, 287n50; and leaks to media and Congress, 199; and liaison with conservatives, 133–134; and loyalty programs, 199–208, 220, 291n8, 294n17; and Martin Luther King, 174–175; and media, 163–164, 184–185; and Media (Pa.) raid, 149–150; and Nixon administration, 289n64; and Official and Confidential Files, 10, 92, 281n1, 281n3; and politics of anti-communism, 135, 137–155, 166–168, 177, 180, 291n8; and reports to White House, xiv, 67–68, 86, 87, 93, 95, 102–103, 157–160, 284n24; and Reserve Index, 258 n40; and restrictions of 1965–1966, 15, 17, 18, 20–21, 25–26, 28–29, 32–33, 35, 38, 113–114, 126–128, 130, 188, 238, 255n42; and restrictions on informers, 36, 188, 286n45; and Security Index, 256n11, 256n15, 258n41; and sensitivity toward conservatives, 168; and separate filing procedures, 102, 106–107, 125–127, 129–131, 157–158, 191, 269n20; and smear tactics, 187; and seventeen wiretap records, 115–116; and termination of COINTELPRO, 148–151; and Truman's 1950 directive, 60, 78–81; and wiretapping, 102, 108–111, 174–175, 180, 182–184, 285n43, 288 n53
Hopkins, Harry, 159
Horrock, Nicholas, 240

324   Spying on Americans

House Committee on Agriculture,
171
House Committee on the Judiciary,
10
House Committee on Un-American
Activities (HUAC; Dies Commit-
tee; House Internal Security Com-
mittee), 66, 76, 101, 134, 135,
157, 162, 164, 197, 283n22
House Subcommittee on Civil and
Constitutional Rights, 154
House Subcommittee on Civil Serv-
ice, 199
House Subcommittee on Govern-
ment Information and Individual
Rights, 129
H.R. 66, 199
H.R. 6051, 242
Huddleston, Walter, 242
Hull, Cordell, 68, 70
Hummer, Ed, 129, 164
Humphrey, Hubert, and request for
FBI political assistance, 181–182
Humphrey, Ronald, 119, 240
Hunt, E. Howard, 190
Huston, Tom Charles, 13, 14, 20;
and conservative anti-communism,
16–17; and FBI Director Hoover's
restrictions, 21; and Huston Plan,
22, 29–32, 34; and IRS, 189; and
politics of anti-communism, 189–
190; and relations with Sullivan,
17, 19; and strategy to bypass
Hoover, 23, 30
Huston Plan, 11, 13–39, 91, 116,
122, 123, 132, 188, 254n32; and
break-ins, 254n41; and insubordination, 40
Hutchins, Robert Maynard, 158

Ibershof, Will, 123
Ickes, Harold, 163, 165
Independent Voters of Illinois (IVI),
159
Inlet, 186–187
Inouye, Daniel, 239, 241, 242
Institute for Pacific Relations (IPR),
161
Intelligence Evaluation Committee
(IEC), 36–37
Interdepartmental Committee on In-
ternal Security (ICIS), 78, 167

Interdepartmental Intelligence Conference (IIC), 78, 79, 84–86, 167
Internal Revenue Service (IRS), 15,
17, 112, 266n53; and FBI, 286
n46; and political investigations
during Kennedy years, 169; and
political investigations during
Nixon years, 188–189
Internal Security Act of 1950 (Mc-
Carran Act), 40, 48–53, 56–58,
134, 135n, 224, 256n15, 257n21;
and repeal of emergency detention title, 59–60, 87–88
internal security bureaucracy: and
abuses of power, 39, 125–131,
195; and Congress, 234–235; and
executive oversight, 12, 136–149,
230–231; and insubordination, 22,
30, 35, 43–44, 55, 70, 76–78, 87,
93, 99–100, 103–105, 110–111,
136–155, 247n4, 255n8, 256n15,
261n14, 269n20, 279n21; and lawlessness, 48, 58–61, 94–95, 121–
132, 234; and political activities,
40, 63, 118, 156, 258n41
International Council of Christian
Churches, 156, 166
Irvine v. California, 108–109
ITT World Communications, 120

Jackson, C. D., 83
Jackson, Henry, 188
Jackson, Robert, 42, 98–99, 110,
197; and Custodial Detention, 262
n22; and wiretapping, 267n9
Jencks v. U.S., 135
Jenkins, Walter, 181
Jenner, William, 214
Jewish Defense League, 194
Jewish War Veterans, 162
Johnson, Hiram, 158
Johnson, Louis, 120, 256n15
Johnson, Lyndon, 17, 147, 193; and
COINTELPRO, 145–147, 279n21;
and FBI political reports, 175–
186, 287n52; and FBI political
surveillance authority, 86, 265n45;
and Hoover's retirement, 149; and
loyalty program, 220–223; and
Operation CHAOS, 131; and Se-
curity Index program, 56; and
surveillance of South Vietnamese

and prominent Republicans in 1968, 185–186; and wiretapping, 272n43
Johnson, Marlin, 182
Johnson, Robert, xii
Johnson, Walter, 4, 7
Johnson Act of 1934, 97
Johnson administration, 192; and COINTELPRO, 140–148; and Ku Klux Klan, 140–141; and loyalty program, 220–223; and 1964 FBI investigations, 288n55; and Operation CHAOS, 287n50; and Operation MINARET, 121–122; and oversight of FBI, 142–145; and Security Index program, 56–58
Joint Anti-Fascist Refugee Committee, 162
Justice Department Appropriation Act of 1941, 197

Kalb, Marvin, 192
Katz v. U.S., 17
Katzenbach, Nicholas, 67, 112; and Black v. U.S., 272n40; and COINTELPRO, 144; and oversight of FBI, 113, 142–143; and wiretapping, 17–18, 114, 126–127, 180, 182–183, 192–193, 272n43, 272n46
Kearney, John, 128, 237
Keeney, John, 274n55
Keith, Damon, 123–125
Kelley, Clarence, 65, 93; and ADEX, 63; and FBI break-ins, 127–128; and FBI investigative authority, 93; and loyalty program, 226–227; and Operation MINARET, 124–125; and wiretapping legislation, 95, 117–118
Kelly, John, Jr., 101
Kennan, George, 4–5, 47
Kennedy, Edward, 118, 190, 239
Kennedy, John F., 110, 265n45; and FBI political reports, 167–168, 170–174; and investigation of leaks, 170; and investigation of steel companies, 170; and loyalty program, 218–220; and sugar quota legislation, 170–171
Kennedy, Robert, 10, 67, 179, 181, 184, 192, 219, 288n53; and CO-

INTELPRO, 138–140; and FBI, 140; and FBI political reports, 167; and FBI political surveillance authority, 84–86; and FBI reports on, 181; and investigation of steel companies, 170; and IRS, 169; and microphone surveillance, 174–175, 288n55; and Security Index, 56; and wiretapping, 110–112, 171, 173–175, 271n36, 285n43
Kennedy administration, 192; and COINTELPRO, 138–140; and electronic surveillance, 112, 170–171; and FBI political surveillance authority, 83–86; and internal security policy, 85, 167; and loyalty program, 218–220; and political uses of intelligence agencies, 169–171, 284n30, 284n32; and Security Index, 56
King, Martin Luther, Jr., 112–113, 172–175, 180–181, 184, 271n36, 286n46
Kissinger, Henry, 10, 15, 115, 231; and Operation CHAOS, 189; and wiretapping, 191–194
Kleindienst, Richard, 8; and ADEX, 63; and FBI investigative authority, 88–89
Knoxville (Tenn.) Area Human Relations Council, 167
Kraft, Joseph, 179, 190–191, 252n2
Krogh, Egil, 20, 21, 190
Kroll, Jack, 161
Ku Klux Klan, 142–145, 168

Ladd, D. Milton, 44–45, 49, 52–53, 129, 133, 201, 212, 256n9; and "educational" program, 163; and 1948 directive, 76–77; and Security Index, 256n11
Ladejinsky, Wolf, 211
Lake, Anthony, 156, 192–193
Landon, Alfred, 68
Lasky, Victor, 250n14
Lay, James, xii
League for Fair Play, 159
Lend Lease, 159
Levi, Edward: and CIA mail opening, 238; and COINTELPRO, 154–155; and FBI guidelines, 93, 154, 235–236; and FBI political

326   Spying on Americans

Levi, Edward (*cont.*)
surveillance authority, 260n6; and Hoover's Official and Confidential Files, 10, 281n1; and wiretapping legislation, 118
Lewis, Fulton, Jr., 6
liberals: and anti-communism, 232; and anti-war dissent, 177–178, 181; and Cold War, 197; and Huston Plan, 13; and presidency, 4, 6–7
Liddy, G. Gordon, 190–191
Lilienthal, David, 162
Lindbergh, Charles, 158, 159
Lippman, Walter, 4
Lisagor, Peter, 179
Lockard, Duane, 65
Loeb, William, 169
Long, Edward, 112–113, 130
Lord, Winston, 192
Loyalty Review Board, 206, 208–209
loyalty/security programs, xiii, 180, 196–228; and FBI reports, 134
Lubenow, Thomas, 165
Lumumba, Patrice, xii

Macy, John, 220–222
Magruder, Jeb, 193
mail opening (mail intercepts), 10, 26, 128–132; and CIA, 230, 234; and FBI, 15, 18–19, 112, 269n20; and Huston Plan, 29, 33
Mailer, Norman, 56
Manion, Clarence, 6
Mansfield, Mike, 149, 235
Marcantonio, Vito, 42, 158
March, Frederick, 101
March on Washington, 173
Mardian, Robert, 37, 61, 115, 191, 193–194, 224–225, 265n48
Maroney, Kevin, 280n39
Marshall, Burke, 140
Mathias, Charles McC., Jr., 239, 242
Matthews, J. B., 161
McCarran, Pat, 232
McCarthy, Eugene, 181
McCarthy, Joseph, Jr., 54, 79, 82, 83, 156, 161, 196, 231, 263n30
McCarthyism, 134, 208, 249n9; and conservative politics, 17; and executive privilege, 6–7, 264n39; and Harry Dexter White, 82–83;

and impact of, 231; and intelligence agencies, 179; and Nixon administration, 189–190
McClellan, John, 4, 117, 119, 239
McCloskey, Paul, 190
McCone, John, 176
McCormick, Robert, 158
McGranery, James, and Security Index program, 51–54
McGrath, J. Howard, 47, 48; and electronic surveillance, 102–103, 105–107, 270n24; and loyalty program, 208, 295n24; and Security Index program, 48–49, 256n15, 257n21; and Truman's 1950 directive, 79
McGuire, M. F., 42
McHarry, Charles, 165
McHugh, Ray, 151, 165
McInerney, James, 49, 51
McIntyre, Carl, 166, 188
McKim, E. D., 160
McLane, James, 172
Media (Pa.) raid, 148–150, 273n52
Merkin, Edmund, 170
Messersmith, George, 73
military intelligence agencies, 44, 70, 135; and domestic surveillance, 88, 120–121, 178–179, 223, 276n62, 282n9; and electronic surveillance, 120–122, 124–125
Miller, Edward: and FBI break-ins, 128, 237–239, 254n41; and FBI investigative authority, 89
Mississippi Freedom Democratic Party (MFDP), 180–181
Mitchell, Harry, 199, 204–205
Mitchell, John, 16, 21, 67, 190; and ADEX, 61–62; and FBI break-ins, 239; and FBI investigative authority, 87–88; and Huston Plan, 32–33, 36–38, 254n32; and oversight of FBI, 142, 145, 149; and Security Index program, 60–61; and wiretapping, 115–116
Montgomery, Ed, 165
Moore, Donald, 19
Moore, George, 146
Moose, Richard, 192
Morgenthau, Hans, 4
Morley, Felix, 6, 232
Morse, Wayne, 156, 177

Moss, John, 119, 241
Moyer, L. V., 208
Moyers, Bill, 181, 220
Moynihan, Daniel, 242
Murphy, Charles, 79, 104
Murphy, Frank, 73; and FDR's 1939 directive, 72–74
Muskie, Edmund, 95, 149, 156; and Nixon surveillance, 193–194

Nation of Islam (Black Muslims), 156, 165, 225
National Association for the Advancement of Colored People (NAACP), 135–136, 159, 166–167, 284n24, 285n43
National Broadcasting Company (NBC), 121
National Council of Arts, Sciences and Professions (NCASP), 162
National Lawyers Guild, 102–103, 156, 162, 165, 167
National Mobilization Office for Demonstrations at the National Democratic Convention, 182–185
national security: and abuses of power, 38–39, 44–47, 58–61, 64, 94, 156, 179, 191–195, 229–231, 239, 274n52; and electronic surveillance, 95, 100, 107–111, 113–114, 116–119; and politics of, xiii, 7, 12, 14, 113, 115, 122–125, 132, 137–138, 149, 170–171, 183–186, 192–194
National Security Act of 1947, 5, 16, 131, 236
National Security Agency (NSA), 22, 94, 118, 240, 270n24; and FBI, 19, 27; and Huston Plan, 25, 38; and legislative charter, 242–243; and loyalty program, 196, 210, 223; and Operation MINARET, 15, 35, 121–125; and Operation SHAMROCK, 120–121; and separate filing procedures, 16, 121–122, 275n61
National Security Council (NSC), xiv, 11, 45, 47, 77–78, 84, 85, 95, 110, 166–167, 185, 219, 233, 236, 243, 263n34; and loyalty program, 209; and oversight of FBI, 78–82;

and record-keeping procedures, xii–xiii
National Student Association (NSA), 17
Nelson, Donald, 159
Nelson, Gaylord, 116–118, 239; and joint congressional oversight committee, 149, 151
Neutrality Acts of 1935–1937, 97, 158
New Left, 23, 165, 176, 179, 194, 223, 289n65; and COINTELPRO, 143, 147–149, 151–152; and FBI investigation of, 86; and Nixon administration, 16, 22, 36, 187; and Security Index program, 57–59
New Mobilization Committee to End the War in Vietnam, 194
New York Times, 9, 163, 170, 191, 192, 240; and executive privilege claims, 7
Newsweek, 169, 170
Nichols, Louis, 129, 157, 164
Nichols, William, 121
Niles, David, 101
Nixon, Richard, 11, 19, 59, 89, 92, 211, 232; and abuses of power, 16, 128, 131–132, 247n4, 252n2, 273n50; and Alger Hiss, 164; and electronic surveillance, 95, 115–116, 192–194, 252n3; and Executive Order 11605, 224–225, 265 n48; and Executive Order 11785, 226; and executive privilege, 6, 8–9; and FBI break-ins, 128, 239, 254n41, 259n42; and FBI reports, 95, 186–194; and Huston Plan, 13–14, 30–39, 71, 91; and IRS, 189; and leaks, 190–194, 225; and Operation CHAOS, 131; and politics of anti-communism, 14, 86, 186; and presidential powers, 9, 15, 132, 230, 254n32; and rationalizing decision-making, 186–188, 190; and Watergate Affair, 116
Nixon administration, 13; and abuses of power, 10, 11, 92, 122–123, 149, 151; and break-ins, 128, 259 n42; and FBI, 142, 145, 149, 190, 252n2, 289n64; and IRS, 188–189; and liaison with Sullivan, 273 n52; and Operation MINARET,

Nixon administration (*cont.*)
122–125; and Security Index program, 58–61; and separate filing procedures, 115–116; and White House secret police, 186, 190, 252n; and wiretapping, 115–117, 273n50, 289n72
Norman, Lloyd, 170
Nye Committee, 97

Office of Naval Intelligence, 44, 70
Office of Strategic Services (OSS), 160
Official and Confidential Files, 128, 129n, 157, 281n1, 281n3
O'Konski, Alvin, 161
Olney, Warren, III, 107
Omnibus Crime Control and Safe Streets Act of 1968, 3–4, 95–96, 114–115, 239
Operation CHAOS, 131–132, 287 n50
Operation MINARET, 121–125
Operation SHAMROCK, 120–121, 253n22, 256n15, 275n61
Oppenheimer, J. Robert, 82–83, 162, 166, 211
Oswald, Lee Harvey, 56
Otepka, Otto, 169, 218–219, 232, 301n50
Oumansky, Constantine, 67–69

Parker, Barrington, 152
Pastore, John, 10, 92
Pauley, Edwin, 163
Pauling, Linus, 165
Peace Party, 176
Pegler, Westbrook, 161
Pennsylvania v. Nelson, 135, 260n6
Perkins, Frances, 204–205
Petersen, Henry, 124–125, 151–154, 226–227
Petersen Committee, 151–154
Polish American Congress, 159–160
Pommerening, Glen, 226–227
Post Office: and COINTELPRO, 143–144; and mail opening programs, 130
presidency: and emergency detention programs, 42–43, 45–46, 54–58; and inherent powers, 3–4, 63–66, 91–92, 94, 96–97, 99–100,

236–237, 239–240; and intelligence agencies, xi, xiii, 11–15, 25–26, 34–36, 38–40, 72, 80, 93, 99–100, 103–105, 132, 136–155, 247n4; and national security, 8, 62, 107–109, 114–119, 132, 215–218, 240–241
press, 84, 121, 191–194; and the FBI, 133–134, 142, 144, 148–152
Princeton University, and conference on FBI, 88
Progressive party, 101, 156
Public Law 733, 210, 213

Rabaut, Louis, 200
Radford, Charles, II, 194
Ragan, John, 190, 190n, 252n3
Ramparts, 17, 286n45
Randolph, Jennings, 199
Rankin, John, 200
Rauh, Joseph, 102–103
RCA Global, 120
Red Squads, 223, 303n57
Reed, Bill, 65–66
Reeves, Albert, 101
Rehnquist, William, 65
Reserve Index, 55–56, 62, 172, 258 n40
Reuther, Walter, 161
Ribicoff, Abraham, 235
Richardson, Elliot, 92; and FBI investigative authority, 90–92; and Operation MINARET, 124–125
Richardson, Seth, 208
Riha, Thomas, 18, 253n9
Roberts, Owen, 98
Robinson, Edward G., 101
Rockefeller Commission on the CIA, 10
Rogers, William, 167, 214–215; and COINTELPRO, 137
Rogovin, Mitchell, 169
Roosevelt, Eleanor, 156, 165–166
Roosevelt, Franklin D., 5–6, 70–71, 215, 231, 261n16; and Civil Service Commission, 198; and Custodial Detention program, 42–43; and FBI political surveillance authority, 12, 66–69, 73, 75–79, 86, 93, 153, 203, 259n5, 261n19; and loyalty program, 197–198; and political investigations, 156–160;

and wiretapping, 98–100, 102–104, 106, 109–110, 267n9
Rosenberg, Julius, 83
Rossiter, Clinton, 4
Rostow, Walt Whitman, 219; and Operation CHAOS, 287n50
Ruckelshaus, William, 128
Rusk, Dean, 56, 84, 138, 219
Russell, Bertrand, 165
Ryan, Sylvester, 101

S. 1566, 239–240
S. 2525, 242–243
S. 2820, 116–118
S. 3197, 118–119, 239
S. Res. 21, 10–11, 92
S. Res. 400, 235
Safire, William, 192, 250n14
Sanders, Bill, 13
Saxbe, William, 10, 92, 117; and COINTELPRO, 152–154
Schlesinger, Arthur, Jr., 9
Schorr, Daniel, 156, 187
Scranton Commission on Campus Unrest, 66
Sears, John, 192
secrecy: and abuses of power, 12–13, 24–25, 32, 41, 43–44, 71, 94, 109, 155, 189, 191–194; and classification restrictions, xi, xiii–xiv, 5–6, 11, 84, 92–93, 122, 137–138, 170, 180, 237
Secret Service, 121, 124, 265n45
Security Index, 36, 43–61, 87, 136, 147, 201, 225, 256n10, 256n11, 258n25, 258n41
Seigenthaler, John, 169
Senate Committee on Armed Services, 10
Senate Committee on Foreign Relations, 10, 177
Senate Committee on the Judiciary, 3; and Subcommittee on Administrative Practice and Procedure, 17, 112, 234, 266n53; and Subcommittee on Constitutional Rights, 65, 88–90, 110, 222–223, 276n62, 301n54; and Subcommittee on Internal Security, 83, 161, 219–220
Senate Select Committee on Intelligence, 119, 151, 235, 240–243

Senate Select Committee on Intelligence Activities (Church Committee), xii–xiv, 10–11, 28, 33, 69, 92, 94, 118, 127, 143, 151, 234–235, 244, 260n6, 261n9, 269n20, 271n29, 275n61
Senate Select Committee on Presidential Campaign Activities (Ervin or Watergate Committee), 7–8, 10, 13, 37, 89, 91, 116, 122–123, 131–132
separate filing procedures, xi–xii, 19, 94, 114, 132, 156; and emergency detention programs, 43–44, 48; and FBI, 102, 105–107, 112, 115–116, 125–131, 185, 191–194, 269 n20, 276n66, 281n1; and Huston Plan, 13–14, 32, 39; and NSA, 16, 121–122, 275n61
seventeen wiretaps (NSC or Kissinger wiretaps), 95, 115–116, 191–194; and separate filing procedures, 273n50
Sharpe, Justice, 37
Shepherd, Mark, 223–224
Signals Intelligence Service, 120
Smith, Gerald L. K., 166
Smith, Harold, 160
Smith, Hedrick, 192
Smith, J. Bromley, 185
Smith, T. J., 62–63
Smith Act of 1940, 42, 45, 134–136
Sneider, Richard, 192
Snyder, John, 207
Socialist Workers Party (SWP), 161, 165; and COINTELPRO, 139–140, 143; and FBI break-ins, 127, 269n20
Sokolsky, George, 161, 165, 232
Sonnenfeldt, Helmut, 192
Souers, Sidney, 78, 160, 256n15
South Korea, 14–15
South Vietnam, 185–186
Southern Christian Leadership Conference (SCLC), 156, 172, 180, 187
Southern Regional Council, 173
Special Service Staff (SSS), 189
Spingarn, Stephen, 76–77, 204, 207
Stephens, Thomas, 165
Stern, Carl, 151–152, 280n39
Stevens, John, 55, 241

Stolley, Richard, 179
Stone, Harlan Fiske, and restrictions on FBI, 255n8, 260n6
Strauss, Lewis, 81–83
Strul, Gene, 165
Student Nonviolent Coordinating Committee (SNCC), 112, 272n46
Students for a Democratic Society (SDS), 59, 176–177, 183–184, 188, 272n46, 286n45
Subcommittee of Senate Committee on Expenditures in the Executive Department, 76
subversive activities: and electronic surveillance, 94–95, 99, 108–109, 111; and emergency detention, 44–45, 55–56; and FBI investigations, 60–61, 66–67, 69–70, 75–81, 83–86, 90–92, 94, 265n45; and politics of, 14–17, 22, 71–72, 162, 166–167, 175–179, 183–186, 200–201, 224–226
Subversive Activities Control Board (SACB), 134–136, 224–225
Sullivan, William, 35, 39, 94, 148, 173–174, 229–230, 259n49, 289 n65; and FBI break-ins, 126, 128; and FBI investigations of congressmen, 165; and Hoover's restrictions of 1965–1966, 18, 20; and Huston Plan, 15–17, 19, 21–29, 34, 40; and Nixon White House, 192–194, 273n52; and Operation SHAMROCK, 253n22; and separate filing procedures, 115–116; and wiretapping, 183–184, 191

Taft, Robert, 5–6, 158, 232
Tamm, E. A., 73, 129
Temporary Commission on Employee Loyalty, 200–202, 204, 256n10, 292n9
terrorism, and politics of, 92, 95, 118, 152, 237, 243
Texas Instruments, 223–224
Thomas, Norman, 158, 165
Thrower, Russell, 189
Thurmond, Strom, 239
Time, 169, 273n50
Toledano, Ralph de, 165
Tolson, Clyde, 27, 60, 129; and CO-INTELPRO, 137; and FBI break-ins, 126–127

Tompkins, William, 212–213
Tordella, Louis, 19–20, 35
Trohan, Walter, 5, 164–165, 232
Truman, Harry S, 4–5, 67, 82–83, 231–234; and classification restrictions, 6; and Executive Order 9835, 202; and Executive Order 10241, 208; and executive privilege, 220, 249n6; and FBI, xiv, 102, 160–164, 168, 205–206; and FBI political surveillance authority, 76–78, 85, 87, 263n28; and Operation SHAMROCK, 120; and Security Index program, 45–46, 54, 256n15; and wiretapping, 99–104, 256n15, 268n12
Truman administration: and loyalty program, 199–209; and McCarthy, 263n30; and Operation SHAMROCK, 120
Truong, David, 119, 240
Turrou, Leon, 71

Ulasewicz, Anthony, 190, 190n
United Auto Workers (UAW), 161, 166
United States Intelligence Board (USIB), 22, 229
U.S. Supreme Court, 8, 65–66, 97–100, 104, 106, 112, 116, 135, 188, 259n5; and loyalty programs, 213, 215; and wiretapping, 17, 98, 108, 194, 214, 273n50
U.S. v. Ayres, 122–125
U.S. v. Baltch, 112, 130, 269n20
U.S. v. Black, 126–127
U.S. v. Butenko, 96
U.S. v. Coplon, 130
U.S. v. Nardone, 97–98, 110
U.S. v. Nixon, 8, 66
U.S. v. U.S. District Court, 66, 124, 116, 194, 238, 239

Vanech, A. Devitt, 199–200, 205–206
Vaughan, Harry, 160, 162
VIDEM, 175
Vietnam War, 7, 14, 17, 132, 186, 219; and anti-war dissent, 147, 177–179, 194; and conservative anti-communism, 175–179, 183–186, 191–192

Villard, Oswald, 158
Vincent, John Carter, 211
Vinson, Fred, 113

Wackenhut Corporation, 190n
Wallace, George, 173
Wallace, Henry, 101, 156, 161–163
Walter, Francis, 214
Wannall, W. Raymond, 66
War Powers Act of 1973, 9
Ward, Jimmy, 165
Warren Commission, 179
Washington Post, 103, 149; and executive privilege, 7
Watergate Affair, 7–8, 89, 116, 273 n52; and political impact, 63, 91, 94–95, 118, 132
Watson, Edwin, 159
Watson, Marvin, 142–143, 177, 179–181, 288n57
Webb, James, 104
Webster, William, 237
Welles, Sumner, 159
Welsh, Richard, 235
Western Union International, 120
Whearty, Raymond, 50–51
Wherry, Kenneth, 200
White, Byron, 56, 84

White, Harry Dexter, 82–83, 211
White, Lee, 218, 220
White House Plumbers Group, 8, 116, 123, 132, 186, 190–191, 252
Whitehead, Don, 134, 141, 261n9
Wigglesworth, Richard, 200
Wilson, Charles E., xiii, 54, 82–83
Wilson, Lyle, 165
Winchell, Walter, 133, 165
wiretapping, 11, 13, 19–20, 25, 29, 33, 105, 127–129, 133, 201; and legislation, 3–4, 117–119, 239–240; and Nixon administration, 192–194; and politics of, 17, 100, 120, 178, 192–194, 288n53; and restrictions on, 15, 18–19, 114, 255n42; and separate filing procedures, 115–116
Woltman, Frederick, 165
Workers Alliance, 158
World War II, 40–41, 73–76, 158–160

Yalta Conference, 5
Yates v. U.S., 135, 214
Yeagley, J. Walter, 86, 221, 289n64
Young Americans for Freedom, 17